Policy Concertation and Social Partnership in Western Europe

POLICY CONCERTATION AND SOCIAL PARTNERSHIP IN WESTERN EUROPE

Lessons for the 21st Century

Edited by
Stefan Berger and Hugh Compston

Berghahn Books
New York • Oxford

First published in 2002 by

Berghahn Books
www.berghahnbooks.com

Editorial offices:
604 West 115th Street, New York NY 10025, USA
3 NewTec Place, Magdalen Road, Oxford OX4 1RE, UK

Library of Congress Cataloging-in-Publication Data
Policy concertation and social partnership in Western Europe : lessons for the 21st century / edited by Stefan Berger and Hugh Compston.
p. cm.
Includes bibliographical references and index.
ISBN 1-57181-702-6 (alk. paper)--ISBN 1-57181-494-9 (pbk. : alk. paper)
1. Corporate state--Europe, Western. 2. Industrial relations--Europe, Western. I. Berger, Stefan. II. Compston, Hugh, 1955–

HD3616.E385 P65 2002
338.94--dc21

2001035610

British Library Cataloguing in Publication Data
A catalogue record for this book is available
from the British Library.

Printed in the United States on acid-free paper.

ISBN 1-57181-702-6 (hardback)
ISBN 1-57181-494-9 (paperback)

Contents

PART II COMPARISONS AND CONCLUSIONS

List of Tables

List of Figures

List of Appendices

Notes on Contributors

Gino Bedani is Professor of Italian at the University of Wales, Swansea, and has published many books and articles on Italian politics including *Politics and Ideology in the Italian Workers' Movement* (1995), 'Pluralism, Integralism, and the Framing of the Republican Constitution in Italy: the Role of the Catholic Left', in *Sguardi sull'Italia. Miscellanea dedicata a Francesco Villari*, ed. G Bedani, Z. Baranski, A.L. Lepschy and B. Richardson (1997), and 'The Dossettiani and the Concept of the Secular State in the Constitutional Debates: 1946–7', in *Modern Italy*, vol.1/2 (1996).

Stefan Berger is Professor of History at the University of Glamorgan and has published numerous books and articles on comparative labour history and on historiography including *Social Democracy and the Working Class in Nineteenth and Twentieth Century Germany* (2000), *Nationalism, Labour and Ethnicity* (with A. Smith, 1999), *Writing National Histories* (with M. Donovan and K. Passmore, 1999), and *The British Labour Party and the German Social Democrats, 1900–1931* (1994, German edition 1997).

Hugh Compston is senior Lecturer in European Politics in the School of European Studies, Cardiff University, and researches in the area of comparative public policy and political economy. Among recent publications are *The New Politics of Unemployment: Radical Policy Initiatives in Western Europe* (edited, 1996), 'Union Power, Policy Making and Unemployment in Western Europe, 1972–1993', *Comparative Political Studies* (December 1997), and 'The End of Policy Concertation? Western Europe Since the Single European Act', *Journal of European Public Policy*, vol. 5/4 (1998).

Peter Dorey is Lecturer in Politics in the School of European Studies, Cardiff University. Recent publications include *British Politics Since 1945* (1995),

The Conservative Party and the Trade Unions (1995), *The Major Premiership* (edited, 1999) and *Wage Politics in Britain* (2001). His book *The Labour Party and Constitutional Reform* will be published in 2002.

James Fulcher is Senior Lecturer in Sociology at the University of Leicester. His main research interests are the development of industrial relations, the labour movement and the state in Sweden, and the bureaucratisation of the Japanese state and its consequences for the development of Japanese society. Major publications include *Labour Movements, Employers, and the State: Conflict and Cooperation in Britain and Sweden* (1991), and *Sociology* (with John Scott, 1999).

Bruce Haddock is Professor of Modern European Political and Social Theory in the School of European Studies, Cardiff University, Fellow of the Royal Historical Society and Professorial Fellow of the Collingwood Society. Publications include *An Introduction to Historical Thought* (1980), *Vico's Political Thought* (1986), *The Politics of the Italian National Identity* (2000, ed. with Gino Bedani) and numerous articles and essays on themes ranging from political theory to Italian history and politics.

Anton Hemerijck is Senior Lecturer in the Department of Public Administration, Leiden University, and Visiting Fellow at the Max Planck Institute for the Study of Societies in Cologne. His research focuses on comparative public policy, welfare state studies, political economy, and institutional policy analysis.

Bernhard Kittel is Research Fellow at the Max-Planck-Institute for the Study of Societies, Cologne, while on leave as Lecturer in the Department of Government, University of Vienna. He has published numerous articles in the fields of comparative industrial relations and political economy, social partnership and comparative methodology. Recent publications include *International Markets and National Labour Relations* (with Franz Traxler and Sabine Blaschke, 2001), 'The Bargaining System and Performance. A Comparison of 18 OECD Countries' (with Franz Traxler), *Gesetzgebung in Österreich* (with Emmerich Tálos, 2001) and *Comparative Political Studies* (2000).

Jeremy Leaman is Senior Lecturer in German Studies at Loughborough University. Publications include *The Political Economy of West Germany 1945–1985* (1988) and *The Bundesbank Myth* (2000) as well as numerous chapters and articles on the political economy of twentieth-century Germany. He is currently engaged on a comparative study of social democratic taxation policy in Germany and Britain. He is managing editor of both *The Journal of European Area Studies* and *Debatte: Review of Contemporary German Affairs*.

Jill Lewis is Lecturer in History at the University of Wales, Swansea, and has published widely on Austrian twentieth-century history, in particular the Austrian labour movement. Major publications include *Fascism and the Working Class in Austria* (1991), and 'Auf einem Seile tanzen: Die Anfänge des Marshall-Planes und des Kalten Krieges in Österreich' in *80 Dollar: 50 Jahre ERP-Fonds und Marshall-Plan in Österreich 1948–1998*, ed. Günter Bischof and Dieter Stiefel (1999).

Mikkel Mailand is Research Fellow at the Employment Relations Research Centre (FAOS), University of Copenhagen. His research focuses on issues such as tripartism, active labour market policy and further education and training, and he is the author of *Den Danske Model Lokalt og Regionalt – konsensus og samarbejde i arbejdsmarkedspolitiske netværk* (*The Danish Model at Local and Regional Level – Consensus and Cooperation in Labour Market Policy*).

Miguel Martinez Lucio is Senior Lecturer in Industrial Labour Studies, University of Leeds. He has published on trade unionism and change in relation to employment and politics, and is currently working on issues relating to privatisation and employment relations in the European Union. Publications include 'Constructing the Post-Fordist State? The Politics of Flexibility and Labour Markets in Contemporary Spain' (with Paul Blyton), reprinted in Bob Jessop (ed.) *Regulation Theory: Selected Writings* (2000), 'Trade Unions and Networking in the Context of Change: Evaluating the Outcomes of Decentralisation in Industrial Relations' (with Syd Weston), *Economic and Industrial Democracy* (May 1995) and *The Politics of Quality and the Management of Change in the Public Sector* (with Ian Kirkpatrick, 1995).

Susan Milner is Reader in European Studies at the University of Bath. She has written several articles and book chapters on trade unions, employment relations and employment policies in France and at European Union level, including *The Dilemma of Internationalism: French Syndicalism and the International Labour Movement* (1990). She is currently working on a comparative study of employment relations practice in France and the United Kingdom.

Emmet O'Connor is Senior Lecturer in Politics at the University of Ulster, Magee College. He has published widely on Irish labour history, including *Syndicalism in Ireland* (1988) and *A Labour History of Ireland, 1924–1960* (1992), and is co-editor of *Saothar*, the journal of the Irish Labour History Society.

Rory O'Donnell is Jean Monnet Professor in European Business at the Graduate School of Business, University College Dublin, and has published extensively on a wide range of subjects including the European Union, the Irish economy, the Irish social partnership and public policy making.

Nick Parsons is Senior Lecturer in French and Director of French Studies in the School of European Studies, Cardiff University. He has published a number of articles on French and British industrial relations and is the author of *Employee Participation in Europe: a Case Study of the British and French Gas Industries* (1997). He is currently working on a study of recent change in French industrial relations.

Victor Pestoff is Professor of Political Science and Head of Department at Södertörns Högskola in Stockholm. His main current field of research is the social economy of Sweden. Recent publications in English include *Between the Market and Politics: Co-operatives in Sweden* (1991 and 1996) and *Beyond the Market and State: Social Enterprises and Civil Democracy in a Welfare Society* (1998).

Robert Robinson is Professor of International Studies and Economics at the Universidad Pontificia Comillas, Madrid, and Head of Studies in the Faculty of Economics and Management. He is currently conducting research into direct investment in Spain.

Hans Slomp is Senior Lecturer in the Political Science Department, University of Nijmegen. His main field of research is comparative labour relations, and recent publications include *Between Bargaining and Politics: An Introduction to European Labor Relations* (1998) and *European Politics into the Twenty-First Century: Integration and Division* (2000).

Carsten Strøby Jensen is Associate Professor at the Employment Relations Research Centre (FAOS), University of Copenhagen. He has worked on labour market issues (industrial relations) and European integration (political sociology) for many years, and has published in journals such as the *European Journal of Industrial Relations, Industrial Relations Journal* and *Journal of Common Market Studies*.

Emmerich Tálos is a professor at the Department of Government, University of Vienna, and has published numerous books and articles on the welfare state, social partnership, political development, fascism, poverty and gender politics. Recent publications on social partnership include *Sozialpartnerschaft. Kontinuität und Wandel eines Modells* (1993), *Sozialpartnerschaft und EU* (with F. Karlhofer, 1996), and *Zukunft der Sozialpartnerschaft. Veränderungsdynamik und Reformbedarf* (with F. Karlhofer, 1999).

Damian Thomas is the Research and Development Officer with the Association of Higher and Civil Public Servants (AHCPS). His research interests include social partnership in Ireland and Europe and the role of interest groups in the policy process.

Chris Williams is Professor at the University of Glamorgan, where he is the Director of the Centre for Modern and Contemporary Wales. His main field of research is British and Welsh political and social history, and his major publications are *Democratic Rhondda: Politics and Society, 1885–1951* (1996), *Capitalism, Community and Conflict: The South Wales Coalfield, 1898–1947* (1998), and *The Labour Party in Wales, 1900–2000* (edited with Duncan Tanner and Deian Hopkin, 2000).

PREFACE

This book is about the political dynamics of policy concertation, defined as the codetermination of public policy by means of agreements struck between governments, employers and trade unions. Policy concertation can take a number of forms, including social pacts in which governments trade policy concessions for wage restraint, such as those agreed in the 1990s in Ireland and Italy, and longer-term processes of continuous political exchange such as the Austrian Social Partnership. It is important because it is a mode of policy making in which employers and trade unions have guaranteed influence over public policy. Whether policy concertation takes place or not therefore affects the content of public policy and thus, over time, the nature of society as a whole.

The differing incidence of policy concertation in Western democracies is often explained in terms of the varying incidence of corporatist systems of interest intermediation, but these days such explanations no longer work very well. In this book we go beyond neo-corporatism to examine a number of alternative and complementary explanations, notably the influence of the ideas and values of social partnership, a topic that has been virtually ignored in the English-language literature. To do this we have brought together historians, political scientists and other social scientists from a number of West European countries to employ a common research format to produce paired historical and political country studies of policy concertation in ten West European democracies. The results of these studies are then used as the basis for three comparative analyses designed to identify the main determinants of policy concertation in Western Europe as a whole.

Carrying out a project involving twenty-three contributors from ten different countries is a big task, and we are grateful to the European Commission Directorate-General on Employment and Social Affairs for the grant that made it possible. We would like in particular to thank Daniel Vaughan-Whitehead of Directorate D for his advice and assistance. The financing of a workshop in Cardiff in September 1998 to consider preliminary drafts was especially worthwhile. We would also like to thank Cardiff University for its financial support, and the administrative staff whose assistance was vital: Bridget Bradley, Graham Edwards, Laura James, Mike Joynson and Helen Muir. Thanks are also due to those who made time to be interviewed for this project, who are too numerous to list here but are acknowledged by name in the relevant chapters. The kindness of interviewees was crucial to the success of this study.

Most of all, however, we would like to thank the contributors to this book for their time, effort and insight. We especially appreciate the extent to which they kept to the common research format despite considerable temptation to deviate. It is thanks to the contributors that we have been able to produce a study of policy concertation that takes national specificities into account in analysing individual countries while enabling us, the editors, to cast at least some light on the general political logic of policy concertation.

Stefan Berger
Hugh Compston

INTRODUCTION

THE STRANGE PERSISTENCE OF POLICY CONCERTATION

Hugh Compston

The Importance of Policy Concertation

It matters who makes public policy. In general we assume that ultimately it is the government that makes public policy through law making and legally authorised executive action, albeit influenced by other political actors, business and labour among them. This can be described as a pluralist view of policy making. In some cases the influence of business and labour may be very great, but governments still retain the last word.

But in many countries public policy in at least some areas is the outcome of explicit negotiated formal or informal agreements between the government, business as represented by peak employer confederations, and labour as represented by peak trade union confederations. This is policy concertation: the codetermination of public policy by governments, employers and trade unions. Policy concertation takes different institutional forms in different countries, but its essence is the same: because the government no longer has the last word on the shaping of public policy, policy concertation is different *in kind* to pluralist policy making. For this reason alone it merits our attention. Although it is usually discussed under the broader rubric of 'corporatism', we prefer the term 'policy concertation' because it is less ambiguous.

Another reason to focus on policy concertation is that it affects the content of public policy.

While employers and trade unions may or may not have influence in pluralist systems of policy making, the very existence of policy concertation means that they *must* have influence. If employers and trade unions (and the government) do not stand to gain from entering the agreements that are the essence of policy concertation, they have no reason to come to an agreement and policy concertation will not occur. If concertation over public policy does occur, therefore, we must infer that all participants did gain, and therefore that employers and unions influenced public policy. In some cases one or more of the participants may have a weak bargaining position, but the same logic holds: there is no motivation to enter an agreement unless the policy outcome is at least less unfavourable than the outcome of not agreeing.

The existence of policy concertation therefore influences the content of public policy by ruling out types of policy decisions that are unacceptable to employers and/or trade unions (unions, for example, are not going to agree to anti-union legislation) and by producing policies that the government would not otherwise have instituted, such as tax cuts agreed in exchange for wage restraint. In addition, the agreement of business and trade unions may render feasible policy options not previously open to the government. Wage restraint, for instance, may make expansionary fiscal policy less risky.

Whether policy concertation takes place does matter.

The Purpose of this Book

Historically, policy concertation has been especially prominent in countries such as Austria, Sweden and the Netherlands but, as we shall see, in most countries it exists in at least some areas of public policy, especially employment and social policy.

But can this continue? The 1990s, according to many observers, have seen the victory of the market as the principal means by which economic and social life is regulated. This implies that policy concertation is dead or dying, and that trade unions and business organisations are now being excluded from the making of public policy. Yet it is clear that during the 1990s trade unions and employers' associations have been involved in social pacts and other forms of participation in policy making in a number of West European countries, including Germany and Italy as well as Austria and Ireland.[1] If neo-liberalism is so strong, why have union confederations and employer groups continued to be involved in policy making? Previous studies in this area have tended to explain policy concertation in terms of the organisation of interest representation, but it seems clear that corporatist structures – large, encompassing organisations of capital and labour – are eroding. Yet policy concertation continues. This implies that corporatist explanations are no longer adequate, at least by themselves.

How, then, can the incidence and nature of policy concertation be explained? The aim of this book is to make progress towards a better explanation of the dynamics of policy concertation by assembling historical and political case studies of policy concertation in ten West European countries written to a common format, then subjecting these to systematic comparative analysis. Particular attention is given to the role of ideas, such as notions of social partnership. The ten West European countries covered are the five biggest – France, Germany, Britain, Italy and Spain – plus five smaller countries: Austria, the Netherlands, Denmark, Sweden and Ireland. Each of these is the subject of paired historical and political chapters covering the period up to 1989 and the period 1990–7 respectively. The comparative analysis is contained in three concluding chapters.

The purpose of this Introduction is threefold. First, to provide a clear definition of our central notion of policy concertation. Second, to set our study in the context of previous theories as they relate to the dynamics of policy concertation. Finally, to set out the precise format of the book.

Policy Concertation Defined

The involvement of business and trade unions in the making of public policy at the macro level is often discussed in the context of (neo)corporatism. Because this term has been used by different writers to mean rather different things, including what I mean by policy concertation, it is useful to approach the definition of policy concertation by clearly distinguishing it from corporatism.

In the article that inspired the modern renaissance of interest in the idea of corporatism, Philippe Schmitter defined it as:

> a system of interest representation in which the constituent elements are organised into a limited number of singular, compulsory, non-competitive, hierarchically ordered and functionally differentiated categories, recognised or licensed (if not created) by the state and granted a deliberate representational monopoly within their respective categories in exchange for observing certain controls on their selection of leaders and articulation of demands and supports.[2]

Although corporatism as defined here has implications for policy making, it is a pattern of organisation rather than a mode of policy making as such. Schmitter's collaborator Gerhard Lehmbruch, however, defined corporatism not as a system of interest representation but as:

> an institutionalised pattern of policy formation in which large interest groups cooperate with each other and with public authorities not only in the articulation ... of interests but ... in the 'authoritative allocation of values' and in the implementation of such policies.[3]

Given that the two definitions refer to two distinct albeit related phenomena, Schmitter suggested in the early 1980s that the term 'concertation' should be used to refer to the type of policy formation described by Lehmbruch so that the word 'corporatism' could be defined unambiguously as a system of interest intermediation.[4]

It is this distinction that constitutes the basis of the definition of policy concertation used here. However in concentrating on *policy* concertation, this study takes on an explicitly public policy perspective: the focus is on the way in which employers and trade unions are involved in the making of decisions that are ultimately the exclusive province of the state, in particular decisions on the contents of legislation, regulations and administrative orders. This is in contrast to what might be called an economic or industrial relations perspective, which concentrates primarily on the way in which the state becomes involved in decisions normally taken by employers and trade unions, such as wage setting. This type of concertation can be termed 'wage concertation' in order to clearly distinguish it from policy concertation, although the two are closely linked in practice.

Hence policy concertation is defined for the purposes of this study as the codetermination of public policy by governments, employer organisations and trade union confederations. More specifically, the study focuses on policy concertation between government representatives and representatives of peak employer and/or trade union organisations about the formation of government policy in areas including fiscal policy, monetary policy, industrial policy, trade policy, labour market policy, employment law, social welfare and regional policy.

The critical distinction made is between policy concertation understood as discussions that lead to agreements on policy, that is, to government commitments to adopt particular policies, and discussions that do *not* lead to such commitments. In this way concertation is sharply distinguished from consultation.

This is not always an easy distinction to apply in practice, however, despite its theoretical clarity, so a few remarks on its empirical use in this book are in order.

First, 'policy concertation' is not simply a synonym for employer and/or trade union influence on government, despite the fact that it does entail influence, because influence can also be exerted via consultative mechanisms such as lobbying and involvement in advisory committees. Because we wish clearly to distinguish between policy-making processes in which decisions are taken jointly, generally in face to face meetings, and policy-making processes in which negotiations take place but the authoritative decision is taken afterwards by the government acting alone, even where it seems clear that its decision has been heavily influenced by other political actors, we *exclude* lobbying and participation in formal consultation processes or task forces, working groups and other government committees from the category of policy concertation *unless* it is quite clear that agreements involving government commitments on public policy are actually struck in these forums.

The only major qualification to this procedural rule is our inclusion in the category of policy concertation of instances where the government passes legislation or alters administrative rules to implement the terms of joint decisions already taken by employers and unions, as is often the case in labour law. This is because such cases constitute tacit agreements and, moreover, are also likely to have been explicitly agreed by the government at the time the apparently bipartite employer–union negotiations were taking place.

Second, some areas of economic life, notably employment, are regulated partly by legislation and partly by collective agreements. In some countries, such as France, legislation is dominant, while in others, such as Denmark, collective agreements are dominant. Since the focus of our interest is public policy as such, rather than regulation as such, concertation over legislative changes is counted as policy concertation, but concertation leading to collective agreements is not.

Third, the involvement of employers and unions in the implementation of public policy is counted as policy concertation only insofar as this involves employer and union representatives actually *making* public policy in the process of implementing it, for instance via deciding the detailed regulations that determine how framework laws are applied in practice in the field of social security.

Theoretical Context

There are a number of theories that are relevant to the task of explaining the nature and incidence of policy concertation as defined above, although not all are explicitly intended for this purpose. These can be divided into theories relating to the rise of policy concertation, theories that assert that policy concertation is in decline due to contemporary liberalising trends, and theories that attempt to explain the persistence of policy concertation in the 1990s.

The Rise of Policy Concertation

The minimum condition for policy concertation to take place is the willingness of organised interests to negotiate and to compromise sufficiently to reach agreements. This has generally been attributed mainly to two major historical trends.

The first is the postwar extension of the role of the state. As the Keynesian state began to intervene more and more in the economy in order to secure goals such as full employment and monetary stability for which it had become held responsible by the electorate, it became dependent on the consent and cooperation of other economic actors if its policies were to work. For this reason governments were attracted by the prospect of gaining additional control over the economy if they could persuade unions and business to cooperate, and were prepared to concede influence in policy making in order to get this cooperation. In this connection incomes policies, while not necessarily essential elements of policy concertation, are seen as particularly important. If inflation caused by excessive wage rises could be avoided, it was believed that both real wages and employment would benefit, and during the 1970s in particular agreements were reached in a number of West European countries whereby wage restraint was exchanged for concessions on non-wage elements of income such as tax and transfer payments.[5] Streeck argues more specifically that the expansion of policy concertation in the 1970s was in large part a reaction to the turmoil of 1968–9 and the economic problems beginning in 1973, and that it was an attempt to control inflation and unemployment simultaneously in countries with strong labour movements.[6]

The second main trend is the development of large and powerful interest groups, especially trade unions. There are two differing arguments as to why this is important. The first is that the rise of powerful trade union movements forces governments to negotiate with them on policy matters: the union power theory. The second is that the development of corporatist systems of interest intermediation – large, unified and centralised organisations representing employers and employees – means that the organisations involved can no longer externalise the economic costs of their actions. If a trade union in a single industry makes excessive wage claims, it may be possible for the employers in that industry to pass these on in the form of higher prices to the rest of society, but if a union movement that encompasses most of a nation's workforce makes excessive wage claims, the resultant price rises hit everyone, including union members. For this reason an encompassing union movement is expected to be more open to using wage restraint as a bargaining counter in negotiations with the government over public policy.[7]

Corporatism is also considered to facilitate negotiations by limiting the number of participants and giving to leaders of trade union confederations and employer peak associations the ability to make binding commitments on behalf of their members, which is essential if political exchange is to take place on a continuing basis. In the case of trade unions, for example, their leadership must be able to secure rank and file compliance with commitments on issues such as wage restraint if they are to be able to bargain effectively with business and the government, and getting this compliance is likely to be easier for highly centralised national trade union confederations with few if any organisational rivals – although it can also be achieved for smaller union movements via the government passing legislation to make agreements reached with employer associations and trade unions binding for all relevant employers and employees. Crouch suggests that this capacity to act strategically is enhanced by having within organisations strong vertical relations of interdependence both up and down, so that the leadership requires the consent of lower levels as well as having the power to make commitments on their behalf.[8]

In addition to these two historical trends, a number of other factors have been identified as being causes of inter-country differences in the incidence of policy concertation. First, it has been suggested that the greater prevalence of policy concertation in northern compared to southern Europe indicates that it is more likely to be established where the state is perceived as being reasonably neutral by both business and trade unions, rather than as an enemy.[9] Historically, policy concertation has been associated with governments in which the working class has a voice via the party system, as such governments tend to give unions privileged access to state decision making. Peter Katzenstein argues that economic openness facilitates the development of policy concertation because vulnerability to price competition for exports and from imports makes wage restraint especially important, thus providing a strong incentive for governments to offer trade unions and employers a role in policy making in exchange for their cooperation. It has also been argued that policy concertation is facilitated by consociationalism, since political elites are already socialised into conflict management via top-level bargaining. Furthermore, a consensus among economists that policy concertation is valuable would obviously contribute to its legitimation. There is also the view that political culture is important, especially that of the labour movement: if norms of equality and solidarity are strong, for example, this may inhibit competition within the union movement over issues such as wage differentials and thereby facilitate compliance with incomes policies and therefore union involvement in the making of public policy.[10]

A number of authors consider that additional organisational factors are also important. Policy concertation is argued to be more stable where the partners participate in the implementation of policies through permanent inter-organisational networks, such as the Austrian Parity Commission and associated committees, on the grounds that this gives participants such high stakes in concertation that the option of exit becomes very costly. In addition, policy concertation at the national level is facilitated by links between the state and organised interests at sectoral level, because these links provide an institutional basis for widened forms of cooperation.[11] Crouch argues that generalised political exchange involving a dense web of exchanges between business, unions and government is more stable than single big exchanges such as social pacts because success is not dependent on the outcome of a single set of negotiations.[12] Policy concertation has been found to be more successful where top-level horizontal networks cover several policy domains: as policies in one domain affect others, peak organisations need to be linked with parliament, agencies such as the central bank, the major advisory councils in the areas of social security, health and the labour market, and intellectual and economic elites.[13]

Finally, Hemerijck argues that corporatist governance, defined as ongoing negotiations within a problem-solving style of joint decision making, is a function of the institutional integration of organised interests (ranging from ad hoc advice to official participation in decision making and implementation) and societal support for the resultant policies, defined as the objective capacity and strategic willingness of organised interests to engage in political exchange.[14]

In summary, according to the political economy literature the main reasons for the development of policy concertation were the emergence of a willingness on the part of governments to trade policy concessions for certain commitments by employers and/or trade unions, and the development of corporatist systems of interest representation. Other important factors were labour party participation in government, economic openness, consociationalism, economic consensus, egalitarian political cultures, degree of societal support, and the extensive institutionalisation of contacts between employers, trade unions and the state.

The Threat of Liberalising Trends

Perhaps the most common current view of the future of policy concertation is that it is on the way out due to inexorable social and economic trends.

For policy concertation to come to an end, one or more of the participants must withdraw from the process of negotiating government policy. Scholars have identified two main recent developments in this regard: withdrawals by governments, for example the British Conservative government in 1979, and withdrawals by business peak organisations, for example the Swedish employer confederation SAF in the early 1990s. Although trade union confederations on occasion walk out of negotiations with the government and business, there is little sign recently of union withdrawal from policy concertation as such.

A number of scholars have attributed the declining support of governments and business organisations for policy concertation to shifts in position caused by liberalising social and economic changes. These shifts in position can be grouped into three categories:

1. *Business neo-liberalism:* A shift in business preferences towards deregulation and decentralised bargaining due to increased competition and market instability stemming from internationalisation and the development of new technology, leading to pressures on firms to increase the diversity and flexibility of production, technology and social organisation.[15] Windolf argues that as a result employers are seeking to create productivity coalitions at firm level between employers and workers by offering their employees greater job security and participation in strategic decision-making in exchange for cooperation with management and commitment to company goals.[16] In addition, the increased mobility of capital due to trade and financial liberalisation is commonly recognised as leading to a general improvement in the power position of business *vis-à-vis* trade unions and government, making it less necessary for business to make concessions in order to achieve its goals;

2. *Government neo-liberalism:* A shift in government economic policy towards market liberalism and deregulation from the late 1970s due to a decline in the efficacy of national economic policy caused by increased economic interdependence and pressure from international monetary agencies and powerful international investors for deflationary policies. This made it difficult if not impossible to use fiscal and monetary measures to offer employment tradeoffs to trade unions in exchange for wage restraint, thus impeding successful policy concertation. At the same time higher unemployment lessened the perceived need for concertation by helping to bring down inflation. The impact of these trends was amplified by a shift to the Right in the composition of governments in a number of countries during the 1980s. Declining economic sovereignty also led to a transfer of policy competences to the European Union in an effort to recover economic sovereignty at the European level, thus narrowing the scope of policy actually

or potentially subject to national-level concertation. Finally, policy concertation was rendered less attractive for the government to the extent that it was made more difficult by business withdrawing its support.[17]

3. *Trade union weakness:* A decline in the bargaining power of trade unions – their ability to reward governments and business for including them in policy making, and to punish them if they are excluded – as a result of their declining ability effectively to represent the working class due to the increasing heterogeneity of the workforce, which in turn is caused by the differentiation of social structures and collective interests that has resulted from technological progress and increasing education. Thus trade union alliances with social democratic parties were weakened by the emergence of a large and well-educated middle class and a broadening of the range of issues on the political agenda; new social movements such as the environmental and peace movements competed for the allegiance of union members; trade union unity was weakened by the decline of working-class subcultures based on mass manufacturing; male trade union leaderships were challenged by the feminisation of the workforce; the emergence of large and growing service sector unions led to an erosion in the dominance of manual trade unions and especially export industry unions, which are considered to have a greater interest in wage restraint and therefore policy concertation than more protected domestic-based unions; the development of large public sectors led to the emergence of militant trade unions opposed to the cuts in public services that export unions saw as necessary; and employers increasingly encouraged company unionism and the formation of productivity coalitions between individual employers and their workforces.[18]

The significance of these shifts is that the liberalising trends on which they are based are seen as irreversible, which implies a secular decline in the incidence and extent of policy concertation. Because the trends are general in nature rather than nation-specific, this decline would be expected to take place in all countries.

A related but distinct view is that liberalising trends have led to electoral fragmentation, weaker governments and more power for national parliaments, prompting organised interests to divert attention and resources from policy concertation with the government to lobbying members of parliament at the same time as increased pressures on ministers and administrative decision makers were making them less positive towards the time-consuming processes of policy concertation.[19]

The Persistence of Policy Concertation in the 1990s

We have already noted that policy concertation continues to be important in a number of West European countries despite the existence of the liberalising trends described above. Contemporary theorists have put forward three main explanations for this.

The first is that the effects of liberalising trends are overrated. The argument that policy concertation has become more difficult due to a trend towards decentralised collective bargaining is undermined by recent findings that there is no general convergence of collective bargaining on a decentralised model.[20] In addition, the persistence of policy concertation bears out the argument of Katzenstein that far from destroying policy concertation, economic openness stimulates it due to the perceived need to maximise competitiveness by enlisting the cooperation of business and trade unions in order to make the most of the few economic instruments still available to national governments.[21]

The second explanation for the persistence of policy concertation is that it varies according to cyclical and country-specific factors, but in no particular direction. For example, policy concertation is likely to be more difficult to sustain where there are large budget deficits, as these impede governments from offering spending increases or tax cuts in exchange for wage restraint.[22] When the budget is in balance again, however, we might expect a resumption of policy concertation. Similarly, where policy concertation is interrupted due to conservative governments coming to power, we might expect a resumption if and when social democratic parties return to office, as they have in the late 1990s.[23] Crouch argues more generally that the nature and extent of policy concertation depends mainly on individual state traditions, for example the relationship of organised groups to modernisation in previous centuries, the extent to which guild and functional chamber traditions carried over into the twentieth century, and the power of labour parties in politics.[24] This implies that customary practices of policy concertation are likely to persist despite general international trends.

The third view is that contemporary trends are altering the content of policy concertation rather than destroying it. In support of this view, it is argued that wage restraint remains important to national competitiveness, thus providing a continuing incentive for governments and employers to engage in policy concertation. This is especially true of those countries that have entered Economic and Monetary Union (EMU), since for these countries it is no longer possible to devalue national currencies in order to retrieve a loss of competitiveness due to excessive wage rises. Unless trade unions are destroyed altogether above the firm level, decentralised bargaining is likely in many cases to lead to leapfrogging wage rises rather than to wage restraint, which means that there is still a role for incomes policy agreements and therefore policy concertation at a central level even if many details are decentralised to industry or firm level. Furthermore, since West European countries need to compete with newly industrialising countries on the basis of quality rather than labour costs, firms are required not only to be more flexible but also to invest more in capital goods, human capital and research and development, and to build trust in relations with their workforces. This requires long-term planning and support from the external environment to supply public goods in the form of incomes policy, hard-currency policy, provision of general skills, and industrial policy, plus a cooperative relationship with trade unions. Hence the importance of what Traxler calls 'supply-side corporatism'. Traxler argues that where this functionally well-adapted form of concertation already exists, it is likely to remain, although unlikely to develop where it is presently absent.[25]

Plan of the Book

To what extent can any of these theories explain the incidence and nature of policy concertation in Western Europe up to 1997? Or are new theories needed? To answer these questions we commissioned twenty-two historians and political scientists to use a common research format to produce paired historical and political chapters on each of the ten countries covered. These countries, with the names of the authors of the relevant historical and political chapters respectively, are Austria (Jill Lewis, Emmerich Tálos/Bernhard Kittel), Britain (Chris Williams, Peter Dorey), Denmark (Carsten Strøby Jensen, Mikkel Mailand), France (Susan Milner, Nick Parsons), Germany (Stefan Berger, Jeremy Leaman), Ireland (Emmet O'Connor, Rory O'Donnell/Damian Thomas), Italy (Gino Bedani, Bruce Haddock), the Netherlands (Anton Hemerijck, Hans Slomp), Spain (Robert Robinson, Miguel Martinez Lucio) and Sweden (James Fulcher, Victor Pestoff). These country case studies are then subjected to systematic comparative analysis in three concluding chapters written by the editors.

Each historical chapter describes the incidence and nature of policy concertation up to 1989 and analyses the extent to which this can be explained by factors such as the development of peak employer associations and trade union confederations and the relationship of both with the state, the role of two world wars in stimulating the development of corporatist structures, the impact of specific national and regional political cultures, and the history of support for associated ideas and values, in particular arguments both for and against policy concertation.

These chapters reveal, among other things, that, in our selection of ten countries, over the course of the twentieth-century policy concertation was most significant in Austria, the Netherlands and Sweden, and least significant in France and Germany. Britain, Denmark, Ireland, Italy and Spain occupied a middle position. Policy concertation first became noticeable in the First World War, but efforts to establish it on a lasting basis between the wars were unsuccessful apart from in Sweden, although policy concertation of a more restricted sort took place within the authoritarian corporatist systems set up in the 1920s and 1930s in Italy, Spain, Germany and Austria. Policy concertation was also important in the Second World War, and became well established after the war in most countries in the areas of employment and social policy. In Austria and the Netherlands it became central to policy making, while Swedish policy concertation broadened and deepened. However episodes of broader policy concertation elsewhere were more sporadic. The authors identify a wide variety of causal influences on the observed pattern of policy concertation, including economic motivations, external threat, political expediency, organisational factors, political culture, ideology, and the balance of power between capital and labour.

Each political chapter describes in detail the nature, forums and workings of policy concertation during the period 1990–7 by providing accounts of formal institutional participation in policy making and summaries of the contents of social pacts, incomes policy deals and similar agreements, then goes on to provide a similarly detailed account of associated concepts and of arguments both for and against policy concertation. Particular attention is paid to the views of governments, peak employer associations, and trade union confederations as expressed in official documents such as communiqués relating to policy concertation, election propaganda and conference documents. Attention is also paid to the views of the population at large as indicated by opinion polls. Each chapter then presents an explanation of the observed pattern of policy concertation in the 1990s, with particular reference to the role of ideas, values and arguments.

Among the findings of the political chapters are that during the 1990s policy concertation on employment and social policy was ubiquitous in all ten countries apart from Britain, but concertation on a wide range of public policy was mainly restricted to Austria, Ireland and Italy. In the Netherlands and Sweden, where concertation on a broad range of public policy had been standard practice for decades, its scope became restricted to employment and social policy, as elsewhere. The political chapters also reveal that advocates of policy concertation sought to legitimate it mainly through arguing that it reduces conflicts and brings economic benefits, while opponents argued most commonly that it is undemocratic. As with the historical chapters, the authors of the political chapters identify a wide range of causal influences on the incidence and nature of policy concertation.

The first of the three concluding chapters, by Hugh Compston, draws together some of the main findings of the political country chapters and carries out an exploratory comparative analysis of the role of ideas and arguments in explaining the scope of policy concertation in Western Europe during the 1990s. This suggests that the simplest explanation in terms of political rhetoric of why policy concertation is wider and deeper in Austria than elsewhere is that the Social Partnership is both representative of, and supported by, organisational members and the population in general. The simplest explanation in terms of political rhetoric of why broad policy concertation was limited mainly to Austria, Ireland and Italy is that it is only in these three countries that governments, employers and trade unions all agree that policy concertation is economically beneficial.

The second of the three chapters, by Stefan Berger, compares the findings of the historical chapters to evaluate the role of a number of factors as causal influences on policy concertation and consultation in Western Europe up to 1989. Five factors are identified as being especially important: an accommodationist state, a homogenous political culture, highly centralised and powerful interest organisations closely linked to political parties, a set of supporting ideas and values, and wartime experience of policy concertation.

The final chapter, by Hugh Compston, develops a general theory of the dynamics of policy concertation in Western Europe during the twentieth century as a whole. This posits that the incidence of broad policy concertation in Western Europe is a function of just three variables: the existence or non-existence of a relevant problem such as war or inflation, the degree of economic agreement among the relevant political actors, and the capacity of these actors to implement their sides of bargains. Examination of the findings of the national case studies shows that the incidence of broad policy concertation can be almost completely explained in terms of these three variables.

Bibliography

Calmfors, Lars, 'Centralisation of Wage Bargaining and Unemployment – A Survey', *OECD Economic Studies* vol. 21 (1993): 161–91.

Christiansen, Peter Munk, and Hilmar Rommetvedt, 'From Corporatism to Lobbyism? Parliaments, Executives and Organised Interests in Denmark and Norway', *Scandinavian Political Studies* vol.22, no.3 (1999): 195–218.

Compston, Hugh, 'The End of National Policy Concertation? Western Europe Since the Single European Act', *Journal of European Public Policy* vol. 5, no. 3 (1998): 507–526.

Crepaz, Markus, 'From Semisovereignty to Sovereignty: The Decline of Corporatism and the Rise of Parliament in Austria', *Comparative Politics* vol.27: 45–65.

Crouch, Colin, *Industrial Relations and the European State Tradition.* Oxford: Clarendon Press, 1993.

Hemerijck, Anton C., 'Corporatist Immobility in the Netherlands', in *Organized Industrial Relations in Europe: What Future?* ed. Colin Crouch and Franz Traxler, Aldershot: Avebury, 1995.

Katzenstein, Peter, *Small States and World Markets.* NY: Cornell University Press, 1985.

Lash, Scott, and John Urry, *The End of Organized Capitalism.* London: Polity Press, 1987.

Lehmbruch, Gerhard, 'Liberal Corporatism and Party Government', in *Trends Towards Corporatist Intermediation*, ed. Philippe C. Schmitter and Gerhard Lehmbruch, London: Sage, 1979.

Lehmbruch, Gerhard, 'Concluding Remarks: Problems for Future Research on Corporatist Intermediation and Policy-Making', in *Trends Towards Corporatist Intermediation*, ed. Philippe C. Schmitter and Gerhard Lehmbruch, London: Sage, 1979.

Lehmbruch, Gerhard, 'Introduction: Neo-Corporatism in Comparative Perspective', in *Patterns of Corporatist Policy Making*, ed. Gerhard Lehmbruch and Philippe C. Schmitter, London: Sage, 1982.

Lehmbruch, Gerhard, 'Concertation and the Structure of Corporatist Networks', in *Order and Conflict in Contemporary Capitalism*, ed. John H. Goldthorpe, Oxford: Clarendon Press, 1984.

Olson, Mancur, *The Rise and Decline of Nations.* New Haven: Yale University Press, 1982.

Regini, Marino, 'Organized Interests and the Regulation of European Economies', paper prepared for the Séminaire RECO 'La Réorganisation des Etats Européen', MRASH Grenoble, 18–19 September 1997.

Rhodes, Martin, 'Globalisation, Labour Markets and Welfare States: A Future of "Competitive Corporatism"?', paper prepared for the Bern Joint Sessions of the European Consortium for Political Research, 1997.

Schmitter, Philippe C., 'Still the Century of Corporatism?', in *Trends Towards Corporatist Intermediation*, ed. Philippe C. Schmitter and Gerhard Lehmbruch. London: Sage, 1979.

Schmitter, Philippe C., 'Reflections on Where the Theory of Neo-Corporatism Has Gone and Where the Praxis of Neo-Corporatism May Be Going', in *Patterns of Corporatist Policy-Making*, ed. Gerhard Lehmbruch and Philippe C. Schmitter. London: Sage, 1982.

Scholten, Ilja, 'Introduction: Corporatist and Consociational Arrangements', in *Political Stability and Neo-Corporatism*, ed. Ilja Scholten, London: Sage, 1987.

Slomp, Hans, 'European Labor Relations and the Prospects of Tripartism', in *Participation in Public Policy-Making: The Role of Trade Unions and Employers' Associations*, ed. Tiziano Treu, Berlin and New York: Walter de Gruyter, 1992.

Streeck, Wolfgang, 'From National Corporatism to Transnational Pluralism: European Interest Politics and the Single Market', in *Participation in Public Policy-Making: The Role of Trade Unions and Employers' Associations*, ed. Tiziano Treu, Berlin and New York: Walter de Gruyter, 1992.

Traxler, Franz, 'From Demand-side to Supply-side Corporatism? Austria's Labour Relations and Public Policy', in *Organized Industrial Relations in Europe: What Future?* ed. Colin Crouch and Franz Traxler, Aldershot: Avebury, 1995.

Traxler, Franz, 'Farewell to Labour Market Associations? Organized Versus Disorganized Decentralization as a Map for Industrial Relations', in *Organized Industrial Relations in Europe: What Future?* ed. Colin Crouch and Franz Traxler, Aldershot: Avebury, 1995.

Treu, Tiziano, 'Tripartite Social Policy-Making: An Overview', in *Participation in Public Policy-Making: The Role of Trade Unions and Employers' Associations*, ed. Tiziano Treu, Berlin and New York: Walter de Gruyter, 1992.

Visser, Jelle, and Anton Hemerijck, *'A Dutch Miracle': Job Growth, Welfare Reform and Corporatism in the Netherlands*, Amsterdam: Amsterdam University Press, 1997.

Wallerstein, Michael, Miriam Golden and Peter Lange, 'Unions, Employers' Associations, and Wage-Setting Institutions in Northern and Central Europe, 1950–1992', *Industrial and Labor Relations Review* vol.50, no.3 (April 1997): 379–401.

Windolf, Paul, 'Productivity Coalitions and the Future of European Corporatism', *Industrial Relations* vol. 28, no. 1 (1989): 1–20.

Notes

1. Hugh Compston, 'The End of National Policy Concertation? Western Europe Since the Single European Act', *Journal of European Public Policy* vol.5, no.3 (1998): 507–26.
2. Philippe C. Schmitter, 'Still the Century of Corporatism?', in *Trends Towards Corporatist Intermediation*, ed. Philippe C. Schmitter and Gerhard Lehmbruch, London, Sage, 1979: 7–52.

3. Gerhard Lehmbruch, 'Liberal Corporatism and Party Government', in *Trends Towards Corporatist Intermediation*, ed. Philippe C. Schmitter and Gerhard Lehmbruch, London, Sage, 1979: 147–83.
4. Philippe Schmitter, 'Reflections on Where the Theory of Neo-Corporatism Has Gone and Where the Praxis of Neo-Corporatism May Be Going', in *Patterns of Corporatist Policy-Making*, ed. Gerhard Lehmbruch and Philippe C. Schmitter, London, Sage, 1982: 263.
5. Lehmbruch, 'Liberal Corporatism': 153–4; Gerhard Lehmbruch, 'Introduction: Neo-Corporatism in Comparative Perspective', in *Patterns of Corporatist Policy-Making*, ed. Gerhard Lehmbruch and Philippe C. Schmitter, London, Sage, 1982: 26; Gerhard Lehmbruch, 'Concertation and the Structure of Corporatist Networks', in *Order and Conflict in Contemporary Capitalism*, ed. John H. Goldthorpe, Oxford, Clarendon Press, 1984: 64, 73.
6. Wolfgang Streeck, 'From National Corporatism to Transnational Pluralism: European Interest Politics and the Single Market', in *Participation in Public Policy-Making: The Role of Trade Unions and Employers' Associations,* ed. Tiziano Treu, Berlin and New York, Walter de Gruyter, 1992: 99–100.
7. Mancur Olson, *The Rise and Decline of Nations.* New Haven, Yale University Press, 1982; Lars Calmfors, 'Centralisation of Wage Bargaining and Unemployment – A Survey', *OECD Economic Studies* vol. 21 (1993): 161–91.
8. Lehmbruch, 'Liberal Corporatism': 167–8; Hans Slomp, 'European Labor Relations and the Prospects of Tripartism', in *Participation in Public Policy-Making: The Role of Trade Unions and Employers' Associations,* ed. Tiziano Treu, Berlin and New York, Walter de Gruyter, 1992: 163; Colin Crouch, *Industrial Relations and the European State Tradition,* Oxford, Clarendon Press, 1993: 54–55, 289.
9. Anton C. Hemerijck, 'Corporatist Immobility in the Netherlands', in *Organized Industrial Relations in Europe: What Future?* ed. Colin Crouch and Franz Traxler, Aldershot, Avebury, 1995; Slomp, 'European Labor Relations': 163.
10. Lehmbruch, 'Liberal Corporatism': 168–72; Gerhard Lehmbruch, 'Concluding Remarks: Problems for Future Research on Corporatist Intermediation and Policy-Making', in *Trends Towards Corporatist Intermediation*, ed. Philippe C. Schmitter and Gerhard Lehmbruch, London, Sage, 1979: 304; Lehmbruch, 'Concertation and the Structure of Corporatist Networks': 74–5; Peter Katzenstein, *Small States and World Markets*, NY: Cornell University Press, 1985.
11. Lehmbruch, 'Introduction: Neo-Corporatism in Comparative Perspective': 24; Lehmbruch, 'Concertation and the Structure of Corporatist Networks': 63–4.
12. Crouch, *Industrial Relations and the European State Tradition*: 53, 62.
13. Ilja Scholten, 'Introduction: Corporatist and Consociational Arrangements', in *Political Stability and Neo-Corporatism*, ed. Ilja Scholten, London, Sage, 1987: 28–30.
14. Anton C. Hemerijck, 'Corporatist Immobility in the Netherlands'. See also Jelle Visser and Anton Hemerijck, *'A Dutch Miracle': Job Growth, Welfare Reform and Corporatism in the Netherlands*, Amsterdam, Amsterdam University Press, 1997: 66–79.
15. Scott Lash and John Urry, *The End of Organized Capitalism.* London, Polity Press, 1987; Streeck, 'From National Corporatism to Transnational Pluralism': 118–119; Hemerijck, 'Corporatist Immobility in the Netherlands': 183.
16. Paul Windolf, 'Productivity Coalitions and the Future of European Corporatism', *Industrial Relations* vol. 28, no. 1 (1989): 1–20.
17. Lash and Urry, *The End of Organized Capitalism*: 234; Streeck, 'From National Corporatism to Transnational Pluralism': 106–111; Crouch, *Industrial Relations and the European State Tradition*: 260; Hemerijck, 'Corporatist Immobility in the Netherlands': 184.
18. Lash and Urry, *The End of Organized Capitalism*: chapter 8; Streeck, 'From National Corporatism to Transnational Pluralism': 118–119; Hemerijck, 'Corporatist Immobility in the Netherlands': 183; Windolf, 'Productivity Coalitions'; Crouch, *Industrial Relations and the European State Tradition*: 242.
19. Peter Munk Christiansen and Hilmar Rommetvedt, 'From Corporatism to Lobbyism? Parliaments, Executives and Organised Interests in Denmark and Norway', *Scandinavian Political Studies* vol.22, no.3 (1999): 195–218. See also Markus Crepaz, 'From Semisov-

ereignty to Sovereignty: The Decline of Corporatism and the Rise of Parliament in Austria', *Comparative Politics* vol.27: 45–65.

20. Franz Traxler, 'Farewell to Labour Market Associations? Organized Versus Disorganized Decentralization as a Map for Industrial Relations', in *Organized Industrial Relations in Europe: What Future?* ed. Colin Crouch and Franz Traxler, Aldershot, Avebury, 1995: 6–8; Michael Wallerstein, Miriam Golden and Peter Lange, 'Unions, Employers' Associations, and Wage-Setting Institutions in Northern and Central Europe, 1950–1992', *Industrial and Labor Relations Review*, vol.50, no.3 (April 1997): 379–401.
21. Katzenstein, *Small States and World Markets.*
22. Traxler, 'Farewell to Labour Market Associations?': 15.
23. Hemerijck, 'Corporatist Immobility in the Netherlands': 183.
24. Crouch, *Industrial Relations and the European State Tradition*: chapters 9–11.
25. Franz Traxler, 'From Demand-side to Supply-side Corporatism? Austria's Labour Relations and Public Policy', in *Organized Industrial Relations in Europe: What Future?* ed. Colin Crouch and Franz Traxler, Aldershot, Avebury, 1995: 281–282; Traxler, 'Farewell to Labour Market Associations?': 13–14. See also Tiziano Treu, 'Tripartite Social Policy Making: An Overview', in *Participation in Public Policy Making: The Role of Trade Unions and Employers' Associations*, ed. Tiziano Treu, Berlin and New York, Walter de Gruyter, 1992; Martin Rhodes, 'Globalisation, Labour Markets and Welfare States: A Future of "Competitive Corporatism"?', paper prepared for the Bern Joint Sessions of the European Consortium for Political Research, 1997; Crouch, *Industrial Relations and the European State Tradition*: 345–350; Marino Regini, 'Organized Interests and the Regulation of European Economies', paper prepared for the Séminaire RECO 'La Réorganisation des Etats Européen', MRASH Grenoble, 18–19 September 1997.

PART I

COUNTRY STUDIES

Chapter 1

Austria in Historical Perspective: From Civil War to Social Partnership

Jill Lewis

The contrast between the histories of Austria's two republics is great. The First Republic (1918–34) was dubbed the 'state which no-one wanted'.[1] Dismissed as economically unviable, it was destroyed by civil war and fascism. Austrian prospects after 1945 seemed little better and yet the Second Republic became an economic and political success. This transformation has been attributed to two basic principles underlying the political culture of the Second Republic:[2] corporatism in domestic political and economic decision making, and neutrality, which dominated foreign policy until the collapse of the Communist bloc and Austria's membership of the European Union in 1995. Both principles identified conflict as the greatest threat to the survival of an independent and prosperous Austrian state.

The main purpose of this article is to trace the ideological and institutional roots of Social Partnership in nineteenth- and twentieth-century Austria. The question of the use of the term 'Social Partnership' in the Austrian context refers not only to the values underlying the postwar culture of consensus, but also to the institutional and behavioural framework of the shared decision-making process. The difference between this and comparable systems of concertationalism is that the Austrian system has become formalised and is a permanent factor in policy making, possessing certain legal and quasi-legal rights. It is also complex and fluid, having expanded and adapted to the changing circumstances of Austrian domestic and foreign politics. Whether the system can continue to adapt has been the topic of heated debate.[3]

Since 1963 Austria has had a permanent and institutional system of forums designed to facilitate the operation of the Social Partnership and collective decision making. The system is centralised, hierarchical and labyrinthine. It is dominated by a joint commission, the Parity Commission, on which sit representatives of the government, peak associations (the Social Partners) and experts, and which acts as an umbrella organisation for an ever-evolving system of commissions, committees and subcommittees. First set up in 1957, the Parity Commission was originally designed as an informal, voluntary and temporary body comprising four government ministers, including the chancellor, two representatives of each of the three economic Chambers (representing employers, employees and agriculture), and two from the Austrian Trade Union Federation (ÖGB). Its remit was to tackle the immediate threat of inflation and to draw up a stable wages and prices policy.[4] In 1963 the Parity Commission became a permanent institution and its two existing subcommittees, on Prices and Wages, which formulated prices and incomes policy recommendations, were joined by a third body, the Advisory Committee on Economic and Social Questions, whose task was to gather information on wider socioeconomic matters (such as social welfare, taxation and fiscal questions) and to provide a forum for discussion. Membership included not only representatives of government and the peak organisations, but also experts from the National Bank, economic research institutes, universities and the Central Office of Statistics.[5] The actual work of the Advisory Committee was, and still is, carried out by a large number of subcommittees and working parties that offer specific policy recommendations to the Parity Commission, which in turn submits these to the relevant government ministries. The actual policy-making processes within the committees of the Parity Commission vary considerably, with some meeting far more often than others. Bargaining is carried out in private, the object of the exercise being to present unanimous policy recommendations to government. Should compromise at the committee level prove impossible, issues are resolved by a committee of the presidents of the four major Social Partners. This system of subcommittees has allowed the Social Partnership to respond to rapid changes in Austrian domestic and foreign policy: for instance, in 1992 a (fourth) subcommittee for international affairs was set up within the Parity Commission, following Austria's entry into the European Union and the opening of the East European markets.[6]

The Social Partnership is, therefore, an extensive, institutional and centralised system of shared, elite decision making. Despite this, the Parity Commission itself has no explicit constitutional status – although its members, the Social Partners, do – but operates on the basis of unanimous public policy recommendations reached by privately negotiated consensus and compromise. As Bernd Marin puts it:

> The Parity Commission is not enshrined in the Constitution either as the centre for cooperation between the [peak] associations or as an advisory organ to the federal government … . Nor does [it] have any fixed meeting place where it may be found, nor an address where it may be reached. It has no telephone number, no headed paper, nor any office personnel of its own.[7]

Attempts to detail its structure are hampered by the fluidity and informality of its plethora of constituent committees. Its role is also difficult to define:

whilst the scope of its activities has greatly increased since the 1960s, the extent of its actual influence has fluctuated and its ability to determine wages and prices policy ended in 1992.[8]

The enlargement of the scope of the Parity Commission in 1963 and its promotion from a temporary to a permanent body was significant, for this required agreement that policy consultation must be regular and sustained, and instigated the involvement of the Social Partners in the formation of social and economic policy beyond the sphere of wages and prices. Tálos contends that a core feature of the Austrian Social Partnership was the acknowledgement by the peak associations that they shared common long-term goals which could not be dealt with effectively on an ad hoc basis.[9] The year 1963, for him, marks the real foundation of the Austrian Social Partnership, the institutionalised basis of Austro-corporatism or cooperative, concerted policy making. But this narrow definition raises several problems, for it implies that the term 'Social Partnership' is inappropriate when applied to both the less formal collective decision-making structures of most other European states, and those which already existed in Austria. For instance, although the Parity Commission first became a formal institution in 1963, it had existed informally since 1957, and the convention of including peak organisations in negotiations on wages and prices was an integral part of the new consensus politics which was established during the first ten years of postwar reconstruction. Was the Austrian Social Partnership founded in 1945, 1957 or 1963? If a wider definition of Social Partnership is adopted, i.e. a system of values which underpin concertational policy making, the term can be applied to the period of informal collective decision making after the Second World War, when the culture of consensus was developing, but the institutions had not been fully established. If 'Social Partnership' refers to an institutional system, the answer must be 1963, and the Austrian Social Partnership is a '*Sonderfall*', a model that is specific to Austria, arising from historical traditions and the unique circumstances of postwar Austria. And yet, as this book clearly shows, similar trends occurred simultaneously throughout Europe.[10]

It is the contention of this article that there were institutional and ideological traditions in Austria that contributed to the emergence of concertation politics, but that these should not be exaggerated. Forms of centralised and bureaucratic concertation policy formation had existed in the Habsburg Empire, the First Republic, and the *Ständestaat,* but with limited success. Catholic corporatism and socialist reformism, the universalist ideologies that underpinned the Christian Social and Social Democratic Parties respectively, both advocated state-regulated capitalism, but for different reasons and, until 1945, these fuelled confrontational rather than consensus politics. The key difference after 1945 was the level of elite consensus and the endorsement of political compromise. Conflicting economic and class interests did not disappear, but the elites agreed that these should not be pursued at the expense of the common goals of high economic growth, low unemployment and political stability. The culture of political and class conflict was replaced by widespread and close collaboration between a few centralised and hierarchical peak associations, the political parties and the government.

The Empire

It is tempting to argue that the complex and bureaucratic nature of the Social Partnership, its semi-transparent structure and its emphasis on secret negotiations followed by unanimous decisions, are themselves legacies of the Habsburg Empire, where the red tape of the state administration was said to thwart change for fear of its consequences. Indeed, the institutional seeds of Austro-corporatism do lie in the nineteenth century, when all aspects of policy were dominated by the central issue of preserving the multinational Empire in the face of rising nationalist demands. The fundamental economic aim of Austrian governments was to consolidate the Empire by creating an economic autarky which would bind together the disparate regions into a single economic unit, using incentives such as loans, tax exemptions and privileges to encourage industrial development and deflect conflicting national and regional demands. The last internal customs barriers were removed in 1849 and 1860 and strict import restrictions and protectionist tariffs were employed to deter foreign trade. Economic cartelisation followed, with the banks playing an unusually important role in industrial development and economic policy formation.[11] A centralised state administered by a professional bureaucracy had arisen from the administrative and economic reforms of the late eighteenth century, and until the First World War economic decision making was dominated by civil servants and governed by the single consideration of political survival. The centralisation and bureaucratisation of the state administration led not only to the growth of a vast and cumbersome civil service (estimated to number 126,230 in 1842) but also to the professionalisation of policy formation and the involvement in this of expert advisers from relevant fields.[12] A semi-autonomous economic planning body, the *Kommerzdirektorium,* had been set up by Metternich in 1818 and by the second half of the nineteenth century there were over fifty commissions and boards which advised government on social and economic policy.[13] Centralised policy making also required detailed information from the regions and this led to the first direct root of the Social Partnership. In December 1848 a law was passed setting up a Chamber of Trade (*Handels- und Gewerbekammer* to represent trade, industry and commerce, to advise the government on economic matters and to report annually on the state of trade and industry to the Ministry of Trade. Its role was gradually extended as local chambers were established throughout the Empire, coordinating and representing the interests of divergent regional and economic sectors – at both local and state levels – and disseminating economic and technical information to their members. Initially there was little to distinguish the Austrian Chambers of Trade from those which had been set up earlier in Britain and France. However, in 1861, the Liberal government cautiously extended the franchise to the industrial bourgeoisie, creating a separate electoral curia for members of the Chambers, a privilege that they retained until the introduction of male adult suffrage in 1907.[14] They remained the official voice of trade and industry even after the 1880s and 1890s, when economic protectionism encouraged the rapid growth of Austrian banks, industrial cartels and independent employers' associations. The employers' organisations, the most influential of which was the Association of Austrian Industrialists, did not enjoy the same legal rights as the Chambers of Trade, but they had an even greater influence on tariffs and economic policy making.[15] The Chambers of Trade were the first statutory peak association in Austria and the model for the Chambers of Labour and Agriculture which were established in the First Republic and became key actors in the Austrian Social Partnership in the Second Republic.

Ideological links with the Social Partnership can also be found in the Imperial Catholic and Socialist political movements, principally in Catholic corporatism and Austro-Marxist theories of the state. Although their underlying principles were diametrically opposed, both advocated state intervention. The decline of Austrian Liberalism at the end of the nineteenth century coincided with the revival of Catholic corporatist theories, notably those of Karl von Vogelsang, the intellectual leader of Catholic Social Reform and the embryonic Christian Social Party. Vogelsang's utopian and backward-looking panacea condemned modern capitalism for its individualism and lack of Christian morality and proposed a homogeneous corporate society of economic estates based on Christian moral principles, social duty, and administered by strict state control. State intervention and immediate social reform were necessary to obviate the evils of capitalism, but these should be protective, fostering self-help and the organic regeneration of society on corporatist lines.[16] Vogelsang chaired the 1883 parliamentary committee, (one of the first to include representatives of labour), which led to laws establishing factory inspections, accident and sickness insurance, and limitations to the working day and to the use of child and female labour.[17] But welfare reforms were merely a palliative measure and Vogelsang's long-term goal was to halt economic concentration and recreate an economy dominated by guild production, bound by a social contract between employers and labour. Under Karl Lueger's leadership the Christian Social Party replaced anti-capitalist social theory with populist rhetoric. The corporate body became the tax-paying, property-owning petty bourgeoisie that made up Lueger's Viennese constituency. Modernism was combined with vitriolic attacks on 'Jewish' capital, social welfare was transformed into 'communalism' and public ownership of public utilities, and anti-liberalism became anti-socialism.[18]

Between 1892 and 1906 Leopold Kunschak founded a union movement based on the papal encyclical *Rerum Novarum* and concepts of social consensus based on Catholic values, compromise between employers and workers, and the rejection of class conflict and the use of the strike. Despite the strength of Catholicism in the country, the movement failed to attract support from industrial workers and antagonised Catholic Conservatives, whose vision of a corporate society did not include the proletariat.[19] But corporatism continued to influence Catholic intellectuals such as Franz M. Schindler and Ignaz Seipel, both of whom advocated occupational estates, but rejected neo-Romantic organic corporatism, and Othmar Spann, whose theory of universalism separated political and economic roles within the organic state.[20]

Despite labour representation on Vogelsang's social welfare committee and on accident insurance boards, antagonism to organised labour in the Empire largely excluded its participation in policy formation. Government proposals for a separate Chamber of Labour in 1886 and for a separate Labour Ministry in 1908 both failed and adult male suffrage was resisted until 1907. Local socialist unions had existed since 1867 and voluntary collective bargaining and coalition rights had been granted, but the frequent use of anti-terrorist laws, combined with fierce internal divisions between radicals and moderates, undermined unity and weakened the movement. In 1889, at Hainfeld, Victor Adler succeeded in bridging sectional schisms to establish the Social Democratic Workers' Party (SDAP), and four years later the first Socialist trade union congress was held: the party and the unions were, according to Adler, the 'Siamese twins' of Austrian socialism.[21] Two aspects of the Austrian socialist movement are important in the context of the roots of the Social Partnership. The first is the central tenet of unity and party discipline, which underpinned the success and strength of the SDAP, preventing the growth of a tangible Communist Party in the First Republic. Fears of internal conflict also fostered a centralised and paternalistic political party in which there was little direct grass-roots democracy, despite the huge growth in party membership and its vast network of clubs and societies. The relationship with the Socialist Trade Union Commission was truly symbiotic, with interacting leaderships and common goals, but the political party was in the dominant role. Policy was made by the party's executive committee, and unanimously endorsed by the annual national conference. Rank-and-file dissent became more vocal in the early 1930s, but party discipline was re-established in the Second Republic, a factor that was crucial for the development of the Social Partnership.

The second critical characteristic of Austrian socialism lay in the Austro-Marxist theory of the neutral state, which was developed by Rudolf Hilferding, Karl Renner and Otto Bauer. Hilferding argued that the growth of cartelisation and 'finance capital' led to 'organised capitalism' with greater state intervention in economic planning and social welfare programmes. Socialism could be achieved by seizing state power, rather than by abolishing the state, and building upon the social and economic reforms of bourgeois governments. Whilst retaining the language of class conflict and revolution, the Austro-Marxists encouraged participation in the political system in order to bring about reform. Bauer was to develop this theory yet further in the First Republic.

Economic policy making in the Habsburg Empire was bureaucratic, centralised and had created formal and informal structures for consultation, but these remained essentially bipartite, largely excluding organised labour. This continued in the early years of the First World War, when all political activity, including Parliament, was banned for the duration. The 1912 War Service Law introduced military control into factories, suspending most existing labour regulations and increasing the powers of employers. Deteriorating output and a great increase in unofficial strikes forced a change of policy: in 1917 Complaints Commissions were established with powers to impose compulsory arbitration in disputes between workers and employers over working conditions and to set legally enforceable wage rates for workers covered by the War Services Law. The Commissions included representatives of the Army, government ministries, employers' associations and the trade unions, and were thus the first examples of tripartite consultation and of compulsory collective bargaining.[22] In the same year the General Commission for the Wartime and Transitional Economy was set up, comprising representatives of the Chamber of Trade, unions, sickness funds, industrial groups and political parties.[23] The government announced the creation of a Ministry of Social Welfare in October 1917.

In the final year of the war the Austrian state turned to concertational politics, but out of crisis rather than conviction. The political characteristics of the disintegrating Habsburg Empire indicated a tradition of centralised decision making, corporate identities and weak liberalism, which manifested itself in the belief in state intervention, but with little consultation. These are necessary, but not sufficient criteria for concertational politics. The missing ingredient was consensus, as the history of the First Republic clearly shows.

The First Republic

The collapse of the Empire led to political stalemate in which, for a short period, the basis for institutionalised industrial relations and cooperative economic policy formation appeared. An Industrial Commission, the first 'parity commission' with equal representation for employers' organisations and unions, was established to draw up a coordinated policy for the transition to a peacetime economy. Its remit was wide and initially covered all aspects of the deconstruction of the wartime economy, but its central task was the demobilisation of labour from the war industries, job creation and unemployment insurance.[24] The birth of the Industrial Commission spanned the end of the war, but the vocabulary used to describe its ethos was to reappear in the 1950s. In one of the first meetings in 1918, Karl Renner, representing labour, spoke of the common interests which bound industry and labour: he argued that the prevailing crisis of industrial production could only be overcome through industrial self-government in which industry and labour would recognise a common interest in maintaining industrial productivity. There should be consultation between the two sides, but only between leading figures.[25] His views were endorsed by Anton Hueber, the leader of the Trade Union Commission, Richard Riedl, the general commissioner, and Heinrich Vetter of the Reichsverband der österreichischen Industrie. But the Industrial Commission was short-lived: by 1921 the Christian Social Party was in government and rising unemployment had begun to weaken labour power. The government and employers withdrew their support. Attempts to revive tripartite policy concertation in 1930 foundered on the issues of credit unions and unemployment benefit. The Free Trade Unions (formerly the Socialist Trade Union Commission) refused to take part in further talks on the grounds that there was no basis for long-term consensus with the employers.[26] By this time political polarisation had deteriorated into open class conflict.

Renner's concept of industrial collaboration between employers and labour was not an anomaly within the SDAP. Otto Bauer's analysis of the 1918 Austrian Revolution recognised two phases in the progress towards socialism.[27] The first was the political seizure of power, in which the existing state authority and institutions of power would be overthrown, but after which capitalist inequalities would remain. Socialism itself could only be achieved by a long-term process of transition and education, during which creative legislation would protect and extend the rights of the working class, whilst economic reorganisation would train them in the skills necessary to run an industrial economy. The key to Bauer's philosophy lay in his theory of the 'Balance of Class Forces' drawn from Marx's '18th Brumaire' and what became known as 'Bonapartism'. Marx argued that in extraordinary circumstances, when the relative strengths of opposing classes were roughly equal, the state could maintain an existence independent of class domination. At this stage, according to Bauer, the peaceful transformation of property relations through legislation was possible.[28]

The SDAP's 1919 electoral programme, which was drawn up by Bauer, advocated a staggered progression towards the socialisation of large-scale industry, landed estates and the banks. Individual companies would be run by joint boards including representatives of the state, workers and consumers. Smaller companies would be controlled by industrial boards, on which employers' organisations also sat, which would control buying and selling, prices, wages and rationalisation policies. Companies employing more than twenty workers would be legally obliged to set up factory councils elected by the workers, which would have joint control over all questions concerning workers' rights and working conditions. Socialisation of key economic sectors, the restructuring of industrial relations, and the expansion of welfare reforms were the basis of the SDAP's plans for the development of socialism.

By October 1920, when the SDAP left the governing coalition, many laws setting up the institutional framework for the transition to socialism had been passed, although the socialisation programme had been almost totally scuppered and the role of workers in factory management was ignored. The 1919 Factory Council Law was attacked by the trade unions, who complained that strong local workers' bodies would foster syndicalism; they succeeded in limiting the remit of the factory councils to the supervision of workers' welfare, the monitoring of the implementation of labour laws, and negotiations over local piece-rate agreements. National wage negotiations were conducted by the trade unions, and disputes over unfair dismissal or collective contracts were adjudicated by the Complaints Commissions, renamed Conciliation Offices, which retained their tripartite structure. The factory councils played no role in industrial management, but were given minimum consultation rights in the form of compulsory fortnightly meetings with employers, and access to annual profit and loss accounts. As unemployment soared, the powers of the unions and factory councils to enforce labour laws declined.[29]

The Chambers of Labour were the most important new peak institutions of the First Republic. These bodies were federally organised, with a central policy-making national conference, and were the legal representatives of workers' interests, paralleling the Chambers of Trade. They were required to draw up reports for the government on social legislation and the state of the labour market, collect labour statistics, and represent labour in negotiations with other organisations. All draft legislation relating to industry, commerce or labour relations had to be submitted to them for comment. The Chambers were also responsible for educating workers in labour law and retraining the unemployed. Membership was compulsory for all workers covered by sickness insurance and representatives were elected by proportional representation, ensuring the participation of the Catholic trade unions, but the domination of the Free Unions.[30] Until the removal of their autonomy in 1933, the Chambers of Labour provided an essential role in the professionalisation of the labour movement.

In 1923 provincial Chambers of Agriculture were also established to represent the interests of farmers and rural communities, presided over by the Conference of the Presidents of the Agricultural Chambers. The Agricultural Chambers were given the same powers as the two existing Chambers, but despite the size and political importance of the rural economy, their influence was not great and they were eclipsed by the rural political parties.[31]

The system of Chambers was the first institutionalised approach in Austria to concerted policy formation, which recognised constitutional, monopolistic and economically diverse interest groups. It was established in the aftermath of war and revolution, when economic and political chaos forced the opposing classes to compromise. This situation did not last. The state was not neutral. After hyperinflation and the collapse of the currency in 1923, economic policy makers were preoccupied with stabilisation. Successive anti-socialist coalition governments placed social welfare at the bottom of their lists of political priorities.[32] Radical social welfare reforms remained on the statute book, including the Factory Council Law, a statutory eight-hour working day, paid holidays, health insurance, unemployment benefit and legally enforceable collective contracts, but they were increasingly ignored by employers, leading to escalating industrial and political conflict.[33] Political and economic compromise was completely dead by 1927. The Christian Social Chancellor, Engelbert Dollfuss, prorogued parliament on a technicality in 1933 and eleven months later banned the SDAP, the largest single political party in the country, and the Free Trade Unions, unleashing civil war. In the light of this, it is difficult to accept the argument of Luther and Müller, that the First Republic should be seen 'as an ultimately unsuccessful attempt at co-operation, rather than as an exclusively confrontational episode in Austria's political history'.[34] Whilst the institutions for concertation politics existed, consensus did not. Compromise had lasted for the first two years, conflict for the next eleven years.

The Ständestaat

Dollfuss's new state returned to the corporatist traditions of the Christian Social Party, combining romantic and economic corporatism, and creating an Austrian variant of fascism. The 1934 constitution proclaimed Austria to be a 'Social, Christian, German state, ... founded upon estates under strong authoritarian leadership'.[35] The surviving independent political parties were replaced by a state-sponsored body, the Fatherland Front. Parliament was replaced by a complex system of six councils, members of which were nominated by the Chancellor's office or provincial governors. In theory, an Economics Council (*Bundeswirtschaftsrat*), whose members were to be delegated from six occupational corporations, representing employers and labour from the basic economic sectors, would advise the government on economic issues. In practice only two corporations, for civil servants and for land and forestry, were set up. Employers were organised into four independent associations, for industry, insurance, trade and transport, and craft trades (*Gewerbebetrieben*), whilst the Catholic and Independent Unions (allied to the native Fascist *Heimwehr* movement) were absorbed into a single union, the Federation of Workers and Salaried Employees. Appointments to all of these bodies were restricted to members of the Fatherland Front.[36]

On paper the structure of the *Ständestaat* allowed independent interest-group participation in policy formation, according to the corporatist principles outlined in the 1931 papal encyclical, *Quadragesimo Anno*. In practice the constitution was a legalistic façade for authoritarian government. The independent labour movement was driven underground, civil rights were removed and members of the advisory councils were government appointees. Agricultural protectionism and fiscal conservatism characterised economic policy, which was greatly influenced by Viktor Kienböck, the president of the National Bank, and sought, unsuccessfully, to achieve a stable currency, stable prices and a balanced budget.[37] Last-minute attempts to negotiate with the illegal labour movement failed and from 1938 to 1945 Austria was absorbed into Nazi Germany and became subject to the policies outlined in Stefan Berger's article in this book.

The Second Republic

Austria's position after the Second World War created conditions in which internal compromise was perceived to be essential for survival. The image of Austria as the 'first victim of Hitlerite oppression' (Moscow Declaration) was studiously nurtured in the Second Republic, despite escalating doubts about the legitimacy of the claim. Much was written about the new spirit of unity that was said to have been forged in the concentration camps, where Social Democrat and Christian Social leaders were both imprisoned.[38] Political cooperation has characterised postwar governments. A grand coalition government of the Socialist Party of Austria and the Austrian People's Party (SPÖ/ÖVP) held office for the first twenty years of the Republic, and introduced a system of proportional representation in the allocation of government and administrative jobs, but it is doubtful that this policy of political cooperation was solely the product of Nazi persecution. One important factor was the ten years of postwar occupation and, in particular, the presence of Soviet troops on one-third of Austrian territory along the European Cold War border between East and West. Protracted negotiations with the Four Power Allied Council for the return of Austrian sovereignty encouraged consensus amongst political parties and peak organisations on economic planning and large-scale state intervention in the economy and in industrial relations. Employers agreed to the nationalisation of key economic sectors and restrictions on their managerial autonomy, whilst the unions abandoned confrontational class conflict in return for participation in policy formation, social welfare gains and long-term economic stability. Both sides became key players in negotiations with government over social and economic questions. The basis for the Social Partnership, therefore, lay in the decade of Occupation.

The institutional structures for concertational politics were similar to those of the First Republic. Laws in 1945 and 1946 re-established the three Chambers, with compulsory membership, and in 1947 a new Factory Council Law was passed. Union sectarianism was minimised by the founding of a centralised non-political trade union federation, the ÖGB, which included Socialist, Catholic and (theoretically) Communist unions, but which was led by Socialist union leaders. Although the ÖGB did not have a constitutional monopoly over trade union organisation, under the 1947 Law on Collective Bargaining it was given sole rights to negotiate wage contracts on behalf of labour, giving it monopoly status in practice. The Federal Economic Chamber (the successor to the Chambers of Trade) negotiated on behalf of the employers, who were unable to create a united front, and so combined the roles played by both the Chamber of Labour and the ÖGB for employees.[39] Overall, the similarities between the First and Second Republics indicate that the institutions could facilitate the development of concertational politics, but they could not create it. Consensus leading to compromise was the product of ideological shifts brought about by the Occupation and the identification of common interests and goals.

One example is the Nationalisation Laws of 1946 and 1947, which brought the bulk of the mining, steel, machinery, chemical and electrical industries into public ownership, along with the three major banks, and created the largest public-sector economy in the Western world.[40] The rationale behind this was not elite conversion to socialism, particularly not on the part of the employers, but the agreed goal of protecting Austrian capital from Soviet reparation claims. In 1945 the Soviet authorities laid claim to all German property in Austria as legitimate war reparations, arguing that almost all productive capital in Austria was, by definition, German, ownership having been transferred during *Anschluss*. The Austrian coalition government, backed by the other three Occupying Powers, responded by nationalising the key industries outside the Soviet sector, establishing them as limited companies.[41] The scale of nationalisation did not result in a planned economy, but what Eduard März has described as an early 'mixed economy'.[42] The companies retained managerial control and operated according to market economy principles, but their political influence was reduced. The Association of Austrian Industrialists, the largest employers' association, no longer represented banking and heavy industry, whilst the nationalisation of these industries provided the government with a lever with which to enforce price restrictions on the private and the public sectors. The nationalisation policy itself also proved that, if the situation was critical, employers would compromise on crucial issues such as property relations, allowing public ownership as long as this did not involve state-run management.

Union leaders were also willing to compromise on the equally critical issue of wage rates. Inflationary tendencies began to threaten the very fragile economy in 1947, and for the next four years wages and prices were regulated by a series of five Wages and Prices Agreements, negotiated by an ad hoc, voluntary, advisory economic commission, the *Wirtschaftskommission,* comprising representatives of the three Chambers and the ÖGB, and then passed to the cabinet for ratification. The first was hastily drawn up in 1947 to combat a severe food crisis, rising agricultural prices and inflationary wage tendencies. It introduced price rises for public utilities and agriculture at over 50 percent, and a sliding scale for wages to cover most, though not all, of the anticipated increase in the cost-of-living, with the provision that the unions could demand further wage increases if the cost-of-living index rose by more than 10 percent in a year. When the index rose by 14.5 percent in six months, union leaders did not put in new wage claims.[43] The interests of their members, they argued, would not be served by competing wage demands, but by long-term economic growth, which required short-term sacrifices. Despite grass-roots protests against successive Wages and Prices Agreements and lower real wages, the ÖGB leadership maintained this policy, accusing the Communist Party and the Soviet authorities of fermenting opposition in order to destabilise the Republic. In 1950 the ÖGB dismissed communist union officials following a widespread strike movement.[44] Union leaders used fears of a Communist coup to consolidate their control over rank-and-file members, urging wage restraint and abandoning the politics of class interests in the name of the national interest and tripartite policy formation. From 1951 onwards the ÖGB president, Böhm, was the leading proponent of institutionalised concertational policy formation, which would give labour a voice in economic decision making beyond the sphere of labour policy.

The employers' attitude to concertational politics was less consistent. Economic recovery required industrial peace, particularly in the precarious political conditions of the Allied Occupation. Economic growth, full employment, a stable currency, wage restraint, low consumer consumption and increased capital investment were all goals which the Federal Economic Chamber and the leading employers' association, the Federation of Austrian Industrialists, shared with the government and the ÖGB. These were also the central policies of the Marshall Plan. Voluntary participation in joint consultation with the other economic interest groups on economic policy was also acceptable to the employers when there was a crisis, but they rejected plans to set up a permanent form of cooperation and agreement between government ministries and the interest groups, arguing that this was unconstitutional and would interfere with the workings of the market.[45]

Consensus politics declined in the mid-1950s at the very time that the Austrian State Treaty was being concluded. Böhm's proposals for a legally constituted consultative institution were spurned again in 1955. Two years later, with rising inflation, a shortage of skilled labour and the threat of strikes, the Federal Economic Chamber agreed to take part in a Parity Commission to look into wages and prices. Initially this was to be another temporary measure, following the precedent of the Wages and Prices Commissions, but the success of its stabilisation policy convinced employers of the benefits of sustained consultation and the permanent structures of the Social Partnership were established. For the next twenty years policy formation was dominated by a tight oligarchy of monopolistic peak associations and political parties.

Conclusion

Austrian postwar reconstruction was based on a close working relationship between the government and centralised peak groups representing labour, employers and agriculture. The formalisation of this relationship between 1957 and 1961 was followed by over two decades of rapid and sustained economic growth, for which the Social Partnership was popularly believed to be responsible, and, despite severe political and economic attacks on the system, the majority of Austrians still consider Social Partnership to be a positive force in political and economic life. Social Partnership is a product of both its historical traditions and the immediate circumstances in which it was born. Whilst institutional and ideological roots can be found in the Empire and the First Republic, a political culture of consensus was missing. In the Second Republic that consensus was established. The geopolitical position of Austria as an outpost of western capitalism and the protracted presence of Soviet troops on Austrian soil produced the conditions for concertational politics and Social Partnership.

Notes

1. Bruno Kreisky, *Zwischen den Zeiten: Erinnerungen aus fünf Jahrzehnten,* Berlin, 1986: 40.
2. Günter Bischof and Anton Pelinka, *Austro-Corporatism: Past, Present, Future*. Contemporary Austrian Studies, vol. 4, New Jersey, 1996: 1.
3. Edgar Grande and Wolfgang C. Müller, 'Sozialpartnerschaftliche Krisensteuerung oder Krise der Sozialpartnerschaft', in: Peter Gerlich et al., *Sozialpartnerschaft in der Krise*, Vienna, 1995: 11–28.
4. Emmerich Tálos and Bernhard Kittel, 'Roots of Austro-Corporatism: Institutional Preconditions and Cooperation Before and After 1945', in Bischof and Pelinka, *Austro-Corporatism*, 43.
5. Bernd Marin, *Die Paritätische Kommission: Aufgeklärter Technokorporatismus in Österreich,* Vienna, 1982: 258.
6. See the article by Tálos and Kittel in this book.
7. Marin, *Die Paritätische Kommission*, 15f.
8. Robert Fannion, 'Institutional Evolution: Constructing a New Place for the Chambers Beyond Austria's Social Partnership', Arbeiterkammerbibliothek, Vienna, 1996: 1.
9. Emmerich Tálos, 'Sozialpartnerschaft': in Gerlich et al., *Sozialpartnerschaft,* 58.
10. Gerlich et al, *Sozialpartnerschaft*, 355–66.
11. N.T. Gross, 'The Habsburg Monarchy', in *The Fontana Economic History of Europe,* ed. Carlo M. Cipolla, vol. 1: 228–78.
12. C.A. Macartney, *The Habsburg Monarchy, 1790–1918,* London, 1973: 263.
13. Tálos, 'Sozialpartnerschaft', 44.
14. Ferdinand Tremel, 'Der Binnenhandel und seine Organisation. Der Fremdenverkehr', in: *Die Wirtschaftliche Entwicklung*, ed. Alois Brusati, Vienna, 1973, vol. 1 of *Die Habsburgmonarchie 1848–1918*, eds. A. Wandruszka and P. Urbanitsch: 394–395.
15. Der Central-Verband der Industriellen Österreichs was founded in 1892 and der Bund österreichischer Industrieller in 1897. Josef Mentschl, 'Das österreichische Unternehmertum', in: *Die Habsburgmonarchie 1848–1918*, ed. Alois Brusatti, Vienna, 1973, vol. 1, 261. (On cartelisation, see David Good, *The Economic Rise of the Habsburg Empire, 1750–1914*, Berkeley, 1984, ch. 7.)
16. Margarete Grandner, 'Conservative Social Politics in Austria, 1880–1980', *Austrian History Yearbook*, vol. 27 (1996): 77–109.
17. Charles A. Gulick, *Austria from Habsburg to Hitler*, Berkeley, 1948, vol. 1: 181.
18. John W. Boyer, *Political Radicalism in Late Imperial Vienna*, Chicago, 1981: 184–247.
19. John W. Boyer, *Culture and Political Crisis in Vienna*, Chicago, 1995: 312–13.
20. Alfred Diamant, *Austrian Catholics and the First Republic: Democracy, Capitalism and the Social Order*, Princeton, 1960: 229–240.
21. Wolfgang Maderthaner, 'Die Entwicklung der Organisationsstruktur der deutschen Sozialdemokratie in Österreich 1889 bis 1913', in *Sozialdemokratie und Habsburgerstaat,* ed. Wolfgang Maderthaner, Vienna, 1988: 30.
22. Grandner, 'Conservative Social Politics in Austria', 64–5.
23. Peter Fischer, 'Ansätze zu Sozialpartnerschaft am Beginn der Ersten Republik', in *Historische Wurzeln der Sozialpartnerschaft,* ed. Gerald Stourzh and Margarete Grandner, Vienna, 1986: 225–42.
24. Tálos, 'Sozialpartnerschaft', 49.
25. Fischer, 'Ansätze zu Sozialpartnerschaft', 229.
26. Tálos, 'Sozialpartnerschaft', 50.

27. Otto Bauer, *The Austrian Revolution,* trans. J.H. Stenning, New York,1970: *Der Weg zum Sozialismus,* Berlin, 1919.
28. Jill Lewis, *Fascism and the Working Class in Austria, 1918–1934,* Oxford, 1991: 50–7.
29. Ibid., 109–22.
30. Gulick, *Austria from Habsburg to Hitler,* vol.1: 223–6.
31. Alfred Klose, 'Die Interessenverbände', in *Österreich 1918–1938*, ed. Erika Weinzierl and Kurt Skalnik, Styria, 1983: vol.1: 331–43.
32. Anton Staudinger, 'Christlichsoziale Partei..' in *Österreich 1918–1938*, ed. Erika Weinzierl and Kurt Skalnik, 255.
33. Max Lederer, 'Social Legislation in the Republic of Austria', *International Labour Review*, vol. II, Nos. 2–3, May–June 1921: 133–59.
34. Kurt Richard Luther and Wolfgang C. Müller, *Politics in Austria: Still a case of Consociationalism*, London, 1992: 7.
35. Jill Lewis, 'Austria', in *Fascists and Conservatives,* ed. Martin Blinkhorn, London, 1990: 99.
36. Ibid.
37. Siegfried Mattl, 'Die Finanzdiktatur: Wirtschaftspolitik in Österreich, 1933–1938', in *'Austrofaschismus': Beiträge über Politik, Ökonomie und Kultur 1934–1938*, ed. E. Tálos and W. Neugebauer, Vienna, 1985: 133–60.
38. Reinhard Sieder, Heinz Steinert and Emmerich Tálos, 'Wirtschaft, Gesellschaft und Politik in der Zweiten Republik. Eine Einführung', in *Österreich 1945–1995: Gesellschaft, Politik, Kultur,* ed. Reinhard Sieder, Heinz Steinert, Emmerich Tálos, Vienna, 1996: 9–11.
39. Tálos and Kittel, 'Roots of Austro-Corporatism', 34.
40. Eduard März, 'Austria's Economic Development 1945–85', in *Austria: A Study in Achievement*, ed. Jim Sweeney and Josef Weidenholzer, Aldershot, 1988: 32.
41. Jill Lewis, 'Auf einem Seile tanzen: Die Anfänge des Marshall-Planes und des Kalten Krieges in Österreich', in *'80 Dollar': 50 Jahre ERP-Fonds und Marshall-Plan in Österreich 1948–1998,* ed. Günter Bischof and Dieter Stiefel, Vienna, 1999: 305–7.
42. Eduard März, *Österreichs Wirtschaft zwischen Ost und West,* Vienna, 1965: 19.
43. Jill Lewis, 'Auf einem Seile tanzen', 309.
44. Fritz Klenner, *Die österreichischen Gewerkschaften,* vol.2, Vienna, 1953: 1460–76.
45. Tálos, 'Sozialpartnerschaft', 68–70.

CHAPTER 2

AUSTRIA IN THE 1990S: THE ROUTINE OF SOCIAL PARTNERSHIP IN QUESTION?

Emmerich Tálos and Bernhard Kittel

Introduction

'Austro-corporatism', the Austrian variant of social partnership, has both undergone some important changes and exhibited a large amount of continuity during the 1990s. Developments in the economic, institutional and political environment in which the Austrian political system is embedded have had their repercussions on the conditions and functioning of the Austrian socio-policy making system,[1] but at the same time social partnership has changed due to these developments and problems of internal aggregation within the core organisations, so that the changes which we will describe in this chapter do not point to a system transformation but to a realignment of the policy making network to the challenges set by the new environment. The evidence we find does not favour the proposition of a 'de-austrification', as has recently been argued, but points towards gradual realignments in terms of power, influence and importance without sacrificing the basic institutional, organisational, and behavioural patterns.[2]

While policy concertation is generally defined in this book as the co-determination of public policy by means of agreements made between governments and employer organisations and trade union confederations, this notion must be specified more precisely to capture the distinctiveness of the Austrian Social Partnership.[3] In the Austrian context, social partnership is more than a complex of underlying conceptions and values that legitimate the participation of the interest associations of workers and employers in the process of policy making. 'Social Partnership' refers to the whole complex of policy making and encompasses two dimensions of policy concertation: *Konzertierung* and *Akkordierung*. While the former generally refers to the participation of interest associations in governmental policy formulation and policy making, the latter focuses on their participation in the explicit search for, and realisation of, compromises between either the government and the peak interest associations or between the peak associations alone.

Policy Concertation in Austria

Austrian social partnership has a long tradition and is characterised by a high degree of informality in the relations among the actors. Although the actors themselves are highly institutionalised – being either highly monopolised and centralised organisations, agents set up by public law, or both – any account referring to formal institutions as the central feature of social partnership misses the point. It is the very institutionalisation and strength of the actors themselves that makes them able to rely less on institutionalised forms of interaction than on informal face-to-face contacts for reaching consensus about political matters. If formal 'social pacts' – as have been concluded elsewhere in Europe during the 1990s and which are regarded as a renewal of corporatist policy making[4] – were necessary in Austria, this would indicate a severe problem of social partnership. The sole formal peak level agreement in the 1990s which comes close to a 'social pact', the agreement between the large interest associations (the 'big four') of November 1992, was concluded during a period of communication problems between labour and capital, and as this agreement was a reaffirmation of the common understanding of the procedure of interest intermediation and the handling of conflict, its existence points to sand in the wheels of social partnership.

Key terms used in Austrian politics to refer to important aspects of social partnership are summarised in Table 2.1. Austrian social partnership is an attempt to coordinate various dimensions of socioeconomic policy making in an 'enlightened', technocratic policy-making process aiming at a long-run consolidation of interests. This entails two closely interrelated though distinct approaches to interest intermediation. On the one hand, social partnership in a narrow sense relates to the autonomous interaction of the trade unions and the employers' organisations in incomes policy.[5] In a broader sense, social partnership refers to the participation of the interest associations in political decision-making processes and agreements which may not only be tripartite but may even imply that the major interest associations negotiate draft legislation in socioeconomic policy areas without government interference. In extreme cases the government then presents the draft as it is to parliament for approval. As the same highly centralised and monopolistically organized associations have crucial roles in both forms of social partnership, this distinction has little importance in practice; from an analytical point of view it is, however, the clue to understanding the distinctive density of the Austrian policy-making network.

Table 2.1. *Key Terms in Austria*

Term	Meaning
Sozialpartnerschaft	Network of close, formally and informally institutionalised interactions, *Konzertierung*, and *Akkordierung* between the trade union organisation ÖGB, the Chamber of Labour BAK, the Economic Chamber WKÖ, the Chambers of Agriculture PKLWK, and government agencies
Sozialpartner	Term referring to all agents of social partnership excluding government agencies, although often only the ÖGB and the WKÖ are meant
Konzertierung	Participation of interest associations in policy formulation and policy making
Akkordierung	Participation of interest associations in policy making with the explicit search for, and realisation of, tri- or bipartite compromises
Kooperativ-konzertierte Politik (Konsenspolitik)	Policy style based on cooperation and concertation between the government and all major interest organisations, in which political decisions stem from bargained compromises between the actors
Kammer	(Chamber) interest organisation under public law to which the state has transferred areas of autonomous regulation of public issues relevant only to the constituency of the organisation
Beiräte/Kommissionen	Advisory councils charged with strategic and evaluative concerns attached to public institutions in which the social partners, among others, have a seat and often dominate. In many instances, this seat is allocated to them by law

Source: see text.

A core characteristic of the Austrian political system is the importance of the monopolised and centralised interest associations in policy-formation processes. The most important interest organisations, the 'big four', are the single trade union organisation (*Österreichischer Gewerkschaftsbund*, ÖGB), the Federal Chamber of Labour (*Bundesarbeitskammer*, BAK), the Austrian Federal Economic Chamber (*Wirtschaftskammer Österreich*, WKÖ), and the Chambers of Agriculture, usually represented by their peak association (*Präsidentenkonferenz der Landwirtschaftskammern*, PKLWK). The chambers are politically privileged in that they are established by law, have compulsory membership and possess the right to comment on government bills before these are decided in the council of ministers and forwarded to parliament.

Labour is thus represented by two organisations, ÖGB and BAK. The trade union is more concerned with workers' immediate interests, while the Chamber's role as a 'think tank' and service organisation for members is to provide background information for both trade union policy and, in particular, government social policy. In practice, the distinction has become somewhat blurred, notably because the BAK has extended its member services after a legitimation crisis in the early 1990s. The employers' side is almost completely monopolised by the WKÖ, which is concerned with both the political and the industrial relations dimensions of interest representation.[6]

The interest organisations are closely interlocked with the two dominant parties *Sozialdemokratische Partei Österreichs* (SPÖ) and *Österreichische Volkspartei* (ÖVP), linking the workers' organisations to the former and the employers' and the agricultural organisations to the latter.[7] These links are exemplified by the accumulation of both party and interest organisation positions by leading officials. Such 'vertical' interrelationships are combined with numerous horizontal interactions between the interest organisations both in the political and the industrial relations arena, resulting in the dense network of cooperation, *Konzertierung*, and *Akkordierung*, to which the notion of social partnership refers.

The structure of Austrian social partnership is highly differentiated. At the central level, the above-mentioned peak organisations of workers and employers take on two tasks. They set the framework for lower-level bipartite bargaining on diverse aspects of wages and working conditions and they are involved in policy-making processes.

At the intermediate level the Austrian system of social partnership is based on sectorally defined suborganisations of the ÖGB and the WKÖ. These 'Fachgewerkschaften' and 'Fachverbände' play the key role in wage setting in that they negotiate the actual wage levels for each industry. Usually, the metal sector is the first to negotiate on wage levels, setting a precedent for the negotiations in all other sectors.[8] In addition, the sectoral level has attained growing importance during the last decade due to the delegation to sectoral bargaining of the detailed specification of framework agreements negotiated by the peak organisations. This process has been especially prominent in working time policy. The 1997 amendment to the working time law explicitly transfers the task of determining the conditions of working time flexibilisation to the sectoral organisations of the interest associations.[9]

At the enterprise level, the relations between workers and employers are institutionalised in legally established works councils. These are entitled to bargain over the details of working conditions inside the framework set by the central and sectoral levels. Until the 1980s the trade unions had a firm grip on these bargaining processes via a close link to the enterprise worker representatives who mostly were trade union members. This close relationship has weakened during the 1990s as more and more council workers, especially in the white-collar sector, are no longer trade union members.[10]

Given the focus on policy concertation, we concentrate on the central level of social partnership which is in effect the sole important level when it comes to analysing the impact of interest organisations on political decision-making processes. Typically, from the 1960s to the 1980s, the decision-making processes dominated by social partnership consist of the following steps. First, informal consultations are held between the ministry in question, the SPÖ and the ÖVP (irrespective of which party is in government), and the 'big four' interest associations, from which results a first draft of a govern-

Table 2.2. *Forums of Concertation in Austria*

Name	Description
Parity Commission	Consultative body of the WKÖ, the BAK, the ÖGB and the PKLWK, presided over by the chancellor, in which the government participates without voting rights. Subcommittees on wages and prices (and since 1992 on international affairs) provide forums for discussing the economic situation in specific economic sectors, while more general macroeconomic issues are discussed in the Parity Commission itself; the Advisory Council for Economic and Social Affairs provides studies which lay down the common understanding of all participating actors
Parliamentary Commissions	(a) top representatives of interest organisations have a seat in parliament on either SPÖ or ÖVP ticket and thus consult within parliament, (b) parliamentary commissions invite experts from the social partners to discuss controversial issues
Government mediation	(tripartism) Ministers invite representatives from all social partners to discuss and decide controversial issues on both a regular and ad hoc basis
Bipartite negotiations	BAK (and ÖGB) and WKÖ are regularly asked by the government to work out a joint proposal for a specific regulation
Consultation	Social partners comment on government draft legislation within the framework of a formal consultation routine
Advisory councils	Policy area-specific discussion forums in which the social partners are able to articulate their interests
Informal negotiations	Contacts between social partners occur at all occasions and times, at all organisational levels, and in all imaginable places, according to perceived necessity

Source: see text.

ment bill. This process may take a long time if some of the actors disagree and can take place in any forum in which the involved actors meet, although certain patterns with regard to policy areas can be distinguished (see Tables 2.2 and 2.3). Second, the chambers officially review the draft, which is then revised and amended. This procedure is sometimes repeated several times.[11] After having reached broad consensus about the contents, the draft is passed by the council of ministers and forwarded to the parliament where some, often only minor, corrections are added. Because peak representatives of important interest associations hold important posts in the SPÖ or ÖVP and party seats in parliament, and because they hold core positions in parliamentary commissions, these corrections may again be based on compromises negotiated outside parliament between the interest organisations and/or between them and the two dominant parties.

In a second type of decision-making procedure, a draft bill is introduced into parliament on the initiative of one or more parties. Although neither

Table 2.3. *Policy Concertation and Public Policy in Austria*

Type of Policy Making	Policy Areas Covered
Concertation (in the sense of *Konzertierung* (between government and peak associations))	Social policy, fiscal policy, monetary policy, investment policy, industrial policy, trade policy, social welfare
Concertation (in the sense of *Akkordierung* (between peak associations))	Labour law, jobcreation and training, employment, equal opportunity policy
Konzertierung without *Akkordierung* (Government decision with individual participation of social partners)	Many fields in economic policy, some areas in social policy, consumer policy, environmental policy, some fields in judicial policy, some fields in technology policy
Government decision with *Konzertierung* and often *Akkordierung* between social partners	EU-issues
Government decision without, or with marginal influence of, social partners	Interior policy, many fields in judicial policy, foreign policy, some fields in technology policy, media policy, school policy

Source: see text.

Note: It is impossible to make a clear distinction across policy areas between concertation and consultation in Austrian policy making because government commitments to adopt particular policies agreed in tripartite discussions are seldom made explicit. Concertation in Austria is more a process of finding a common understanding which is then implemented by government policies. If no understanding can be reached, the issue is either left for further negotiations or the government attempts to impose either its own view or a policy close to the minimum consensus. Thus all policy areas which the editors have asked us to classify – fiscal policy, monetary policy, investment policy, industrial policy, trade policy, jobcreation and training, employment and social welfare – are the object of consultation, often with an option for concertation. However, we cannot classify these policy areas as merely the objects of consultation because all actors have the power to veto policies to which they do not adhere but may choose not to make use of this power for the sake of political and economic stability. The categories above, which are based on the terms used in Austrian politics, are meant as a classification of the dominant pattern observed in different policy areas. They do not capture changes and fluctuations over time.

interest organisations nor ministry need to be involved in such initiatives, it is often the case that preliminary bargaining processes with or between the social partners[12] are used to accelerate processing of a bill.

Thus, in practice a multitude of decision-making processes are possible ranging from the 'full procedure' to party initiatives in parliament that are or are not based on accords between the interest associations. Recent research has revealed that policy-making processes are much more diverse across different policy areas than the notion of encompassing social partnership suggests: there are several areas in which interest organisations do not coordinate their interests but act much more like lobbying pressure groups, and other areas in which the interest organisations are not involved at all (see Table 2.3).[13]

The Debate over Concertation: Challenges to Social Partnership

From the late 1950s to the late 1980s social partnership was accepted by virtually all influential organisations in Austrian society. Although some commentators questioned the legal basis of decision making by *Konzertierung* and *Akkordierung*, the economic and social success story of the 1960s and 1970s and the Christian-social ideological background of social consensus of the employers silenced all critique.[14]

Apart from fundamental opposition from the communist party (KPÖ), criticism is most fervently put forward by the minority parties in parliament. During all of the Second Republic, the right-wing *Freiheitliche Partei Österreichs* (FPÖ) has attacked both the interest organisations and the institution of social partnership as a dominant pattern of decision making in Austria, focusing on its alleged functioning as a 'second government' without election-based legitimacy and control. More specifically, this party's critique focuses on compulsory membership. In addition, in 1997 the FPÖ challenged the monopoly position of the ÖGB by constituting its own trade union organisation, which, however, has not been able to obtain bargaining rights up to the time of writing. Leaders argue that the domain of social partnership should be reduced to core arenas and be diminished at the macro level in favour of transferring bargaining to the enterprise level.

Similar points are made by the *Liberales Forum* (LIF), a liberal group that left the FPÖ in 1993. This party argues in favour of abolishing compulsory membership and reducing the influence of social partnership to its core function of finding compromises between workers and employers. The criticism of the large influence of social partnership on policy making, often at the expense of parliament, is shared by the Green Party. However, contrary to FPÖ and LIF, the Greens accept unconditionally the ÖGB and the Chamber of Labour as the genuine interest representatives of the workers and employees.

The main arguments for and against social partnership are summarised in Table 2.4.

The increased importance of these arguments in public debate led to a serious legitimation crisis of the Chambers in the early 1990s, focused not only on the issue of compulsory membership but also on bureaucratism, lack of democracy, sluggishness and lack of innovation. In addition, the interest associations themselves and their top officials have been subjected to increasing criticism. In recent years the number of members taking part in the elections in the Chambers has fallen, and ÖGB membership is in decline.[15]

The public debate on these issues led the government to urge the BAK, the WKÖ and the Chambers of Agriculture to question their constituencies on

Table 2.4. *Key Arguments in Austria*

Proponent	Argument
For	
Peak interest associations, government	Economic performance: positive effect on economic performance (unemployment, inflation)
Peak interest associations	Political performance: low level of open social conflict
Peak interest associations, government	Representational performance I: direct participation of large interest groups in policy making
Peak interest associations	Representational performance II: high acceptance by both constituency and population
Peak interest associations	Organisational performance: high level of service to constituency
Against	
Government (partly), media, opposition parties	Inefficient, slow, not innovative
Opposition parties	Undemocratic
Opposition parties	Does not represent minority interests; mandatory membership in Chambers
Opposition parties	Low representativeness
Enterprises, Federation of Austrian Industry	Unfavourable cost/benefit outcome, expensive

Source: see text.

their opinion on the status of the Chambers as an interest representation established by law, for which compulsory membership was regarded as a necessary prerequisite. These referenda took place during 1995 and 1996. With a participation rate of 66.6 percent (in the BAK) and 36.4 percent (in the WKÖ), 90.6 percent and 81.7 percent respectively of those participating voted in favour of the continuing existence of the Chambers. Despite this result, however, the need for the peak representatives to concentrate on motivating their constituencies led to a more adversarial tone between the interest associations in public debate which did not contribute to their ability to find compromises.

The above-cited results have calmed down public debate, although now and then criticisms are still articulated by large enterprises, which are less and less willing to pay their considerable membership dues to the WKÖ. For example, in June 1998 the Federation of Austrian Industry (IV) proposed that membership in the WKÖ be made optional if a firm was a member of the IV. However the WKÖ responded negatively, and this idea lacks broad support (even within the IV) for the time being. Nevertheless, there remains awareness of the need for further organisational reform. The basic orientation of this was laid down in the agreement between the social partners of November 1992, although its implementation was interrupted by the referenda on compulsory membership.

Regarding the acceptance of social partnership in the population we can note considerable continuity. In spite of up and down movements and a slight backwards tendency, the existing surveys show clearly that even in the changing context of social partnership, a remarkable majority considers social partnership to be favourable for Austria (60 percent in 1997 compared to 63 percent in 1990 and 69 percent in 1983). Only a small minority is convinced that it isn't (12 percent in 1997 compared to 6 percent in both 1990 and 1983). Similarly, the problem-solving competence of social partnership is confirmed by a majority of 57 percent (1994); only 26 percent denies this. This correlates with the finding that only a small minority of the respondents is in favour of abolishing social partnership (10 percent in 1994 as compared to 13 percent in 1990), while more than half of the respondents deny the need for abolition (64 percent in 1994 as compared to 58 percent in 1990).[16]

Patterns of Change and Continuity in Austro-Corporatism

Institutional Framework

The changes in the economic, political, and organisational environment of social partnership did not leave this mode of policy formation unaffected. The most visible changes in institutional perspective concern the Parity Commission with its institutions (the full assembly, the subcommittees on wages, prices and international affairs and the Advisory Council for Economic and Social Affairs), which has been regarded as a core institution of social partnership.[17] In all of these committees the ÖGB, BAK, WKÖ and PKLWK are represented with one vote each, while ministers and government officials participate in the full assembly without voting rights.

Formally, wage bargaining can still only be undertaken by sectoral trade union organisations after having been sanctioned to do so by the subcommittee on wages, but during the 1980s the subcommittee on prices lost its importance due to the deregulation of the prices of virtually all products, and currently serves as an occasional meeting place for discussing economic developments in specific sectors. Although the full assembly of the Parity Commission was never more than a forum in which wages and prices were formally decided, and this function was undercut by the loss of function of the subcommittee on prices, it was given a new formal task as a discussion forum for economic policy in the November 1992 agreement.

In contrast to its lack of relevance in relation to the effective decision-making process, the Parity Commission remains important due to the fact that it brings together the main actors in socioeconomic decision-making processes in a regular manner to discuss perspectives and clarify positions, the details of which can then be finalised in negotiations at the level of experts. In this respect the meetings of the presidents of the four large interest organisations are the most important because these are where the conflictual questions are dealt with. Thus the Parity Commission with its subcommittees can be considered to be a forum that provides the institutional framework and gives some ritual and continuity to the relations between the interest associations and to their contacts with the state.

Following a number of years of diminished ability on the part of the WKÖ and the ÖGB to agree on common views of economic policy during the early 1990s, the Advisory Council for Economic and Social Affairs gained both importance and status after having completed a series of economic studies during 1997 and 1998. In June 1998, a joint analysis of economic policies still open to political intervention in an era of increasing economic internationalisation not only reaffirmed the ability of the interest associations to agree upon common frameworks for policy orientation, but also renewed the activity of the full assembly of the Parity Commission as a forum for discussion of economic policy.[18]

In addition, there is no evidence that essential institutional prerequisites of Austro-corporatism, such as compulsory membership of the Chambers and central cooperative forums like the Parity Commission, will be abolished. The formal institutionalisation of the influence of the interest associations via their right to comment on government bills and their standing in parliament, plus the pervasive and widely differentiated informal institutionalisation of concertation, means that the loss of importance of the Parity Commission is hardly noticeable in practice. In fact, the influence of the interest associations has even increased in various fields, for example the preparation of Austrian positions on European policy and the administration of labour market policy.[19]

The Practice of Concertation

While scholarly observers have usually focused on the institutions of social partnership, officials in the interest organisations tend to put more weight on the behavioural dimension. For them, the Parity Commission is one of many forums of *Konzertierung* and *Akkordierung*, along with formal and informal advisory councils to ministries and public institutions, bargaining processes between the coalition parties, and informal meetings between interest organisation officials. From this perspective social partnership is not an institutional setting but a mode of policy making characterised by actively seeking compromise with the opposite peak association.

All actors have to be able to rely on the ability of the other actors to stick to compromises struck at peak-level negotiations. Thus, the ability to participate in these processes depends on the ability of the peak organisations to focus their strategic orientation on long-term and economy-wide issues, to enforce decisions made at the top level on lower-level units, and to silence more particularistic rank-and-file opposition. The high level of centralisation of the Austrian interest organisations combined with the high level of monopolisation of the core organisations is particularly well fitted to provide the peak actors with the necessary amount of trustworthiness in political exchange.

The relationship between the core interest associations has become much more complex in recent years. In this regard we have to stress the difference between two levels of action: the political and the expert level. The experts constitute a dense network, sometimes even cross-cutting associational affiliations, in which the actors have built up a joint, technocratic understanding of socioeconomic policy making (with differing emphases) and know the others' limits very well. Individuals are gradually socialised into this approach by carefully designed career paths within the interest organisations. This means that negotiations are led by people who have internalised a consensus-oriented style of policy making.

At the political level, and in ideological terms, there has been much continuity in the basic orientation of the interest organisations since the end of the Second World War.[20] However, representing special interests while keeping the entire economy under consideration does not imply converging views about sociopolitical values among the interest organisations, nor does it mean the end of conflict and dissent. Yet this model is characterised by both widespread consensus on the main objectives for the entire economy (economic growth, low unemployment, stable currency, international competitiveness) that must be kept in mind while pursuing special interests, and the search for consensual problem solving, which was reaffirmed by the November 1992 agreement. This is known in Austria as the 'class struggle at the negotiating table'. Strikes and lock-outs have not been abolished altogether, but they are only used as a last resort.[21]

Overall, the positions on macroeconomic perspectives of the economic interest associations coincide with those of the two major parties and the government, namely the inclusion of the interest associations in the policy-making process and in the implementation of policy, and agreement to realise the necessary goals for the entire economy by way of negotiations.

However, although the peak-level organisations and the chamber bureaucracies tend to stick to this orientation, in recent years it has come under strain by increasing internal opposition from rank-and-file organisations, followed by a more particularistic orientation both in public debate and in bargaining processes, which has increased the number and intensified the character of conflicts. This has meant a more pronounced conflict of interests at the political level, particularly visible in the redesign of social policy, e.g. in working time flexibilisation, unemployment insurance, old age pensions, but also in vocational training, labour costs and the regulation of dismissal payments.[22]

While at the expert level agreements can still be reached, the presidents of the associations, and also political functionaries, now stand for more confrontational strategies which are often meant to avoid internal disputes. The WKÖ in particular has in recent years become less able to enforce peak-level agreements on dissenting member organisations, being less centralistically organised than the ÖGB or the BAK. Given the increasingly competitive macroeconomic environment, the peak associations have more difficulty in persuading members of the adequacy of a compromise. A recent example of the decreased commitment to political exchange is the amendment to the trade regulations in 1997. In order to align the farmers on the side of the coalition in favour of becoming a member of the European Union, the WKÖ and the PKLWK struck a compromise according to which the chambers of agriculture would persuade the farmers to vote in favour of the European Union in exchange for a liberalisation of trade regulation, thus increasing the farmers' earnings possibilities outside their traditional tasks (to the disadvantage of small business and retail trade). However, after Austria had entered the European Union, the WKÖ did not stick to the agreement due to pressures exerted by sectoral organisations. Only after intervention by peak representatives of the ÖVP was a new compromise struck on somewhat less favourable terms for the farmers.[23]

In the ÖGB, the more particularistic orientation is manifest in repeated internal conflicts between sector unions, in particular between the white-collar employees' union *Gewerkschaft der Privatangestellten* (GPA), which has become the largest union, and the blue-collar worker unions, among which the *Gewerkschaft Metall, Bergbau, Energie* (GMBE) is the most influential. These differences make the process of interest aggregation and the internal acceptance of peak-level decisions more difficult. In consequence, the relations between the 'social partners' have been perceived in public as being more antagonistic and less dominated by attempts at *Akkordierung*, although practical work is effectively perceived as business as usual by the representatives of the interest associations.

Regarding the relations between the interest associations and the state, the 1990s have witnessed a clear emancipatory development of government from the 'social partners'. The cabinet of chancellor Vranitzky was less responsive to interest organisation pressures than previous governments. Most observers agree that this was due to the need to consolidate the state budget, which forced the government to legislate cuts in the social security system. In a first attempt, the SPÖ-ÖVP government proposed a savings pact in 1994 aimed at consolidating the budget for 1995. However, given that it was not based on a prior consensus established with the interest associations, this proposal was torn apart by the ÖGB. Only after difficult renegotiations between the government and the ÖGB was a considerably restricted compromise struck and the budget adopted. Because the 1996 budget was in even greater need of consolidation, the government did not risk a renewed conflict with the interest associations and involved them in the negotiation process from the very beginning, although the compromise eventually reached by the 'social partners' turned out to be based on a flawed calculation of the extent to which the budget needed to be consolidated by the government. However, given the preference of the SPÖ – under pressure from the ÖGB – for greater reliance on increases in state revenue, which was not reconcilable with the strict expenditure-side approach of the ÖVP, these negotiations did not lead to a compromise at party level and resulted in the resignation of the ÖVP from the cabinet. After the new elections were won by the SPÖ a new savings pact was negotiated in early 1996 in close cooperation with the interest organisations. This eventually led to

Austria meeting the Maastricht criteria for participating in the Euro project without severe societal disruption.[24]

The reform of old age pensions in 1997 reveals the multidimensionality of conflicts with particular clarity. The SPÖ-ÖVP government announced far-reaching changes in the pension system without prior consultation with the interest associations and legislated the reform against strong opposition by the workers' associations, although the associations were involved in the ensuing negotiations about details. The employers, too, were opposed to the reform on the grounds that it did not go far enough. Under these conditions not only was it impossible to find a compromise between the interest associations, but in addition the relations between SPÖ and ÖGB were strained as never before during the Second Republic. In the end, however, the interest associations accepted a compromise proposal close to the initially announced government plan, although without accord between themselves.[25]

The core area of *Akkordierung*, working regulations, has been less challenged. However, government has gained more influence in this area too. An instructive example of this constellation is the amendment to the working time law in 1997. While the existing law was based on a peak-level agreement between the interest associations enacted by parliament in 1969, the 1997 amendment was bargained between the interest associations in the context of strong government pressure for flexibilisation and repeated government interventions in the bargaining process. Thus although the decision itself rested in the realm of the interest associations, the bargaining process was strongly influenced by government pressure.[26]

These episodes illustrate three developments. First, the government more and more succeeds in both setting the agenda and formulating policies, the details of which are then – although reluctantly – specified by the interest associations. Second, except for the reform of old-age pensions, the interest associations have retained enough power to prevent legislation which interferes with their, or their consituency's, vested interests. While the ÖGB has more difficulties in imposing its preferences on policy, the WKÖ finds itself more often in accord with the government's options. Thus although we observe a large amount of continuity in the participation of associations in policy making, in comparison with former practice the government is less likely to wait for basic decisions to be taken by the interest associations or to formally delegate the decision to the interest associations. Third, and related to the former two points, given the more particularistic orientation of interest organisation policy in practice, they are only able to reach agreement on lower common denominators. This is often considered both by the government and in public opinion as impeding necessary reforms.

Some observers argue that parliament has gained an increased role in the decision-making process.[27] The increased number and strength of opposition parties and the decreased number of interest organisation representatives in parliament give the impression that parliament has gained more influence on the final result. However the representatives of interest associations still hold core positions and are able to intervene if their interests are not met. On the other hand, their parliamentary parties more often stand for a different position, so that they have to vote in favour of regulations not completely in line with their interest organisation's position. This, however, is not indicative of a stronger parliament, but reflects the greater influence government has, given that the coalition parties usually vote in favour of government proposals.

Conclusion

Despite encompassing transformation of the economic, institutional and political environment of Austro-corporatism, as well as the weakening of the internal organisational structure of the interest associations, the basic element of providing a forum for interest intermediation and a platform for consensus bargaining between the large societal groups has remained remarkably stable over the last decade. Several fields of social and economic policy making are still heavily dependent on the cooperation of the large interest associations, either via *Konzertierung* and/or *Akkordierung* or via *Konzertierung* without *Akkordierung*, although conflicts and areas of dissension have increased.

Although we observe a withering away of core institutions like the Parity Commission, this process does not entail a decline in importance of concertation. There are still many formal and informal forums in which political exchange can take place; negotiations, which at no time were restricted to or even dominated by the Parity Commission, were increasingly transferred to more informal and less regular meetings.

However, there is indeed change in the procedural terms of decision making. Concertation is declining and has been overlaid by arrangements dominated by government and by the use of privileged access to the government on the part of the interest associations which act to a larger extent than before as lobbyists for their constituency. The government has gained importance in agenda setting and the formulation of policies, mostly due to a need for policy reforms on which the social partner organisations cannot reach consensus by themselves due to internal restrictions on bargaining positions. Parliament has gained in terms of discourse, but not in terms of actual influence over policy content. Thus although the social partner organisations have lost their encompassing power, they still remain centres of expertise which are able to impress their interests on policy making to a large extent.

In many – though by far not all – areas of Austrian politics, *Konzertierung* via intermediation and under the leadership of the government is the rule, although there is less *Akkordierung* between the 'social partners' and government. Thus in Austria the notion of social partnership does not refer to partial social pacts as elsewhere in Europe during the 1990s, but points to a durable and rather robust pattern of day-to-day policy making which is capable of solving conflicts in a routine of cooperation. In short: social partnership is changing, but no end of the 'Austrian way' is in view.*

*Since the completion of this chapter (Spring 1999), the coalition government formed by the FPÖ and the ÖVP in February 2000 has cut out the labour associations from privileged participation in policy-making processes. Whether this will result in a long-term departure of the Austrian political system from social partnership remains to be seen. See: E. Tálos and B. Kittel, *Gesetzgebung in Österreich. Netzwerke, Akteure und Interaktionen in politischen Entscheidungsprozessen*, Vienna, 2001.

Notes

1. See E. Tálos, 'Corporatism – The Austrian Model', in *Contemporary Austrian Politics,* ed. V. Lauber, Boulder 1996: 103–23; F. Traxler, 'From Demand-side to Supply-side Corporatism? Austria's Labour Relations and Public Policy', in *Organised Industrial Relations in Europe: What Future?,* ed. C. Crouch and F. Traxler, Aldershot, 1995: 271–86.
2. A. Pelinka, 'Die Entaustrifizierung Österreichs. Zum Wandel des politischen Systems 1945–1995', *Österreichische Zeitschrift für Politikwissenschaft* 24, no. 1 (1995): 5–16; for a critique see B. Kittel, 'Entaustrifizierung? Die Grenzen des Wandels des österreichischen politischen Systems', *Neue Politische Literatur* 43, no. 2 (1998): 290–300.
3. But note that this differs from Lehmbruch's concept of corporatist concertation, which does not encompass the importance of agreements but simply refers to privileged access of peak interest associations to policy making under the condition of a joint understanding of their orientation towards macroeconomic goals. G. Lehmbruch, 'Concertation and the Structure of Corporatist Networks', in *Order and Conflict in Contemporary Capitalism,* ed. J.H. Goldthorpe, Oxford, 1984: 60–80.
4. P C. Schmitter and J. Grote, 'Der korporatistische Sisyphus: Vergangenheit, Gegenwart und Zukunft', *Politische Vierteljahresschrift*, Vol. 38, no. 3 (1997): 530–54; A. Ferner and R. Hyman, eds, *Changing Industrial Relations in Europe*, Oxford, 1998.
5. For an overview of developments in this dimension see F. Traxler, 'Austria: Still the Country of Corporatism', in *Changing Industrial Relations in Europe*, ed. A. Ferner and R. Hyman, Oxford, 1998: 239–61.
6. The Federation of Austrian Industry, *Industriellenvereinigung (IV)*, has an important role as a pressure group, restricted to industry, on its own, but not as a partner in wage bargaining.
7. There are a few exceptions because both the ÖGB and the chambers are constituted as non-affiliated associations. But due to the overarching dominance of the social democratic trade unionists in the ÖGB and the BAK, and of the ÖVP-associated employers in the WKÖ, policy within these associations is in practice defined by these groups.
8. P. Rosner, 'Lohnbewegung und Bewegung der Lohnpolitik', in *Zukunft der Sozialpartnerschaft. Veränderungsdynamik und Reformbedarf*, ed. F. Karlhofer and E. Tálos, Vienna, 1999.
9. B. Kittel, 'Deaustrification? The Policy-area-specific Evolution of Social Partnership', West European Politics 23, no. 1 (2000): 108–129.
10. J. Flecker and M. Krenn, 'Betriebliche Arbeitsbeziehungen im Wandel der Sozialpartnerschaft', in *Zukunft der Sozialpartnerschaft. Veränderungsdynamik und Reformbedarf*, eds. F. Karlhofer and E. Tálos, Vienna, 1999.
11. For example, the 1989 amendment to the law on unemployment insurance was vetoed five times by the ÖVP on behalf of the WKÖ in the council of ministers because no agreement was reached in tripartite negotiations between the government, the ÖGB and BAK and the WKÖ. See E. Tálos and B. Kittel, 'Sozialpartnerschaft und Sozialpolitik', in *Zukunft der Sozialpartnerschaft. Veränderungsdynamik und Reformbedarf*, ed. F. Karlhofer and E. Tálos, Vienna, 1999.
12. Whether a draft is presented to parliament as a government bill or a party initiative is of minor importance to interest organisation officials as long as they maintain leverage over the contents. Given the fact that they are informally represented in crucial positions in Par-

liament, this condition is virtually omnipresent. See H. Fischer, 'Das Parlament', in *Handbuch des politischen Systems Österreichs*, 3rd edn, eds H. Dachs et al., Vienna, 1997: 99–121.

13. B. Kittel and E. Tálos, 'Interessenvermittlung und politischer Entscheidungsprozeß: Sozialpartnerschaft in den 1990er Jahren, in *Zukunft der Sozialpartnerschaft. Veränderungsdynamik und Reformbedarf*, ed. F. Karlhofer and E. Tálos, Vienna, 1999; see also W.C. Müller, 'Die Rolle der Parteien bei Entstehung und Entwicklung der Sozialpartnerschaft. Eine handlungslogische und empirische Analyse, in *Sozialpartnerschaft in der Krise*, ed. P. Gerlich et al., Vienna, 1985: 135–224.
14. E. Tálos, 'Sozialpartnerschaft: Zur Entwicklung und Entwicklungsdynamik kooperativ-konzertierter Politik in Österreich', in *Sozialpartnerschaft in der Krise. Leistungen und Grenzen des Neokorporatismus in Österreich*, ed. P. Gerlich, E. Grande, and W. C. Müller, Vienna, 1985: 41–84. For further references see B. Kittel and H. Gröger, 'Sozialpartnerschaft im Spiegel der österreichischen Politikwissenschaft, *Österreichische Zeitschrift für Politikwissenschaft*, vol. 26, no. 2 (1997): 209–23.
15. F. Karlhofer, 'Verbände: Organisation, Mitgliederintegration, Regierbarkeit', in *Zukunft der Sozialpartnerschaft. Veränderungsdynamik und Reformbedarf*, ed. F. Karlhofer and E. Tálos, Vienna, 1999; A. Pelinka and C. Smekal, eds, *Kammern auf dem Prüfstand*, Vienna, 1996.
16. SWS-Telefonumfrage Nr. 97, Februar/März 1997, Arbeit und Wirtschaft 12/1994, SWS FB 301, Oktober 1994.
17. B. Marin, *Die Paritätische Kommission. Aufgeklärter Technokorporatismus in Österreich*, Vienna, 1982; A. Pelinka, *Sozialpartnerschaft und Interessenverbände* (Politische Bildung no. 52/53), Vienna, 1986.
18. *Wirtschaftspolitische Handlungsspielräume*, Beirat für Wirtschafts- und Sozialfragen, no. 73, Vienna, 1998.
19. Kittel and Tálos, 'Interessenvermittlung und politischer Entscheidungsprozeß'.
20. See J. Lewis in this volume. Cf. Tálos, 'Corporatism – the Austrian model'; E. Tálos and B. Kittel, 'Roots of Austrocorporatism: Institutional Preconditions and Cooperation before and after 1945', in *Austro-corporatism: Past, Present, Future* (Contemporary Austrian Studies IV), ed. G. Bischof and A. Pelinka, New Brunswick, 1996: 21–52.
21. Surveys show that members of the interest associations support the attempt to avoid conflicts. In 1990 more than half of those questioned preferred to have economic and social decisions determined through negotiations between the state, business and labour groups. Only 3 percent supported decisions arrived at by active conflicts such as strikes (Sozialwissenschaftliche Studiengesellschaft FP 269, 1990).
22. See, e.g., Tálos and Kittel, 'Sozialpartnerschaft und Sozialpolitik'; P. Rosner, 'Lohnbewegung und Bewegung der Lohnpolitik', in *Zukunft der Sozialpartnerschaft. Veränderungsdynamik und Reformbedarf*, eds F. Karlhofer and E. Tálos, Vienna 1999; E. Tálos and K. Wörister, 'Soziale Sicherung in Österreich nach 1945', in *Soziale Sicherung im Wandel. Österreich und seine Nachbarstaaten. Ein Vergleich*, ed. E. Tálos, Vienna 1998: 211–88.
23. G. Fellner, 'Die Gewerbeordnung 1997', in *Sozialpartnerschaft und Entscheidungsprozesse*, eds E. Tálos and B. Kittel, project report, University of Vienna.
24. M. Sebald, *Sozialpartnerschaft und Sparpolitik: zum Wandel politischer Entscheidungsprozesse am Beispiel der Strukturanpassungsgesetze 1995 und 1996*, M.A. thesis, University of Vienna, 1998.
25. Tálos and Kittel, 'Sozialpartnerschaft und Sozialpolitik'.
26. Kittel and Tálos, 'Interessenvermittlung und politischer Entscheidungsprozeß'.
27. M.L.L. Crepaz, 'From Semisovereignty to Sovereignty. The Decline of Corporatism and Rise of Parliament in Austria', *Comparative Politics*, 27, no. 1 (1994): 45–65.

Chapter 3

Britain in Historical Perspective: From War Concertation to the Destruction of the Social Contract

Chris Williams

Introduction: Perspectives

The history of social partnership in Britain is largely one of absence.[1] The term has been little used in descriptions of twentieth-century Britain. 'Corporatism', however, has attracted some attention, although British corporatism has been regarded as a relative failure, and the British state viewed as exhibiting one of the weakest varieties of corporatism in Western Europe.[2]

Two notable exceptions to the orthodox interpretation demand brief consideration. J. T. Winkler's prediction that 'a corporatist economic system is the most likely development for the United Kingdom', was made in 1976, but within three years it, like many assumptions about the prospects for consensual government and the adherence of the state to Keynesian economic orthodoxy, could be consigned to an intellectual scrap heap.[3] History has a habit of discrediting prophets, and Winkler's assumptions are now more revealing as an indication of a particular policy conjuncture in the mid-1970s than as an accurate assessment of the importance of corporatist management to the British state.

Keith Middlemas's work represents a more serious challenge to orthodox assumptions about the historic fragility of social partnership in Britain.[4] Middlemas has argued that, from the Great War to 'Thatcherism', British government has been characterised by 'corporate bias', defined as 'the tendency of industrial, trade union and financial institutions to make reciprocal arrangements with each other and with government while avoiding overt conflict'.[5] Trade unions and employers' associations are seen as having been transformed from interest groups into 'governing institutions'. Middlemas's empirical work commands respect, but his analysis remains unpersuasive. In a European context, the British state's very survival throughout a century of turmoil warrants explanation, and Middlemas is correct in calling attention to this. Yet it is difficult to agree with him that, without 'corporate bias' and its implicit policy concertation between government, capital and labour, social revolution would have resulted. The labour movement's non-revolutionary character, the ruling class's essential unity, the state's flexibility in accommodating the political demands of burgeoning social groups, and Britain's avoidance of military defeat all prepared the ground for compromise and conciliation in industrial relations. Furthermore, Middlemas's argument that 'corporate bias' was, rather than being explicit and clearly identifiable, instead a 'code', 'a sort of *outillage mental* acquired by the leaders of institutions as part of their political apprenticeship', resists verification.[6] With the evidence ambiguous at best, most historians have not endorsed Middlemas's thesis.

Although here it is argued that British government, industry and trade unionism have been underpinned by essentially non-corporatist assumptions, the absence of a strong tradition in favour of social partnership should not be seen as antipathetic to a political culture that has prized harmony, consensus and constitutionalism. Moreover, significant efforts have occasionally been made to engineer greater cooperation over industrial and economic matters. The exigencies of two world wars provided vigorous boosts to tripartite policy concertation, and the aftermath of both the Great War and the General Strike of 1926 witnessed moves towards establishing greater common ground between capital and labour. In the 1960s and 1970s Conservative and Labour administrations made spasmodic attempts to build a permanent structure for social partnership, in the name of economic progress and social peace. However, their failure opened sufficient political space to allow the success of Thatcherism's adversarial rhetoric and economic neo-liberalism, which relegated social partnership to the historical margins.

War, Strife and Planning: Social Partnership to 1939

Before 1914 barely any conception of social partnership existed in civil society. Although the late nineteenth century had seen the emergence of a 'new liberalism' that encouraged some politicians to contemplate state intervention in social welfare, there was no encouragement for more directive planning or cooperation involving employers and trade unions. In industrial relations the gradual development of mechanisms of conciliation and arbitration in which the state was implicated had hardly been welcomed either by the trade union movement or employers. The former was deeply suspicious of the state and keen to preserve its legal freedoms and right to free collective bargaining, whilst the latter was uneasy about any infringement on its managerial prerogative or restriction of its power to launch counter-attacks against trade unions. The relevant government departments (the Home Office and the Board of Trade), aware of the labyrinthine difficulties they confronted in such politically explosive matters, exhibited marked reluctance to involve themselves any further than was necessary.

The demands of 'total war', the first in which the state had been involved, transformed the peacetime situation of 'arm's length' relationships between the putative social partners. The catalyst was the munitions crisis of 1915, accompanied by serious industrial unrest. Agreements were sought with unions and employers in the armaments industries, government control extended over coal and shipping, and places found in government for leading employers and representatives of trade unions. Union membership and recognition blossomed: the 4,145,000 trade unionists of 1914 swelled to 8,348,000 by 1920. Continued rumblings of industrial unrest plus, from 1917, discontent over food shortages and rent increases, forced the government to give serious consideration to the grievances of the working class. The 1917 Commission of Enquiry into Industrial Unrest gave voice to mounting concern over the gulf between labour and capital, and the Whitley Report of 1917 led to the establishment of 'Whitley councils', including representatives of employers and unions, to discuss issues ranging from wages to employment and from workforce education to management efficiency.

The demands that war placed on both sides of industry generated significant organisational changes. The Trades Union Congress (TUC), little more than a loosely organised pressure group before 1914, began transforming itself into the labour movement's 'civil service', with an expanded administration and a more coherent and representative committee system. In the aftermath of the collapse of the 'Triple Alliance' of railwaymen's, miners' and transport workers' unions in 1921 the TUC established itself as the unchallenged 'peak' organisation of the trade union movement.

Amongst employers, concerns that their interests were subordinated to those of industrial peace were critical in the foundation of the Federation of British Industries (FBI) in 1916. Sir Charles Macara, president of the Master Cotton Spinners' Federation, was one of a number of prominent businessmen who observed that:

> Labour is organising along broad lines; Capital has no corresponding Organisation, and it is essential that such an organisation should be formed now, so that Capital and Labour may confer with the Government on equal terms, and in some cases co-operate.[7]

The FBI rapidly developed a strong financial base and a competent administration, but had to face resentment and hostility from already-existing employers' organisations. Ultimately this found expression in the creation of a second 'peak' organisation, the National Confederation of Employers' Organisations (NCEO) (later the British Employers' Confederation (BEC)), in 1919.

Notwithstanding that the Great War witnessed great consultation and cooperation with trade unions and employers, orchestrated by and channelled through the state, these developments were viewed by all parties as temporary measures in a state of emergency, to be discontinued once peace returned. Amongst trade unionists there was growing momentum for more radical solutions than those involving merely a place at a negotiating table, including demands for workers' control and nationalisation of key industries. Speaking at the 1917 TUC conference, miners' leader Frank Hodges denounced Whitley councils on the basis that they assumed the interests of labour and capital could be reconciled, arguing instead 'there never could be permanent relations between employer and employed'.[8] Employers desired rapid 'decontrol', and, when the immediate postwar economic boom was succeeded by a harsh economic climate, government was happy to wash its hands of the seemingly intractable problem of industrial relations.

Admittedly, for a moment in 1919, a 'corporatist' solution appeared feasible in the form of the National Industrial Conference (NIC), which brought together employers and trade union representatives, and was hailed as an alternative to the strife of direct action and 'Bolshevistic' menace. But although the NIC's Provisional Joint Committee recommended that it be established permanently and recognised as 'the official consultative authority to the Government upon industrial relations', the project fell victim to the lack of consensus over the value of policy concertation, and the NIC dissolved itself in 1921. The Triple Alliance and other major unions were hostile, and the government was reluctant to commit itself to taking advice from an extra-parliamentary body on matters that it preferred to leave to private interests to resolve.

Standing on the sidelines and hoping for industrial peace yielded poor results, as the industrial relations climate of the 1920s demonstrated. After the General Strike and miners' strike of 1926, progressive employers and pragmatic trade unionists again attempted to find common ground, in the 'Mond–Turner' talks of 1927–8 (named after the businessman Sir Alfred Mond and the TUC Chairman Ben Turner), and their sequel, the TUC–FBI–NCEO talks of 1929–33. The genesis of these discussions was the desire of some far-sighted employers to encourage industrial rationalisation (for which the cooperation of labour was a prerequisite), and the TUC's need to re-establish its sense of direction following the calamities of 1926, the Trades Disputes Act of 1927, and a steady fall in union membership (to 4,842,000 by 1930). For unions, incentives included the possibility of formal, and general, recognition, an employers' commitment to restrain from victimising union activists, and the possibility of having a voice in economic policy making via a 'National Industrial Council'. Such inducements headed off leftist criticism that cooperation signalled an acceptance of capitalism.

However, the 'Mond group' of employers found it more difficult to stimulate enthusiasm amongst employers' associations than influential trade unionists Walter Citrine and Ernest Bevin did to generate recognition amongst trade unionists that cooperation offered the best way forward. Both FBI and NCEO rejected the recommendations of the Mond–Turner Interim Joint Report. Such hostility could be traced partly to a latent reluctance to grant official recognition to trade unions as purportedly equal partners in industry, and to widespread suspicion of the unrepresentative 'Mond-group's' motives. Most NCEO member federations were relatively unreconstructed in their attitude towards the ills of industry: preferring less, not more, economic intervention from either state or labour movement. Subsequent talks between the TUC, FBI and NCEO made little headway, and did not presage any immediate advances in industrial cooperation.

Throughout the 1930s trade unions and employers stood apart, and successive governments refrained from trying to bring them together. The decade did witness the circulation of a number of schemes of a 'corporatist' flavour, some influenced by developments in Mussolini's Italy, but none made any significant impact on policy. Although they were supported by a range of politicians and business leaders, including Harold Macmillan, the second Lord Melchett (the son of Sir Alfred Mond) and Lord Eustace Percy, quite apart from Oswald Mosley and his British Union of Fascists, their contribution remained in the field of intellectual debate. Overall, in terms of social partnership, the inter-war years were a period of false starts, missed opportunities, and frustrated visions. It was the hot blast of war, again, which turned some of these dreams into a form of reality.

War, Reconstruction and Growth: Social Partnership 1939–62

The extraordinary circumstances of the Second World War led to the development of the most extensive system of social partnership ever witnessed in Britain. As the economy was mobilised to meet the demands of a conflict on whose outcome rested the very existence of the state itself, so mechanisms of central management and direction replaced the free market. The contrast with the Great War was marked: at its height in 1917, government expenditure had measured 37 percent of Gross National Product, but at its Second World War peak in 1943, it reached 54 percent.[9] The state coordinated the direction of productive capacity and manpower resources for military and economic purposes, and entered into negotiations, compacts and bargains with employers and trade unions. There was a proliferation of bipartite and tripartite machinery aimed at maximising efficiency in industrial production and minimising labour unrest, with a concomitant growth in the number of civil servants assigned to oil its moving parts.

Although new government ministries (Production, Supply, Food, Fuel and Power) played important roles in this expanding structure, the central hub was the Ministry of Labour and, from May 1940, the Minister of Labour, Ernest Bevin. He inherited a National Joint Advisory Council (NJAC) including thirty representatives taken equally from the TUC and from the BEC, whose task it was to advise on manpower issues. Bevin established a smaller and more coherent Joint Consultative Committee, and committed himself not only to a more dynamic and constructive policy, but also to winning the wholehearted support of the trade union movement of which he himself was the outstanding representative.

Bevin sensed that consent, rather than coercion, was the key to success, despite having various legal remedies at his disposal with which to combat strike activity. He saw appealing for wage restraint as preferable to imposing statutory wage limits. Drawing employers and union leaders into the processes of government (through the NJAC, the National Production Advisory Council for Industry, and Whitley Councils) was a canny method of implicating them in the consensus. The trade union movement responded well to its wartime responsibilities. Losing some of its residual suspicion towards the state, in 1944 the TUC proclaimed itself in favour of maintaining a 'decisive share in the actual control of the economic life of the nation', possibly through a national industrial council that would bring employers and trade unions together to advise government.

Nevertheless, in terms of industrial policy, it is possible to overstate the importance of the wartime consensus. Although commitment to a welfare state and full employment gathered considerable cross-party support, it is difficult to see wartime social partnership as more than a temporary expedient. Whilst the Labour Party was ostensibly in favour of economic planning, it had no designs ready to sustain or extend industrial controls. Aneurin Bevan (on the left of the political spectrum) and *The Economist* (on the right), accused Bevin of having 'corporatist' (by which they meant illiberal) intentions, but Bevin defended the consultative mechanisms he had pioneered as an aid, not a threat, to parliamentary democracy.[10] The unions wished to maintain an input into government thinking, but wanted nothing to prevent the restoration of free collective bargaining. Civil servants had no enthusiasm for perpetuating intervention, and industrialists were resolutely opposed to anything other than a return to unfettered 'normalcy' and *laissez-faire*. Not only was the experience of wartime explicitly not a launching pad for a permanent structure of social partnership, but in peacetime, the cracks gradually began to appear in the tripartite compact.

Labour's 1945 election victory horrified many businessmen, who were almost transfixed by fear of the wholesale nationalisation of industry. As it was, Labour's programme of public ownership, although radical, contained few surprises. Moreover, its reluctance to institute a fully planned (rather than a managed) economy, presented little threat to the autonomy of private enterprise. Direct control of labour was abandoned, and emphasis placed more on tempering demand than channelling supply. As far as the government's attitude towards employers was concerned, a voluntary system of consultation was maintained, with a view to enlisting industrialists' support in creating a favourable climate for wage restraint rather than desiring direct collaboration in economic development.

For the unions there were more obvious benefits to be had from close bipartism. The government required a self-denying ordnance over wages, but in return could offer nationalisation, full employment, the welfare state, and the rhetoric of 'New Jerusalem'. Sealing the bargain was a commitment (involving tacit cooperation from employers) to price stability. The fact that economic management did not extend to a formal incomes policy was the outcome of trade union hostility and a lack of demand from Labour itself for such intervention.

This lack of demand is partly explained by the historic and organic links between the Labour Party and the trade union movement, but it is also true that the Labour government did not enter wholeheartedly into economic planning. Planning was 'a god that was forgotten', lost in the crevasse opening up between 'totalitarianism' and 'democracy' in the Cold War era.[11] There was an Economic Planning Council and a brief Ministry of Economic Affairs, but the government's Economic Surveys remained suggestive rather than directive. Ideas for a 'national plan' foundered on the indifference of a government seeking, after 1947, to 'consolidate'.

The Conservative administrations of the 1950s felt no compulsion to take up Labour's loose ends. Responding to FBI worries that business autonomy had been infringed, they proclaimed themselves against planning, and concentrated on fostering economic growth whilst maintaining wage restraint. However, by the mid-1950s this latter objective was becoming less attainable, with a groundswell of industrial unrest. Attempts to re-establish a tripartite structure in 1957, with the Council for Prices, Productivity and Incomes, proved unsuccessful as the unions became increasingly alienated from the government. By the early 1960s concerns were expressed over the faltering of consensus and over the wastefulness of a 'Stop-Go' economic policy that appeared pitifully amateurish in comparison with the more streamlined and successful indicative planning being practised elsewhere, particularly in France. As Ben Pimlott writes, 'talk of imaginative planning experiments abroad was on every up-to-date politician's lips'.[12] Accordingly, for the first time outside the extraordinary demands of world war, the state embarked on a series of social partnership strategies that aimed not only to reverse Britain's relative economic decline but also to provide the remedy for industrial unrest.

'Neddy', 'White Heat' and the 'New Capitalism': Social Partnership 1962–79

The first experiment in social partnership was the establishment by the Conservative Macmillan government of the National Economic Development Council (NEDC, or 'Neddy') in 1962. This was the outcome of a shift in thinking by the Conservatives and FBI, reassured by European comparisons that tripartite planning did not lead to socialism and a loss of independence, and encouraged by prospects of economic growth. The government's desire to control wages led it to contemplate a permanent incomes policy, but it recognised that the unions would not accept so baldly stated an objective. Entangling the TUC in a tripartite body of wider scope might, nevertheless, permit effective understanding over wages.

Neddy was an explicitly tripartite body, with representatives from employers, trade unions and the state. Its task was to set targets for production, and establish guidelines to influence pay awards. It was followed by the creation of similarly comprised Economic Development Councils ('Little Neddies') for specific industries. Finally a National Incomes Commission (NIC or 'Nicky') was to have power to arbitrate in wage disputes.

This impressive apparatus made a sluggish start. Trade union suspicions were not assuaged: if anything, the establishment of Nicky exacerbated TUC hostility and they refused to cooperate with it. The TUC also resisted interference from Neddy in free collective bargaining. But gradually union leaders, and prominent industrialists, appreciated the opportunities that Neddy provided to voice concerns and ideas over economic matters. Although this was hardly 'planning by partnership', as the Conservatives claimed, it was an important means whereby the two sides of industry could reconcile themselves to both the mixed economy and the responsibility of the government for sound economic management.

Ultimately it was Harold Wilson's Labour Party, rather than the Conservatives, that capitalised on a public mood propitious for promises of planning. Wilson believed that 'a comprehensive plan of national development can recreate a dynamic sense of national purpose and restore our place in the world', and at the 1964 General Election he advocated the harnessing of economic planning to the 'white heat' of the 'scientific revolution'.[13] This was to be 'planning with teeth', with a new Department of Economic Affairs (DEA) responsible for energising the economy and having parity with the Treasury. The prospect of an enlarging economic cake appealed to leaders of private enterprise and trade unions, and held out the possibility that the often conflicting demands of both might be reconciled.

The DEA, headed by George Brown, harnessed Neddy to it in an advisory capacity, increased the number of little Neddies, and began working on a National Plan to blueprint economic development for five years. When published in September 1965 this heralded 25 percent economic growth by 1970. Integral to growth would be a National Board for Prices and Incomes (NBPI) ensuring that wages remained within manageable limits. Roger Opie has suggested:

> For many people it was a great moment. But it was to be only a moment. Indeed one could date the life-cycle of the Plan as 'conceived October 1964, born September 1965, died (possibly murdered) July 1966'.[14]

Received with enthusiasm by the government's social partners, the National Plan did not possess the range of directive weaponry necessary to fulfil its promises. It remained voluntary and indicative in nature, long on theory (and data) but desperately short in practice. Critically, with the Wilson government in a life-or-death struggle against devaluation, it was never accorded the priority necessary to be more than a wish list. With deflation taking precedence over economic growth, the National Plan was shelved less than a year after its launch. For Ben Pimlott, the demise of the National Plan took with it 'Labour's short-lived reputation ... as the party of efficiency and modernity'.[15]

The Wilson government's interventionism was not confined to the DEA and the National Plan, but nothing matched their scope and appeal. The Industrial Reconstruction Corporation (IRC) was founded with £150 million of funds and the brief to promote mergers, reorganisation and rationalisation where economic benefits might accrue. After 1968 the Ministry of Technology had power to invest in nascent or vulnerable manufacturing industries via the Industrial Expansion Act. These innovations were relatively tame (in comparison with the expectations aroused by the DEA) and productive of friction with the Confederation of British Industry (CBI), created from the 1965 merger of FBI, BEC and the National Association of British Manufacturers. The CBI entertained exaggerated fears that the activities of the IRC and Ministry of Technology represented 'back-door' public ownership.

More significant in the demise of tripartism was the feud that developed between government and trade unions. It had been expected that a Labour administration would work effectively with the TUC, and Wilson had indicated that he had no desire to move beyond a voluntary incomes policy. The December 1964 *Joint Statement of Intent on Productivity, Prices and Incomes* represented a commitment on the part of employers and unions to wage restraint, but by 1966 Wilson decided more was needed, and the Prices and Incomes Bill, which requested that increases be vetted by the NBPI, resulted in the resignation of trade unionist Frank Cousins as Minister of Technology. As levels of industrial disputes and wage claims rose, so the perception grew, in government and in society at large, that the role of the unions needed reforming.

Barbara Castle, Secretary of State for Employment and Productivity, was charged with resolving this seemingly perpetual conundrum. Her 1969 White Paper *In Place of Strife* proposed the strongest intervention by the state in union affairs since the Trades Disputes Act of 1927, and occasioned, if anything, a greater level of hostility. With provision for the use of strike ballots, 'conciliation pauses' and prosecutions by an Industrial Relations Court, the issue split the Parliamentary Labour Party, the Labour Party's National Executive Committee, and the Cabinet. Although the TUC allowed Wilson to withdraw, saving face with a 'solemn and binding agreement' that it would apply greater self-regulation, *In Place of Strife* destroyed much residual trust between the Labour Party and the trade union movement.

In terms of social partnership, the 1970s was a farcical repeat of the tragedies of the 1960s, albeit after a brief pause at the beginning of the Heath government of 1970–4. Initially the incoming Conservative administration aimed to rein in state intervention and, in the matter of trade union reform, to succeed where Labour had failed. The NBPI and IRC were abolished, the Industrial Expansion Act scaled down, and the Industrial Relations Act of 1971 enacted variants of the provisions of *In Place of Strife*. But when economic recession bit in 1972, Heath changed tack, re-embracing the virtues of corporate planning in terms that emphasised the responsibility that all social partners had for ensuring economic prosperity. The 'new capitalism' aimed to generate economic growth within the context of a 'civilised society'.

In fact, Heath had his hands full, for the remainder of his premiership, with industrial relations problems, including two national strikes by the National Union of Mineworkers. Talks aimed at securing the TUC's consent to voluntary pay restraint failed, and statutory pay restraint, in a three-tier Prices and Incomes Bill, led to escalating conflict between government and unions. This allowed Wilson, in opposition, to reinvent the Labour Party–TUC relationship with a 'social contract', holding out the prospect of peaceable relations under a future Labour administration. Even the CBI lost patience with Heath, believing that his failure to secure TUC cooperation was undermining the economy. When the Heath government fell in February 1974, many Conservatives turned their backs on both economic planning and social partnership, with serious consequences for the approach of the next Tory government.

In 1976 Wilson wrote that his Cabinet was engaged in 'almost constant consultation with industry, with the Confederation of British Industry, the Trades Union Congress, and with both together'.[16] One presumes it was incomes policy that dominated such discussions, as that issue preoccupied the 1974–9 Labour governments of Wilson and James Callaghan. Planning received a new lease of life with the establishment of the National Enterprise Board and a system of planning agreements, but neither found much favour with the CBI, and were overwhelmed by the industrial relations and wider economic crises. Initially the 'social contract' held up well, with the TUC accepting wage restraint, but by autumn 1977 there were mounting calls for a return to free collective bargaining. Ultimately, trade union aspirations clashed with the government's counter-inflationary strategy, and, in the 'winter of discontent' of 1978–9 the last vestiges of the bipartite compact dissolved, corroded by bitter industrial strife that discredited both parties and opened the way to a Conservative administration that would have little truck with what were seemingly bankrupt notions of social partnership.

Conclusion: The Fragility of Social Partnership in Britain

Kenneth O. Morgan has suggested that 'if there is one supreme casualty in British public life between 1945 and 1989 it is the ethos of planning'.[17] This may be so, but economic planning, and the social partnership fundamental to its success, have never been given the priority necessary to allow their potential to be tested fully. Outside the specific, temporary conditions of wartime, social partnership on a grand scale was attempted once, by the 1964–70 Wilson governments, and even then was rapidly subordinated to the battle against devaluation.

The reasons for the relative absence of social partnership in Britain are easily identifiable. Some stem from the very nature of the social 'partners' themselves: business peak associations have generally been suspicious of government intervention, and have always had to be mindful of the conservative instincts of elements of their membership. Similarly the TUC, although able to exercise more consistent leadership over the trade union movement, could only do so by recognising the constraints on its initiative imposed by an attachment to free collective bargaining. Any infringement of that principle might yield unbearable tensions within its own ranks that could jeopardise the TUC leadership itself.

Nor can the state escape blame for the limited and abortive attempts made at policy concertation and economic *dirigisme*. The civil service has never shown itself enthusiastic or adept at proactive intervention in the industrial economy, in part because of close links between the hegemonic Treasury and the City of London, but also because historical and cultural factors have preserved a generalist, rather than a specialist, administrative ethos. Furthermore, no government has been prepared to invest the energy and political capital necessary to implement a system of social partnership that would be central to a directed economy.

All these restraints are rooted in an essentially liberal political culture. Attachment to principles of parliamentary democracy, and of individual citizenship and equality before the law, has been the most effective, long-term constraint on social partnership. In wartime, corporatist planning has been reluctantly accepted. Always the expectation was that it would be withdrawn at the peace. Historians and commentators of interventionist bent may lament what they see as a failure to carry forward the systems that had delivered wartime success, but it has been they, and not the governments of the day, who have been out of step with the prevailing mood of the British people, their corporate institutions and their state.

Notes

1. I would like to thank Kevin Passmore, Sara Spalding and Harri Williams for their advice and support.
2. Andrew Cox, 'The failure of corporatist state forms and policies in postwar Britain', in *The Corporate State: Corporatism and the State Tradition in Western Europe*, ed. Andrew Cox and Noel O'Sullivan, Aldershot, 1988: 198–223; Alan Cawson, *Corporatism and Political Theory*, Oxford, 1986: 99.
3. J.T. Winkler, 'Corporatism', *Archives Européennes de Sociologie* 17 (1976): 100–36.
4. See his *Politics in Industrial Society: The Experience of the British System since 1911*, London, 1979, and the three volumes of *Power, Competition and the State*, Basingstoke, 1986, 1990, 1991.
5. Middlemas, *Power*, 1: 1.
6. Middlemas, *Politics*, 371. See review by Michael Dintenfass in *Bulletin of the Society for the Study of Labour History* 41 (1980): 63–5.
7. Cited in John Turner, 'The Politics of "Organised Business" in the First World War', in *Businessmen and Politics: Studies of business activity in British politics, 1900–1945*, ed. John Turner, London, 1984: 33–49: 35.
8. Cited in John R. Raynes, *Coal and Its Conflicts*, London, 1928: 156.
9. Peter Howlett, 'The wartime economy, 1939–1945', in *The Economic History of Britain since 1700, Vol. 3, 1939–1992*, ed. Roderick Floud and Donald McCloskey, Cambridge, 1994: 1–31: 9–10.

10. Alan Bullock, *The Life and Times of Ernest Bevin, Vol.2: Minister of Labour 1940–1945*, London, 1967: 275.
11. Stephen Brooke, 'Problems of "Socialist Planning": Evan Durbin and the Labour Government of 1945', *Historical Journal* 34 (1991): 687–702: 687.
12. Ben Pimlott, *Harold Wilson*, London, 1992: 276.
13. Cited in Roger Opie, 'Economic Planning and Growth', in *The Managed Economy,* ed. Charles Feinstein, Oxford, 1983: 147–68: 149.
14. Opie, 'Economic Planning', 159.
15. Pimlott, *Harold Wilson*, 364.
16. Harold Wilson, *The Governance of Britain*, London, 1977: 146.
17. Kenneth O. Morgan, *The People's Peace: British History 1945–1989*, Oxford, 1990: 509.

Chapter 4

Britain in the 1990s: The Absence of Policy Concertation

Peter Dorey

> ... no matter which party or parties form the government ... a corporatist system will be introduced in Britain by 1980. This will represent the completion of a new structure which both Labour and Tory governments have been building pragmatically, hesitantly, gropingly, piecemeal, but inexorably, since the early 1960s.
>
> Ray Pahl and Jack Winkler, 'The Coming Corporatism'

> We have rejected the TUC; we have rejected the CBI. We do not see them coming back again. We gave up the corporate state.
>
> Lord Young, *The Financial Times*

Introduction: Historical Background and Context

During the 1960s and 1970s, successive governments in Britain sought a partnership with the trade unions (via the Trades Union Congress, hereafter TUC) and employers' representatives (via the Confederation of British Industry, hereafter CBI). This 'tripartism' was not derived from any explicit theory about social partnership – indeed, the term itself was hardly ever used (see Table 4.1 for the terms variously deployed) – but tended to reflect pragmatic responses by Labour and Conservative governments in the context of growing concern about the relative decline of the British economy.

Indeed, what was perhaps most notable about these various forms of 'social partnership' was the degree to which they were primarily concerned with securing wage restraint from the trade unions, for 'excessive' wage increases were widely deemed to be responsible for fuelling inflation, reduc-

Table 4.1. *Key Terms in Britain*

Term	Meaning
Social partnership (trade unions)	TUC, CBI and government jointly pursuing common economic, industrial and social policies
Corporatism/Tripartism (political parties)	Used pejoratively to depict incorporation of the TUC and CBI into economic policy making during the 1960s and 1970s
Sectional interests (Conservative Party)	Pejorative allusion to producer groups, particularly trade unions, allegedly pursuing their own 'selfish' interests to the detriment of the national interest
Free collective bargaining (trade unions primarily, but also political parties)	Negotiations concerning pay and conditions of employment conducted between trade union and employers' representatives, free from government intervention or direction
National Economic Assessment (Labour Party during 1980s and early 1990s)	Proposed exchange of information and views between ministers, trade union leaders and employers' representatives in order to facilitate common agreement on economic policies, but without reverting to corporatism.
National interest (political parties)	Subordination of 'sectional' [trade union] interests to the 'national interest', as defined by government

Source: see text.

ing profitability, deterring investment, generating unemployment, and generally undermining competitiveness. As such, to the extent that 'social partnership' was ever pursued in Britain, it was inextricably linked to the pursuit of incomes policies and restraining wage increases.

However, the 1979 general election heralded the end of any such 'social partnership', for the new Conservative government, strongly influenced by New Right philosophy, accused the trade unions themselves of weakening the British economy. A new approach to governing Britain was deemed necessary, one that rejected 'social partnership' and thus excluded the TUC and the CBI from economic decision making.[1] The ensuing Conservative governments insisted that:

> The ability of the economy to change and adapt was hampered by the combination of corporatism and powerful unions ... Corporatism limited competition and the birth of new firms whilst, at the same time, encouraging protectionism and restrictions designed to help existing firms.[2]

Consequently the 1979–97 Conservative governments explicitly reduced trade union involvement in policy making, with economic and industrial decisions henceforth to be determined solely in the context of market forces and on the basis of commercial criteria. At the same time, ministers decreed that by abandoning social partnership, consumer interests would prevail over the interests of producers, for it was held that 'corporatism is never concerned with the individual, but only with the collectivity, never with the consumer, but only with the producer'.[3]

Alongside a battery of legislation to regulate and restrict the activities and powers of Britain's trade unions,[4] the Thatcher-Major governments systematically reduced unions' involvement in all spheres of policy making, thereby making it quite clear that organised labour was no longer to be viewed as a social partner.

Recent Developments

Downgrading and Dismantling the NEDC

The most obvious symbol of the rejection of social partnership in Britain during the 1980s and 1990s was the abolition of the National Economic Development Council (NEDC) in 1992, following the Conservative Party's fourth successive election victory in April of that year. Throughout the 1980s the NEDC had steadily been downgraded, and was increasingly treated with contempt by Conservative ministers who viewed it as 'a symbol of a half-hearted corporatist past which had no place in a Britain which had decisively turned its back on the corporate State.'[5]

Consequently, until its abolition in 1992, the NEDC met with diminishing frequency, so that what had previously been monthly meetings were, after the 1987 election victory, reduced to just four meetings per annum. Furthermore, cabinet ministers increasingly delegated attendance at NEDC meetings to their junior ministers, or even their departmental officials, making no secret of their view that the NEDC was a waste of ministerial time. Meanwhile, many of the NEDC's thirty-eight Sector Working Parties (the so-called 'little Neddies' which corresponded to specific industries) were abolished.

In finally abolishing the NEDC in 1992, the Conservative government made it unequivocally clear that there was no longer any formal or institutional role for the trade unions as social partners. They were no longer deemed entitled to any role in economic policy making.

Reducing trade union representation on other tripartite bodies

Alongside the downgrading and subsequent abolition of the NEDC, two other trends symbolised the Conservative governments' rejection of social partnership in Britain during the 1980s and 1990s. Firstly, various other tripartite bodies were abolished, or had their objectives significantly altered. For example, the National Enterprise Board was abolished, whilst ACAS had its remit amended by the 1993 Trade Union Reform & Employment Rights Act, whereupon it was no longer concerned to encourage *collective* bargaining.

Secondly, trade union representation on various tripartite bodies was reduced whilst employers, businessmen or other private sector representatives were usually granted a corresponding increase in membership. For example, until 1987 the trade unions had enjoyed equal representation – three members – with employers on the Manpower Services Commission (MSC), an agency originally established in 1973 in order to develop and coordinate policies to reduce unemployment. In 1987, however, the Thatcher government announced that the MSC was to be renamed the Training Commission, whereupon the Secretary of State for Employment would be empowered to offer employers' representatives an extra six seats (yielding them a total of nine), whilst trade union representation remained at three.

Subsequent reorganisation saw the Training Commission replaced by two new bodies, the Training Agency, and a local network of Training and Enterprise Councils (TECs).[6] On the Training Agency two-thirds of the membership comprised senior representatives from industry and commerce, whilst at least two-thirds of the TECs' membership was provided by employers, thus ensuring that 'the representation of trade union interests dwindled from its customary parity with employers' interests.'[7] On the thirteen TECs established by the beginning of 1990 there were 122 representatives from the private sector compared to just nine trade unionists.[8] Two years later, when the number of TECs had increased to eighty-two, the trade unions were represented on just fifty-eight out of the 1,136 'seats', or about 5 percent of the total representation on these bodies.[9]

Reducing ministerial contact with the TUC

The Conservative governments also presided over a diminution of contacts between ministers and the TUC. For example, 1985 witnessed twenty-three TUC meetings with ministers and one with the Prime Minister, but in 1987, there were only eleven meetings between ministers and the TUC, and none with the Prime Minister. When TUC leaders met the Chancellor of the Exchequer in 1993, it was the first such meeting for five years.[10]

This reduction in the number of meetings between ministers and the TUC was matched by a decline in the effectiveness or success (from the trade unions' point of view) of such meetings; a quantitative *and* qualitative decline. For example, whereas the TUC had deemed 47 percent of its meetings with the 1978 Labour government to have been successful, it considered less than 19 percent of its meetings with the 1984 Conservative government to have proved a success.[11] On the occasions when Conservative ministers did still meet the TUC, it was invariably to inform – rather than to consult – about the government's decisions and objectives.

Rejection of incomes policies

The 1979–97 Conservative governments' rejection of 'social partnership' was also derived from their eschewal of incomes policies. This was prompted by four main considerations.

Firstly, these governments held that the primary cause of inflation was excessive increases in the money supply, rather than wages and salaries per se, although large pay increases were certainly deemed to cause unemployment due to employees and trade union members 'pricing themselves out of work'. Incomes policies were thus deemed irrelevant to the curbing of inflation, thereby further obviating the need for a partnership with the trade unions.

Secondly, Conservative governments were unwilling to enter into the type of exchange relationships with the social partners – particularly the trade unions – which incomes policies invariably entailed. Given their hostility towards the welfare state, it is inconceivable that Conservative ministers would have contemplated offering the trade unions improvements in the 'social wage', for example, in return for TUC acceptance of wage restraint. Instead, higher unemployment was the Conservatives' preferred means of encouraging 'responsible' pay bargaining by the trade unions.

Thirdly, this unwillingness to enter into such 'exchange relationships' reflected ministerial determination to restore the authority and autonomy of government and the state. Only by returning to 'high politics', Thatcherite Conservatives believed, could the competence and legitimacy of Britain's governing institutions be restored.

Fourthly and finally, the Thatcher and Major governments rejected incomes policies due to recognition that the TUC was unable or unwilling to impose agreements on its affiliated members. Previous postwar incomes policies had frequently been abandoned in the wake of 'rebellions' by ordinary workers, usually after two or three successive years of pay restraint. This persuaded many Conservative ministers that incomes policies were not only wrong in principle but also unworkable in practice, for trade union leaders had repeatedly proved unable to 'deliver' the compliance of their members.

'New Labour': No Revival of Social Partnership

Meanwhile, the latter half of the 1980s witnessed the main Opposition party, the Labour Party, moving steadily to the right in response to crushing electoral defeats in 1983 and 1987. This rightward trajectory has been maintained during the 1990s, particularly following the Labour Party's fourth consecutive election defeat in 1992. Indeed this last defeat was instrumental in convincing many senior Labour politicians – and a few trade union leaders – that the Party's organisational and financial links with the trade unions were an electoral liability as well as a serious impediment to winning the cautious confidence of the business community.

The last ten years have thus witnessed the Labour Party loosening its links with the trade unions whilst Tony Blair, having become leader in July 1994, has repeatedly claimed that the unions will not be granted any preferential treatment or automatic 'insider' status.[12]

In so doing, 'New Labour' has vigorously sought to dispel any expectations – or fears – that it will seek to revive some kind of tripartite forum in which the TUC and CBI sit down alongside government ministers jointly to determine economic policies. Blair himself is emphatic that 'the re-creation or importation of a model of the corporate state popular a generation ago [is] out of date and impractical'.[13] Yet in spite of such pronouncements by key figures in 'New Labour' – most notably Tony Blair himself, Peter Mandelson and Stephen Byers – many trade unions have still been surprised at just how disdainfully they have been treated since the Labour Party was elected in May 1997 with a phenomenal 179–seat parliamentary majority. It has been widely noted that Tony Blair has very little time or respect for the trade unions, yet accords the utmost respect to the views and recommendations of employers and the business community.[14] Although the Labour Party entered office with a few minimal commitments to policies favoured by the trade unions, most notably statutory trade union recognition and the minimum wage, even these appear to have been pursued grudgingly by Blair.

Meanwhile, although trade union leaders have enjoyed regular access to Labour ministers, including the Prime Minister himself, this certainly does not constitute social partnership as defined in the context of this study. Frequency of meetings with ministers should not be construed as evidence of significant influence on policy outputs. Indeed, the trade unions' influence on economic and industrial policies seems considerably less than that exerted by the CBI on behalf of Britain's employers. As such, to speak of the emergence of genuine social partnership in Britain is woefully inaccurate and inappropriate.

Furthermore, most meetings between trade union leaders and Labour ministers (including, on occasions, Tony Blair himself) have either concerned specific policy commitments, such as the minimum wage and statutory union recognition, or policies germane to a specific department. In other words, rather than a series of regular and institutionalised meetings at macro level jointly to determine economic and industrial policies, many contacts between trade union leaders and ministers have been at the sectoral level, dealing with issues on an ad hoc basis. For example, trade unions representing local government employees have met appropriate ministers to discuss the Compulsory Competitive Tendering of local and public services, whilst union leaders representing health service employees have met the Health Secretary to discuss the structure of pay bargaining in the NHS, and the Private Finance Initiative.

It should also be noted that Compulsory Competitive Tendering and the Private Finance Initiative were both introduced by the previous Conservative governments in order to encourage greater private sector involvement in what remains of the public sector, yet these initiatives have also been embraced and extended by 'New Labour' in spite of trade union opposition, particularly from public sector unions.

These bilateral and meso-level contacts with the Blair government therefore fall far short of European-style social partnership and as such must have proved somewhat disappointing to John Monks, General Secretary of the TUC, who has repeatedly called for a new partnership between the trade unions, business community and the state in which virtually the whole range of economic, industrial and social policies are discussed and jointly determined.[15]

The TUC itself, meanwhile, has called upon the Chancellor of the Exchequer, Gordon Brown, to 'convene national social partnership discussions on how best to combine real wage increases, low inflation and high employment, including discussions on productivity, investment and the role of the social wage',[16] whilst the TUC's 1997 annual conference approved a resolution supporting 'the principle of a social partnership between unions, employers and the Government' which would 'involve unions in the widest possible discussions on the future direction of the economy ... together with the development of enlightened social policies'.[17] The arguments advanced both for and against (overwhelmingly the latter) social partnership are delineated in Table 4.2.

Table 4.2. *Key Arguments in Britain*

Proponent	Argument
For	
TUC	Securing agreement and cooperation vis-à-vis policies which will achieve low inflation, new jobs, sustainable economic growth, higher investment, improved living standards, and eradicate poverty
'One nation' Conservatives	Promote moderation and responsibility by both sides of industry in order to reverse Britain's relative economic decline, and to temper the worst excesses and injustices of the unfettered free market which might otherwise lead to social division and unrest
Against	
Most Conservatives	Unwarranted state intervention and political interference in economic affairs and operation of market economy
Most Conservatives	Privileges and empowers producer groups such as trade unions, at the expense of individuals and consumers
Most Conservatives	Impedes and impinges upon managerial authority, and prevents employers taking decisions based on purely commercial criteria (profitability, competitiveness, etc)
Most Conservatives	Compromises or undermines autonomy and authority of the state, and sovereignty of Parliament
Labour Party	Desire to distance itself from trade unions, who are seen as electoral liability
Labour Party	New determination to forge links with, and gain the trust of, the business community, thereby further marginalising the Conservative Party (which has previously been the party of capital in Britain)
Labour Party	Economic and industrial changes of last twenty years render concertation and corporatism obsolete
Employers	No need or desire to share power or authority with trade unions; management's right to manage has been restored during last two decades.

Source: see text

Yet John Monks readily admits that – at present – his and the TUC's support for such a social partnership is not shared by employers, nor does it appear particularly popular amongst many Labour ministers, least of all those most closely identified or associated with 'New' Labour.[18] Consequently, whilst trade union leaders in Britain are enjoying more regular contacts with government ministers than they did under the Conservatives, these fall far short of a genuine social partnership. As one commentator has pointed out:

> This is not a partnership on the model of Scandinavia, Germany or Italy. There is no national-level corporate machinery, no tripartite ... board, no commission that negotiates on pay settlements ... There is neither an actual, nor an implied, social contract.

Instead, it is suggested that what Britain is witnessing under the Blair government is 'an experiment in employer-led partnership, in which the State plays an enabling, but not a persuading role, and when pushed, will tend to side with the employers.'[19]

Advocacy of other forms of social partnership

Instead, New Labour urges other, or new, forms of partnership, most notably between government and the private sector (via such measures as the Private Finance Initiative) and between employers and employees in the workplace. Neither of these modes of partnership provides the trade unions with a role in national-level economic policy making.

Furthermore, New Labour's advocacy of partnership in the workplace – like that of the previous Conservative government – is one in which management's right to manage is sacrosanct. Such 'partnership' generally involves little more than management keeping the workforce better informed of its plans and policies, rather than any genuine process of bargaining and negotiation between capital and labour. In this respect 'employees and their representatives remain shut out of key decisions which might affect them.'[20]

Even in companies where there have been moves to create more substantive forums for consultation, such as the supermarket chain Tesco, it could be argued that part of the rationale is to 'replace traditional union bargaining with a hierarchy of interlocking staff forums', whilst in a number of other companies, such as Blue Circle, Legal & General, United Distillers and Welsh Water, 'most ... partnership agreements have effectively boiled down to trading flexibility for job security'.[21]

Furthermore, whilst the Blair government appears enthusiastic about greater partnership within the workplace – possibly seeing such arrangements as a 'third way' between adversarial, conflictual industrial relations on the one hand, and authoritarian 'macho management' on the other – it remains just as resistant as the CBI to EU measures promoting greater partnership in the workplace, insisting instead on the principles of competitiveness, flexibility, and subsidiarity. For 'New Labour', partnership in the workplace is acceptable only if it is introduced or endorsed voluntarily by employers, rather than demanded by employees from below or imposed by the EU from above.

Employers' contacts with the Blair government

Many of Britain's employers have been pleasantly surprised at just how open and amenable to them the Blair government has been since being elected. Admittedly the CBI was less than happy with the proposals on statutory trade union recognition, but on a range of other issues – most notably the details concerning the minimum wage – employers' representatives have found New Labour to be highly sympathetic to their views and values.

Not only have employers' representatives from the CBI enjoyed regular contacts with both the Prime Minister and the Chancellor, they have also been regular visitors to the Department of Trade and Industry, whose concern to promote enterprise and competition in the British economy, partly by reducing bureaucratic and administrative burdens on industry, has further endeared the Blair government to the CBI.

Their various meetings with Tony Blair, Gordon Brown, and the former Trade and Industry Secretary Peter Mandelson (replaced in December by a fellow arch-moderniser and Blairite, Stephen Byers) have persuaded CBI officials that on a whole range of economic and industrial issues they and the Blair government not only share similar objectives but often speak the same language.

Furthermore, on some of the Blair government's policy commitments to the trade unions, most notably the minimum wage, the CBI has succeeded in securing significant concessions from ministers, most notably in ensuring that the hourly rate was set at £3.60, rather than the £4.15+ that many trade unions had campaigned for.

In addition to enjoying regular meetings with various ministers, employers' representatives and industrialists have also been awarded posts on a plethora of working parties, government taskforces, advisory committees and commissions established by the Blair government to examine a range of policy initiatives and proposals. Such generous representation has not been enjoyed by the trade unions, which reinforces the impression that Tony Blair in particular is far more concerned to develop a partnership with the CBI and the business community than with the trade unions.[22]

This, of course, partly reflects a political calculation on Blair's part, namely that 'New Labour' needs to work hard to retain the trust of employers and industrialists, whereas trade union support is virtually assured, if only on the grounds that however little New Labour actually delivers to the unions, it will still be significantly more than they would obtain from another Conservative government. The underlying assumption is that the trade unions now need a Labour government rather more than New Labour needs the trade unions. This, too, further militates against the development of a genuine social partnership.

Long-Term Factors

Yet in some respects, the political trends of the last twenty years have merely reflected and reinforced a variety of wider or longer-term factors which have militated against the establishment of a genuine social partnership in Britain, most notably the British notion of parliamentary sovereignty, suspicion of the state by the putative social partners, Britain's liberal political culture, the sectionalism and short-termism of the 'social partners', and changes in the character and structure of the state and political administration in Britain during the last two decades.

Parliamentary sovereignty

A central component of Britain's uncodified constitution is that of the sovereignty of Parliament. In declaring that no entity or organisation enjoys political authority over and above that of Parliament itself, the doctrine of parliamentary sovereignty also maintains that Parliament's authority is – or ought to be – indivisible. Yet genuine social partnership would entail government sharing its authority and decision-making power with the leaders of the trade unions and employers' representatives, thereby compromising Parliament's sovereignty. Indeed, this is precisely one of the reasons cited by some Conservatives in their ideological attack on corporatism and social partnership since 1979.[23]

Another dimension of parliamentary sovereignty that is widely deemed to render social partnership inappropriate in Britain concerns the mode of representation involved. Whereas Britain's parliamentary democracy – the 'Westminster model' – is formally based on the territorial representation of individual voters in geographically-based electoral constituencies, with each constituency represented by an individual MP, social partnership entails functional representation, via the 'peak associations' of Capital and Labour (the CBI and TUC respectively).

Yet the 'social partners' would not be accountable either to Parliament or to the electorate, and as such:

> the notion of absolute parliamentary sovereignty which is central to ... the Westminster Model is, by definition, a formidable barrier to explicit and open power-sharing between the State and organised groups of producers.[24]

Thus the concept of parliamentary sovereignty, which Britain's Eurosceptics invoke against further European integration, is also deployed as an argument against social partnership in contemporary Britain.

Suspicion of the state by the social partners

Both capital and labour share a long-standing suspicion of the state in Britain. Organised labour has invariably suspected that state intervention in industrial relations would either be to the advantage of employers (by placing legal restrictions on trade unionism), or would offer the trade unions benefits only in return for a corresponding reduction in their autonomy and activities. Given that Britain's trade unions have primarily been committed to *free* collective bargaining, they have jealously guarded their autonomy against what they perceive to be state interference in their activities.

Meanwhile, Britain's employers have tended to evince equal antipathy towards what they see as state interference in industrial relations. However, much of their fear has been that state intervention might well be to the advantage of organised labour, thereby impinging upon management's right to manage and challenging the power of Capital. As Coates has observed:

> industrial leaders have invariably seen in ... government intervention an unacceptable challenge to their commercial and personal autonomy. They have feared that power-sharing and social equality would be the price extracted from them by the state for its intervention, because of the politicians' need to draw trade union support to their common and collective endeavour.[25]

Such suspicion of the state is one of the major factors underpinning the putative social partners' traditional support for *voluntarism* in Britain, whereby employers and trade union officials have preferred to bargain with each other directly, rather than have their respective objectives mediated through the state. This joint commitment to industrial self-government has further militated against any genuine commitment to social partnership.

Admittedly, the two 'social partners' have not always rejected tripartism in practice – they clearly did not reject it during much of the 1960s and 1970s – but it has meant that instances of social partnership in Britain at 'peak' or macro level have been fragile and unstable, with both the TUC and the CBI wary of becoming too closely incorporated into governmental decision making and policy implementation, not least because of the extent to which such incorporation would entail surrendering their autonomy and independence whilst also alienating their affiliated members who are more concerned with tangible, short-term gains. Furthermore, sporadic recourse to tripartism has invariably been based on pragmatism, not principle.

Britain's liberal political culture

The suspicions which capital and labour have traditionally harboured concerning the state can also be viewed as part of a wider commitment to liberal *laissez-faire* values in British society, and this too has militated against social partnership in Britain. A number of commentators have traced the hegemony of a predominantly liberal ideology back to Britain's Industrial Revolution, which was predominantly voluntaristic and society-centred. In other words, industrialisation in Britain was *not* the product of an active or deliberate drive by the state to modernise the economy, but evolved piecemeal over a seventy-year period from about 1780 to 1850.[26] Yet whilst:

> The minimalist state of late-eighteenth century and early-nineteenth century England was appropriate for an industrial pioneer, in which economic devel-

> opment could take place slowly and gradually, through a series of small, piecemeal steps ... Once Britain's old followers had begun to overtake her ... roles were reversed ... But the values and assumptions of her pioneering days still survived ... [27]

In similar vein, Crouch has explained how, in Britain, the:

> lengthy development of industrialization in a context of individualism and restricted State involvement imparted a deep liberalism to political, legal and economic institutions to which neither corporatist industrial relations nor state-regulated capitalism could be easily wedded.[28]

As such, Cox has referred to the 'cultural commitment of British people to liberal social values and parliamentary forms of representation' as constituting 'crucially important factors which constrain the state's role and make state intervention ... illegitimate.' Consequently, social partnership has been doomed in Britain due partly 'to the anti-state, liberal values of the mass of the population',[29] whilst Shonfield has noted the extent to which 'the old instinctive suspicion of positive government, which purports to identify the needs of the community ... [has] remained as vigorous as ever.'[30]

Short-termism and sectionalism of the 'social partners'

Each of the 'social partners' in Britain is characterised by a notable degree of short-termism, which further discourages their involvement in the type of longer-term strategy, and recognition of a superior national interest, implied by social partnership. The trade unions, for example, have invariably been primarily concerned with the immediate material interests of their members in the workplace through bargaining with employers over terms and conditions of employment.

This in turn has fostered considerable sectionalism amongst the trade unions, with membership based primarily on occupation or industry rather than class position or political affiliation. This has further militated against their commitment to social partnership, for this would entail subordinating the short-term, material interests of trade union members in their particular occupation or industry to some nebulous notion of the long-term 'national interest' as defined by government or the state. Besides, as the trade unions have discovered all too often in the past, the 'national interest' invariably entails a requirement that they practise wage restraint, but with little, if any, corresponding restraint required of the business community *vis-à-vis* dividends and profits.

Yet also fatal to the potential for social partnership in Britain has been the dominance of financial capital and 'the City' over manufacturing and industrial capital, for it is the former which have proved especially hostile to the degree of political intervention and longer-term economic planning which genuine social partnership would entail. [31]

This is because financial capital and the City in Britain have been primarily concerned with short-term yields and returns, whereby 'the structure of the City's money, securities and other markets is orientated towards the rapid turnover of marketable assets, rather than to direct involvement with the financing of industrial production.'[32]

The changing character of the British state

The period since 1979 has also witnessed changes in the character of the British state itself, and these too have militated decisively against social partnership. The changes derive in large part from the withdrawal or 'rolling back' of the state from much of the economy as a consequence of such measures as privatisation, contracting out, market testing, agencification, and the granting of independence to the Bank of England. Indeed, these measures have ensured that the British state itself is now much more fragmented than hitherto.

Yet whilst these measures reflect changes in the British state's relationship *vis-à-vis* the domestic economy and civil society, the character of the state has also obviously been affected by the processes of Europeanisation and globalisation. Indeed, the cumulative effect of these ongoing endogenous and exogenous developments is deemed by some to represent a 'hollowing out' of the state, entailing 'the loss of functions upwards to the European Union, downwards to special-purpose bodies, and outwards to agencies.'[33]

According to Rhodes, these changes in the character and competence of the British state are also resulting in the development of a 'new governance', entailing both the increasing number and complexity of 'self-organizing, inter-organizational networks' which enjoy a 'significant degree of autonomy from the State', and thus 'resist central guidance'.[34]

These dual processes, the 'hollowing out' of the state and the development of a 'new governance', compounded the disintegration of any remaining vestiges of social partnership in Britain during the 1980s and 1990s. Indeed in conjunction with the other factors discussed in this chapter, they are likely to ensure that social partnership in Britain remains redundant.

Notes

1. Peter Dorey, *The Conservative Party and the Trade Unions*, London, 1995: 145–8, 183–6; Keith Joseph, *Solving the Union Problem is the Key to Britain's Recovery*, London, 1979; David McCrone, Brian Elliott and Frank Bechhofer, 'Corporatism and the New Right', in Richard Scase, ed., *Industrial Societies*, London, 1989: 44–63.
2. Department of Trade & Industry, *DTI – Department for Enterprise*, London, 1988: 1.
3. Timothy Raison, *Power and Parliament*, Oxford, 1979: 37.
4. Between 1979 and 1997, six major Acts of Parliament were introduced *vis-à-vis* the trade unions, the cumulative effect being to: outlaw the closed shop (compulsory trade union membership), prohibit secondary or 'solidarity' industrial action, strictly limit picketing, narrowly redefine the definition of a lawful 'trade dispute', and require secret ballots for trade union members prior to strike action, and for the election of trade union leaders.
5. Nigel Lawson, *The View from No.11*, London, 1992: 714.
6. For a fuller discussion of these developments, see David Marsh, *The New Politics of British Trade Unionism*, Basingstoke, 1992: 126–34.

7. J. Cassels, 'Reflections on tripartism', *Policy Studies* 3 (1989).
8. *Employment Gazette*, July 1990: 366.
9. John McIlroy, *Trade Unions in Britain Today*, 2nd edn, Manchester, 1995: 207.
10. Ibid, 204.
11. N. Mitchell, 'Changing pressure group politics: the case of the TUC 1976–1984', *British Journal of Political Science*, 17(4), 1987.
12. See, for example, Peter Dorey, 'The Blairite betrayal: New Labour and the trade unions', in Gerald Taylor, ed., *The Impact of New Labour*, Basingstoke, 1999.
13. Tony Blair, *New Britain: My Vision of a Young Country*, London, 1996: 109.
14. See, for example, Ian Bell, untitled article, Comment page, *Observer* 22 March 1998; Joy Johnson, 'The weak link takes the strain', *New Statesman*, 31 January 1997; Seamus Milne, 'Silenced voices', *Guardian* 12 May 1997; Seamus Milne, 'Blair's blast sends a seafront shiver through the unions at Brighton', *Guardian* 13 September 1997; Patrick Wintour, 'Downing Street opens door to trade unions', *Guardian,* 31 August 1997.
15. Interview with author, 6 November 1998.
16. TUC: *Economic Policy and Social Partnership,* London, 1998: 34. See also, TUC: *Partners for Progress: Next Steps for the New Unionism*, London, 1997: 1, and *passim.*
17. TUC: *Congress Report 1997*, 62–4.
18. Interview with author, 6 November 1998.
19. John Lloyd: 'Take your partners', *New Statesman Trade Union Guide 1999*, iii and v.
20. David Guest and Riccardo Peccei,*The Partnership Company*, London, 1998.
21. Seamus Milne: 'Tesco embrace of union opens way to "new era"', *Guardian* 14 March 1998.
22. See, for example, Steve Richards, 'What is the point of having businessmen in a government?', *Independent* (Review Section) 18 February 1999: 3.
23. See, for example, Raison, *Power and Parliament,* 33.
24. David Marquand, *The Unprincipled Society*, London, 1988: 173. See also, David Coates, *The Context of British Politics*, London, 1984: 244–6.
25. David Coates, *The Question of UK Decline*, Hemel Hempstead, 1994: 207.
26. See, for example, Coates, *Context of British Politics*, 50; Andrew Gamble, *Britain in Decline*, London, 1981: 68–75; Marquand, *The Unprincipled Society*, 91–174, *passim.*
27. Marquand, *The Unprincipled Society,* 148.
28. Colin Crouch, 'The State, Capital and liberal democracy', in David Held et al., eds, *States and Societies*, Oxford, 1983: 321.
29. Andrew Cox, 'The failure of corporatist state forms and policies in post-war Britain', in *The Corporate State*, ed. Andrew Cox and Noel O'Sullivan, Aldershot, 1988: 201, 220.
30. Andrew Shonfield, *Modern Capitalism*, London, 1965: 93.
31. See, for example, Coates, *Context of British Politics*, 58–67, 77; Frank Longstreth, 'The City, industry and the State', in *State and Economy in Contemporary Capitalism*, ed. Colin Crouch, London, 1979: 160–1.
32. Geoffrey Ingham, 'Divisions within the dominant class and British exceptionalism', in *Social Class and the Division of Labour*, ed. Anthony Giddens and G. McKenzie, Cambridge, 1982: 220. For a fuller discussion, see Geoffrey Ingham, *Capitalism Divided: The City and Industry in British Social Development*, London, 1984; Coates, *Question of UK Decline*, 51–4; Will Hutton, *The State We're In*, London, 1996.
33. R.A.W. Rhodes, *Understanding Governance*, Buckingham, 1997: 17. For a fuller exposition, see R.A.W. Rhodes, 'The hollowing out of the State', *Political Quarterly* 65 (1994).
34. Rhodes, *Understanding Governance*, 53, 59; see also, W. Kickert, 'Complexity, governance and dynamics: conceptual explorations of public network management', in *Modern Governance*, ed. J Kooiman, London, 1993: 275.

CHAPTER 5

DENMARK IN HISTORICAL PERSPECTIVE: TOWARDS CONFLICT-BASED CONSENSUS

Carsten Strøby Jensen

Introduction

When analysing social partnership in Denmark, the most important historical month is September 1899; this month is furthermore significant when attempting to comprehend existing relations between government, trade unions and employers in Denmark. In September 1899, trade unions and employers reached a settlement after a four-month conflict. Appropriately enough the settlement was coined the September Compromise of 1899. Since then, the September agreement has served as the framework for labour market cooperation in Denmark. Likewise the agreement played a major role in dividing the tasks of the government and the tasks of the social partners; this is the case concerning labour market issues, but also in relation to public policy in general. Furthermore the September Compromise gave rise to a system where the relationship between the social partners could be characterised by conflict-based consensus.

In describing the system of conflict-based consensus, it is important to point out that the relationship between the labour market parties is based fundamentally on an awareness of and agreement that trade unions and employers' organisations have conflicting interests. Consequently, there seems to be a high degree of consensus among the disputing parties as to what the conflict is about. The relationship between the social partners is characterised by: massive union support among employees, a strong centralised collective bargaining system constituted by trade unions and employers' organisations, a close relationship between the state and collective bargaining parties and a fundamental set of regulatory rules in the labour market, where emphasis is put on agreements reached by the labour market participants, not legislation.

With the advent of the September Compromise, employers established their right to lead and distribute work while in return accepting the organisational and bargaining rights of their employees.[1] This has meant that trade unions have secured a large percentage of workers – 80 percent of all workers are union members. The fact that employers early on accepted the organisational and bargaining rights of workers has induced Danish companies to come to terms with employees being union members. The labour market parties have had a strong organisational basis since the beginning of this century. This has meant that the state/government in many cases has involved the social partners in decisions regarding different policy areas – mostly through ad hoc committees. In many cases, labour market parties have therefore been involved directly or indirectly in processes which could be defined as policy concertation.

The State and Interest Groups

Throughout the twentieth century the state has involved the labour market parties and other interest groups (e.g. agriculture) in pre-legislative work.

> In essence the Danish tradition implies, that affected interests are involved in drafting and executing political decisions whenever the affected interests are organised, i.e. when actions turn out to have decisive consequences for members ... Such norms of involvement, thought to have been established since the first half of the century, supposedly have and still make up the constitutive cooperative foundation among organisational, political and administrative authorities.[2]

The number of committees, commissions and boards – where for instance businesses are represented – have increased throughout the century. By 1914 'private interest groups were operative in 18 public commissions'.[3] In 1946, 413 interest organisations were active participants in more than 200 public boards and in 1980 this number peaked at 732.[4] Concerned parties are involved in decision-making processes to the extent that they are affected by them.[5]

However, this form of participant involvement merely represents one of many social partnership modes. In Denmark, a tradition of close contact exists between the Danish Social Democratic Party (and left-wing parties) and unions on the one side and leading executive business representatives and the Conservative Party (*Konservative Folkeparti*) on the other side. By way of constituting the political backbone of the Danish Social Democratic Party, unions have been active participants in discussions concerning key Social Democratic political initiatives, even to the extent that they set the policy agenda. This has been particularly the case with regard to the development of the welfare state.

Trade Unions and Employers' Organisations

In Denmark there is a tradition of limited competition among trade unions. Discrepancies and disputes between trade unions are for the most part handled within the organisations themselves. This has helped strengthen trade unions when dealing with either employers or the government. Traditionally unions in Denmark are organised under peak organisations, according to the educational background of members. In Denmark there are three such peak organisations: the Danish Confederation of Trade Unions *(Landesorganisationen i Danmark,* LO), the Confederation of Salaried Employees and Civil Servants in Denmark *(Funkionærernes og Tjenestemændenes Fællesråd,* FTF) and the Danish Association of Professional Associations (*Akademikernes Centralorganisation,* AC). LO is traditionally perceived as the dominant peak organisation and consists first and foremost of unions organising skilled and unskilled manual labour, although non-managerial white-collar workers are also organised under this peak organisation. FTF unions organise members who have obtained intermediate educational skills such as teachers, nurses and pedagogical staff. AC unions organise academic and highly educated personnel; some key AC members include lawyers, economists and doctors. The Danish Social Democratic Party and LO have traditionally been affiliated with one another and formal as well as informal ties have characterised their relationship. In broad terms both organisations consider themselves as being part of the same labour movement. The peak organisations of FTF and AC came into existence as a reaction to LO's tight connection with the Social Democratic Party. The aim of FTF and AC was to establish politically independent organisations.

The majority of Danish companies are typically small and medium-size businesses. The peak organisations of Danish employers are: the Danish Employers' Confederation (*Dansk Arbejdsgiverforening,* DA), the Danish Employers' Association for the Financial Sector (*Finanssektorens Arbejdsgiverforening,* FA) and the Danish Confederation of Employers' Associations in Agriculture (*Sammenslutningen af Landbrugets Arbejdsgiverforeninge,* SALA). *Finanssektorens Arbejdsgiverforening* and *Sammenslutningen af Landbrugets Arbejdsgiverforeninge* both represent a limited amount of employer interest and will therefore not be mentioned further in this article. DA, on the other hand, represents a vast range of Danish employers' interests and is looked upon, in relation to the Danish state and parliamentary system, as the dominant and most important employers' organisation. DA members come from of a number of trade- and business-based organisations.

State intervention in labour market matters has been limited. The two sides of industry have been cooperation-oriented to a considerable degree. When it comes to questions concerning minimum wage and maximum working hours the workers in effect have no legislative rights.[6] The only rights workers have in such matters are those which have been agreed upon in collective bargaining rounds.[7] Thus, in the twentieth century, ideologically there has been consensus among management and labour and the big political parties that, wherever possible, the parties should negotiate labour market standards such as wages, working hours et cetera. Moreover there has been a general agreement that the parties themselves should handle the resolution of the conflicts between them.

The construction and development of labour market regulation and rights have thus taken place when labour market organisations have made or broken deals. By contrast, social policy is implemented through legislation and therefore this area pertains to the dealings of the state and municipal authorities. Labour market organisations are the bearers of responsibility in creating and securing rights inside the company gate through collective bargaining (questions of wages, terms of notice, maximum working hours and so on). But it is the duty of the government to secure regulation and rights outside the company gate. This is the case when issues like unemployment,[8] healthcare, daycare, rehabilitation, care of the elderly et cetera are on the agenda.

Even though labour market parties hold no direct responsibility in areas concerning welfare state policy, traditionally they get to influence these policy matters. By participating in pre-legislative committees, labour market parties have (from the 1930s onwards) had the opportunity to voice their opinion to the government. Discussions about the welfare state between unions and the Social Democratic Party have been going on ever since.

Parliamentary Development in Denmark – Labour Market Politics and Political Intervention

As we have seen above, the Danish state plays a limited role in regulating the labour market. The leading political parties in the Danish political system have traditionally had strong ties to both sides in the labour market. Because both sides in general have prioritised non-governmental intervention in the labour market, the political system has accepted that it plays a passive role. It has been found politically appropriate that labour market organisations resolve their own conflicts.

A significant background factor in understanding the unobtrusive governmental position toward labour market regulation can be found in the character of the Danish parliamentary system. In comparison with other European countries, Danish postwar Parliament workings have not been characterised by block politics in the same degree as elsewhere. Neither socialist nor conservative governments have held positions of parliamentary majority for long periods of time. Instead they had to enter coalitions with centrist parties, which in turn contributed to the development of a consensus-oriented political culture.[9] A balancing-out of important political and wider societal interest has therefore taken place.

This parliamentary situation has made it difficult for labour market parties to gain advantages over one another through legislative initiatives. Labour market organisations in general and LO in particular have thus never been certain of securing support from the Social Democratic Party through legislation when the question of workers' interests has been on the agenda. Although the government has been Social Democratic for a more or less uninterrupted period from the 1930s to the 1980s, they have never single-handedly held a parliamentary majority in the Danish Parliament. They were never able to secure trade union demands through legislation.

Social partnership also played a central part during WWII when both labour market parties supported the Danish government's policy of cooperation with the German occupying forces. Increasingly, in the postwar era, the state and labour market organisations have acted in cooperation in the area of labour market politics. Over the last two decades, for example, the state has sought to implement new and better educational schemes.

Conclusion – Conflict-Based Consensus

The compromises and settlements of the past have created the institutional framework in which the labour market parties operate today. Conflict-based consensus in Denmark has no tradition of establishing permanent institutions of social partnership. Instead ad hoc committees have been formed and the spirit of social partnership is kept alive through the contacts between the major political parties and the labour market parties. At the same time a well-functioning division of labour has left labour market and social policies to the state.

The idea of social partnership as an ideological project has never had much importance in Danish society. It is not a concept that has played a major role in the programmes of either employers or trade unions. However, if we look at the importance of social partnership as a practical project it can hardly be overestimated. The state and the political system have always been willing to involve the labour market parties in the political process, traditionally through numerous boards and commissions.

Notes

1. J. Due, J.S. Madsen, C. Strøby Jensen, L. Kjerulf Petersen, *The Survival of the Danish Model – A Historical Sociological Analysis of the Danish System of Collective Bargaining*, Jurist- og Økonomforbundets Forlag, Copenhagen, 1994.
2. P.M. Christiansen, 'Interesseorganisationer, centraladministration og udvikingen af nye indflydelsesstrategier', pp. 119–54, in K. Ronit, *Interesseorganisationer i dansk politik*, Jurist- og Økonomforbundets Forlag, Copenhagen, 1998: 130.
3. Ibid.
4. Ibid., 131.
5. O. Olsen and N. Sidenius 'The Politics in Private Business Cooperative and Public Enterprise – Denmark', Research report nr. 4/91, Department of Political Science, Aarhus University, 1991.
6. Though it should be noted that there exists EU legislation in the area of maximum work hours. The limit has been set to 48 hours per week. Attempts to implement EU legislation in Denmark via collective bargaining (not legislation) have been made.

7. Naturally there also exist individual agreements/contracts elsewhere in the labour market. The majority of workers are nevertheless not covered by such agreements.
8. Peak organisations administer unemployment funds in the same way that employers and employees contribute towards financing unemployment funds. The state is the largest financial contributor when it comes to unemployment funds.
9. E. Damgaard, 'Parlamentarismens danske tilstande', in E. Damgaard, ed., *Parlamentarisk forandring i Norden*, 1995: 15–43.

CHAPTER 6

DENMARK IN THE 1990S: STATUS QUO OR A MORE SELF-CONFIDENT STATE?

Mikkel Mailand

Introduction

The involvement of labour market parties has for a long time been an integral part of policy formulation and implementation in Denmark. Policy concertation, the more centralised, formal and binding part of this involvement, is the focus here. Concertation is defined as co-determination of public policy by governments, peak employer associations and/or trade union confederations – that is, discussions that lead to government commitments to adopt particular policies. Social partnership is defined as concertation plus the values and ideas that legitimate it.

Policy concertation in Denmark differs from one policy area to another. Four important policy areas have been selected for this analysis: economic policies (fiscal policy, monetary policy and incomes policy), labour market policy (employment service, job creation, training and social insurance), social policy, and employment law (focusing on regulation of the work environment).

The first part of the chapter will outline the economic, organisational and political context of social partnership in Denmark. The second part will outline the developments in concertation in the 1990s. The third part will focus on the development of the idea of social partnership. The fourth part will try to explain the changes in concertation as well as in its underlying ideas.

The Context

The economic context of social partnership has changed significantly during the 1990s. After a short upturn in the economy in the mid-1980s, unemployment was still on the rise at the beginning of the 1990s. It peaked in 1993 when 12.3 percent of the population registered as unemployed.[1] Since then unemployment has declined to 7.2 percent (April 1998). One reason for this fall in unemployment is the creation of new jobs in the private sector. Another reason is a reduction in the size of the labour force due to the large number of persons temporarily taking part in active labour market measures or leave schemes. In contrast to the upturn in the mid-1980s, neither overheating of the economy, skills shortages nor wage inflation has followed the recent economic upturn.

The most important organisational development started in the 1980s, although it gradually lost its momentum in the mid-1990s. Changes made in organisations and in collective bargaining structures during the past decade have boosted the position of large, new, sector-wide organisations and cartels, particularly the position of *Dansk Industri* (Danish Manufacturing) on the employers' side and *CO-Industri* (Central Organisation for Manufacturing Workers) on the employees' side. This development has led to a corresponding decline in power and influence for the traditional peak organisations, *DA* (Danish Employers' Confederation) and *LO* (Federation of Danish Trade Unions), leading the political system to regard them as being less capable of acting as key negotiating counterparts than before. These changes have thus posed problems for concertation, because concertation in Denmark traditionally means that the government and Parliament are only prepared to grant influence to the parties if – and this is an important proviso – there is a single, unified employer association and a single, unified trade union federation capable of achieving a mutual compromise on the relevant issues. However, the sector/branch organisations are unlikely to usurp or inherit the role of the peak organisations, if it is decided to maintain the level of influence hitherto granted to the labour market organisations, because the organisational structure at the sectoral level is too fragmented.

Hence the current problem is that the organisational structure poses a representational problem which is difficult to solve, at least until the division of power between the two levels (peak organisation and sector organisation) has been clarified and the sector-wide organisations (with a few exceptions) acquire the necessary cohesion and coverage. The situation is further complicated by the merging of sectors as a result of technological and economic development.[2]

The political context also changed in the 1990s. With the help of some small centre-right parties, the Social Democratic Party came to power in 1993 after twelve years in opposition to a liberal-conservative government. This has had consequences for concertation, because the new government initially seemed more committed to concertation than the previous one. However developments have not been straightforward and different paths have been followed in the four important areas of concertation. As with most Danish governments, the new Social Democratic government is a minority government and is therefore dependent on cooperation with the opposition.

Another change in the political context is the relationship between the interest-organisations and political parties, or more precisely the relationship between the Social Democratic Party and the LO. The formal links were cut in the mid-1990s and informal links have also been weakened, which has left LO frustrated. However LO has recently established closer contacts with the Liberal Party, the leading party of the opposition, although it is still too early to pass judgement on the sustainability of this contact. A further analysis of the LO-government relationship will be presented below.

Concertation in Four Policy Areas

Concertation can be found in several policy areas in Denmark. This section will focus on concertation in economic policy as well as in labour market policy, work environment legislation and social policy. These policy areas are selected either because of their importance for policy and politics in general (economic policy) or because they contain a substantial share of the overall amount of concertation or concertation-like involvement (the remainder).

Economic policy

There has been no concertation in relation to incomes policy since 1987. This is contrary to the developments of the 1970s and the beginning of the 1980s, though consistent with the voluntaristic tradition of the Danish model of industrial relations according to which wages and conditions are negotiated between trade unions and employers' organisations.

In 1987 the peak organisations and the government signed the so-called 'declaration of intent' (*hensigts-erklæringen*). This stated that wage increases in Denmark should be maintained at a rather low level in comparison to countries considered to be the main competitors of the Danish economy. Between 1987 and 1996 wage moderation was a shared objective of the labour market parties and the government, even though there was no formal concertation in relation to incomes policy during this period.[3] In 1997 tripartite talks on economic policy took place for the first time in a decade, but the government and the labour market parties failed to reach an agreement.[4] Moreover, in 1998 LO withdrew from the 1987 'declaration of intent'. The president of the LO, Hans Jensen, justified the decision by referring to government intervention in the 1998 bargaining round:

> The trade union movement can no longer be co-responsible for the development in overall costs that the government's intervention will entail, as LO has had no influence on the intervention.[5]

At the same time LO proposed to replace the joint statement with a broader 'social contract'. The Danish Prime Minister, Poul Nyrup Rasmussen, reacted promptly by inviting LO and DA to tripartite talks. Although tripartite talks about a social contract never materialised, talks concerning a new labour market reform took place in the autumn of 1998 and will be analysed below.

In relation to fiscal policy and monetary policy there has been no concertation in the 1990s. Although the peak organisations are represented on the board of the National Bank and in the Economic Council, neither of these boards has been involved in concertation.

Labour market policy

Denmark has a two-tier system for activation (job creation and training) and social benefits for the unemployed. The majority of the workforce (85 percent) are members of an unemployment insurance fund. If these people become unemployed, they are activated through the labour market policy system. The unemployed who are not eligible for unemployment benefits are the responsibility of the municipalities. They may receive social security at a level which, for persons with children, amounts to 80 percent of the maximum unemployment benefits.[6]

Labour market policy has become an increasingly important part of labour market regulation. It is also a policy area in which the labour market parties are closely involved in discussion and negotiation, some of which leads to government commitments on policy and can therefore be called concertation. This takes place in temporary pre-legislative committees and in permanent tripartite committees at the national level. Other forms of labour market policy involvement take place in regional policy implementation boards. The permanent national and regional tripartite bodies have been built up slowly since the 1960s, but only received substantial competency recognition in the 1990s.

The most important single example of concertation is the labour market reform that came into force in 1994. The reform was modelled on the recommendations of the intensive pre-legislative work undertaken by a tripartite committee, *Zeuthen-udvalget*. The reform decentralised authority to fourteen Regional Labour Market Councils in relation to the identification of target groups of unemployed for early activation, guidelines for activation instruments, guidelines for Public Employment Services provision of labour, and measures to prevent labour shortages. This decentralisation also meant increased policy influence for the labour market parties, counties and municipalities due to their representation in the Regional Labour Market Councils.

Not all authority was decentralised. The reform also included the introduction of framework budgeting and management by objectives: the tripartite National Labour Market Council (*Landsarbejdsrådet*) specifies the Regional Councils' objectives and result requirements. Moreover, the Ministry of Labour allocates a budget framework to each region.[7]

However, soon after the introduction of this ambitious reform the government and the Ministry of Labour began to recentralise competences by adding several adjustments to the reform, causing frustration in the Regional Labour Market Councils. This tendency to reduce the influence of the labour market parties was continued in 1999 when the labour market parties were excluded from the pre-legislative working committee on a new labour market reform, the main goal of which, according to the pre-legislative working committee, is to create 200,000 new jobs by 2005.[8] But even though the intention of the government was to keep the labour market influence at a minimum, they were invited to tripartite talks on the reform in autumn 1998, that is, after the pre-legislative committee had finished its work. Contrary to the expectations of the government, the labour market parties reached an agreement on most important issues that became the basis for a 'joint conclusion paper' (*fælles konklussions papir)*. This paper limited the room for manoeuvre of the government and Parliament and became the core of the new reform passed by Parliament.

The view of most commentators was that the surprising agreement between LO and DA had to do with the fact that LO desperately needed to make itself visible after years on the sidelines in bargaining on wages and conditions as well as in labour market policy. Hence, LO accepted such controversial suggestions as a shortening of the period for which unemployment benefits are paid and the elimination of particular benefit regulations concerning unemployment benefits for people aged 50–54. However, the compromises turned out to have some negative repercussions for LO in that one of the most powerful unions within the organisation, the General Workers Union in Denmark (*Specialarbejderforbundet i Danmark (SiD)*) opted out of the agreement. The SiD opt-out is unlikely to have any bearing on the progress of the reform, but has created some tensions within the labour movement.

It is too early to say if the tripartite talks on the labour market reform will be followed by talks on more general issues and if a permanent forum for intersectoral concertation will be established, as was proposed by LO in the beginning of autumn 1998. The unsuccessful attempt by the government to control the political game around the labour market reform in 1998 has probably not increased the willingness of government to establish such a forum.

Overall, the development in this policy area in the second half of the 1990s seems to be a tendency to reduce some of the influence the labour market parties had obtained at the beginning of the decade. However, the political processes around the 1998 labour market reform show that this development is not straightforward.

Social Policy

Social policy differs from active labour market policy on a number of points. The labour market parties, LO and DA, have never had the same influence on social policy as they have had on labour market policy, either in influencing the content of laws or in the implementation and administration of these. Implementation and administration of social policy is still in the hands of the counties and municipalities.

However, the two policy areas have been moving closer to one another and labour market policy now has more influence on social policy than previously. This is because attempts to employ and re-employ persons previously on early retirement have increasingly become an important part of social policy. This can be seen as a kind of 'workfare' similar to such schemes in labour market policy, and therefore necessitates involvement of the labour market parties.

This involvement has taken several forms. One such is on the border between social policy and the industrial relations system. It is related to the introduction of so-called social chapters (*sociale kapitler*) in collective agreements from 1995 onwards. The social chapters are an attempt by the government to commit the social partners to preserve and create jobs on special terms of employment for disabled people, in order to avoid social exclusion and limit the number of persons who take early retirement. By 1998 most collective agreements contained a social chapter. The introduction of these was followed up by evaluations and recommendations by two tripartite boards, *Skånejobudvalget I* and *Skånejobudvalget II*, but no concertation took place in these bodies.

The second form of involvement of the labour market parties is via the new local tripartite boards (*lokale koordinations-udvalg*) that have been established at municipal level to facilitate the process of re-employing disabled people. These boards were made compulsory in 1998. Moreover, two national tripartite boards were added: *Rådet for den sociale indsats på det rummelige arbejdsmarked* and *Det centrale koordinationsudvalg*. However, the role of all these is consultative and is not likely to lead to concertation in the foreseeable future.

A third form of involvement is the so-called 'four-partite talks' (*fir-parts forhandlinger)* between the government, LO, DA, and subnational authorities represented by the National Association of Local Authorities in Denmark (KL) and the Danish Confederation of County Councils (ARF), but again these talks are a forum for consultation, not concertation.

In contrast to these examples, there was no increase in the involvement of the labour market parties in the 1998 reform of the twenty-year-old Social Policy Act. This, and other social policy legislation in the 1990s, was passed by Parliament without tripartite committees being set up. The formal involvement of the labour market parties took the form of hearings. Overall, the influence of labour market policy on social policy legislation was limited.

Summing up, there has been no concertation in social policy apart from areas affected by active labour market policy. The involvement of the labour market parties in the policy-making process in this area has increased during the decade, but has taken the form of consultation, not concertation. It is too early to say if the consultation could lead to concertation at a later stage.

Work environment

The work environment has, in contrast to wages and working conditions, always been regulated by legislation in Denmark. The first laws concerning the work environment were some of the first laws of the Danish welfare state, being passed in the late nineteenth century before the industrial relations system had been established.

The labour market parties have several channels of influence in matters pertaining to the regulation of the work environment. One such channel is through their representation in the Working Environment Council, *Arbejdsmiljørådet,* which takes part in the formulation of new rules and can through its own initiative raise questions regarding the work environment. A second channel is through the twelve bipartite Sector Councils for the Work Environment, *Branchesikkerhedsrådene*. These councils provide an advisory service and are allowed to set up advisory services for specific branches/sectors. Moreover, all enterprises with more than five employees must elect a safety representative and all enterprises with more than twenty employees must form a safety committee.

At the beginning of the 1990s the influence of the labour market parties on the regulation of the working environment increased. Firstly, the labour market parties were instructed to commit themselves to carry out some of the preventive work.[9] Secondly, through their representation in the permanent tripartite bodies and pre-legislative work, the labour market parties have had a profound influence on overall environmental policy. Concertation has taken place in at least two important cases: the government action plan to prevent repetitive and monotonous work *(ensidigt gentaget arbejde)* and the action plan 'Improved Work Environment Year 2005' from 1994 (*Rent arbejdsmiljø år 2005).*

However, towards the end of the 1990s concertation in this area ran into serious problems. In 1997, the high and increasing number of industrial injuries fuelled a debate on the new Work Environment Act, which was part of the government action plan from 1994. The Minister of Labour had lost her patience with the labour market parties:

> It is simply unacceptable that employees die at work, and that society will have to spend millions on hospital bills – the government is impatient; now that our economy is improving and more jobs are being created we would like to see safer workplaces.[10]

Therefore the new reform of the twenty-year-old Work Environment Act gave the minister increased control of the new Branch Work Environment Councils (*Branchearbejdsmilljøråd*) – a new version of what were previously known as the Sector Councils for the Working Environment. DA criticised the Minister of Labour for what it saw as a lack of consultation of the social partners in pre-legislative work, and furthermore found the hasty process by which the law was passed in Parliament to be totally unacceptable. Moreover, DA argued that the new law increased centralisation and bureaucracy and decided to opt out of the Working Environment Council, leaving the tripartite system in a shambles. LO complained that the process was contrary to tradition and characterised by secretiveness but nevertheless asked DA to return to the tripartite system. This occurred in June 1998 when the new Minister of Labour stated that the government would only intervene in the Branch Work Environment Councils if the work of the councils was in conflict with the government's action plan for the Work Environment.

Developments in the scope of concertation in this policy area in the 1990s have been more or less the same as in labour market policy: an increase in concertation at the beginning of the decade, followed by a decrease towards the end.

Summing up on policy concertation

The overall picture is that governments extended the role of concertation at the beginning of the 1990s but withdrew some of the influence of labour market parties in the late 1990s. Although this development was not straightforward in any of the policy areas, Table 6.1 reveals that it was highly visible in labour market policy and in the regulation of the work environment. Developments have taken another path in social policy: there has never been concertation including the labour market parties in pre-legislative work in this policy area, and the tripartite committees set up in the second half of the decade are forums for consultation, not for concertation. In economic policy no concertation took place throughout the decade.

A trend towards less involvement in pre-legislative committees and other ad hoc forums was also identified by a recent quantitative analysis of developments in the relationships between interest-organisations and the state in all policy areas.[11] However, the labour market parties' frequency of 'important contacts' with the ministries, Parliament and the government, other than pre-legislative work and other ad hoc forums, increased according to this analysis. It seems that the involvement of the labour market parties has

Table 6.1. *Policy Concertation in Denmark*

Content	Forums
Economic policy	None
Labour market policy	
Steering Regional Labour Market Councils etc.	National Labour Market Council (permanent)
Preparing Labour Market Reform '94 etc.	Zeuthen-udvalget (1991–2)
Bargaining on Labour Market Reform Stage 3	Tripartite talks (1998)
Social policy	None
Labour law	
Codetermination of work environment rules	Working Environment Council (permanent)
Codetermination of the government action plan 'Improved Work Environment Year 2005'	Working Environment Council (permanent)

Source: see text

not decreased, but has changed from concertation and consultation, especially in the pre-legislative phases, towards more informal relationships in other phases of the political cycle.[12]

The Ideas of Social Partnership – Continuity and Renewal

The ideas of, and arguments for, social partnership, which are summarised in Tables 6.2 and 6.3, do not always distinguish between concertation and consultation. The most important idea underlying concertation as well as other forms of involvement of labour market parties in Denmark is still what can be called conflict-based consensus,[13] which means that all three actors (the state, employers' organisations and employees' organisations) recognise conflicts of interest but agree about the rules of the game and prefer agreed settlements to imposed solutions. Although the forms of involvement have changed, the underlying idea has not. This idea or norm was first created on a bipartite basis in form of the so-called 'September Compromise' (*Septemberforliget*) struck in 1899 between the peak organisations of the employers and the employees. Conflict-based consensus has since spread its importance from labour market regulation to other policy areas. Moreover, despite the LO opt-out of the 'declaration of intent', the government and labour market parties still have a more or less common understanding of the economy and of what the content of social policy and labour market policy should be.

But other ideas pertaining to concertation and consultation have changed in the late 1980s and the 1990s. First, the concept of social solidarity has changed. Solidaristic wage policy is not so much on the agenda any longer.

Table 6.2. *Key terms in Denmark*

Term	Meaning
Trepartsforhandlinger	Temporary tripartite concertation, should lead to government commitment to adopt certain policies
Treparts-drøftelser	Temporary tripartite consultation, not necessarily aiming for government commitments
Treparts-samarbejdet	Tripartite cooperation, refers to the work of the permanent tri- and 'four-partite' boards, committees and councils at national as well as regional/local level
Firparts-drøftelser	'Four-partite' consultation in social policy, where the national federation of the municipalities is a powerful actor
Socialt partnerskab	Social partnership, refers to various kind of bipartite (employer-employee) or tripartite cooperation inside or outside the state apparatus at national as well as regional/local level

Table 6.3. *Key Arguments in Denmark*

Proponent	Argument
For	
LO	A broad social contract including social, labour market, industrial policy etc. is needed because the instruments of economic policy are no longer sufficient
The opposition	Will not add to the labour market parties' proposals for a labour market reform, because it could create further trade union resistance
Against	
Former minister of labour	The labour market parties do not deliver results. They want the government to pay, but themselves to control the regulation of the work environment
Some civil servants	The labour market parties discourage change in the tripartite boards

Sources: see text.

Solidarity is now more about refusing social benefits if these are not needed. Some examples of this development are the tightening of benefit conditions in social and labour market policy schemes; LO's suggestion that social benefits to a greater extent should be targeted towards those who are worst off; the recent change in the rules for early retirement; and the wish of the opposition and DA to lower the level of pensions due to the ageing of the population. Moreover the employers are, as something new, also being asked for solidarity or 'social responsibility' (*socialt ansvar*) as part of workfare in social policy. Perhaps this intimates a first step in the direction of moving the Danish welfare state closer towards the continental model.[14]

A second change is related to the actors' own ideas about who should be included in concertation and consultation. The influence of the counties and municipalities has increased considerably in the 1980s and in the 1990s. Over time, the DA and LO representatives at all levels have come to accept the representatives of counties and the municipalities in tripartite work, but there has been some sluggishness in this process. In labour market policy the representatives of the counties and municipalities are still not treated as equal partners.

Concertation has not been questioned as much in Denmark as in some other countries.[15] In all its various forms, the involvement of labour market parties in policy making is so integrated into Danish politics that its advantages and drawbacks are not often on the agenda. However, a few arguments for and against are heard from time to time.[16]

In 1998 the LO explicitly called for a social contract, arguing that new challenges have appeared in many policy areas since the 1987 'declaration of intent' and that a new forum for concertation should be set up, to include other policy areas as well as economic policy.

The attitude of DA and its member organisations towards social partnership has been cooler, but not hostile. One anonymous source in DA explains the approach of DA and its powerful affiliated organisation Danish Manufacturing (*Dansk Industri*) as 'businesslike: you do not initiate it yourself, but if it seems to benefit your members, the willingness to make an agreement is there.'

Arguments against concertation are also rare among the opposition. It is interesting to note that the leader of the Liberal Party indirectly supported concertation in relation to the new labour market reform 1998 when he justified the opposition's acceptance of the LO/DA 'joint conclusion paper' as the core in the reform: 'We have no interest in creating difficulties for the leaders of LO by proposing new demands not already in the agreement.'[17]

The post-concertation opt-out of SiD from the labour market reform and the DA opt-out from the permanent tripartite work environment forums cannot be taken as an expression of unwillingness to engage in concertation. What these organisations questioned was the results and the forms of the concertation processes, not concertation in itself.

However, arguments against social partnership are heard. A fundamental criticism was raised by a frustrated former Minister of Labour during the crises in the reform of the Work Environment Act:

> It is my impression that employers and sometimes the unions perceive tripartite cooperation as two parties playing a role whilst expecting the government to finance whatever they decide. Well, let me tell you that this is not how the government sees it. When it is the government who pays it is only fair that I, as the minister in charge, put forward demands and raise issues relating to political objectives.[18]

Critiques addressing concertation can also be found among civil servants in parts of the state apparatus, for instance the Ministry of Labour and the Ministry of Education. The content of this criticism is that the involvement of the labour market parties discourages changes because the labour market parties act in a conservative way. This criticism is also found among some parliamentary politicians but it is very rarely stated officially.[19]

Explaining Danish Social Partnership in the 1990s

The first conclusion to be drawn from this analysis is that social partnership is still essential to policy making in Denmark in that concertation supported by the idea or norm of conflict-based consensus still plays an important role in policy making. Secondly, there have been trends towards less concertation and more involvement through other channels in the second half of the 1990s, although this development is not the same in every policy area and is not straightforward in any policy area. There are several possible explanations for this change in the extent of concertation.

One possible explanation is that the change towards a post-Fordist society diminishes the role of the labour market parties. This view can be perceived as the backdrop of the criticism of the social partners as being conservative and unable to deliver results. Binding kinds of involvement such as concertation have therefore been abandoned. That the involvement of the labour market parties has not been questioned more fundamentally could, according to this explanation, be because this development is new – hence, more criticism could be expected in the near future. This very general explanation partly explains recent developments, but it is difficult to verify.

A second possible explanation has to do with the development of the organisations themselves. As described in relation to matters concerning the organisational context, the development of large, new, sector-wide organisations and cartels in the 1980s and the 1990s led to a decline in power and influence for the traditional peak organisations DA and LO, so that the political system now regards them as being less capable of acting as key negotiating counterparts than previously. This power-balance related argument also seems reasonable.

A third explanation could be that the change has to do with changes in the ideas of social partnership. But, as was argued previously, the most important idea of social partnership, conflict-based consensus, has been left fairly uncontested. The changed ideas of social solidarity and of inclusion in concertation and consultation are unlikely to explain the decrease in concertation.

A fourth possible explanation is that the speed of the political cycle has increased: the time it takes from a problem being formulated as a political problem to the formulation and implementation of a solution has been reduced and therefore the pre-legislative processes are considered to be too long.[20] This more technical explanation has some explanatory power but it ignores the fact that the pre-legislative committees often commit the government more than informal relations do. This development has therefore had consequences for the power relations between the government and the interest organisations. It is not only a technical change.

All four arguments have to do with long-term trends. It is also possible, however, that some of the changes in the extension of concertation are short term or have more to do with personal relations or the strategic choices of the actors than with long-term structural changes. This argument is supported by the return of DA to the tripartite work of regulation of the working environment after the change of Minister of Labour, and by the political game centred on the labour market reform of 1998. By limiting the focus to the four policy areas of this analysis, it is still too soon to say if the trend towards a more self-assured state is a short-term or a long-term one, but in any case it is important to be aware that the developments of the latter part of the 1990s have not led to ending the involvement of the labour market parties in policy making.

Notes

1. P.L.S. Consult and P. Jensen, *Labour Market Studies – Denmark*, Brussels, 1997.
2. J. Due, J. S. Madsen, C.S. Jensen et al., *Towards Multi-level Regulation of Employment Relations. 5–years Research Programme 1998–2003 – an outline proposal*, FAOS, Industrial Relations Research Group, Department of Sociology, University of Copenhagen, Copenhagen 1998: 26–7.
3. J. Due, J.S. Madsen, M. Mailand, *Partssamarbejdet i den danske model,* Forskningsnotat, August 1997: 6.
4. K.F. Petersen, 'Tripartite talks on the 1998 bargaining round'. *Eironline*, December 1997.
5. K.F.V. Petersen, 'LO opt out of the 1987 joint statement and for a social contract', *Eironline*, May 1998.
6. P. Kongshøj Madsen, 'Denmark – Active and Passive Labour Market Policies in Denmark', *Sysdem Trends,* no. 28 (1997): 15.
7. PLS Consult and P. Jensen, *Labour Market Studies-Denmark,* 41.
8. Arbejdsministeriet et al., *Videreførelse af den aktive arbejdsmarkedspolitik. 2005–udvalget om videreførelse af arbejdsmarkedsreformerne.* Copenhagen, 1998.
9. J. Due and J.S. Madsen, eds., 'Arbejdsmarkedets parter og den fremtidige arbejdsmiljøindstas', in *Arbejdsmiljøinstitutet 1946–96 – en jubilærumsbog med tre bud på fremtiden,* Arbejdsmiljøinstitutet, Copenhagen, 1996: 163–84.
10. K.F.V. Petersen, 'Disagreement on the proposed new Danish Work Environment Act', *Eironline*, May 1997.
11. P.M. Kristiansen, 'Interesseorganisationer, centraladministration og udvikling af nye indflydelsesstrategier', in *Interesseorganisationer i dansk politik*, ed. K. Ronit, Copenhagen, 1998: 119–54. In this analysis, however, the trend begins in the mid-1980s.
12. The importance of the informal contacts between the state apparatus and the labour market parties has also been stressed by other Danish researchers. See J. Due and J.S. Madsen, *Forligsmagerne*, Copenhagen, 1996, and O.K. Petersen, 'Interesseorganisationer og den parlamentariske styreform', in *Interesseorganisationerne i dansk politik*, ed. K. Ronit, Copenhagen, 1998: 197–232.
13. See also Strøby Jensen, this volume.
14. C.J.Jensen, 'The Winner Takes It All – Valfærd, arbejdsmarked og social politik i europæisk belysning', *Social Politik*, special issue, 1998.
15. Petersen, 'Interesseorganisationerne og den parlamentariske styreform', 198.
16. The arguments here relate only to tripartite concertation. Critiques concerning the dominant position of LO and DA and/or its affiliated organisations in bargaining of pay and conditions are not included.
17. K.F.V. Petersen, 'Tripartite agreement reached on content of new labour market reform', *Eironline*, October 1998.
18. K.F.V. Petersen, 'Problems of implementing the newly amended Work Environment Act', *Eironline*, August 1997.
19. *Mandag Morgen*, 26 January 1997; *Mandag Morgen*, 9 March 1998.
20. Kristiansen,'Interesseorganisationer, centraladministration og udvikling af nye indflydelsesstrategier', 148.

CHAPTER 7

FRANCE IN HISTORICAL PERSPECTIVE: THE IMPOSSIBILITY OF PARTNERSHIP

Susan Milner

Introduction

France is commonly characterised as having low levels of macroeconomic policy concertation. History helps to identify several reasons for this: notably slow and patchy industrialisation and a distrust of intermediate associations dating back to the *Ancien Régime*, as well as strong tendencies of the national political culture which ran throughout the nineteenth and twentieth centuries and which impeded the formation of a partnership culture. Low levels of interpersonal and societal trust have been identified by various observers since Alexis de Tocqueville, who wrote of France at the time of the 1789 Revolution that 'nowhere else in the world were citizens less inclined to join forces and stand by each other in emergencies'.[1] Ideological polarisation weakened political currents favourable to concertation (centre-left technocracy, social catholicism and social democracy), which tended to deviate into more radical or authoritarian versions. Concertation developed only episodically, in response to specific political and economic circumstances, and was heavily state-driven.

In the twentieth century, the impact of war was particularly strong. The war effort provided both the need and justification for concertation: the imperative of productivism and industrial rationalisation; legitimation of state power; and a discourse of national unity. It gave trade unions access to decision-making institutions as well as ideological legitimation as defenders of the nation and the republic. It also mitigated the fiercely independent tendency of employers and downgraded private profit. The importance of wartime experience suggests the inertia of underlying structures and values favourable to concertation, in line with the accepted view that social reform in France is always precipitated by crisis rather than by a process of incremental and consensual change. In such circumstances concertation failed to take root and was easily swept away, although some elements – notably its more technocratic features – were incorporated into the state's practice.

In general terms, the relationship between social 'partners' has been marked by low levels of trust and a wide gulf between labour and management. At the same time, both trade unions and employers have been fearful of the state, jealously guarding their autonomy. At times, this has led to temporary alliances between the 'social partners'. But the fundamental imbalance in the relationship between unions and employers makes such an alliance impossible in the longer term, and unions tend to look towards the state instead, both dependent and resentful. Politically, this ambiguous attitude also found expression in the Communist Party (PCF), which maintained the discourse of antagonistic class interests whilst pragmatically claiming its place at the table.

From Outlaws to Social Partners? Trade Unions, Employers and the State in the *Belle Époque*

Work-based associations, such as trade unions and employers' organisations, were assimilated with cartels and outlawed by the Revolution (Le Chapelier law of 1791). The revolutionary tradition thus sought to set up a direct relationship between the republican state and the citizen: a protective state with its own internal checks and balances (notably constitutionalism) rather than a liberal state relying on civil society. Employers for their part looked to the state to protect their commercial interests and to maintain public order. Within the private firm, they insisted on complete freedom of action. Although willing to join with other employers to quell unrest, employers did not develop coordinated actions, as in Germany with lockouts. Some employers, particularly in eastern France, developed paternalistic policies of social welfare, such as the Le Creusot model steelworks in Burgundy. Employers and engineers of this type were close to various branches of the social Catholic movement (led by Albert de Mun and René de la Tour du Pin) or to the Catholic sociologist Frédéric Le Play's charitable social reform movement. Many of them had been influenced by the experience of war and defeat in 1870, and they linked national military decline with social hygiene.[2] However, by the 1880s such experiments in 'moralizing paternalism' had clearly failed to contain working-class militancy.[3]

Nineteenth-century uprisings (particularly the failed workers' republic of 1848) left behind two lasting traditions in the French labour movement: a revolutionary tradition strongly associated with anarchosyndicalism, stressing direct action and distrust of parliamentary politics; and a republican tradition based on the union of middle-class radicalism and the proletariat against reaction. Both of these currents found their way into the pre-1914

Confédération Générale du Travail (CGT), although the combined effect of employer resistance and state repression gave primacy to revolutionary syndicalism. Founded in 1895, the CGT was a minority movement, representing less than 2 percent of the workforce. Trade unions had been legalised only in 1884, and prior to this date labour organisation had been forced underground. The economic and political climate was particularly unpropitious to the development of a mass labour movement.

The relatively slow development of capitalism also hampered moves towards state regulation of labour relations, other than by the direct use of force. The beginnings of labour legislation in the 1870s, particularly laws on industrial accidents and work inspectors in 1874, coincided with the first attempts at creating state institutions to deal with labour issues: the *Conseil Supérieur du Travail* and the *Office du Travail* dated from 1891. However, the function of these institutions was limited to compilation of statistics, and the labour inspectorate lacked any real authority.

The socialist Alexandre Millerand was responsible for the first systematic attempts to defuse worker unrest and encourage more consensual labour through ambitious but unsuccessful plans for compulsory arbitration.[4] A group of reformist socialists, led by Albert Thomas, continued to promote Millerand's ideas of social integration, but they met with little response until the war.

By 1914, the state realised that trade unionism posed little threat: labour militantism 'went into hibernation' once the troops had been called.[5] Still, striking workers in mining and munitions factories posed a threat to production. Thomas, in various ministerial positions with responsibility for munitions from 1914, set up obligatory conciliation and arbitration committees in arms factories in 1917 and established a system of workers' delegates. Assisted by other socialist ministers such as Marcel Sembat, Thomas promoted labour leaders as official spokespeople.[6] At first reluctant, many major employers accepted the practice of bargaining within the firm for the duration of the war. But such experiments remained limited, and did not take root.

Nevertheless, some elements of the wartime attempts to modernise industrial relations and create the conditions for economic planning had a longer-term influence. Étienne Clémentel, at the Ministry of Trade, remained in power longer than Thomas (from 1915 to 1920), and Jean Monnet, the later head of economic planning after 1946 and founding father of the European Coal and Steel Community, served as his *directeur de cabinet*.[7] A Radical politician, Clémentel sowed the seeds of state intervention in industry, although with an emphasis on bureaucratic planning rather than social partnership. However, he was rapidly marginalised after 1919 as the state disengaged from its wartime involvement in the economy.

Many CGT leaders seized the opportunity for greater involvement in decision making. Under Léon Jouhaux's reformist leadership, the CGT moved towards a new relationship with the state.[8] Its 'minimum programme', agreed in 1918 and inspired by President Wilson's Twenty-one

Points, saw a role for labour in postwar economic recovery, including presence on a tripartite National Economic Council. Nationalisation formed the basis of the CGT's new economic policy, which marked a clear departure from revolutionary syndicalism's 'class-against-class' militancy. It corresponded to changes within the structure of the organised workforce: civil servants, teachers and postal workers flocked to the CGT and reinforced the new state-centred line.

Following the expulsion of dissidents, who set up a rival confederation, the CGT was now free to pursue its 'policy of presence'. But as union membership fell during the Depression, employers felt no compulsion to bargain, either in the workplace or at national level. The state made only limited moves towards the unions' economic agenda. When the CGT's demand for a National Economic Council failed to find a response, the confederation was reduced to setting up its own council of economic planning experts, which the government simply ignored.

On the other hand, the state's relationship with employers underwent major change, as armaments brought the major metalworking, vehicle and aircraft producers into the state's orbit, as well as the key energy sector.[9] It was no coincidence that the first sector to organise – and still the best organised and most vocal today – was the mining and metal employers. State relations with the banking and credit agencies also grew particularly close from the 1910s. In 1919, the Ministry of Commerce and Industry invited the employers' federations and associations to form a peak organisation.[10] Created in direct response to the state's need for an 'interlocutor', the *Confédération Générale de la Production Française* (CGPF) had little influence over its constituent associations, but formed the kernel of a lobbying group which would mobilise only later, in response to a more direct and universal threat: left government.

The Popular Front: The 'Social Summit' as a Defining Moment?

Centre-left governments from the mid-1920s began to grant some of the CGT's demands for more say in decision making: in 1925, the *Cartel des Gauches* government finally set up a National Economic Council. But the ideological confrontation between left and far-right polarised French political life and made tripartite coexistence impossible.

The political demands for bread and work[11] which brought the Popular Front to office also meant a revival of the unions as channels for popular discontent. Anti-fascism served to reunite the CGT and its communist-led rival shortly before the united left was swept into office on a wave of working-class expectation. Union membership rocketed to five and a half million, and a wave of strike action and occupations across France propelled the unions to the forefront of economic policy making.

The Popular Front's economic policy was based on demand-led recovery. Thanks to the opposition of both the Radicals and the PCF, the united left's programme failed to take up the structural reforms – including state-led planning and the nationalisation of key industries and banks – advocated by Jouhaux and his political allies in the socialist party ('planism').[12] Some nationalisation took place, mainly of arms and aeronautical industries (1937), whilst the state virtually took over the governing body of the *Banque de France*. But it did not form part of a structural reform of the economy. Wages policy and anti-unemployment measures formed the main planks of Léon Blum's 'New Deal'. The Matignon summit, convened by Blum in June 1936 in order to get France back to work, gave unions a landmark deal: wage rises, reduced working time and the introduction of elected works delegates. Employers, frightened by the spectre of social revolution, could do nothing to resist. But by March 1937 recovery had halted, and by June 1937 Blum was out of office. Employers quickly reversed the concessions.

The Popular Front experiment left a lasting mark on relations between unions, employers and the state. It set the precedent for national-level 'summits' to defuse industrial unrest. It taught the biggest union confederation that the most immediate and universal way to satisfy demands was to look to the state, and particularly to work for electoral victory of the left. It left the employers with a visceral fear of left-wing government, but also taught them that they needed to organise as a class. In 1936, the CGPF became the confederation of *patrons* (bosses) rather than 'producers', marking a retreat from state-led productivism. It reorganised its internal structure and began to think more seriously about defending the enterprise's cause in dealings with the state. However, it still had no coherent policy to promote.

Vichy: The Culture of Corporatism

The period of Vichy government (July 1940–August 1944) saw an experiment of another kind: the authoritarian state banned the existing employers' and union organisations and attempted to set up a corporatist state with strong fascistic overtones. Vichy corporatism emphasised the protection of French business and strong statism, as well as a nostalgic ruralism. Underpinning it lay the notion that class divisions could be overcome by working together in the national interest. A former socialist MP, Vice-President Pierre Laval, launched the campaign for 'Work, Family, Fatherland'. The Labour Charter of October 1941, presented by Minister of Labour René Belin (formerly Jouhaux's right-hand man), made membership of state-sponsored trade unions compulsory, and set up workplace committees in all large firms in order to encourage harmony between workers and employers. The National Revolution also included the introduction of health benefits for workers and special categories (widows, the elderly) and a minimum wage.

Vichy's discourse of social 'harmony' had close ideological ties with a strand of (Catholic) employer paternalism, seen for example in the *Centre des Jeunes Patrons* (CJP). Set up in 1938, the CJP was strongly influenced by de Mun's conservative Catholic social reform movement of the 1880s, which aimed to turn workers away from radical demands by binding them into the workplace. Despite this ideological affinity, many Catholic employers turned away from the Vichy regime because of its links with the German occupier.

Some have seen Vichy as the employers' and ruling classes' revenge for 1936: certainly the nationalistic, corporatist discourse sought deliberately to quash the working-class strength symbolised by the Popular Front. The extent of active support for Vichyite corporatism is difficult to gauge, however. Certainly, on the employers' side, the Vichy regime's emphasis on discipline and its productivism chimed with many large employers' wishes. According to Robert Paxton, corporatism enabled France's notoriously risk-averse employers to protect themselves against both class struggle and competition.[13] The dissolution of the General Confederation of Small and Medium Sized Enterprises (*Confédération Générale des Petites et Moyennes Entreprises,* CGPME) may have been necessary to counterbalance the outlawing of independent trade unions, but in reality it continued to exist, and several leading employers, such as CJP president Jean Mersch, moved in Vichy circles. The main friend of business in the Vichy administration was Jean Bichelonne, Laval's junior minister for industrial production, who introduced sectoral 'organisation committees' in August 1940. Organisation committees, set up to distribute raw materials among the different sectors of activity, found favour among large employers who saw them as a means of protecting themselves against German demands and of influencing government policy.[14]

Employers saw less advantage in Vichy's new social order, particularly the works committees. Among employers as a whole, passive cooperation with the state seems to have been the norm, and it was widespread enough for works committees to function in many companies: ninety-one committees were functioning in 1941, and 234 in 1944. Among trade unionists too, passive collaboration allowed the committees to function, although there is evidence that trade unionists may have used them for militant rather than collaborative activities.[15]

Important parts of Vichy-style corporatism proved attractive to currents within the employers' organisations and the trade unions, and it may therefore be seen as an historical thread in France's political culture. But it took an authoritation state and foreign coercion to impose the corporatist solution, which fell into discredit after the war. Nevertheless, elements of Vichyite corporatism continued into the postwar period. Shorn of its authoritarian ideology, technocracy was perfectly in tune with the reconstruction drive of the postwar period.

Postwar Planning and Limited Macroeconomic Concertation

The legacy of Vichy is also seen in a negative sense: workers (especially trade unionists) had been prominent in the Resistance against German occupation and the Vichy regime. Trade unions' opposition to Vichy – and, conversely, active collaboration with the Germans by prominent employers like Louis

Renault – legitimated them and integrated them into the nation as never before. Membership rocketed to an all-time high of five million for the CGT and another million for the Catholic CFTC (*Confédération Française des Travailleurs Chrétiens*). With the left (including the PCF, fêted as the party of Resistance martyrs) in power, and a programme of social partnership put forward by the National Council of the Resistance, the CGT looked set to obtain its say in decision making.

The ideology of Resistance and social justice also pushed Christian democracy leftwards, away from the nationalistic right that had been discredited by its links with Vichy. For the first time in France's history, a significant Christian Democrat party emerged and became strongly associated with the new Republic: the *Mouvement Républicain Populaire* (MRP), which participated in twenty-three of the twenty-seven governments between 1944 and 1948 and acted as the fulcrum of the parliamentary system.[16] The MRP supported nationalisation, economic planning and the welfare state in the Liberation period. At that time, it enjoyed a close relationship with the CFTC and gained a significant number of working-class votes in strongly Catholic areas of France. However, during the 1950s the MRP moved to the right, thanks largely to fear of communism, whilst progressive leaders began to gather support within the CFTC and pushed the confederation leftwards.

There were also strong economic imperatives driving the postwar consensus. Jean Monnet's technocratic vision struck a chord with modernisers on the left and right, whilst free-market liberals had been discredited by their links with the tainted Third Republic. Productivist values required the integration of the working class, especially the organised groups with the most potential for disruption: the communists and their CGT allies. But pacification of the communists was short-lived. The PCF ministers were expelled from government in 1947 following a strike wave which both the party and the CGT had difficulty controlling. Worker unrest led to concrete victories, but these did not last as employers clawed back concessions, and devaluations diminished the effect of wage increases.

The programme of the National Council of the Resistance laid down the basis of economic policy making: the establishment of a 'real economic and social democracy', sweeping away 'feudal' vested interests; rational organisation of the economy in which individual interests would be subordinated to the general interest; the intensification of production according to a plan drawn up by the state after consultation with the representatives of all those involved in production; nationalisation of all the major means of production, sources of energy and mineral wealth, insurance companies and the main banks; support for cooperatives; workers' rights to access to management and administrative functions and more generally workers' participation in economic decision making.[17] In practice, this meant economic planning, nationalisation, and consultation of unions and employers in the Economic and Social Council. Workers' rights to consultation within the firm took the form of elected workplace committees (*comités d'entreprise*), although the committees' powers were strictly contained within a collaborative framework which effectively limited them to organising social activities. Nevertheless, the introduction of elected committees in large firms gave the leading union confederations, especially the CGT, an important new power base.

Nationalisation concerned mainly energy, aeronautics and insurance and banking. In general, the competitive sector was left untouched (with the notable exception of Renault). The nationalisation of the utilities was to give the state a strategic role in economic planning, particularly in Monnet's first Plan (1947–1952). It also gave trade unions a new voice, since they were heavily represented in the energy sector. The miners especially were the heroes of the Liberation period, symbolising the new production drive exalted by PCF leader Maurice Thorez (deputy prime minister in 1947). In return, they gained special status with job guarantees and an elaborate system of bonuses. However, nationalisation definitely meant state control rather than worker control, and it was not until the Auroux laws in 1981–2 that formal mechanisms for consultation were set up. Instead, pressure was exerted by rank-and-file mobilisation.

The Plan was central to the postwar economic miracle (4.8 percent average annual growth 1949–61, 5.4 percent 1961–73). Its function was to define priorities and set production targets, which were largely met by the 1950s (already by the Second Plan there was overproduction, leading to financial imbalances). It also provided a framework for regional planning, with department-based planning agencies introduced later in the 1960s and 1970s and subsequently regionally-based agencies. After the initial period of indicative planning, the Plan became an instrument of targeted industrial policy in the 1970s. In the context of economic crisis from 1973, planning became at first more selective and then more general in the late 1980s and 1990s, opening up grand debates rather than setting specific tasks. The Plan was essentially technocratic and state-driven, despite its structure which involved employers' and trade union representatives on the planning commissions. Its culture was bureaucratic and its links with the private sector 'tenuous'.[18] Moreover, the Plan did not create a culture of partnership because it failed to dissipate the long-standing distrust between employers and unions. Employers looked to the state rather than to the unions. Unions found themselves the junior partner, complaining that issues had been settled between the state and employers in private. In response, the CGT and the Worker's Force (*Force Ouvrière*, FO) virtually boycotted the Plan from the 1950s until 1981.

More generally, the postwar settlement laid the foundations of an interventionist state. With its control of the financial sector, the state was able to use monetary policy as an instrument of economic regulation, especially from the 1950s.[19] The state also sought to influence economic activity through wages, notably the guaranteed minimum wage, which was to serve as a baseline for collective bargaining. The expansion of the domestic market created the conditions for economic growth, fed by remarkable productivity gains.

The establishment of the contributions-based social security system in 1945–7 played an important part in the stimulation of consumer demand. It also gave employers and trade unions a new role in the complex system of administration of contributions and benefits, based on the bipartite basic regime (*régime général*), plus a series of bipartite sector-specific basic regimes and complementary regimes for status groups (created by a series of national-level collective agreements in the late 1940s and 1950s), with mutual organisations in the voluntary sector filling in the gaps. The bipartite administration of social insurance funds marked a significant change in employer-union relations, requiring a socially 'responsible' attitude on both sides and a measure of cooperation between them. It also 'nationalised' their activities to an important degree, encouraging a state-centred rather than workplace-oriented strategy.[20]

The Economic and Social Council introduced ad hoc consultation of employers and trade unions (alongside representatives of other social groups such as consumers' and family associations), rather than policy concertation. The ESC was to be consulted by legislators on draft legislation before the parliamentary stage, or invited to give opinions on matters that might form the basis of legislation. Moreover, social policy rather than macroeconomic policy came under the remit of the ESC, which was particularly concerned with regulating relationships between the social partners.[21] The ESC therefore forms part of a network of consultative organs set up by the state to boost its effectiveness in social legislation.

As with other bipartite or mixed institutions, the ESC may have had the effect of bringing employers and unions together and encouraging a more cooperative culture. There are also suggestions that involvement in consultative bodies may have boosted smaller, moderate unions with specific expertise, such as the CGC (*Confédération Générale des Cadres*: supervisory staff union, set up in 1946) and the Catholic CFTC, with its links with church-based voluntary associations also represented on the ESC and its interest in family policy. However, consultation was too limited and state-driven for any real cooperation to develop, and the 'revolutionary' unions were able to use the bodies to denounce government policy. Such pluralism – or fragmentation – of interests worked against the emergence of neo-corporatism, as it occurred in mainly northern European countries in the 1960s and 1970s.

To sum up, the immediate postwar period legitimated a participative culture and brought previously marginalised groups – particularly the PCF and the workerist CGT – into the polity. Not only was this culture the ideological glue France needed after the wartime divisions, it chimed with the technocratic drive for modernisation. But already by 1947, with the eviction of the Communists, the glue was weakening. 'Modernisation' was the key word which defined the general interest and provided the basis for social and political consensus. Employers, unions and the state agreed on the overriding objective of rapid economic growth and the expansion of the domestic market. However, the mobilising power of modernisation was too weak to bridge the ideological divide on redistributive issues, revealed in the political instability of the Fourth Republic. Unlike after 1918, employers found their position weakened in relation to the state and to unions, and this accounts for many of the institutional changes which took place. But fear of communism meant that the balance of power was never tipped far the other way.

Gaullist Attempts at Modernisation

The Gaullist Fifth Republic, born in 1958, maintained the consultative apparatus of the Fourth Republic intact, but with some important cultural differences. The participative consensus of the 1946 constitution gave way to a discourse of national interest embodied in a strong executive. Political parties and interest groups were seen as inimical to national unity. Technocratic planning still included consultation (especially where, as earlier with Monnet, this allowed bodies to bypass parliament) but the executive (that is, particularly after 1962, the President) decided.

However, the employers and unions proved implacably resistant to incorporation. The Gaullist modernisation project had the effect of strengthening the employers' position. In 1958, France's entry into the Common Market forced them to abandon protectionism and embrace competition. From now on, France's national interest would be defined by the position of its leading firms on world markets. The rehabilitation of the business ethic – and the employers' counter-offensive – had begun.

For the two leading unions, the CGT and the French Democratic Workers' Confederation (*Confédération Française Démocratique du Travail,* CFDT), the existence of a seemingly entrenched right-wing state, coupled with the absence of social reform, led to direct confrontation with the state, associated by the CGT with the interests of large capital ('state monopoly capitalism thesis'). In the 1960s, they boycotted planning meetings and centred their action on protests against state reduction in social security benefits and planned pit closures. Social tensions exploded in the strike and protest movements of May–June 1968. President de Gaulle, bewildered by the social movements, could not provide any solutions, apart from the curious 1969 referendum which coupled regional reform with the creation of an interest-based upper house. Later in the early 1970s, his successor Georges Pompidou, assisted by Gaullist Jacques Chaban-Delmas and his centre-left adviser Jacques Delors, tried to introduce a systematic modernisation of social relations in France by encouraging collective bargaining and bipartism.

The strike movement had the effect of (temporarily) shifting the balance of power away from employers, who had to concede recognition of workplace unions. But the employers' position was shifting anyway. Rather than wholesale opposition, they began to develop a new social policy based on bipartism, in order to retake the initiative from the state. These shifts on the part of employers and the state led to a new 'contractualisation' of social relations in the early 1970s, which saw a series of national-level agreements on employment and training as well as branch-level bargaining. The state took a leading role in defining the bipartite agenda, as for example in 1970 with the generalisation of salaried status. But the employers were active partners in this enterprise, particularly in social insurance. They had opposed the move from social insurance to universal redistribution implicit in the social security system, fearing that demand for services would create an impossible financial burden on companies. The need to define policy on social security prompted employers to organise, and became increasingly central to its lobbying strategy as the burden increased after the mid-1970s. In response to employers' criticisms, the social security system was reformed in 1967: three groups of risk (age, family and sickness) were separated and financial responsibility was conferred on administrators. Employer and trade union representatives were to be elected rather than designated. Also prompted by the state, the employers took the initiative in setting up unemployment insurance funds. The practice of bipartite talks and agreements on employment dates from this period, although it was eclipsed in the 1980s by government initiatives, particularly on active labour market policies.

As regards macroeconomic policy, the 1970s saw the end of the Keynesian consensus. The liberal right-wing administration after 1976 brought in an austerity policy, which united all the unions in opposition. The old system was in crisis.

The Mitterrand Years: The New Pluralism?

Mitterrand's manifesto in the 1981 presidential election promised an end to the austerity programme, with the creation of public-sector jobs and the stimulation of demand-led growth. It also contained elements close to the heart of the CFDT (which in the late 1970s turned away from political campaigning towards a workplace-centred strategy): industrial democracy and political decentralisation. The CFDT supplied several advisers to the new government in these areas. With its campaign promises – reminiscent of 1936 – to milk the rich and nationalise industry, the left government scared employers onto the offensive. But the reflationary experiment was short-lived. Even the nationalisations of 1981–2 gave way to pragmatic, hands-off management, then partial privatisation, before wholesale privatisation under the cohabitation government (1986–8), then Mitterrand's 'neither-nor' acceptance of the mixed economy, and finally further privatisation in the 1990s. Old-fashioned *dirigisme* was not revived by the socialists, who on the contrary presided over the marketisation of social and economic relations in France.[22]

True to his criticisms of Gaullist authoritarianism, Mitterrand increased consultation of various social groups which constituted power networks for his allies, and which showed disruptive potential during the 1980s, such as students. Employers – or rather particular networks of employers – enjoyed extensive informal access to decision makers, especially as the new French capitalism blurred the dividing lines between public and private ownership. Trade unions represented only one set of interests in this pluralistic consultation, which continued to be state-driven and state-led. Increasingly, consultation of trade unions became ritualistic and disconnected from policy as their membership dwindled. Most union confederations called for growth policies at election time (although by 1988 they had abandoned any pretence of political directives to their membership), yet the CFDT broke ranks early on when in 1982 its general secretary Edmond Maire was one of the first public figures to call for austerity measures. Union presence in the public sector remained high, however, and constituted a powerful check on policy making: thus, for example, Rocard's much-vaunted reform of the '*service public*' came to nothing.

Employers took advantage of their position of strength to redefine collective bargaining and microeconomic policy, in line with the new orthodoxy of 'flexibility'. Under these conditions, tripartism was unlikely to flourish, although bipartism was set for a revival. The discourse of 'social partnership' promoted in the 1980s, at least partly under the influence of the European Community, may to some extent be seen as a social-democratic gloss on neo-liberal adjustment policies. It also marks, and serves to legitimise, the retreat of the state from its overwhelming welfare and fiscal commitments. But it also reveals the limits of neo-liberalism, in terms of public opinion and worries about economic sustainability, as evidenced in the 1995 presidential election.

Conclusion

This overview shows the importance of class antagonisms in French history, exemplified in the PCF's prominence in postwar political life. The discourse and institutions of social partnership, promoted by reformist socialists and left Catholics, came to the forefront at times of national crisis which necessitated unity, at the price of some of the hard left's demands. But the depth of class antagonism meant that such moments were short-lived and usually led to employer reorganisation and counter-offensive. Christian democracy was hampered by the legacy of revolution, which pushed it into confrontation with the republic and associated it with the right, whilst Christian trade unionism followed an independent path. The failure of the French socialist party to invent a French form of social democracy also weighs heavy in this history.[23] For much of the twentieth century, the strength of French communism and the workerist tradition caused the socialist party to retain a revolutionary discourse whilst the practice of coalition government after 1945 created a gulf between rhetoric and day-to-day policy making. At the same time, trade union weakness, division and distrust of political parties precluded the emergence of a mass union following for social democracy as in Germany.

Wartime experiences steadily strengthened the role of the state throughout the twentieth century, even if its reliance on employers and unions diminished in peacetime. As state intervention weakened the organisational capacity of both employers and unions, a vicious circle developed: distrust between employers and unions had the effect of further increasing the role of the state as intermediary. Horror of 'face-to-face' relationships[24] created the need for 'social summits' and for state legislation in place of bargaining: for example, the state's ability to extend collective agreements across a region, a sector or even nationally aggravates the 'free-rider' problem of union membership and contributes to a hollowing-out of social relations in which the symbolic value of agreements counts for more than their practical application. The heavy hand of the state allowed little room for social partnership to flourish, and made militancy seem an easier option for the unions, thus reproducing the vicious circle.

Notes

1. A. de Tocqueville, *The Old Régime and the French Revolution*, New York,1955: 83. See also M. Crozier, *The Bureaucratic Phenomenon*, Chicago, 1964; F. Fukayama, *Trust. The Social Virtues and the Creation of Prosperity*, London and New York, 1995: 113–26.
2. One such figure was Émile Cheysson, a leading member of the *Société d'Économie Sociale* which became a vehicle for Le Play's followers, who was appointed director of the Le Creusot works and in this capacity advocated greater worker participation in social welfare provision: see P. Rabinow, *French Modern. Norms and Forms of the Social Environment*, Chicago and London, 1989: 97–8.
3. Rabinow, *French Modern*, 110. On de Mun, see also J.-L. Mayeur, *Des partis catholiques à la démocratie chrétienne: XIXe–XXe siècles*, Paris, 1980: 85–6.
4. J.-M. Mayeur and M. Rebérioux, *The Third Republic from its Origins to the Great War 1871–1914*, trans. J.R. Foster, Cambridge, 1984: 237.
5. J.-J. Becker, *The Great War and the French People*, trans. A. Pomerans, Leamington Spa, 1985: 69.
6. J. Horne, *Labour at War. France and Britain 1914–1918*, Oxford, 1991: 67–8.
7. Rabinow, *French Modern*, 325–6.
8. B. Georges and D. Tintant, *Léon Jouhaux. Cinquante ans de syndicalisme*, vol.I, Paris, 1962; see also Horne, *Labour at War*, 127.
9. See H. Chapman, *State Capitalism and Working-Class Radicalism in the French Aircraft Industry*, Berkeley, 1991.
10. The statutes of the CGPF reveal the state-driven nature of the project, defining its objectives as 'to study and defend the interests of national work; to contribute to the development of France's production and export strength; to coordinate the efforts of the sectoral [employers'] unions and associated professions': J.-D. Reynaud, *Les Syndicats en France*, vol. II (Textes et documents), Paris, 1975: 34.
11. See J. Jackson, *The Popular Front in France. Defending Democracy, 1934–1938*, Cambridge, 1988.
12. See Jackson, *The Popular Front in France*, 79–80.
13. R.O. Paxton, *Vichy France, Old Guard and New Order,* London, 1972: 204–13.
14. B. Brizay, *Le Patronat. Histoire, structure, stratégie du CNPF*, Paris, 1975: 53–7.
15. P. Fridenson and J.-L. Robert, 'Les ouvriers dans la France de la Seconde Guerre Mondiale. Un bilan', *Le Mouvement Social*, no.158, janvier–mars (1992): 117–47.
16. See R.E.M. Irving, *Christian Democracy in France*, London and New York, 1973: 217–22.
17. Programme du Conseil National de la Résistance, établi en séance plénière le 15 mars 1944 sous le nom de Programme d'action de la Résistance. Reproduced in Reynaud, *Les Syndicats en France*, vol. II, 302–4.
18. P. Hall, *Governing the Economy. The Politics of State Intervention in Britain and France*, Cambridge, 1986: 87.

19. J.-F. Eck, *Histoire de l'économie française depuis 1945*, Paris, 1988: 13–22.
20. See S. Milner, 'What about the workers? The trade unions' short century', in *France after Napoleon*, ed. M. Alexander, London, 1999.
21. Thus, Jean-Daniel Reynaud cites the 1971 law on collective bargaining as a prime example of the usefulness of such consultation: the text adopted in Parliament took account of the ESC's deliberations, since it directly concerned the ESC's members: see Reynaud, *Les Syndicats en France*, vol. I, 262.
22. See V. Schmidt, 'An end to French exceptionalism? The transformation of business under Mitterrand', in A. Daley et al., *The Mitterrand Era*, New York and Basingstoke, 1996: 117–40.
23. See S. Padgett and William E. Paterson, *A History of Social Democracy in Postwar Europe*, London and New York, 1991; P. Anderson and P. Camiller, *Mapping the West European Left*, London and New York, 1994.
24. On the difficulty of face-to-face relationships and the resulting bureaucratisation of economic, social and political life in France, see M. Crozier, *The Bureaucratic Phenomenon*, Chicago, 1964, especially 213–22.

CHAPTER 8

FRANCE IN THE 1990S: STRUGGLING WITH THE WEIGHT OF HISTORY

Nick Parsons[1]

Introduction: The Context of Policy-Making in the 1990s

The state has traditionally played a predominant role in the regulation of social relations in France, due to the weakness of trade union and employer organisations and their hostility towards each other. A mutual recognition of legitimacy and bargaining culture has been largely absent and both sides have sought the intervention of the state to regulate relations between them, usually through legislation. For most of the postwar period, the trade union movement has been ideologically divided between the communist-inspired Confédération Générale du Travail (CGT), the socialist-leaning Confédération Française Démocratique du Travail (CFDT) and the 'apolitical' Force Ouvrière (FO).[2] Although periods of unity have been achieved between the CFDT and the CGT, division has been the rule. Although the Conseil National du Patronat Française (CNPF) is the main umbrella organisation on the employers' side, divisions exist here too, notably between large- and small-scale business, the latter having its own organisation to represent its interests, the Confédération Générale des Petites et Moyennes Entreprises (CGPME). Furthermore, both sides have traditionally exercised weak control over their base. Under such circumstances, national-level tripartite policy concertation has, historically, been virtually impossible, with consensus being the exception, and conflict and state arbitration the rule.[3]

However, trade union and employer organisations can, in theory, intervene in national-level policy processes through collective bargaining, consultative bodies and the management of social security funds, as well as through their everyday lobbying activities. In the 1990s such activities have taken place in the context of changing presidential and parliamentary majorities. Constant throughout these political changes, however, has been a continuing decline of trade union strength – now only about 9 percent of French workers are unionised, the lowest level of any industrialised nation.[4] On the economic front, policy has remained remarkably consistent given the changes in government. Indeed, since the mid-1980s governments of both left and right have followed the main deflationary and deregulatory orientations of the 'competitive disinflation' policy begun by Pierre Bérégovoy in 1984.[5] Much of this policy has been implemented under the impulsion of the construction of the Single European Market and the need to reduce the budget deficit to 3 percent of GDP in order to meet the Maastricht criteria for entry into the EMU.

Concertation, Collective Bargaining and Legal Regulation

One of the peculiarities of the French system of social regulation concerns the articulation between collective bargaining and the law. While collective bargaining at the national level is now well-established in some areas, such as vocational training and the management of social insurance funds, in other areas the intervention of the state is necessary, or requested, by employers and/or trade unions to ensure the survival of an agreement by giving it the force of law (for example, the 1990 agreement and subsequent law on the use of temporary work contracts). The state may also use the threat, or passing, of legislation to push the trade unions and employers into negotiating on particular issues. This is often seen as 'facilitating' legislation, as the state takes stock of the situation after a few years to see whether the law should stand, be amended, or be scrapped in the light of agreements negotiated on the issue by the trade unions and employers. Such is the case, for example, with the reduction of working time to 35 hours per week (see below). Furthermore, lower-level agreements can be extended by the state to cover the whole economy if this is considered desirable.

Table 8.1 gives a global view of the extent of collective bargaining between the peak organisations of employers and labour from the late 1980s to the mid-1990s. The figures are divided into new agreements and addenda to, or updating of, existing agreements (codicils).

The bulk of these agreements reflect the important role played by the peak employer and trade union organisations in the management of the

Table 8.1. *France: Number of National Level Agreements Between Trade Unions and Employers*

	1988	1989	1990	1991	1992	1993	1994	1995	1996	1997
Agreements	6	6	7	1	5	6	2	5	3	6
Codicils	44	39	41	36	52	58	61	37	54	37

Source: European Industrial Relations Review

vocational training system and pension and social security funds. In the latter case, they generally concern adjustments to levels of receipts and expenditure. However, since 1994 there has also been a trend towards agreements aimed at stimulating employment. In 1994 the *allocation pour le remplacement de l'emploi* (ARPE) was set up. This is a fund managed by the UNEDIC unemployment insurance fund that enables workers who have paid forty years of contributions to retire even if they have not reached the legal retirement age of 60, in return for the recruitment of unemployed people. In 1995 national agreements paved the way for branch-level negotiations on the annualisation and reduction of working hours. In the following two years various agreements have been signed aimed at facilitating the employment of those facing redundancy, the young and the long-term unemployed.[6]

Thus, the peak organisations of capital and labour can exercise an important influence over social security and employment issues through collective bargaining. However, it should be remembered that whether agreements are transposed into law or not, or whether they are a response to legislation or not, this bargaining takes place over a narrow range of issues and cannot be seen as evidence of a generalised political exchange between the state and the organised representatives of capital and labour. Indeed, wages are rarely the subject of national intersectoral bargaining (the statutes of the CNPF do not allow it to negotiate wages on behalf of its members), but are the subject of branch- and company-level bargaining,[7] which reduces the capacity of unions to offer something in exchange for favourable legislation. Of course this does not preclude the possibility of informal deals being brokered at this level. However the increasingly decentralised nature of wage bargaining along with national union confederations' lack of control over their base would suggest that this is unlikely due to the problem of delivery at lower levels.

The problem of delivery is not confined to the hypothetical case of national wage bargaining, as the attempts to reduce working time in order to stimulate employment amply demonstrate. Following a 'five-year employment law' passed in 1993, which allowed for the annualisation of hours at company level, an agreement was signed at the intersectoral level in October 1995 that linked the annualisation of hours with a reduction in working time. The application of this was to be the subject of branch-level negotiations. The mediocre results of these negotiations, however, led to the Robien Law of July 1996, which exempted companies from certain social charges if they reduced working time by at least 10 percent, and used this to save or create jobs.[8] In spite of the wave of negotiations that this law gave rise to at company level, the Left preferred a blanket reduction across the economy to a 35-hour week and announced that a national tripartite conference on employment, working time and wages would be organised to discuss the issue. In the face of stiff opposition to the idea of a 35-hour legal working week from the employers' lobby, including threats to boycott the conference, the Prime Minister, Lionel Jospin, announced, at the end of the conference, that the government was to legislate on the matter. The 'Aubry Law', named after the Minister of Labour, was finally adopted by Parliament on 19 May

1998. It was clear that the government's decision had been taken in advance of the conference, perhaps because it feared that without legal compulsion, collective bargaining on the matter would again yield poor results.

A further problem – linked undoubtedly to that of delivery – with national-level collective bargaining as a form of concertation in France concerns the legitimacy of agreements. By law, only one of the five 'representative' trade unions needs to sign an agreement for it to be valid. Thus there is no real need to arrive at a consensus among the peak organisations representing labour and capital in order for an agreement to come into force. Indeed it is rare for all trade unions to sign agreements, the CGT being the most reluctant[9] in order to give itself the freedom to denounce them when they do not achieve their goals or if they disagree with their aims. Thus, for example, an agreement signed in October 1995 allowing for non-trade union members to be mandated by unions to negotiate on behalf of the workforce in small and medium- sized companies lacking trade union representation was validated by parliament in spite of not being signed by either the CGT or FO.

Bipartism and the Welfare State

The system of social security that has developed in France since the Second World War has devolved the management of funds covering family allowances, sickness benefits, pensions and unemployment insurance to employer and trade union peak organisations.[10] In the 1990s many of these funds have faced severe financial problems. Although many national-level agreements signed during the 1990s have aimed to balance the budgets of these funds, the state has sought to increase its control over the system in order to reduce public expenditure.[11]

In 1995, the announcement of the reform of the social security system, named the 'Juppé Plan' after the then Prime Minister, was greeted, in November and December of that year, by the most serious strike wave seen in France since 1968. The CGT and FO were vehemently opposed to the reforms in the name of the defence of 'guaranteed rights', while the government was supported by the CFDT.[12] In the end, the bulk of the reforms were passed by decree the following year in spite of the strong opposition they aroused. These reforms reinforced State control over the social security system by establishing the principle of an annual vote in Parliament of a 'law on the financing of social security', which sets out the spending objectives for each fund. In addition, the representatives of capital and labour are joined in the management of these funds by 'qualified individuals' named by the government. Furthermore, trade union and employer control over the funds is also weakened, and State control reinforced, by changes to the way contributions are collected. This has shifted from being employer and employee contributions based on wages to being financed partly by general taxation through the 'general social contribution', a tax set up by the Rocard government in 1988, and the 'repayment of the social debt', a tax set up as part of the 'Juppé Plan' to balance the social security budget.[13]

Tripartism

The main tripartite bodies through which peak employer and trade union organisations can hope to influence government policy-making are purely consultative ones: the Economic and Social Council (ESC) and the Planning Commissions.

Both are made up of representatives of peak employer and trade union organisations, as well as other interest groups such as consumers, and 'qualified individuals' nominated by the government. The ESC gives advisory opinions on all bills before they go before the National Assembly. The Planning Commissions were established after the Second World War to develop a consensus around medium-term government policy and come under the tutelage of the state via the General Planning Commissariat (GPC). Regional and sectoral commissions, as well as those set up to examine specific policy areas (for example, employment) feed into indicative Five-Year Plans via the GPC. Their influence has declined since the 1960s, but the Rocard government tried to breath new life into the process at the end of the 1980s.[14] In the 1990s the tenth and eleventh National Plans have aimed at preparing France for entry into the single European market and combating unemployment.

Other tripartite consultations occur on an ad hoc basis, particularly through the government's calling of 'social summits' to discuss urgent questions that need addressing. Thus, the Juppé government of 1995–7 held several such summits, dealing notably with youth unemployment and working time following the social unrest of November–December 1995. More recently, Lionel Jospin used the same device to discuss unemployment, working time and wages on 10 October 1997, at the end of which he announced plans for the reduction of the legal working week to 35 hours. Apart from these high profile summits, the leaders of peak employer and trade union organisations have a privileged access to ministers and are generally seen in face-to-face meetings while legislation that may affect their interests is being drawn up.[15]

However this consultation remains underdeveloped, and is essentially limited to the State testing the strength of opposition to its policies.[16] Thus both the National Planning Commissions and the ESC appear to be bodies through which the government explains and informs the peak employer and union organisations of its policies, rather than bodies in which a genuine consensus is sought. Indeed the CGT denounced the neo-liberal thrust of the Tenth Plan as 'an offensive, regressive strategy' that would sacrifice social expenditure and protection and the guaranteed rights of workers for the exclusive benefit of financial powers and the free circulation of capital'.[17] The CGT's report goes on to criticise the planning process for having 'evolved in a profoundly authoritarian manner ... The Tenth Plan is not that of the Nation, but has become that of the State, a State more than ever in the service of transnational capital'.[18] When the Plan was submitted to the ESC in 1989, only representatives of the small Catholic union confederation CFTC voted for, while the CGT and FO voted against and the CFDT abstained.[19] The Plan was nevertheless adopted by the National Assembly on 7 October 1989 through the use of Article 49–3 of the French Constitution, a device that eliminates the possibility of parliamentary debate on a text. Likewise, the report of the 'Employment Group' of the Eleventh Plan, which was never implemented because of the change of government in 1993, was generally favourably received by the CFDT but criticised by the CGT, FO and the CNPF (see below).[20]

Outside of these bodies, ad hoc consultations between representatives of the government and peak employer and union organisations do not appear to lead to any generalised political exchange or concertation practices either. Juppé's 1995 social summit did not lead to any agreement on any of the issues discussed, while, as we have seen, the one organised by Lionel Jospin concluded with the latter's announcement of legislation on the 35–hour week without this being the subject of any agreement. Indeed, the announcement provoked the resignation of Jean Gandois from the presidency of the CNPF in protest.

Of course, this does not preclude the possibility of concertation practices on an informal level. Indeed, the announcement in the present government's budget plans for 1999 that business tax would be reduced could be seen as a compensation for employers for the imposition of the 35–hour week.[21] Although a long-standing demand of the CNPF, the reaction of the latter to the 35–hour week does not suggest that the two measures should be seen together as part of a general agreement over the question of the promotion of employment. Indeed, the report of the 'Employment Group' for the Eleventh National Plan suggested that the savings accruing to the state, through the reduction of unemployment resulting from a reduction in working time, could be passed on to businesses through a reduction in their social charges in order not to harm their competitiveness.[22] The CNPF, through its then president, François Périgot, nevertheless declared itself 'totally opposed to any form, whatever the mechanisms, of a general reduction in working time'.[23]

Attitudes Towards Concertation Practices

The reality would thus appear to be that although the representatives of the peak organisations of capital and labour can hope to influence economic and social policy through the means described above, there is little, or nothing, in the way of generalised political exchange and agreement that could be termed 'concertation'. This can be partly explained by the attitudes of the representatives of the state and employer and union peak organisations towards such practices. Table 8.2 gives a summary of the different terms used by the trade unions, employer organisations and the state when referring to concertation, while Table 8.3 summarises the arguments used for and against this idea.

Table 8.2. *Key Terms in France*

Term	Meaning
Social partners (state, media)	Unions and employer organisations in their role of representative institutions for the purposes of social regulation
Social actors (unions, employers)	Used in opposition to the idea of 'social partners' to reject the idea of partnership/joint interests.
Corporatism (all actors)	Defence of sectoral interests (from the restrictive trade *corporations* of feudal France).
Corporatism (unions)	Implication in the co-management of the state/capitalism.
Concertation/consultation (all actors)	Used interchangeably to describe non-binding consultation. For unions this is seen as meaning their views should be taken into account, although some argue this is often not the case.
General will/interest (political parties)	The expression of popular sovereignty as expressed and delegated to political representatives through the ballot box.
Intermediary bodies (political parties)	Pressure groups, including unions.

Source: see text.

Table 8.3. *Key Arguments in France*

Proponent	Argument
For	
CFDT	Necessary to enable the negotiated modernisation of social structures
CFDT	Allows trade unions to influence social change on behalf of wage earners
Against	
Unions, especially CGT and FO	Defence of workers' interests requires trade union independence from political parties, state and employers
CGT, FO	Implies co-management of capitalism/state/general interest
Political parties	Undermines universal suffrage/popular sovereignty/ general will
Political parties	Economic management and decision making is solely the responsibility of political parties in government
CNPF	Prevents flexibility and freedom of management necessary for economic competitiveness

Source: see text.

Although the term 'social partners' is widely used in legal and administrative documents and in the press, the term 'social actors' is preferred by officials of the CNPF, the CGT and FO. Even in the CFDT, the confederation that has more than any other since the 1970s accepted as inevitable the trends of modern capitalism and sought an accommodation with them, the general secretary, Nicole Notat, expresses a preference for the term 'social interlocutors' to that of 'partners', 'which would seem to indicate that we are, more or less, on the same side of the fence'.[24]

Thus, at the level of terminology, the idea of social partnership is rejected by the 'social partners' themselves. Indeed, all the major trade unions in France continually proclaim their independence from the state and political parties, particularly through their statutes, although in the case of the CGT, with its close (but non-organic) links with the French Communist Party, this independence is more myth than reality. Furthermore, the CGT, FO and CFDT all aim to defend workers against capitalist exploitation.[25] The CFDT's statutes are most ambiguous on this point, but nevertheless proclaim that 'it [the CFDT] aims through its action to awaken in workers a consciousness of the conditions of their emancipation'.[26]

Such pronouncements are, of course, only general ideological orientations and may not govern concrete action. The CFDT, for example, has followed an explicitly reformist path since the late 1970s[27] and defended the Juppé reforms of the social security system as a necessary modernisation of the system, given social and economic trends. Moreover, the CFDT's wish would be to negotiate the modernisation of French social structures, and the implications of this, in partnership with the state and employers. In 1992 it proclaimed: 'This wish for autonomy risks coming into conflict with another necessity, particularly evident for a trade union which aims to act upon the whole of society and even to propose projects for social transformation – the need to find one or more partners at the *political* level'.[28] However, this shift towards corporatist conceptions of the role of a trade union should not be exaggerated. Notat never explicitly argues for a trade union role in the definition of economic policy,[29] although the regulation of social questions such as those pertaining to urbanism[30] has obvious implications for budgetary policy.

Even this narrow form of corporatist concertation is rejected by the CGT and FO in favour of the defence of the 'guaranteed rights' of wage earners, something that can only be achieved if trade unions maintain their independence from employer organisations and the state. For Louis Viannet, the former general secretary of the CGT, this rejection of corporatism is associated with the rejection of capitalism: 'If one thinks that there is no other possible system, trade unionism almost legitimately becomes a partner of those who manage society'.[31] The same goes for relations between trade unions and employers.[32] In this way of thinking, state action and legislation is the result of the balance of power between labour and capital, and the role of the trade union is to work for a balance of power favourable to the translation of worker demands into law in order to improve their condition through the extension of their 'guaranteed rights'.[33] Social and economic regulation at the macro level is not part of the functions of a trade union, as these are limited to the defence of wage earners' interests and do not include co-responsibility for the management of capitalism. Compromises may have to be made on demands, but these should never put the 'guaranteed rights' of wage earners in jeopardy – hence the impossibility of compromise bargaining across a range of subjects aimed at macroeconomic and social regulation.

FO comes to a similar conclusion about the role, if not about the preferred means of action, of a trade union from a reformist standpoint. The general resolution adopted at their 1992 Congress by 68 percent of the votes cast proclaims that: 'The management of the State and the definition of the "general interest" is up to political parties, and the exclusive role of trade unions is the defence of their mandators, the wage-earners'. Corporatist practices are therefore condemned without equivocation.[34]

Such a division of labour is also accepted by the main political parties in France, including those of the Left. Thus, for the Socialist Party (PS):

> The state is responsible for preparing the future, and guaranteeing the general interest ... .The 'social authorities' are responsible for negotiating on their own behalf and are not a substitute for universal suffrage which delegates sovereignty to the legitimate representatives of the people. The law embodies the general will.[35]

At the PS's 1994 Congress, Jospin emphasised the role of trade unions as interlocutors with the government, but, again, their role is seen as limited to consultation and negotiating on wages and labour market issues. The then First Secretary of the party, now Prime Minister, affirmed 'the responsibility of the political powers in the economic sphere, and hence their obligation to determine priorities, objectives and the means of obtaining results'.[36] In a similar vein, the PCF has called for increased consultation with tripartite bodies in political decision making, 'to help *those elected to office to take decisions*'.[37]

The Right shares this view of the state as the embodiment of the 'general will', although it is argued that it must play a much less interventionist role in a climate of economic globalisation and increased international competition.[38] Although the role of the 'social partners' in negotiating social change is acknowledged, this is not taken to mean any national-level concertation, particularly over economic policy: 'Budgetary policy depends only on the State'.[39] Indeed since the end of the 1970s, in both rhetoric and practice, the parties of the Right have followed a neo-liberal logic of economic, financial and labour market deregulation and decentralisation to enable companies to react more rapidly to changing product market conditions.[40] Within this conception, the role of the state should be reduced to carrying out its 'essential' functions of ensuring security, the functioning of the justice system, regional planning for 'territorial cohesion' and determining immigration policy.[41] On the non-Gaullist right, the notion of the general interest is bound up with 'The humanist values of the revolutionaries of 1789 *and the ideal of individual development and personal autonomy*..the values of individual liberty and democracy'.[42] For the Gaullist right, interest groups deform the 'general will' by establishing intermediary bodies between the individual and the state:

> The incessant encroachment of the state has led to citizens forming pressure groups in order to better represent their interests .... From a relationship between the citizen and the state based on an awareness of the common good, we have arrived at a power struggle between organised groups seeking to gain increasingly substantial advantages.[43]

Such a development inevitably leads to the weakening of the general interest.

Finally, the CNPF has moved from hostility to company-level bargaining, fearing this would legitimise trade unions and encroach upon the 'sovereignty' of management, to embracing the decentralising tendencies of the Auroux laws of 1982, arguing that 'any flexibility easing the development of the flexible arrangements that companies need ... is positive'.[44] In essence, the employer's organisation has argued for neo-liberal solutions to economic and social management in the name of economic competitiveness in a global market. Thus, in his response to the idea of negotiations covering working time, wages and employment, contained in the conclusions of the 'Employment Group' of the Eleventh Plan, François Périgot asserted that 'we [the CNPF] cannot give our agreement to the proposition aiming to encourage the generalisation of negotiations at national, branch or company levels [as this is] incompatible with the freedom of management that they [companies] need in the context of international competition'.[45]

Conclusion: An Explanation for a Lack of Concertation

In France, then, the structural preconditions for corporatist concertation do not exist. The trade union movement is weak and divided, and the peak employers' federation cannot bargain centrally over wages. Amongst these divisions, however, there is a striking consensus that rejects concertation as a style of policy making. The majority of the actors see the state as an arbiter, acting according to the prevailing balance of power or general will. Within this framework, both unions and employers' organisations reject the idea of a social partnership, seeing their role as defending their specific interests by pressuring the government to legislate in their favour.

These orientations have deep roots in French philosophical, political and industrial history. In the industrial sphere, the anarcho-syndicalist origins and Marxist leanings of large sections of the trade union movement have led, not only to division and weakness, but also to a preferred strategy of opposition to, rather than co-optation into, the co-management of capitalism.[46] The hostility of employers to trade unionism can be seen as both cause and effect of this trade union radicalism. Attempts to render industrial relations more harmonious cannot be seen as paving the way for more policy concertation either. The articulation between legislation and bargaining structures may give employers and unions a role in policy implementation, but as with the 35-hour week, the impetus for change still comes from the state, often against the wishes of one or other of the two sides.

In the political sphere, notions of the primacy of the state can be traced back at least as far as the 1789 Revolution. Indeed, in his influential work, *The Social Contract* (1762), Rousseau expounds his ideas of government through the 'general will' of the people, this being the product of the desires of free individuals. This gives rise to the notion of the state as an arbiter between individual wills, and a certain suspicion of intermediary bodies between the state and the citizens, these being seen as deforming the 'general will' through the promotion of sectional interests. On the non-Gaullist right, such values find modern-day expression in an emphasis on the state as guarantor of individual freedoms, while the Gaullists have traditionally emphasised the state as the embodiment of the nation and of the 'general will' of the people. On the Left, such preoccupations are mirrored by republican and Jacobin conceptions of the interventionist state as the enlightened motor of economic and social progress. None of these value systems allow much space for the intervention of the social partners in national-level social or macroeconomic management. Indeed, such views are reinforced by a technocratic and meritocratic view of government in which a highly competitive education system – with at its summit the *grandes écoles*, such as the *Ecole Nationale d'Administration* – plays a major role in the selection and recruitment of political and administrative elites.[47]

Developments during the 1990s do not look like overthrowing the weight of history in this respect. Firstly, the decentralisation of collective bargaining has gone hand in hand with neo-liberal economic and labour-market policies, trends that have been severely criticised by both the CGT and the FO.[48] Although employers have also been highly critical of government policy – in particular, high social charges related to wage bills have been blamed for reducing the propensity of companies to recruit, and high interest rates are seen as constituting a brake on investment – there is little doubt that their preference is for a decentralised form of social and economic regulation.

Secondly, although the CFDT has recently argued in favour of a limited form of concertation, under 5 percent of the workforce belongs to the confederation (although it can claim about 20 percent of the votes in workplace elections),[49] while the attitude of the CGT, still the most powerful union in France, militates strongly against any moves towards corporatist concertation. Furthermore, such orientations have met with great internal dissent, culminating in the creation of a rival organisation, SUD, in the public sector, while the emergence of other groups of autonomous unions under umbrella organisations during the course of the 1990s means that the French trade union movement appears more divided than ever,[50] a factor that can only harm its capacity to intervene in national-level policy making. In addition to this, other social movements are emerging that directly impinge upon the unions' territory.[51] In particular, the beginning of 1998 saw the occupation of local authority buildings by the unemployed to publicise their plight and to wring concessions out of the government.[52]

Thirdly, a number of current developments may further reduce the capacity of national unions and employers' organisations to intervene in the policy process. In the area of social security, the state has increased its intervention in order to take control of spending, as many social insurance funds have accumulated mounting deficits. This can only reduce the role of the 'social partners' in an area where they have played a major role since the Second World War Furthermore, future developments, such as the probability of legislation on the establishment of private pension funds, are likely to reduce the space for bipartite regulation even further.[53] Lastly, European integration suggests that concertation will take place amongst national governments rather than with national unions and employers' organisations.[54]

The evidence of recent years suggests that the state will try to encourage change in some areas through the articulation between legal regulation and the collective bargaining system. With deep-seated attitudes being difficult to shed, however, the impetus for change will more likely come from the state rather than from the voluntary interaction of the 'social partners', particularly where difficult choices requiring compromise bargaining are concerned. While the CFDT may currently be providing a willing bargaining partner for employers, a large part of the trade union movement will resist any generalised exchange in the name of the defence of 'guaranteed rights'. Likewise, the CNPF remains hostile to any generalised political exchange at the national level in the name of flexibility. Thus, with the state jealously guarding its status as the legitimate incarnation of the will of the people, what could be termed 'pluralist conflict regulation' rather than 'corporatist concertation' would appear likely to characterise public policy making in France for many years to come.

Notes

1. I would like to express my gratitude to The Nuffield Foundation for a research grant that enabled the research necessary for this chapter to be undertaken.
2. In the interests of space I will confine my comments to these three trade unions, as they are the largest recruiting amongst all wage earners in France. The CFTC and the CFE-CGC managerial union are also recognised by the state as representative at the national level, and a host of 'autonomous' unions also exist, particularly in the public sector. Such a narrow focus inevitably overlooks the close relations that exist between some unions and ministries, such as the farmers' union, the FNSEA, and the Ministry for Agriculture (see V. Wright, *The Government and Politics of France*, 3rd edn, London, 1989: 269–70). These, however, concern specific sectors and issues rather than macroeconomic and social regulation.
3. Since 1998 the CNPF has been known as the Mouvement des Entreprises de France (MEDEF). See the following for further information on these points: J-D. Reynaud, *Les syndicats en France,* vol.I, Paris, 1975; S. Lash and J. Urry, *The End of Organized Capitalism*, 3rd edn, Cambridge, 1993; M. Kesselman, 'The New Shape of Labour and Industrial Relations', in *Policymaking in France from de Gaulle to Mitterrand*, ed. P. Godt, London, 1989: 165–75; C. Lane, 'Industrial Order and the Transformation of Industrial Relations: Britain, Germany and France Compared, in *New Frontiers in European Indus-*

trial Relations, ed. R. Hyman and A. Ferner, Oxford, 1994: 167–95; H. Slomp, 'European Labor Relations and the Prospects of Tripartism', in *Participation in Public Policy-Making: The Role of Trade Unions and Employers Associations*, ed. T. Treu, Berlin and New York, 1992: 170.

4. G. Groux, 'Industrial Relations in France: Union Crisis and the "French Exception"', *Journal of Area Studies* 5 (1994): 80–90; D. Andolfatto, 'Le plus faible taux de syndicalisation des pays industrialisés', in *L'Etat de la France 98–99*, Paris, 1998: 481–3.
5. N. Hocblat, 'Politique macroéconomic: une inflexion limitée', in *L'Etat de la France 98–99*, Paris, 1998: 398–407.
6. *European Industrial Relations Review* (EIRR) 274: 27; 284: 29, *Liaisons Sociales Brèf*, 23 March 1998.
7. Exceptions to this may occur at times of deep crisis, such as the agreement following the strike wave of May–June 1968.
8. J-P. Jacquier, *Les Clés du Social en France*, Paris, 1998: 110–11.
9. C. Vincent, 'La politique contractuelle fonde-t-elle les relations sociales?', in *L'Etat de la France 98–99*, Paris, 1998: 536–42.
10. Jacquier, *Les Clés du Social*, 87–8.
11. Ibid., 132–47.
12. R. Mouriaux and F. Subileau, 'Les grèves françaises de l'automne 1995: défence des acquis ou mouvement social?, *Modern and Contemporary France* NS4, no. 3 (1996): 299–306.
13. Jacquier, *Les Clés du Social*, 135–44.
14. V. Wright, *The Government and Politics of France*, 3rd edition, London, 1989: 101–3.
15. Jacquier, *Les Clés du Social*, 87–8.
16. J. Hayward, *The State and the Market Economy*, Brighton, 1986: 172; Jacquier, *Les Clés du Social*, 88.
17. Confédération générale du travail, *La CGT et le Xe Plan*, Paris, 1989: 3–4, my translation.
18. Ibid., 13–14, my translation.
19. Ibid., 189.
20. Commissariat général du Plan, *Choisir l'emploi: rapport du groupe emploi*, Paris, 1993: 149–72.
21. *Le Monde*, 23 July 1998.
22. Commissariat général du Plan, *Choisir l'emploi*, 102.
23. Ibid., 172, my translation.
24. N. Notat, *Je voudrais vous dire*, Paris, 1997: 63, my translation.
25. H. Landier and D. Labbé, *Les organisations syndicales en France: des origines aux difficultés actuelles*, Paris, 1998: 129, my translation; Force Ouvriere, *Compte rendu du XVIIe Congrès Confédéral, 27 février–1 mars, Paris*, Paris, 1996: 580, my translation.
26. Quoted in H. Landier and D. Labbé, *Les organisations syndicales en France*, 134, my translation.
27. Groux, 'Industrial Relations in France', 86–7.
28. Confédération française démocratique du travail, *Notre histoire en marche: histoire et identité CFDT*, Paris, 1992: 39, my translation and italics.
29. Notat, *Je voudrais vous dire*, passim.
30. Ibid., 90.
31. L. Viannet, *Syndicalisme, les nouveaux défis*, Paris, 1995, my translation.
32. Ibid., 108.
33. Ibid., passim.
34. Force Ouvrière, *Compte rendu du XVIIe Congrès Confédéral, 27–30 avril, Lyon*, Paris, 1992: 461, my translation.
35. Parti socialiste, *Avant-projet pour un socialisme d'avenir en France*, Paris, 1991: 107, my translation.
36. Parti socialiste, *Congrès du Parti socialiste de Levin, 18/19/20 novembre 1994, Tome 1: Rapports Statutaires et Motions soumises au vote des militants*, Paris, 1995: 15, my translation.

37. Parti communiste français, *Programme du parti communiste: Programme pour une politique nouvelle de justice, de solidarité, de liberté, de paix*, Paris, 1994: 84, my italics and translation.
38. Parti radical, *Manifestement radical*, Paris, 1996; Rassemblement pour la République, *Projet pour la France et les Français*, Paris, 1998.
39. Rassemblement pour la République, *La réforme maintenant*, Paris, 1993, pages not numbered.
40. N. Hocblat, 'Politique macroéconomic'; Parti républicain, *Prêt pour l'Alternance*, Paris, 1992: 16–18; Parti radical, *Manifestement radical*, 21–2; Rassemblement pour la République, *La France en mouvement*, Paris, 1991: 6; Rassemblement pour la République, *Projet pour la France*.
41. Rassemblement pour la République, *Projet pour la France*, 41–5.
42. Parti radical, *Manifestement radical*, 5–6, my translation, emphasis in original.
43. Rassemblement pour la République, *Projet pour la France*, 43, my translation.
44. Commissariat général du Plan, *Choisir l'emploi*, 172, my translation.
45. Ibid., my translation.
46. Reynaud, *Les syndicats en France*; Landier and Labbé, *Les organisations syndicales en France*, 13–16.
47. S. Hazareesingh, *Political Traditions in Modern France*, Oxford, 1994: 170–1.
48. Groux, 'Industrial Relations in France', 86–7; Vincent, 'La politique contractuelle', 539.
49. Landier and Labbé, *Les organisations syndicales en France*, 31 and 40.
50. Ibid., 143–56.
51. Ibid., 201–4.
52. F. Royall, 'Le mouvement des chômeurs en France de l'hiver 1997–1998', *Modern and Contemporary France* 6, no. 3 (1998): 351–65.
53. P. Concialdi, 'La réforme des retraits, enjeux et débats', in *L'Etat de la France 98–99*, Paris, 1998: 533–6.
54. Jospin explicitly stated that the 1998 plan for employment was the result of concertation at the Extraordinary European Council held in Luxembourg on 21 November 1997: *Plan national d'action pour l'emploi, France, 1998*, La Documentation française, Paris, 1998: 9.

CHAPTER 9

GERMANY IN HISTORICAL PERSPECTIVE: THE GAP BETWEEN THEORY AND PRACTICE

Stefan Berger

Modell Deutschland, as it emerged in the 1970s, was, to many outside observers, based on an ideology of social partnership between employers' and employees' organisations and a state willing to mediate between diverse economic interests. The specific type of tripartite policy concertation, as it developed and flourished in the Federal Republic after 1967, had few direct precursors in pre-1945 Germany when the antagonism between capital and labour often seemed unbridgeable. By contrast, as this chapter will demonstrate, bipartite policy concertation between state and industry had been well established in Germany since the early nineteenth century. The ideas of social partnership and policy concertation were modelled and remodelled under the very different social, economic and political circumstances that existed under the authoritarian constitutional monarchy before 1918, the democratic republic of Weimar, the fascist dictatorship and even under German-style communism in the GDR. This chapter will take the story of the ideals and values of social partnership and their (often inadequate) implementation up to the developments in the FRG in the 1970s, when Social Democrats such as Karl Schiller and Helmut Schmidt experimented with crisis corporatism.

Imperial Germany

In comparison with Germany no other state has had 'a "corporatist" tradition of comparable dimensions, diversity or duration'.[1] Fichte's 'closed commercial state', Adam Müller's organic *Ständestaat*, Hegel's idea of organising society in corporations, as well as the theories of Franz Baader, Karl Marlo and Ludwig Gerlach, all established the credentials of democratic as well as authoritarian variants of corporatism in the German lands well before 1870. Conservative monarchists such as Hermann Wagener and Albert Schäffle essentially aimed at defending the authoritarian capitalist status quo. Proclaiming a 'community of interests' between capital and labour, they argued that the state as the 'central, universal corporation' (*Universalkorporation*) had the task of supervising the smooth functioning of that community. A 'social monarchy' would be capable of overcoming the antagonism between capital and labour, integrate diverse social and economic interests and represent the *bonum commune*.

Nineteenth-century German liberalism also remained sceptical of market forces, and instead, to varying degrees, adhered to ideals of a corporate structuring of society. In 1851, Robert von Mohl, in an influential critique of the free market ideology, suggested that the whole of the social sphere of society should be based on a set of institutionalised relationships, which he called 'corporations'. They were to mediate between the individual on the one hand and the state on the other. Their aim was to make society more cohesive and overcome the social conflict inherent in market economies.[2] The prominent Association for Social Policy (*Verein für Sozialpolitik*) argued for the adoption of institutions that would co-opt the interest organisations of capital and labour into the process of policy making on all levels. Some, like the left-liberal Friedrich Naumann, advocated the ideals of social partnership to integrate workers into the state. In 1907, he had already outlined his vision of a democratised economic sphere of the future in a Reichstag speech, in which he foresaw 'full industrial parliamentarism and finally a system of codetermination of full participation of employees and workers in the labour constitution through workers' councils, labour committees etc.'[3]

Within the state administration, influential civil servants such as Theodor Lohmann developed ideas of social partnership which pointed in the direction of policy concertation. State-sponsored workers' councils would be the starting point for an envisioned new social order in which workers would be the equal partners of employers: ' ... workers will not only have to get a greater share of the profits, they will also have to get a greater say in the management of the economic order.'[4] Making the unions 'equal partners in the reorganisation of industry', that was also the aim of Lujo Brentano who, like Lohmann, lambasted the reactionary attitudes of German employers and championed the 'corporate organisation of capital and labour' under the guidance of a strong state capable of breaking the power of the cartels and enhancing the status of trade unions in German society.[5]

The German lands, and in particular Prussia, had a long history of state intervention in the economy. In the first half of the nineteenth century the state had initiated the foundation of the chambers of commerce. Subsequently the latter had taken over public functions and channelled information and opinions to the state bureaucracy. In effect, they very much functioned as support organisations for state economic policies. In the

1880s, the Prussian Economic Council (*Preußischer Volkswirtschaftsrat*) and the German Economic Senate (*Reichswirtschaftsrat*) were attempts at setting up institutions where the already existing umbrella organisations of German industry, commerce and agriculture could come together to discuss and determine economic and social policies together with the state administration and (carefully chosen) workers' representatives. Although both attempts had failed to take root by the end of the decade, policy concertation between industry and government continued to function through a wide variety of formal consultation processes including memoranda, petitions, deputations and personal contacts. The contacts to the state administration were of particular importance, as the overwhelming number of legislative proposals came not from within Parliament but from the Prussian and Reich bureaucracies. The institutionalised cooperation included the setting up of advisory councils within various ministries on which industrial interests were heavily represented. Leading personnel of industrial pressure groups switched to take a job within the state bureaucracies and vice versa, and the state administration could rely on considerable financial support from industrial pressure groups. State bureaucracies found it increasingly difficult to come to competent economic decision making without the support of the peak organisations of industry.

Of particular importance amongst industrial pressure groups were the Chambers of Commerce, the Central Association of German Industrialists (*Centralverband deutscher Industrieller*, CVDI), the Association of German Industrialists (*Bund deutscher Industrieller*, BdI), the *Hansabund* and the *Langnamverein*. These organisations influenced a wide variety of economic, financial, social and foreign policies, which were of direct interest to their members. In particular, the heavy-industry dominated CVDI had direct access to the chancellor, and the industrialists were never shy about calling for state help. So, for example, the general director of the chemical giant BASF, speaking before a parliamentary commission, compared the state to an architect in 1887. If industry's roof was leaking, he argued, industrialists would come to the state demanding that the state repair the damage.[6]

Imperial Germany witnessed a highly developed interpenetration of business and state interests but the trade unions remained largely excluded. They had developed highly centralised organisations since the 1890s, which were, however, split along ideological lines. The biggest were the socialist free trade unions, followed by sizeable Catholic unions and the small liberal Hirsch–Duncker unions. The socialist free trade unions, under the leadership of Carl Legien, increasingly abandoned their transformatory, revolutionary and anti-capitalist stance and adopted reformist policies. Hence ideas of policy concertation and social partnership began to appeal to them.

The Catholic unions adhered to Catholic social teaching, which was critical of the social consequences of capitalism, but stopped short of demanding a transformation of the economic or political system. The teachings of Karl von Vogelsang, Wilhelm Emmanuel von Ketteler (bishop of Mainz after 1850) and the social encyclical *Rerum Novarum* of 1891 explicitly emphasised that the relationship between labour and capital should be guided by the values of social partnership. Franz Hitze's 600–page *Capital and Labour*, published in 1880, was influential in moving the Catholic Centre Party towards adopting proposals in 1905 which aimed at the setting up of chambers of labour on all levels, including the national one, in which trade unions and employers' federations would be equally represented. Heinrich Pesch's theory of 'solidarism' (*Solidarismus*) and Gustav Gundlach's theory of 'subsidiarity' (*Subsidiarität*) both aimed at a constructive partnership between capital and labour in which the state had important steering functions.

The liberal Hirsch–Duncker unions in Imperial Germany also adhered specifically to an ideology of social partnership between capital and labour. In the 1870s its general secretary, Hirsch, showed himself convinced that 'we live in a period in which the natural harmony between capitalism and labour has momentarily been interrupted by a sudden and massive industrialisation. ... the natural harmony of these two groups will ultimately alleviate these troubles ... '[7]

In Imperial Germany this was, to all intents and purposes, an extraordinarily optimistic assessment of the situation. The exclusion of trade unions from economic policy making only came to an end in the context of the First World War. The Auxiliary Service Law (*Hilfsdienstgesetz*) of December 1916 for the first time gave important rights of consultation and decision making to the trade unions and forced reluctant employers to recognise trade unions as the interest organisations of workers. In the war policy concertation became an important means of keeping the war economy afloat. The state, in close cooperation with industry and unions, began to organise the planning of production, distribution of raw materials and finished products, and established a whole system of controls of the economy and of foreign trade. Tripartite structures now decided on capital investment, the means and the extent of production and distribution. Cartels and trade associations in effect became semi-public bodies. A whole new economic system appeared on the horizon, and when the political system of Imperial Germany collapsed amidst military defeat at the end of the First World War, some saw the wartime economy as a model for the future.

The Weimar Republic

The end of the First World War saw the restructuring of bourgeois Europe along 'pluralist corporatist' lines on a massive scale.[8] The ideology of social partnership and the practice of policy concertation proved vital ingredients of such corporatist crisis management. In 1918–19 two mutually exclusive visions about the re-ordering of the economic system competed with each other: the idea of the 'German collective economy' (*deutsche Gemeinwirtschaft*) put forward by industrialists such as Walther Rathenau, civil servants such as Wichard von Moellendorff and politicians such as Rudolf Wissell, and the notion of a direct alliance between capital and labour which underpinned the foundation of the Central Working Community (*Zentrale Arbeitsgemeinschaft*, ZAG) in November 1918.

According to Rathenau, the wartime economy represented a new type of economic organisation, which served the whole of society rather than the egotistical ambitions of individual entrepreneurs.[9] Whereas Rathenau provided the ethical and philosophical foundations for a new economic system, the conservative Moellendorff penned in the nitty-gritty of the programme.[10] As Under-Secretary of State in the Reich Economics Office, his detailed six-point action programme, published in September 1918, suggested establishing economic chambers (*Wirtschaftskammern*) and chambers of labour on local, regional and national levels. So-called 'expert economic councils' (*Sachwirtschaftsräte*) would advise Reich ministries on macroeconomic policies. Furthermore a Reich Economic Council (*Reichswirtschaftsrat*) would be a forum for economic interest organisations to give their opinion and make suggestions on economic policy making. The Social Democratic trade unionist Rudolf Wissell, economics minister from February to July 1919, emerged as the major supporter of Moellendorff within the cabinet. However, they failed to convince the Social Democratic Party (SPD) led government that their proposals amounted to 'practical socialism'.

Moellendorff and Wissell had been defeated not least by a powerful alliance of industrialists and trade unionists who had come together in November 1918 to sign the Stinnes-Legien pact, which marked the foundation of the ZAG.[11] At the end of the war industrialists saw themselves confronted with the threat of socialisations and the possible transformation of the whole capitalist economic order in the context of the German revolution of 1918–19. To prevent any such radical moves, they signed a deal with the Social Democratic trade unions: the latter promised not vigorously to pursue socialisation in the present economic climate, whilst the employers in turn accepted trade unions as bargaining partners. They also promised to set up workers' councils in the factories and introduce the eight-hour working day. Union representatives perceived the ZAG as an institution which would formulate the common interests of the 'community of producers' incorporating both employers and employees. For them, it was a declaration of intent that in future representatives of employers and employees would cooperate in the spirit of social partnership to settle as many aspects of industrial and economic life as possible. Within the socialist union movement (ADGB), enmity towards the concept of social partnership was strong within the largest and most powerful industrial union, the metalworkers' union (DMV), whose officials continued to campaign for widespread socialisations and more powerful factory councils. Yet, the majority in the ADGB, in line with the Catholic trade union organisation in the Weimar Republic (*Deutcher Gewerkschaftsbund*, DGB) and the liberal Hirsch–Dunker unions, supported the ZAG. However, it never fulfilled those initial far-reaching goals of forming and dominating economic policy making. It continued its existence until January 1924 when the socialist unions withdrew officially in response to the employers' abandonment of the eight-hour day in December 1923. Two major preconditions for the survival of the social partnership ideal were simply not in place in the interwar period: relative economic stability and a willingness of important sections within the employers' federations to accept the values of social partnership.

As far as the employers were concerned, their antagonistic 'class war from above' stance resurfaced quickly once the direct threat of revolution had evaporated. Only a minority of employers in the chemical, optical, electrical and export-oriented textile and engineering industries wanted to cooperate with the state and the unions. Within the main Federation of German Employers' Associations (VDA, founded in 1913) and the Reich Association of German Industry (RdI, founded in April 1919, the first peak organisation in German history uniting a whole economic sector), the reactionary captains of the Ruhr coal, iron and steel industries called the shots. They were extremely well organised in the Association of German Iron and Steel Industrialists (VES) and the so-called Langnam Association. The major industrial pressure groups developed into important political players in their own right, which often managed to bypass Parliament and deal directly with the government. In comparison with their position in Imperial Germany, their status and power was considerably enhanced.

Unions and employers alike tried to influence government, Parliament, ministries and the state bureaucracy so as to push through their own interests. The ZAG was supplanted by an advisory council within the Economics Ministry, where Robert Schmidt in 1919–20 deliberately pursued policies aimed at arriving at a consensus between the interests of labour, industry and commerce. Furthermore the Provisional Reich Economic Council (*Vorläufiger Reichswirtschaftsrat*, RWR) was founded in 1920–21. Here a whole array of interest organisations from industry, finance, commerce, agriculture, small-scale producers and labour were represented to discuss economic and social policies such as export levies and controls, credit problems of German industry, Reichsbank policies, reparations, work hours, currency reform and industrial relations. The number of representatives and the multitude of organisations represented made it a cumbersome, unwieldy and ineffectual institution, which was finally wound up in 1923–24.[12]

In the early years of the republic, the unions were in a strong position to influence government, Parliament and state bureaucracies. For the first time in German history, leading trade unionists such as Robert Schmidt, Gustav Bauer and Rudolf Wissell took ministerial office. Bauer was even Reich chancellor between June 1919 and March 1920. Furthermore the unions established important factions within the SPD, Centre Party and DDP. In particular the DGB had considerable influence on labour and social policies as one of their own, Heinrich Brauns, served continuously as Minister for Labour Affairs between 1920 and 1928. Trade unions campaigned for the extension of public expenditure on housing, for an expansion of the health, disability and social insurance system, for a new unemployment insurance, the restoration of the eight-hour day and modifications to the Labour Courts Law of 1926. For a brief period in 1927–28 it looked as though the spirit of social partnership could be revived in the more favourable macroeconomic climate that characterised the middle years of the republic. In 1927 discussions between state, employers and unions on the long-planned insurance against unemployment came to fruition and the much-celebrated 'Law on Work Exchanges and Unemployment Insurance' was passed in Parliament.

At its 1919 Nuremberg congress the ADGB had underlined its view that the trade unions would be indispensable partners in the running of the economy. Its goal was worker codetermination from the factory level upward to the highest level of national economic planning. Between 1925 and 1928 the head of the ADGB's Research Institute for Economic Affairs, Fritz Naphtali, developed the concept of economic democracy. The democratisation of the economic sphere was to be achieved through extending the powers of works councils and establishing institutions for economic self-administration in which unions would be represented on equal terms with the employers. While the first steps towards economic democracy could already be achieved under capitalism (essentially through state intervention in central processes of economic decision making), full economic democracy, Naphtali insisted, would only be possible in a socialist economy. Hence the transformation of capitalism and the abolition of private ownership of the means of production remained the long-term aim of the ADGB.[13]

Despite denouncing the Weimar Republic as a 'trade union state', employers' federations managed to gain an important say in politics as early as 1918–19. As only lawyers could be admitted to the higher echelons of the German civil service well into the 1920s, politicians and top civil servants alike felt that industrialists and bankers were indispensable as advisers on economic and social policies. Furthermore, employers' federations built up industrial wings in almost every bourgeois political party in the 1920s. Their representatives also had direct access to high-ranking ministerial civil servants, members of the cabinet, the chancellor and the president (in particular after 1925 when Hindenburg became president). Whole ministries or departments within ministries became so-called 'associational fiefdoms' (*Verbandsherzogtümer*) where civil servants and industrialists were united by a common 'ideology of matter-of-factness'.[14] By contrast, the relationship between employers and trade unions was often characterised by bitter and vociferous enmity. It was no coincidence that, in 1930, the managing director of the Langnam association, Max Schlenker, called for a corporate reorganisation of state and society along the lines of fascist Italy.[15]

'Social Partnership' in Nazi Germany

The authoritarian corporatism of the Nazis was based on the exclusion of any independent representation of working-class interests and on a widespread identity of interests between Nazis and the representatives of big industry. The Nazis made it clear right from the start that any tripartite arrangement would work only on one paramount precondition: the subordination of the interests of capital and labour to the interests of the Nazi state, which allegedly pursued the common good of the whole people (*Volkswohl*). On 2 May 1933 the socialist unions were forcibly dissolved. All other independent unions declared their self-dissolution shortly afterwards. And even the National Socialist trade unions (NSBO) were quickly disempowered. On 22 May 1933, the RdI dissolved itself and was amalgamated with the VDA to form the Reich Estate of German Industry. The industrial, commercial and banking sector of the economy was structured into six groups, all of which were subordinate to the Reich Economic Ministry. The state administration took direct control of the industrial sector.

Labour relations were restructured in an authoritarian manner. The National Socialist ideal of the 'factory community' meant that factory managers became 'leaders' whilst the workforce became 'retinue'. The works councils were replaced with powerless 'consultative councils of trust' appointed by the management. Independent unions were replaced by the German Labour Front (DAF), of which both workers and employers had to become members. It had the explicit task to 'mediate between the justified interests of all parties and find compromises which would adequately reflect National Socialist principles'.[16] The first of those principles was, of course, the creation of the 'people's community' (*Volksgemeinschaft*) – an ideological buzz-word which heavily implied the partnership of workers and employers who were meant to cooperate harmoniously in the interest of nation and race. Although, under the leadership of Robert Ley, the DAF developed far-reaching plans for social reform and did battle with the Reich Economic Ministry and the Reich Labour Ministry so as to secure power over as many jurisdictions as possible, at the end of the day it remained a largely powerless instrument of the regime reduced to its first and foremost function: the effective control of the workforce. Most employers rightly dismissed the DAF as a paper tiger.

Whilst the Nazis established a 'directed economy'[17] in which the autonomy of the economic management of the employers was restricted, the overall relationship between big industry and the National Socialist regime was characterised by a good deal of harmonious cooperation. As Norbert Frei has written: 'In the first years of the Third Reich private big business penetrated the political system rather than the other way round.'[18] The chemical giant IG Farben, for example, was a crucial driving force behind the Nazis' first four-year plan of 1936. Given that the nominal head of the four-year plan bureaucracy, Hermann Göring, had virtually no idea about economics, the director of IG Farben's executive board, Carl Krauch, became the mightiest person in this important state bureaucracy. On the one hand, the National Socialist state used the well-organised apparatus of business associations for their own policy-driven economic needs, but, on the other hand, industry extensively used the state and National Socialist organisations to pursue its own economic interests.[19] Under National Socialism formal channels of communication between industry and state were replaced by more personal contacts with representatives of the state bureaucracy and the new

National Socialist institutions (such as the SS). The 'Freundeskreis Himmler' and the 'Deutscher Klub', for example, became important meeting places. Krauch was by no means the only influential industrialist in the state. Wilhelm Zangen, director-general of the Mannesmann group and head of the Reichsgruppe Industrie since October 1938, cooperated closely with the Economics Ministry as well as with the foreign office. In the spring of 1939 he played a leading role in pressing for the occupation of the whole of Czechoslovakia.[20] In the context of the Second World War, representatives of German big business were directly involved in exploiting the economic potential of the occupied areas in Eastern Europe, whilst in the West, the Nazi state, the military authorities and the industrial elites cooperated to achieve a restructuring of the European economies.[21]

Policy Concertation and Social Partnership in a Socialist State? The GDR, 1949–89

In the socialist economy of the GDR any independent representation of employers was unthinkable. According to Marxist theory, the private ownership of the means of production was the basic root of social inequality. Hence the abolition of capitalism had to be the first step towards a more just society. Yet in the GDR any independent representation of workers' interests through trade unions was also impossible. In a socialist state, as (in particular) Wladimir Iljitsch Lenin had argued, trade unions were useful tools for the ruling Communist parties to control the workforce. Unions and the state were both subordinated to the party, which represented the interests of all workers. Hence, economic and social policies in the GDR were determined by the Socialist Unity Party (SED) in close consultation with the ministries for the diverse industries, the trade unions and the managers of the socialist factories. The unions' activities in the GDR were closely interlinked with the state apparatus and the management of the economy. Hence, for the millions of committed Free German Trade Union Movement (FDGB) officials the rhetoric of social partnership might have been an alien one, but the practice was not: they were used to close cooperation and intensive discussion between representatives of unions, management and state (and, the decisive fourth player in this peculiar form of tripartism, the SED) over a whole variety of policy issues and areas. This, one can only assume, prepared them relatively well for their new tasks within the all-German trade unions after 1990.

Social Partnership and Policy Concertation in the Early Federal Republic: The Road Towards *Modell Deutschland*

At the end of the Second World War, those German politicians who had some responsibility for administering the territories of occupied Germany had an overriding interest in running in as smooth a manner as possible an economy characterised by scarcity (*Mangelwirtschaft*). Therefore they needed the cooperation of the industrialists and the 'social peace', which, they hoped, the trade unions could guarantee. For all those reasons, state, industry and labour developed a variety of corporatist concepts between 1945 and 1949, which were based on ideas of policy concertation and sentiments of social partnership.[22]

No one liked to call it corporatism after 1945, as the term was widely associated with National Socialism. Instead, the preferred term was 'economic democracy'. The suggestions discussed under that heading could be a far cry from Naphtali's suggestions in the 1920s but they could equally present themselves as derived from the Weimar debates. Often their explicit aim was to regulate social conflict. Ludwig Erhard, as Bavarian Economics Minister in 1946 and as director of the Bizonal Economic Administration in 1948–49, set up economic advisory councils in which unions and business federations were represented. Likewise, the new unitary trade union organisation, the DGB (which, for the first time in German history, overcame the ideological divisions), suggested economic councils that would advise government. The widest-reaching suggestions for economic councils were passed by the Berlin city council in 1948. They foresaw a fundamental new structure for decision making on economic matters. All those plans were ultimately vetoed by the Allied occupation governments. In particular the Americans argued that the economic sphere should be kept separate from politics.

When the Federal Republic was established in 1949 no coherent attempts were made to institutionalise some of the ideas and concepts vetoed by the Allied occupying powers before 1949. Yet many of the sentiments and values underpinning these ideas remained in place. The negotiations over codetermination in the early 1950s, as well as over the factory councils law of 1952, were carried out with extensive consultation processes involving both the unions and employers' federations. Furthermore the Economics Ministry under Ludwig Erhard retained a number of largely informal contacts with industrialists and union leaders. In fact, quasi-institutionalised consultations took place through the labour union liaison office located in the Ministry and headed by Eberhard Bömcke, who struck up a close relationship to Ludwig Rosenberg, a leading trade unionist who was to become chairman of the DGB.

Throughout the 1950s, the unions were absorbed to a very large extent by a painful process of ideological reorientation, which was to move them away from a concept of unions as opposition force to the existing economic and political order (*Gegenmacht*) and towards the ideas of social partnership and cooperation between capital, labour and the state. Erik Nölting, Rudolf Zorn, Gerhard Weisser, Fritz Baade and Fritz Tarnow were amongst those who paved the way for the acceptance of market forces by DGB and SPD and led the search for some form of consultation between state, capital and labour over questions of economic policy making. Ironically, given the hard-line opposition of the American military government to all forms of corporatism between 1945 and 1949, the harmonious relationship between the DGB and its American counterpart, the American Federation of Labor (AFL), contributed to the willingness of German trade unionists to opt for more cooperation between unions and employers.[23]

Initially the vast majority of industrialists, socialised in the antagonistic climate of industrial relations in the pre-1933 period, were rigorously opposed to any kind of policy concertation with government and unions. They managed to form highly centralised, homogeneous and powerful peak organisations: the Federal Association of German Employers' Federations (BDA) and the Federal Association of German Industry (BDI). Both cultivated their bilateral contacts with ministers and the government, attempting to exclude the unions from decision-making processes as far as possible. Erhard's preference for businessmen over civil servants gave the employers' federations considerable influence in the Economics Ministry. BDI and BDA brought their influence to bear on the appointment of industry-friendly civil servants to important ministerial posts. In West Germany's 'chancellor's democracy' (*Kanzlerdemokratie*) direct access to the chancellor proved to be particularly important.[24] Under Adenauer, the contacts to the business sector went overwhelmingly via Adenauer's confidant, Fritz Berg, chairman of the BDI after 1949. Furthermore, bankers and industrialists such as Robert Pferdmenges and the Werhahn family kept very close contact with the CDU, whilst in Bavaria, the CSU was hopelessly entangled with the Flick group and MBB.[25] In certain sectors and at certain times, business interests were allowed to design and plan economic policies for the government.[26]

The values and sentiments of the German economic elites began to change under the influence of the American occupiers. The Americans arranged study tours for German managers, where they were able to learn about a more responsible, flexible and less authoritarian handling of their employees and their interest organisations.[27] Apart from the American influence, sectoral change in German industry also contributed to the breakthrough of sentiments more amenable to ideas of social partnership and policy concertation. Whilst heavy industry continued to decline, the industries of the Second Industrial Revolution became more important in the German economy overall. They began to dominate the BDA, which was untiring in its efforts to build bridges to the trade union movement in the 1950s. The BDI, dominated by Germany's heavy industry, was far more hostile to any such rapprochement. No doubt, the experience with codetermination also had a positive effect on lessening the antagonism between unions and employers and pushing the peak organisations of both workers and employers towards more cooperation. A marked generational change in industrial circles also helped: those who had served as soldiers in the Second World War before training as managers in the post-1945 era were more critical of the 'master-in-one's-own-house' attitude of their fathers' generation and more amenable to a fundamental restructuring of labour-management relations.

Under CDU-dominated governments, the influence of Catholic social teaching on the emerging sentiments of social partnership should not be underestimated. Here the unions found an important ally in Oswald Nell-

Breuning, whose concept of an 'ordered' or 'organic pluralism' included a harsh critique of the FRG's social market economy and demands for the incorporation of trade unions in economic policy making. Nell-Breuning's fellow Jesuit Johannes Messner went even further and argued that the principle of solidarity between capital and labour should lead to 'the direct and equal co-responsibility and co-determination in the planning, guiding and control of the social economy ... '[28]

As early as 1960 Ludwig Erhard and his associates had initiated a broad public discussion with his proposals for a 'structured society' (*formierte Gesellschaft).* Erhard was dissatisfied with having to rely on appeals to employers and unions for restraint and wanted to establish more institutionalised forms of policy concertation. Increased cooperation of all groups and interests in society would emerge from the recognition that they were mutually dependent on each other and hence would gain by free and voluntary discussions about the best economic and social policies to adopt.

Erhard's ideas were later picked up and realised by a Social Democratic Economics Minister, Karl Schiller. As a committed Keynesian, Schiller, in February 1967, was convinced that it was possible to 'steer' the economy through difficult times with the help of a Concerted Action (*Konzertierte Aktion*). In effect this meant round-table discussions between unions, employers and ministerial officials, which would produce, in Schiller's words, a 'textbook recovery' (*Aufschwung nach Maß*). Given that the Social Democrats emphasised that wage restraint by the unions was the precondition for overcoming the economic difficulties, employers felt attracted. Furthermore, the planners in the Economics Ministry were entirely dependent in their forecasts on data provided by the BDI and BDA. Unionists, on the other hand, hoped that the mechanism of policy concertation, once established, might give them a lever on the more just distribution of wealth in German society. Here, however, they were going to be disappointed. As the former general director of Thyssen, Ernst Wolf Mommsen, in an interview with *Der Spiegel*, argued in 1972:

> This social-liberal coalition has opened the door wide for business interests. It was immensely industry-friendly – not the least because of Herr Schiller. And the chancellor: whom did he invite time and again to his personal receptions? Always the big shots, always the ones with the big names. And Helmut Schmidt has provided industry with an important forum for information exchange in the Armaments Industry Study-Group.[29]

Modell Deutschland, which reached its apogee under Helmut Schmidt in the 1970s, brought huge benefits to the employers whilst the unions, blinded by the 'ideological illusion' of social partnership, remained, at best, junior partners in a relationship primarily designed to guarantee the smooth functioning of the economy and avoid social conflict.

Conclusion

The values and sentiments of social partnership and the practice of policy concertation go back a long way in German history. Under very different political and economic circumstances, policy concertation could take on a range of diverse forms and expressions. Anti-democratic, illiberal and authoritarian theories and institutions of policy concertation stood next to liberal democratic ones. Bismarck's plans contrasted sharply with those of the SPD in the 1880s, although both called for the institutionalisation of economic chambers where employers and unions would be represented. In the Weimar Republic the ADGB recommended 'economic democracy' as a policy concept for the future. It was based on the idea that workers through their interest organisations would participate in and control economic decision making as well as the actual execution of economic policies. Yet the authoritarian, undemocratic form of corporatism won out under National Socialism and brought the concept into disrepute. It was only in the 1960s that institutionalised forms of policy concertation were introduced. Then it was a technocratic, efficiency-based corporatism – reminiscent in some respect of the corporatism championed by civil servants like Moellendorff at the end of the First World War – which advocated policy concertation and social partnership because they were perceived as best suited for the needs of a modern economy.

Employers from the late nineteenth century to the present day were remarkably adept at using the state for their own economic interests. They cultivated their bilateral contacts with the state administration in the hope of providing the most favourable political climate for their business interests. At the same time, however, they adamantly defended their managerial prerogatives and insisted on keeping the state at arm's length. Any interference in economic management was bitterly rejected. When policy concertation measures were endorsed by leading industrialists it was in times of economic crisis when they feared for the worst, such as socialisation or expropriation. At those times, as at the end of both world wars, they felt a need to find mechanisms whereby labour organisations could be tied in. Notions of social partnership and policy concertation became powerful ideologies of capital to protect their own interests and integrate unions in a political-economic system geared towards maintaining international competitiveness of the national economy in an increasingly globalised market place.

Notes

1. Ralph Bowen, *German Theories of the Corporative State with Special Reference to the Period 1870–1919*, New York, 1947: 7.
2. James Sheehan, *German Liberalism in the Nineteenth Century*, Chicago, 1978: 8f.
3. Cited in Karl Dietrich Erdmann, 'Eigentum, Partnerschaft, Mitbestimmung. Zur Theorie des Sozialstaats in Österreich und der Bundesrepublik Deutschland', *GWU* 39, 1988: 405f.

4. Cited in Hans Rothfels, *Theodor Lohmann und die Kampfjahre der staatlichen Sozialpolitik (1871–1905)*, Berlin, 1927: 90.
5. James Sheehan, *The Career of Lujo Brentano. A Study of Liberalism and Social Reform in Imperial Germany*, Chicago, 1966: 159–63.
6. Cited in Hans-Ulrich Wehler, *Deutsche Gesellschaftsgeschichte*, vol. 3: *1848–1914*, Munich, 1995: 667.
7. Cited in Rennie W. Brantz, 'The Hirsch–Duncker Unions in the Weimar Republic, 1918–1933', *IWK* 31 (1995): 156.
8. Charles Maier, *Recasting Bourgeois Europe. Stabilisation in France, Germany and Italy in the Decade after World War I*, Princeton, 1975.
9. Walther Rathenau, *Die neue Wirtschaft*, Berlin, 1918: 32. 30,000 copies of the book were sold in the first month after its publication in January 1918!
10. On Moellendorff see David E. Barclay, 'A Prussian Socialism? Wichard von Moellendorff and the Dilemmas of Economic Planning in Germany', *Central European History* 11 (1978): 50–82.
11. G.D. Feldman and I. Steinisch, *Industrie und Gewerkschaften 1918–1924. Die überforderte Zentralarbeitsgemeinschaft*, Stuttgart, 1985.
12. Gerald Feldman, *The Great Disorder. Politics, Economics and Society in the German Inflation, 1914–1924*, Oxford, 1993: 243, 354.
13. John Moses, 'The Concept of Economic Democracy within the German Socialist Trade Unions during the Weimar Republic', *Labor History* 34 (1978): 45–57.
14. Hans-Peter Ullmann, *Interessenverbände in Deutschland*, Frankfurt-on-Main, 1988: 180.
15. Max Schlenker, 'Gedanken zum neuen Agrarprogramm', *Stahl und Eisen* 50 (1930): 697f.
16. Decree of the Führer and Reich Chancellor of 24 October 1934.
17. K. Hardach, *Wirtschaftsgeschichte Deutschlands im 20. Jahrhundert*, Göttingen, 1976: 77.
18. Norbert Frei, *National Socialist Rule in Germany. The Führer State 1933–1945*, Oxford, 1993: 56.
19. George W. F. Hallgarten and Joachim Radkau, *Deutsche Industrie und Politik von Bismarck bis heute*, Frankfurt-on-Main, 1974: 376.
20. Ibid, 266, 292.
21. For details compare Hans-Erich Volkmann, 'Zum Verhältnis von Großwirtschaft und NS-Regime im Zweiten Weltkrieg', in *Nationalsozialistische Diktatur 1933–1945*, ed. Karl Dietrich Bracher, Manfred Funke and Hans-Adolf Jacobsen, Bonn, 1986: 480–508.
22. Diethelm Prowe, 'Economic Democracy in Post-World War II Germany: Corporatist Crisis Response, 1945–1948', *Journal of Modern History* 57 (1985): 451–82.
23. Michael Fichter, *Besatzungsmacht und Gewerkschaften*, Opladen, 1982.
24. Gabriele Müller-List, 'Adenauer, Unternehmer und Gewerkschaften. Zur Einigung über die Montanmitbestimmung 1950/51', *Vierteljahreshefte für Zeitgeschichte* 33 (1985): 288–309.
25. Hallgarten and Radkau, *Deutsche Industrie*: 450f., 466 and 499.
26. Werner Abelshauser, 'The First Post-Liberal Nation: Stages in the Development of Modern Corporatism in Germany', *European History Quarterly* 14, 1984: 305.
27. Volker R. Berghahn, 'The United States and the Shaping of West Germany's Social Compact, 1945–1966', *International Labor and Working-Class History* 50 (1996): 125–32. See also his more broadly conceived *The Americanisation of West German Industry 1945–1973*, Leamington Spa, 1986.
28. Johannes Messner, *Das Naturrecht. Handbuch zur Gesellschaftsethik, Staatsethik und Wirtschaftsethik*, 4th edn, Munich, 1960: 1037.
29. *Der Spiegel*, 18 December 1972: 28.

Chapter 10

Germany in the 1990s: The Impact of Reunification

Jeremy Leaman

Introduction

The Federal Republic of Germany has often been held up as a paradigm for social partnership and consensual conflict resolution. After the Second World War a set of institutional structures emerged – in part inherited, in part re-established, in part quite new – which have been described variously as 'neo-corporatism', 'consociational democracy' or 'concertation'.[1] In contrast to the authoritarian corporatist traditions, developed under Bismarck and re-established ruthlessly under Hitler, which involved dialogue with agrarian and industrial elites but not with workers' organisations, neo-corporatism was deliberately inclusive and was rooted in a firm, public commitment to parliamentary democracy and civil rights. The traditional preferences of both employers and conservative political forces against cooperation with representatives of the labour movement were set aside, influenced by expediency in defeat and the danger of social unrest, by the acknowledgement of past failure and by the more conciliatory doctrines of social catholicism. On the other hand, the German cultural preference for juridified social relations helped to promote institutional arrangements that went beyond the typical openness of parliamentary democracies to lobbying and external advice. Thus, in addition to irregular consultations in parliamentary hearings and specially commissioned reports, Federal ministries introduced at an early stage Academic Consultative Committees (*Wissenschaftliche Beiräte*), which produce regular commentaries on policy fields. The effectiveness of these committees in the 1950s encouraged the creation of the now firmly entrenched Council of Economic Experts (*Sachverständigenrat zur Begutachtung der Wirtschaft* – SVR) in 1963, which publishes an annual assessment of macroeconomic conditions; since the early 1980s the congruence of socioeconomic opinion between government parties and the SVR has helped strongly to underpin government programmes. The formalised inclusion of outside (academic) experts in policy assessment and planning is clearly seen as a vehicle for both refining those processes and (ostensibly) broadening the strategic policy base beyond the traditional bureaucracy. There has never been a formalised element of tripartism in these consultative bodies, however, in contrast to the Austrian Parity Commissions; the presence of neo-Keynesian economists in the SVR, for example, which were closer to labour interests, was a rare and chance occurrence – Werner Glastetter in 1970s is the one exception which proves the rule; in the 1980s and 1990s the SVR has presented a consistently neo-liberal face.[2]

Germany has a strongly federal system of government, with currently sixteen *Länder* (regional states) responsible for major elements of state policy, including education, policing, transport, housing and the administration of state social services. Each *Land* is also responsible for the assessment and/or the collection of most of the major taxes. All three levels of government (federal, regional, local) enjoy fixed proportions of major tax revenues and also operate within a sophisticated system of fiscal equalisation, which shifts resources both horizontally and vertically to assist structurally weaker regions and local authorities. The German political system is marked by a broad set of institutional checks and balances. The Länder share significant legislative powers with the Federal government. The Upper House of the Federal Parliament, the Bundesrat, is composed of delegates from the individual Länder, and its approval must be sought for the passage of legislation relating to Land regional and local affairs. A powerful Federal Constitutional Court also functions to monitor legislation and judicial practice; all private citizens and interest groups have the right to appeal to the FCC. An additional institutional constraint on federal (and regional) policy making is the existence of an autonomous central bank, now supplemented by the European System of Central Banks. As a result of these checks and balances, legislative processes are generally slow and cumbersome; 'policy immobilism'[3] has been a significant impediment to concerted crisis management, although the higher level of predictability in political culture favours stable relationships between the major political actors, i.e. it helps to maintain institutional continuity and favours the operation of a consensual system for resolving problems.

Stability and continuity characterise government administrations since 1949 at both federal level – which has seen just four changes of government and seven different chancellors – and at regional level. Qualified proportional representation has produced a stable party system involving a Christian Democratic bloc (CDU/CSU), a Social Democratic party (SPD), liberals (FDP) and more recently a pragmatic Green Party. There is some evidence of dealignment recently, particularly with the emergence of extreme right groupings and the survival of the PDS, successor to the East German Socialist Unity Party, in both federal and regional assemblies. Participation rates in both elections and in active politics are high by international standards.

The major interest groups are characterised by high levels of centralisation, concentration and membership:

Trade unions are organised predominantly along 'industrial' lines in national bodies with regional and local representative bodies: engineering workers in IG-Metall (*Industriegewerkschaft Metall*), with nearly 3 million members, media workers in IG-Medien (215,000), public sector workers in the ÖTV (1.87 million) etc. There were at one time seventeen unions, including the police union, under the umbrella of the German Federation of Trade Unions (DGB), but a series of mergers has reduced this to just twelve, with predictions of a further concentration down to as few as five DGB unions. Outside the DGB, which represents over 10 million workers, there is currently a separate White Collar Workers Union (DAG: 489,000), a Christian Federation of Trade Unions (CGB: 316,000) and the German Federation of Civil Servants (BGB: 1.1 million). The DAG is currently involved in negotiations to create a giant service sector union embracing public sector workers (ÖTV), financial services (HBV), media workers and postal workers and which would, if realised, represent over 3.8 million workers and end the separation between DGB and DAG.

Capital interests are organised according, in large measure, to functional categories:

Employers are represented by national branch associations, with regional subgroups, and enjoy a very high membership ratio of over 90 percent; the branch associations are primarily responsible for conducting wage negotiations with respective branch unions within the framework of free collective bargaining. The Federal Association of Employer Federations (BDA) functions as the employers' political lobby in relation to supra-national, national and regional governments.

Industrial associations are likewise organised along branch lines, with a very high membership ratio of over 80 percent and a strong culture of both cooperation and norm setting in commercial contracts. The Federation of German Industry (BDI) comprises thirty-four peak industrial associations and is arguably the most powerful umbrella organisation for German capital, operating as both a national and international lobbyist for industrial interests and as a dominant member of the EU-level peak employers' confederation UNICE.

The eighty-four Chambers of Industry and Commerce (IHKs) are centrally involved in both the accreditation of enterprises and in the coordination, together with state authorities and trade unions, of the highly structured 'dual system' of training in Germany. Membership of the IHKs is, with the exception of craft trades and agriculture, mandatory for all German enterprises and encompasses more than 3 million companies. Their peak association is the German Association of Industry and Commerce (DIHT).

There are a number of smaller organisations representing small- and medium-sized enterprises (ASU) and the professions (BFB), which play a minor but occasionally significant role in policy consultations and/or implementation; the Federal Chamber of Doctors is a particularly influential professional association.

The institutional structures of German corporatism have traditionally varied from one area of concern to another and over time; they have thus involved both trilateral and bilateral links, different levels of commitment from participating groups and thus different qualities of outcome. There are strong trilateral elements within the fields of statutory social insurance, where capital and labour interests monitor the administration of health, pensions, unemployment, accident and – since 1995 – of long-term care insurance, in conjunction with representatives of appropriate state ministries. Likewise, the so-called 'dual system'of training (based in both enterprise and technical college) involves trilateral consultative bodies at central and local policy level as well as statutory bilateral linkages between employers and workforce representatives at enterprise level. Labour law is a separate branch of jurisprudence in Germany, with a specialist Labour Court judge operating trilaterally on a panel with a representative of both labour and capital in litigation procedures; a relatively typical feature of Labour Court proceedings is that the panel will seek to achieve a consensual outcome between conflicting parties before recourse to formal judgement.

Tripartism at the macro-political level was introduced briefly in 1967 under the Grand Coalition in the form of Concerted Action (*Konzertierte Aktion*), based loosely on the British NEDO; this involved non-binding discussions between employer, union and state representatives concerning medium-term macroeconomic targets, in particular relating to wage costs. It achieved the short-term objective of moderating wage settlements, but after 1969 remained ineffectual until its formal collapse in 1977. Trade union hopes of developing a set of tripartite macro-policy institutions along Austrian lines evaporated. Nevertheless, the Concerted Action principle was adopted within the health sector in the 1970s (*Konzertierte Aktion im Gesundheitswesen*) to help in the reform of healthcare provision and above all to resolve longer-term differences between the health insurance funds and the powerful medical associations.[4] In this regard the institution continues to demonstrate some success as well as longer-term viability. At the macroeconomic level tripartism only survives in the institutionalised but informal framework of the Chancellor's 'bungalow discussions' involving industrial/employer representatives, trade union leaders and Federal government representatives in the Chancellor's Bonn residence.[5] As with the formal Concerted Action programme, discussions are non-binding and driven by the spirit of consensualism and (albeit disparate) perceptions of the 'common good' in the context of an institutional culture which still seeks to include the opinions of labour representatives. This constitutes a minor but significant difference between the translation of neo-liberal doctrine in a country with corporatist-consensual traditions (Germany) and a country like Britain with its adversarial traditions: Thatcherite neo-liberalism sought both to weaken trade unions as social institutions and to exclude them from policy formation in a way that would still be resisted by a majority of German conservatives and employers' associations.

Unification and 'Partnership'

The speed of German unification was driven by political not economic imperatives, in particular by the fear of increased immigration.[6] In macroeconomic and fiscal terms it has proved in large measure dysfunctional, compounded by poor economic management:[7] growth rates have been disappointing, the gap between east German output and east German consumption has had to be plugged by west-east transfers, social insurance funds have had to raise contribution rates and state investment has been concentrated on improving the poor economic infrastructure of the East. On the other hand, the phenomenal cost of transforming the five new Länder has been borne without major social unrest and largely in the spirit of national 'solidarity'. The rhetoric of commonality, partnership and consensus has been regularly invoked in relation to taxpayers, civil servants, trade unions and employers; in this process the enlightened self-interest of minimising the social costs of unification and overcoming dangerous structural disparities played a significant role. Within the three-cornered framework of state, employers and trade unions in the west, however, there were significant differences of perspective: while employers – as potential purchasers of east German commercial assets, investors in new enterprises and employers of labour in the east – were most concerned by low levels of productivity and poor infrastructural conditions, trade unions feared the depressive effect of low east German wages on national wage rates and real incomes in the west: low wages as an inducement to invest could thus threaten west German living standards, already depressed by the 7.5 percent 'Solidarity Surcharge' on income tax. In the remarkable situation of unequal economies united under one roof, a remarkable set of deals was struck between branch-based employers' organisations and unions in the course of 1991, in concert with the Federal Government as employer and resource provider, which agreed to a fixed timetable for the incremental but relatively rapid alignment of east and west German wage rates.[8] This was in part predicated on (exceedingly) optimistic forecasts of macroeconomic convergence between east and west within ten years;[9] it still meant that higher unit costs in the east would potentially deter new investors. The immediate gap was essentially bridged by Federal employment subsidies, investment grants, tax breaks and interest subsidies; one additional major concession to employers, however, was the suspension in the five new Länder of codetermination rights (1976 Law) in large industrial companies with more than 2,000 employees. The less significant Works Council arrangements from the 1952 Works Constitution Law were applied in the East, ensuring at least limited consultation rights with regard to working conditions. In general, all other institutional structures of corporatism and 'social partnership' were imposed on the five new Länder: the dual system of training, the Labour Courts, arbitration structures, and parity representation in the monitoring of the social insurance funds. Chambers of industry and commerce, trade associations, employers' federations and trade unions absorbed or created their east German counterparts. Branch-based national collective bargaining remained in place and – unsurprisingly – all employment-related statutes were transferred onto the new territory.[10]

Formal concertation between state, employers and trade unions was virtually absent in the initial stages of unification at the macro-political level, even though there were a number of calls for the resurrection of Concerted Action as an instrument of crisis management.[11] The wage-convergence agreements did not emanate from a formally agreed wages policy but via a set of incremental understandings, some nevertheless deriving from chancellor Kohl's informal 'bungalow discussions' with representatives of corporate peak associations and the larger trade unions. Another by-product of Kohl's informal consultations with representatives of capital and labour was the so-called 'Solidarity Pact' of 13 March 1993, which was designed to accelerate and fund the reconstruction of east Germany. Against the background of severe recession and rising unemployment in the west and the colossal structural weaknesses of the East, both employers and trade unions were prepared to accept the emergency measures, including the burdensome 7.5 percent surcharge on income taxes. The most significant feature of the policy process leading to the Solidarity Pact was the incorporation of both the SPD and the Land heads of government as co-signatories (employers and trade unions were not included).[12] The burden of west-east 'solidarity' was borne by the mass of the population, and willingly. This did not stop commentators criticising both the supply-side bias of the package and the supposed electoral opportunism ('clientelism') of Kohl's emergency programme.[13] Policy concertation in specific sectors like that of social insurance was decisive in facilitating the immediate and trouble-free absorption of the east German population into schemes, for which no accumulated GDR funds were forthcoming. The actuarial anomaly of insurance funds acknowledging the rights of non-contributors (prior to 1990) to pro rata benefits based on length of employment and an entirely notional level of entitlement, was set aside in a series of tripartite discussions in the autumn of 1990. The individual funds were obliged to increase contribution rates markedly; overall, the share of employer and employee contributions to gross wages rose by nearly 18 percent between 1990 and 1998, from 35.8 percent to 42.2 percent. While employer, union and state assent was essentially driven by the extraordinary circumstances of unification and by the absence of alternatives, the fact that the 'social partners' agreed to shoulder the bulk of the financial burden, either through increased marginal wage costs or through higher wage and salary stoppages, indicates the smooth functioning of concertation at sectoral level. Having said that, the increases in employers' marginal wage costs have subsequently been used to fuel demands for legislative reform in the field of social security and in particular for reduced employer contributions. This in turn has increased differences on social policy between employers and trade unions and rendered discussions in other tripartite forums more difficult.

The most significant examples of informal concertation since unification in 1990 have been the periodic discussions concerning the so-called 'alliance for work' (*Bündnis für Arbeit,* see Table 10.1). The phenomenon first arose in a number of sectoral wage agreements, notably in the textile industry and the chemical sector, in which 'no redundancy' clauses and pledges on training were negotiated for wage rate settlements which often left net wage increases below the rate of inflation.[14] In November 1995, IG-Metall chairman, Klaus Zwickel, proposed a nationwide 'alliance for work'; this was taken up by Helmut Kohl in one of his tripartite 'bungalow discussions' in January 1996 which produced a joint communiqué, 'Alliance for Jobs and for Securing the Economic Location', from employers, unions and federal government. Kohl's initiative enjoyed considerable resonance in the early Spring in the run-up to regional elections but foundered in the medium term because of simultaneous cutbacks in job-creation schemes, announced in the government's emergency budget of spring 1996; nevertheless, in May 1997 at a joint press conference with the federal government and employers, Dieter Schulte, head of the DGB, announced a further initiative for a national 'job alliance' after unemployment had risen above 4 million and the labour market in the east had begun to deteriorate again.[15] Despite assurances of additional employment measures and private job creation in the East, the decline in employment continued, reinforced by pre-Maastricht cutbacks. Undeterred, the main motion of the DGB's Executive Committee for its June 1998 Congress contained the demand for an 'alliance for jobs' from the next federal government.[16]

Employers have also directed their lobbying towards social state benefits in general: this resulted, on the one hand, in the introduction in 1995 of Long-Term Care Insurance as a fifth pillar of the statutory social insurance system, which has brought relief to both pension funds and health funds. On the other hand, the Kohl government sought to reduce pensions insurance contributions by raising retirement thresholds and reducing the earnings-related ratio of pensions benefits, and also passed controversial legislation in late 1996 allowing the reduction of sick-pay entitlement from 100 percent to 80 percent of average weekly earnings. While trade unions have been able to stave off the implementation of this cost-relief measure in a number of sectors, involving over 15 million employees,[17] they have been forced to make other concessions on both direct wage cost settlements and on non-statutory benefits. The new Schröder government, meanwhile, has produced proposals for reducing pension insurance contributions through higher federal subsidies funded by increased energy taxes.

The BDI, through its president Hans-Olaf Henkel, has been particularly outspoken in its questioning of key principles of neo-corporatism. Henkel pleaded for the application of the principle of 'subsidiarity' to wage agreements, to social affairs and state economic policy. He applauded the open flouting of branch-based agreements by east German enterprises and the weakness of trade unions in the east. He eschewed 'round tables' – the long-standing symbol of corporatist institutions – expressing a preference for 'sharp-edged decisions' (see Table 10.2). He thus set himself starkly outside the cooperative model of 'social partnership', breaking ranks both with the

Table 10.1. *Key Terms in Germany*

Term	Meaning
'Bungalow-Gespräche'	Informal 'bungalow discussions' originating under Helmut Schmidt in the 1970s and equivalent to the British 'beer and sandwiches' tradition: informal bi- and trilateral consultations between federal government, employers' and trade union leaders. It is significant that this tradition of informal concertation was actively maintained by Helmut Kohl, forming the basis for a temporary 'alliance for jobs' in 1996.
Bündnis für Arbeit	The idea of an 'alliance for work' or 'alliance for jobs' was first mooted in 1995 and has subsequently been deployed both by the Kohl administration and by the Schröder government to achieve a coordinated, tripartite approach to macro policy, notably on wages, investment and working time. In the electoral propaganda of both Greens and Social Democrats it was synonymous with 'Concerted Action' (see below).
Konzertierte Aktion	'Concerted Action' was the misnomer applied to the non-binding discussions inaugurated by the Grand Coalition in 1967 and surviving until 1977, involving the peak organisations of labour (DGB, IG-Metall) capital (BDI, BDA) as well as the federal government and federal bank, which produced a brief voluntary agreement on wage restraint in 1967 and 1968. Plans – actively promoted by trade unions – to develop the institution into a formalised system of macro-political concertation were never taken seriously by the other two parties. The term has been used to describe successful cooperative arrangements within specific sectors (e.g., health) involving a plurality of interested parties.
Mitbestimmung	'Codetermination' is used both to describe the specific institutions of labour representation within German private companies and to denote the inclusion of a plurality of interest groups, above all of organised labour, in macro-political affairs.
Mitspracherechte	Like 'codetermination', the 'rights to inclusion in [political and other] discussions' are a common and significant feature of German political culture.
sozial (adj)	'Sozial' (social) has a stronger positive resonance than in Anglo-Saxon culture, not because it is clearly defined, but because it is more readily associated with distinct and positive features of modern German history: Social Catholicism, Social Liberalism, Social Democracy; it was a popular tag to append to new programmes ('social market economy', 'social partnership') or new parties (Christian Social Union) after the Second World War; the trade union wing of the CDU continues to be organised under the umbrella of the 'Social Committees'.

Table 10.1. *Continued*

Term	Meaning
Soziale Symmetrie	'Social symmetry' first appeared in the late 1960s – as a highly contested term – in the context of income distribution ratios. It re-emerged in a similar context in the 1980s and 1990s. Trade unions employ the term in relation to an assumed balance of social distribution ratios; employers and government ministers (including social democrats) present the term as meaning merely social progress which ensures real income increases for all.
Sozialpartner (n)	The 'social partners' – employers and trade unions – were established as part of common political currency after the War in the wake of the disastrous labour-capital polarities of the years up to 1945; official handbooks, guides to German politics, local address directories include employers' and workers' associations under the rubric of 'social partners'.
Sozialpartnerschaft (n)	'Social partnership' in Germany is shorthand for the consensual system of labour-capital relations which developed in the 1950s within a complex and juridified framework and with the active support of state institutions, notably the labour courts. The frequent use of the term by both employers and trade unionists (as well as all politicians) confirms its embeddedness in German political culture.

Source: see text.

consensual approach of the Employers Federation (BDA) under Hundt and with its commitment to the principle of industry-wide collective bargaining. Henkel's own firm, IBM, was withdrawn demonstratively from the BDA. In 1995 and 1996 there was significant conflict between Henkel and the then president of the BDA, Klaus Murmann; the latter saw grave dangers in the abandonment of national agreements, in terms of increased negotiating costs and the risk of enterprise-based conflict.[18] Other voices, urging moderation and bemoaning the new hostility towards trade unions and collective bargaining, have been heard from within the employers' camp.[19]

The new Red–Green coalition under Gerhard Schröder has made the resurrection of informal tripartism, in the form a new 'alliance for work' initiative, a key element of its initial programme. Both employers and trade unions joined with government leaders in an initial communiqué of an Alliance for Work, Training and Competitiveness on 7 December 1998, but the auguries are not particularly promising, both in terms of a weakening growth cycle and the narrowness of the common ground occupied by all major participants. Employer reluctance has been strengthened by tax reform proposals which favour private households over corporations and by a tougher negotiating process in the 1998–9 wage round. The institutions of consensualism nevertheless survive and the rhetoric of social partnership remains strong.

Table 10.2. *Key Arguments in Germany*

Proponent	Argument
Federal Association of German Employers Federations (BDA)	'Social peace is an indispensable element of the Social Market Economy. Social peace is the result of a dialogue that directs divergent interests to compromises capable of securing majority support. The BDA is committed to making consensus and compromise defining approaches to social policy rather than conflict and struggle.' (March 1999)
	'We need our systems of solidarity to be orientated towards elementary core risks. The community has to step in where the individual cannot help himself. If subsidiarity has priority over solidarity, we will not simply create greater justice in benefit payments, but we will also make the social state affordable once again.' (March 1999)
	'Alliances for jobs belong in the enterprise. Only there can we maintain employment and training places and create new ones.'
	Dieter Hundt, President of the BDA, *Frankfurter Allgemeine Zeitung*, 2 December 1998
Federation of German Industry (BDI)	'The consensus model' is yesterday's model. Everywhere in the world people are recognizing that the principle of subsidiarity should also apply within the economy. ... In Germany we have too many Round Tables and too few quick and hard-edged decisions.'
	Hans-Olaf Henkel, President of the BDI, *Der Spiegel*, January 1998
	'A point has been reached when a policy of compromise at any price can no longer be sustained. The decisive question is not "what will appease the trade unions" but "what will combat unemployment" ... When needs must, one must be prepared for confrontation.'
	Tyl Necker, Vice-President of the BDI, *Die Zeit*, 22 March 1996
German Federation of Trade Unions (DGB)	'A new Alliance for Jobs is necessary, because the rapid reduction of mass unemployment and the targeted realisation of greater social justice is most likely to be achieved in the cooperation of the state, of business and of trade unions.'
	Joint statement of DGB with its constituent unions, 6 October 1998

Table 10.2. *Continued*

Proponent	Argument
Trade Union for the Mining, Chemicals and Energy sectors (IGBCE)	'I hope that all participants [in the tripartite alliance talks] are clear about one thing, that we have no other alternative than to reach such an agreement. This is also historically determined. We have grown up within the corporatist model. Other countries may have developed other working relations; we are dependent on consensus – and overall have not done badly from it.' Hubertus Schmoldt, chair of IGBCE, interview in *Die Zeit*, 3 September 1998
Metal Workers Union (IG-Metall)	'The "Alliance for Jobs" offers the opportunity to re-think (neo-) corporatism, of opening it up socially and thus inducing a change of politics embracing the whole of society.' Wolfgang Schroeder, Analyst within IG-Metall executive board, (with Josef Esser) in: 'Vom Bündnis für Arbeit zum Dritten Weg', *Blätter für deutsche und internationale Politik*, January 1999, p. 57
	'There is strong support for the supposition that a new Alliance for Jobs will involve an "antagonistic conflict partnership" rather than a conflict-free arrangement. Concealed behind the apparently uncontested consensus about the aims of the whole affair are divergent interests. In relation to the goal of full employment and a policy leading to it, the motives of all the participating actors display anything but unanimity, whatever the rhetoric claims'. Horst Schmidthenner, member of executive board of IG-Metall, in: 'Bündnis für Arbeit – schon wieder', *Blätter für deutsche und internationale Politik*, August 1998, p. 844
The Alliance for Jobs, Training and Competitiveness (BDI, BDA, DIHT, Craft Federation, DGB, IG-Metall, DAG, IGBCE, ÖTV, Federal Government)	'The overcoming of the high level of unemployment is the greatest challenge for politics and society in the transition to the new century. ... A positive development in the market for employment and training places requires a continuous cooperation between the state, trade unions and business interests. A close agreement between the participants is particularly urgent. The Alliance for Jobs, Training and Competitiveness is thus designed as a long-standing arrangement and as a process of communication aimed at achieving mutual trust but where divergent interests and differing opinions are articulated.' Extract from Joint Communiqué, Bonn, 7 December 1998

Source: see table.

The Future of Social Partnership in Germany

The debate about the 'consensual' model of politico-economic relations in Germany is being driven by a confident and more powerful corporate sector which has more options for manoeuvre than either unions or state authorities. The public debate is most frequently framed in terms of a crude polarity between a hide-bound 'sclerotic' German model and a more dynamic and flexible Anglo-Saxon model. For more differentiated accounts one has to look to the fringes of academic opinion and to trade union analysts who, typically, have most of the good arguments but less public clout than the orthodox neo-liberal majority in Germany. Heise's critique of the 'sclerosis-flexibility' polarity and of neo-liberalism as macro-policy and ideology[20] is well complemented by comparative studies of the micro level, e.g. by Ebster-Grosz and Pugh, and Casper and Vitols.[21] Neither study draws the simplistic conclusion of a stark alternative – either the British model or further decline via German sclerosis. Both rather seek to identify strengths and weaknesses that can be addressed by 'incremental adaptation' and synergies.

Casper and Vitols identify significant residual strengths of the German model, concluding that Germany's 'competitiveness problem ... has been exaggerated', and that neo-liberal claims of 'structural barriers' are 'inaccurate or only partially true'.[22] In an international comparison of wage bargaining systems, Franz Traxler comes to similar conclusions, underlining that the German system of national–sectoral wage agreements is in line with most other EU countries and that the coordinated management of wage costs allows the successful 'internalisation of externalities' – they become common for all – in a way that eludes decentralised systems in countries such as the USA and the UK.[23]

After ten years of aftershocks from unification and the intensification of globalisation, the defenders of the German model are sensing a fairer wind. The resilience of the system is noted by foreign observers[24] and the economic and electoral advantages of embracing the rhetoric of 'social partnership' and dialogue are being increasingly recognised by both industrial leaders and their political allies.[25] Trade union membership remains high by European standards. There have been one or two demonstrative withdrawals from trade associations and employers federations, but in general the value of centralised interest articulation and intermediation for national and supra-national lobbying and for industrial relations management remains firmly entrenched within German enterprises. The reluctance of the BDA to abandon codetermination and national collective bargaining is not difficult to explain: in the BDA's own words, 'the trans-enterprise regulation of remuneration and other working conditions for a whole sector has contributed decisively to *social peace* in Germany. National wage agreements keep distributional conflicts out of the enterprises'.[26] Social peace has been maintained despite the extraordinary economic dislocation caused by unification and despite the fact that the ratio of wages and salaries to national income (wages ratio) in united Germany has continued to fall, and the gross profits ratio to rise.[27] Furthermore, as long as structural mass unemployment persists and international economic conditions favour German corporate interest in foreign markets for direct investments, Germany's trade unions will continue to play second fiddle and their pronouncements of the 'end of modesty' will remain, sadly, impotent rhetoric.[28] This is the perhaps grim irony of the recent history of German corporatism: the erosion of trade union power and the widening of the disparities in income and wealth distribution are being conducted within the framework of a consensual system designed implicitly to prevent this kind of development; participation by trade unions in corporatist structures was at least traditionally predicated on the assumption of distributional justice or 'social symmetry' (see Table 10.1).

The development of Germany's 'social partnership' in the 1990s demonstrates the functionality of its institutions and its rhetoric (as far as capital is concerned) and the extent to which these are deeply embedded in the cultural values and expectations of the mass of the population. As long as the social security of the population is not threatened, the consensual model of redistributing national wealth in favour of capital will continue to thrive and 'concession bargaining' will continue to reduce corporate costs. A reversal of this pessimistic trend would only seem possible if the valorisation of (German) capital hits the barriers of global crisis, and economists, politicians, trade unionists and corporate leaders take a long, hard look at the self-destructive tenets of neo-liberalism (which seem incapable of acknowledging that labour income is more than just a cost).

Ironically, Germany's institutions of asymmetrical 'social partnership' do contain, in their culture of constructive engagement and dialogue, the potential for addressing some of the core problems – demographic imbalance and the limits of growth – that will face German society in the new century in a far more effective way than the decentralised market mechanisms of the Anglo-Saxon model. The successful introduction of long-term care insurance has been rightly credited in part to the operation of corporatist mechanisms within the social insurance funds and the Federal Labour Ministry.[29] It is likely, however, that the distributional conflicts of the twentieth century will pale into insignificance compared to the challenge of an economic culture that physically, mathematically and ecologically is incapable of growing as fast as the laws of capitalist accumulation currently demand.[30]

Notes

1. See Gerhard Lehmbruch, 'Consociational Democracy, Class Conflict and the New Corporatism', in *Trends Towards Corporatist Intermediation*, ed. G. Lehmbruch and P.C. Schmitter, London and Beverly Hills, 1979; also Gerhard Lehmbruch, 'Concertation and the Structure of Corporatist Networks', in *Order and Conflict in Contemporary Capitalism: Studies in the Political Economy of Western European Nation,* ed. John H. Goldthorpe, Oxford, 1984.
2. A significant result of the homogenisation of economic opinion in the SVR and in government was the formation of the so-called Memorandum Group of alternative economists

and political scientists who, since 1975, have published an annual counter-assessment which challenges the neo-liberal orthodoxy of the SVR's annual report.

3. See Simon Bulmer and Peter Humphreys, 'Kohl, corporatism and congruence: the West German model under challenge', in *The Changing Agenda of West German Public Policy*, ed. S. Bulmer, Aldershot, 1989.
4. See Gerhard Lehmbruch, 'The Institutional Framework of German Regulation', in *The Politics of German Regulation*, ed. K. Dyson, Aldershot, 1992: 39ff; admittedly, the politico-economic composition of Concerted Action in the Health Sector is not the same as its 1967 model; the practitioners (qua labour) wield considerably more power than the commissioning health funds (qua capital), as do the pharmaceutical suppliers of the sector.
5. See M. Donald Hancock, *West Germany. The Politics of Democratic Corporatism*, Chatham (NJ), 1989: 138f; also Bodo Zeuner, 'Von der "Konzertierten Aktion" zum "Bündnis für Arbeit" Neun Thesen zu einem ökonomischen und politischen Lehrstück', in *Frankfurter Rundschau*, 13 November 1996: 11.
6. Migration to Germany was already the highest in Europe, involving hundreds of thousands of political refugees, ethnic Germans from eastern Europe as well as east Germans.
7. See Chris Flockton, 'Germany's long-running fiscal strains: Unification costs or unsustainability of welfare state arrangements', *Debatte* 1 (1998): 79ff.
8. For example, in March 1991 the metal workers' union, IG-Metall, negotiated an incremental scheme with the powerful employers' organisation, Gesamtmetall, which envisaged full convergence of wage rates in the metal-working industry of Mecklenburg-Vorpommern by April 1994; the postponement of convergence was later negotiated for most branches, such that a full alignment of wage rates had only been achieved in five sectors by February 1998: iron and steel, metal-working (Saxony), printing, private banking, office cleaning (Berlin). Civil service pay rates are still only 85percent of western levels, in chemicals 83.8 percent, energy 81.6 percent and agriculture in Mecklenburg-Vorpommern 68.2 percent; see: Reinhard Bispinck et al. 'Von niedrigen Lohnabschlüssen zum "Ende der Bescheidenheit"? Eine tarifpolitische Bilanz des Jahres 1997', *WSI-Mitteilungen* 2 (1998): 78f.
9. A study by Goldmann Sachs in 1992 predicted convergence of GDP per head within ten years, based on average GDP growth of 10 percent per annum; *Borrowed Prosperity: Medium Term Outlook for the East German Economy*, London, May 1992. A more realistic assessment would now see convergence or near convergence within approximately eighty years; thus R. Barro and X. Sala-I-Martin, cited in T. Lange and Geoffrey Pugh, *The Economics of German Unification*, Cheltenham 1998: 135ff.
10. It should be noted that, in the process, significant elements of east German labour law and family law were cancelled: these included generous parental leave provision, company and state childcare provision etc. This weakened still further the position of east German workers on the labour market, in particular that of women.
11. See Claus Noé, 'Lieber ein Runder Tisch als eine Rezession', *Die Zeit*, 31 January 1992; Jürgen Hoffmann, 'Konzertierte Aktion in Neuauflage – Ein Blick zurück in die Zukunft', *Frankfurter Rundschau*, 21 January 1995.
12. See Hugh Compston, 'The end of national policy concertation? Western Europe since the Single European Act', *Journal of European Public Policy,* 5:3 (1998): 515.
13. See, for example W. Bayer and E. Horstkötter, 'Solidarität statt "Solidarpakt"', *Blätter für deutsche und internationale Politik* 3 (1993): 300f.
14. Of the eight years 1990–7, five have produced net falls in real wages and only three net increases in the west; if one includes the unification boom-year of 1990, net real wages in the west actually fell by 0.8 percent in the period to 1997; without 1990 the decline from 1991 has been 5.44 percent; figures from Claus Schäfer, 'Verteilungspolitik: Chronik eines angekündigten politischen Selbstmords', *WSI-Mitteilungen* 10 (1997): 669ff, own calculations.
15. See Reinhardt Bispinck et al., 'Vom "Bündnis für Arbeit" zum Streit um die Entgeltfortzahlung – Eine tarifpolitische Bilanz des Jahres 1996', *WSI-Mitteilungen* 2 (1997); R. Bispinck et al. 'Von niedrigen Lohnabschlüssen zum "Ende der Bescheidenheit"? – Eine tarifpolitische Bilanz des Jahres 1997', *WSI-Mitteilungen*, 2 (1998).

16. Further details, see: Horst Schmitthenner, 'Bündnis für Arbeit – schon wieder?', *Blätter für deutsche und internationale Politik* 7 (1998): 841ff.
17. Bispinck et.al. 'Von niedrigen Lohnabschlüssen', 86.
18. See *Die Welt*, 12 June 1996, 'Murmann stolpert über Streit mit BDI'.
19. Dieter Kirchner, the former director of the Engineering Employers' Federation, Gesamtmetall, accused the current manager-generation of being 'too impatient' and went as far as to say that 'we have a leadership problem' in the ranks of the employers; quoted in: B. Pappenheim, 'Dieter Kirchner geht mit den Arbeitgebern ins Gericht', *Stuttgarter Zeitung*, 28 November 1996; Ernst Niemeier quotes the Swiss banker, Hans-Dieter Vontobel, who had issued a 'plea against the Darwinisation of mores' and against 'vulgar liberalism'; Niemeier, 'Maßlose Gewinnmaximierung zerstört unser Wirtschafts- und Gesellschaftssystem. Die schiefe Globalisierungsdiskussion', *WSI-Mitteilungen* 1 (1998): 39ff.
20. Arno Heise, 'Neoliberale Empfehlungen zur Beschäftigungspolitik in Theorie und Praxis: Großbritannien und Deutschland im Vergleich', *WSI-Mitteilungen* 11 (1997): 758–70.
21. D. Ebster-Grosz, and D. Pugh, *Anglo-German Business Collaboration. Pitfalls and Potentials*, London, 1997; Steven Casper, and Sigurt Vitols, 'The German Model in the 1990s: Problems and Prospects', *Industry and Innovation*, vol. 4:1 (1997).
22. Casper and Vitols, 'The German Model', 8ff.
23. Franz Traxler, 'Nationale Tarifsysteme und wirtschaftliche Internationalisierung. Zur Positionierung des "Modell Deutschland" im internationalen Vergleich', *WSI-Mitteilungen* 4 (1998): 249–55.
24. For example, David Gow, 'The sick man of Europe dances a jig', *Guardian*, 12 August 1998, p. 15.
25. See, for example, Erika Martens, 'Zurück zum Modell D', in *Die Zeit*, 12 March 1998.
26. Thus the BDA, 'Flächentarifvertrag', http://www.arbeitgeber.de
27. Claus Schäfer calculates a further 3.2 percent drop in the adjusted gross wages ratio between 1991 and 1997, 'Verteilungspolitik: Chronik eines angekündigten politischen Selbstmords', *WSI-Mitteilungen* 2 (1998): 669.
28. Klaus Zwickel, head of the engineering workers' union, IG-Metall, had declared 1998 to be the year where workers put an 'end to modesty'.
29. See Lehmbruch, 'The Institutional Framework of German Regulation', 39.
30. Real GDP growth of 2.5 percent is the minimum for maintaining current employment levels; if Germany succeeds in achieving an average of 2.5 percent real growth for the next twenty-nine years (which is by no means certain), society will need to be consuming twice as much as it currently consumes. To maintain this trajectory is a physical and cultural absurdity, but one which the vast majority of economists and politicians are incapable of questioning.

APPENDIX

Gross Wages Ratio [WR] in the EU (Share of Gross Wages and Salaries of Net Social Product/ National Income) 1980–1996 in percent (plus selected EU standardised unemployment rates [U])

Year	Bel		Den		Ger*		Fin		Fra		Lux		Ned		Aus		Port		Swe		Gre		GB		Ire		Italy		Spa	
	WR	U	WR	U	WR	U	WR	U	WR	U	WR	U	WR	U	WR	U	WR	U	WR	U	WR	U	WR	U	WR	U	WR	U	WR	U
1980	71.9		81.4		75.9		72.4		74.9		80.7		73.2		73.2		56.2		82.8		38.0		79.6		71.8		57.8		61.0	
1981	72.3		81.1		76.8		74.3		75.4		82.3		71.6		75.0		57.6		83.5		38.6		80.0		70.9		59.1		61.9	
1982	70.8	10.2	79.1		76.7	5.9	73.1		75.9	8.1	78.4	3.0	70.9	8.2	73.3		58.2	7.8	80.5	3.9	39.9		77.6	11.3	69.4	11.5	58.7	6.8	60.5	15.3
1983	70.0		78.2		74.7		72.8		75.5		77.4		68.9		72.2		57.5		79.1		41.0		75.5		69.1		58.4		60.5	
1984	68.9		76.6		73.7		72.7		74.5		76.1		66.1		72.1		55.3		77.8		40.8		75.0		66.6		56.8		57.3	
1985	67.8		76.6		73.2		74.6		73.6		77.7		65.1		72.1		53.4		78.7		41.5		74.0		64.9		56.7		58.0	
1986	67.3		77.3		72.3		75.1		71.1		75.0		66.4		71.9		52.7		79.2		39.9		75.0		65.6		55.1		57.7	
1987	66.9		80.6		72.6		75.8		70.6		78.2		68.3		72.1		52.3		80.1		39.9		73.7		64.6		55.1		57.4	
1988	65.3		80.1		71.7		74.9		69.8		74.7		67.8		70.7		52.6		80.0		40.2		73.6		61.1		55.0		57.4	
1989	63.6		78.6		71.0		74.9		68.9		73.7		65.8		70.5		52.6		81.5		42.2		74.0		59.9		55.3		57.7	
1990	64.9	6.7	78.0	7.7	70.4	4.8	77.5	3.2	69.8	8.9	77.6	1.7	65.5	6.2	70.0		54.2	4.6	84.2	1.8	43.4		75.5	6.9	58.9	13.4	56.8	9.1	59.2	16.2
1991	66.3		77.7		73.1		82.5		70.0		80.7		66.0		70.7		57.1		83.5		40.8		76.7		60.0		57.3		60.3	
1992	66.6		76.9		73.9		80.4		70.1		80.0		67.3		71.7		58.8		80.9		39.7		75.2		60.7		57.6		60.9	
1993	66.6		76.1		74.2		75.2		70.7		79.0		67.8		72.6		56.0		78.7		38.4		72.9		59.6		57.2		60.7	
1994	65.9		75.0		72.4		71.8		69.5		76.3		65.8		70.9		55.3		76.2		39.0		71.3		59.3		54.8		58.5	
1995	65.3		75.1		71.6		71.0		69.8		77.0		66.9		69.9		55.0		72.9		40.2		71.2		56.7		53.1		56.7	
1996	64.6	9.8	74.9	6.9	70.5	8.9	71.2	15.3	70.2	12.4	76.7	3.3	66.6	6.3	69.0	4.4	55.9	7.3	75.3	10.0	41.7		70.8	8.2	56.4	11.8	53.5	12.0	58.2	22.1
1980 –96 +/–	–7.3		–6.5		–5.4		–1.2		–4.7		–4.0		–6.6		–4.2		–0.3		–7.5		+3.7		–8.8		–15.4		–4.3		–2.8	

Source: Deutsches Institut für Wirtschaftsforschung: 'Anteil der Arbeitseinkommen in fast allen Mitgliedsländern der EU seit 1980 rückläufig', *Wochenbericht* 48/1997

* Germany 1980–90 old territory of the FRG

Chapter 11

Ireland in Historical Perspective: The Legacies of Colonialism – Edging Towards Policy Concertation

Emmet O'Connor

Social partnership in Ireland is the outcome of long-term mediating forces rooted in the colonial legacy, as well as a response to problems in the economy and industrial relations that arose between 1969 and 1987. Three factors have conditioned its evolution. First, independent Ireland (the Irish Free State from 1922, Éire from 1937, and the Republic of Ireland from 1949), inherited a weak, dependent industrial base, leading to a high level of state direction of the economy from 1932 to 1958, and escalating political management of wage determination thereafter as the state withdrew from economic direction. Secondly, the British model of industrial relations and trade union organisation continued to prevail after 1922, but not without opposition from some Irish unions, who wanted a more positive relationship with the state, and a more centralised labour movement. Thirdly, Fianna Fáil, the predominant party since 1932, has always been reliant on working-class support and goodwill towards the trade union movement.

The history of corporatist thinking falls into two phases. Fianna Fáil's first period in office, from 1932 to 1948, was littered with failed corporatist initiatives. Political corporatism was championed by the Catholic Church and fascist sympathisers, and functional corporatism by employers seeking control over the new legislation introduced to promote industrialisation through tariff protection. Initially, Fianna Fáil aimed to encourage capital and labour through populist policies and patriotic appeals. This fruitless approach gave way to statutory controls on industrial relations after 1939; and then a series of corporatist proposals for postwar development, which proved too radical for unions and employers. After 1958, a shift to 'freer trade', a new wave of industrialisation, accelerating inflation and strike activity led to a revival of emphasis on industrial relations reform. Again, Fianna Fáil sought, in the first instance, to engineer voluntary change, this time through tripartite consultative structures. However, whilst tripartism contributed to a more consensual attitude among elites, it took a crisis in free collective bargaining to compel the adoption of centralised bargaining in 1970. Bipartite National Wage Agreements had led to tripartite National Understandings by the end of the decade, the emergence of the term 'social partnership', and a new rhetoric of consensus, based more on the values of harmony and economic efficiency, than on patriotism or morality. Yet, the commitment to social partnership remained tentative, and all sides happily reverted to free collective bargaining in 1981. Fianna Fáil policy was crucial to the sudden switch to deeper social partnership in 1987.

The Colonial Legacy

The union of Ireland with Britain in 1800 created an enduring material basis for class collaboration, and stymied the emergence of class-based politics. From 1830, trade unions endorsed successive nationalist movements in the hope that self-government and tariff protection would reverse the de-industrialisation accompanying Ireland's integration into the British economy.[1] But by the end of the century, anglicisation was leading to the adoption of metropolitan models of labour organisation, politics and industrial relations.

Labour federation dates from 1894, when fifty-two unions founded the Irish Trade Union Congress (ITUC) as a 'parliament of labour', on the pattern of the British TUC.[2] Economic and demographic decline were currently creating doubts about the viability of Irish trade unions, and by 1900 some 75 percent of trade unionists in Ireland belonged to British unions. The TUC model reflected the concomitant mental colonisation. A highly decentralised federation was singularly inappropriate for a fragmented movement, comprising craft, and later general and white-collar unions, and embracing under 50,000 workers, or less than 5 percent of employees, up to 1917. Anglicisation reinforced the sectionalist pattern of trade unionism, and popularised a belief that free collective bargaining, minimal state intervention in industrial relations and labour law, and an antagonistic labour–state relationship, were essential to a free trade unionism.

The British paradigm did not solve the problem of building a bargaining power for a small, disparate working class in an undeveloped economy, and British labour rarely committed sufficient resources to surmount Irish employer militancy. Partial de-anglicisation followed the launch of the Irish Transport and General Workers' Union (ITGWU) in 1909. Committed to the principles of 'Irish unions for Irish workers' and the American industrial unionist idea of 'One Big Union', the ITGWU enjoyed phenomenal expansion during the boom years of 1917 to 1921, and powered a general revival of Irish-based unionism.

Union growth after 1916 was facilitated by state intervention. As the First World War dragged on, the British government extended its control over the economy, making provision for the payment of war bonuses and minimum wage rates. To contain class conflict, statutory regulation intensified after the war. The struggle for national independence, from 1919 to 1922, consolidated state intervention. When Sinn Féin won a majority of Irish constituencies in the 1918 general election, the party convened a national parliament, Dáil Éireann, declared a Republic, and tried to subvert British rule by building a Republican counter-state. In return for cautious support from Labour, Dáil Éireann adopted a social manifesto, the *Democratic Programme*, largely drafted by Congress, the IRA (Irish Republican Army) tolerated widespread use of direct action tactics by trade unions in the postwar militancy, and the Dáil established a Department of Labour which operated conciliation and arbitration courts, though their rationale was primarily 'to oust the British Ministry of Labour which has sought to act as an arbitrator for the settlement of wages in Ireland'.[3]

The national revolution entailed little social change. Congress hopes that the *Democratic Programme* would be implemented were not realised, and independence brought reaction in its train. Sinn Féin split over the Anglo-Irish Treaty, which offered British Dominion status for the Irish Free State, and civil war broke out in 1922–3.[4] The victorious pro-Treaty party, later Cumann na nGaedheal, drew its core vote from big business and strong farmers. Economically, the Free State was little more than a cattle-ranch for Britain. Of its 1.3 million labour force, 670,000 were engaged in agriculture, and 67,000 in manufacture. In 1924, agriculture, food, and drink accounted for 86 percent of exports, and 98 percent of exports went to the United Kingdom.[5] Faced with this crushing dependency, Cumann na nGaedheal discarded the autarkic aims of Sinn Féin for a strategy of maximising agricultural exports in free trade with Britain. Industrial employment remained low, and industrial relations peripheral to public policy. Although the Free State constitution made provision for vocational structures, Cumann na nGaedheal restored the liberal conception of labour-state relations. Machinery of conciliation, arbitration, and wage setting, introduced by the British and Republican states, was abolished, along with the Republic's Department of Labour. The Irish state recognised Westminster legislation enacted before 1922, and did not try to revise the legal mode of industrial relations before 1941. Anti-Treatyites regrouped in 1926 to found Fianna Fáil under Eamon de Valera. Blending political and economic nationalism with an amorphous social radicalism, Fianna Fáil held power from 1932 to 1973 for all but six years. Its ideal of an Irish-owned self-sufficient, mixed economy, remained the national orthodoxy up to 1958, grounded on Fianna Fáil's majority backing in each of the main social classes.

Fianna Fáil's success reinforced Labour's political marginality. Congress had become the ITUC and Labour Party in 1914, and Labour contested general elections from 1922, but up to 1987 it averaged 11.4 percent of the vote.[6] Though some unions affiliated to the Party, Labour's participation in coalition governments was sufficiently intermittent, subordinate and unpredictable to be useless as a strategic calculation, and relations with Labour cabinet ministers were not exceptionally close.

Peak Labour and Employer Federations and the State

The growth and significance of labour and employer federations has been connected closely with state policy. The ITUC became important during the independence struggle, was of slight consequence to its affiliates or public policy under the Cumann na nGaedheal administrations, and acquired renewed importance with the introduction of Fianna Fáil's industrialisation programme in 1932. In 1936, the government pressed the ITUC to tackle the growing problem of inter-union disputes. Congress was itself anxious to become a more centralised body, and discussed a scheme to recast all affiliates as ten industrial unions. The plan was rejected in 1939, largely because of British opposition to a proposal that would, inter alia, make Congress completely Irish-based.[7] The failure to effect internal reform led to attempted statutory reform in the Trade Union Act (1941). It also caused private-sector Irish unions to favour a more statutory mode, provided it conferred greater legal recognition on trade unions, and did not displace voluntarism. Expectations of a fresh labour-state relationship and hostility to alleged 'British domination' triggered a split in Congress in 1945, with the formation of the Congress of Irish Unions (CIU), representing 77,500 workers, as against the ITUC's 146,000. The CIU was soon disappointed with the government's response, including its refusal to legislate against British unions. Indeed, the government prompted exchanges on unity in 1953, and the twins merged as the Irish Congress of Trade Unions (ICTU) in 1959. The subsequent evolution of tripartism and centralised bargaining finally gave Congress a growing authority over its affiliates and an influence on public policy.

The proportion of union membership within Congress has been relatively high since 1917, and about 90 percent since 1940.[8] Congress has also been successful in promoting rationalisation in recent years, and the tally of affiliates in the Republic fell from eighty in 1983 to fifty-two in 1993.[9] The number of trade unionists in Ireland was probably under 90,000 up to 1917, and peaked at some 250,000 in 1920. In the south, unionisation then contracted to a low of 99,500 in 1930, before recovering steadily, with significant growth in the 1930s, from 1946 to 1951, and in the 1960s. The 1980s saw a reversal of this trend, and unionisation falling from a peak of 527,200 in 1980 to 457,300, or 56.2 percent of employees, in 1987.[10] Congress data suggest a modest rise in unionisation in the 1990s.[11]

Employer associations developed largely in response to industrial conflict. The identification of federation with militancy has often discouraged membership, and employer unity has also been hampered by the unorganised structure of industry. In 1993, there were thirteen employer groups in the Republic holding negotiation licences under the Trade Unions Acts, together with divers trade associations with minor industrial relations functions. The biggest licensed body, the only one that is national, rather than industrial, and the only one that specialises in industrial relations, is the Irish Business and Employers' Confederation (IBEC).[12] IBEC's genealogy may be traced to the Dublin Employers' Federation, founded in 1911 as one of a number of contemporary local alliances created to combat generalised strikes. State promotion of native manufacture and the growth of industrial unrest in the 1930s led to a major increase in membership of employer bodies. The Dublin Employers' Federation, renamed the Federated Employers Ltd in 1928, appointed a full-time official in 1937, and amalgamated with some local federations in 1942 to constitute the Federated Union of Employers (FUE). Membership expanded from 451 in 1942 to 1,038 by 1950, and 1,628 by 1970, and the FUE acquired a unique recognition from government in appointments to state bodies, and from the Congresses in the national pay rounds introduced from 1946.[13] In 1989 the FUE was restyled the Federation of Irish Employers (FIE), and in 1993 it merged with the Confederation of Irish Industry, the biggest employer body dealing with matters other than industrial relations, to form IBEC; IBEC represented 3,700 companies, employing 300,000 workers, or 60 percent of employees in private manufacturing and services. The only other sizable negotiating bodies are the Construction Industry Federation, the Irish Pharmaceutical Union and the Society of the Irish Motor Industry; in 1993 they represented 2,188, 1,222 and 1,212 members respectively.[14]

Employer bodies have generally welcomed centralised wage bargaining, but avoided solidaristic militancy, and see their role as representative rather than pro-active.

The Failure of Corporatist Initiatives, 1932–48

The level of state economic direction after 1932 encouraged two varieties of corporatist thinking; one overtly political and social, the other functional. Vocationalism was advocated by the Catholic Church following the publication of *Quadragesimo Anno*, and a blend of vocationalism and Italian corporatism by Fine Gael, formed in 1933 from a merger of Cumann na nGaedheal and the fascist 'Blueshirts'. Vocationalists and corporatists varied in emphasis – the former tended to stress 'organic' democracy, the latter inter-class unity – but both wanted workers', employers' and farmers' syndicates to determine industrial relations, shape economic policy and be represented directly in Parliament; the better to foster social harmony and forge a third way between liberal capitalism and Communism.[15] Fianna Fáil deemed it politic to make a few empty gestures, to vocationalism at least. The new constitution to end Dominion status, ratified in 1937, allowed for the creation of vocational councils – without offering any means or incentive for their establishment. The provision has never been acted upon. The Senate was ostensibly made a vocational chamber – and given an electorate composed substantially of elected politicians, which rendered the vocational dimension a mere technicality. In 1939, the government agreed to an opposition request for a Commission on Vocational Organisation. The Commission issued a weighty report in 1943, which the government ignored. De Valera rejected any imposition of vocationalism, and held that change should come 'from below', but public interest, never great, faded quickly.[16] In reality, Fianna Fáil was notoriously jealous of power, and preferred to direct interest groups through its hegemony of nationalism. It was slow to abandon voluntarism until the wartime Emergency.

The government took a clearer line against calls for functional corporatism. Seán Lemass, Minister for Industry and Commerce from 1932 to 1939, 1941–8, 1951–4, and 1957–9, and Fianna Fáil's key economic strategist, preferred to harness capital and labour through public policy and by consolidating representative organisations sympathetic to government policy.[17] Lemass hoped that the benefits of protectionism for labour – rising union membership, and growth in real wages – together with statutory improvements in working conditions, would induce a cooperative attitude. He also encouraged workers to join Irish- based unions, on the assumption that they would be more sensitive to the national interest. However, strike activity increased after 1932, as did inter-union disputes. If unions were wary of collusion with Lemass, employers took a contrary position. Enthused by opportunities for import substitution, and increasing consultation with government, they were soon abandoning their proclivities for free trade, liberalism, and Fine Gael. The Federation of Irish Industries for example, founded in 1932, confined membership to Irish nationals. In return, the Federation wanted to discharge some of the functions of the Department of Industry and Commerce, and became ever more critical of Lemass's stance.[18] Though Lemass had called for a 'National Economic Council' in opposition, he held to a strict understanding of 'consultation' as Minister. Ten years on, a Departmental report noted: 'It was always made clear to associations and to industrialists generally that consultation was for the purpose of securing advice derived from practical experience: all decisions rested with the Minister who took full responsibility for what the Department did or omitted to do. It was necessary to insist on this position'.[19]

The outbreak of war in 1939 brought renewed appeals from employers for the delegation of Departmental functions, and even Congress suggested the creation of a consultative Economic Council, representing the government, industry, agriculture and labour.[20] Fianna Fáil gave short shrift to these proposals, and tried to tackle neutral Ireland's economic difficulties through the emergency powers in force from 1939 to 1946. Wages, for example, were placed under statutory control in 1940–1. At the same time, the unprecedented authority assumed by the government inspired a series of initiatives so radical that they could be implemented only on the basis of collaboration with capital or labour. The first of these was the Trade Union Act (1941), introduced by Seán MacEntee, who replaced Lemass as Minister for Industry and Commerce between 1939 and 1941. The Act reflected the view, common to Fianna Fáil and Irish unions, that the key to better industrial relations was the rationalisation of trade unions, and aimed to eliminate union multiplicity by granting sole negotiation rights to unions representing a majority of workers in a particular category. British unions were precluded from obtaining such rights. It was rumoured at the time, and subsequently corroborated, that the Act was secretly prompted by William O Brien, General Secretary of the ITGWU, and many regarded it as a corporatist assault on trade union freedom, designed to create a more nationalist, and more compliant, ITGWU-dominated labour movement. A storm of protest ensued. But whilst Congress was nominally united, private sector Irish unions accepted that there was a case for rationalisation, and saw a potential in a new relationship with the state. With a high proportion of low-paid workers, they hoped that legislation might provide a substitute for wage militancy and a platform for membership growth. British unions, on the other hand, were ideologically committed to a residual state mode and, in Éire, were based mainly on craftsmen with a capacity for militancy, while public sector unions had a fixed membership potential. Enveloping the material imperatives, the Act inflamed an old, emotive debate about whether British unions ought to operate in Ireland. If the labour riposte to the Act was ineffective, the controversy, combined with wage control, rattled Fianna Fáil, causing a leakage of working-class votes to the Labour Party. On returning to Industry and Commerce, Lemass restored a more consensual style to Congress-government relations.

Lemass had no intention of undoing the substance of MacEntee's work. He envisaged the retention of wartime controls on capital and labour, proposing in 1942 the creation of a Department of Labour to regulate wages, industrial relations, labour mobility, emigration, welfare, and micro-economies in industry, and in 1944 the appointment of a state commission on wages and economic development.[21] When both ideas proved too far-reaching for de Valera, he tried to interest the Congresses and the FUE in linking wages with economic development. Meeting a further rebuff, he narrowed his immediate objectives to wage regulation, and eventually concluded that wage control could not be sustained. Ironically, his problems were compounded by the sheer inconvenience of negotiating with two antagonistic Congresses.

Another setback for Lemass occurred in 1946, when the Supreme Court found the crucial rationalisation measures in the Trade Union Act (1941) to be unconstitutional. He discussed another regulatory Act with the Congresses, only to find that neither was enthusiastic. His final initiative of the period was the Industrial Prices and Efficiency Bill, which proposed a prices and incomes policy, worker participation in management, and greater state intervention to promote efficiency. The Congresses were positive about aspects of the bill, but Lemass found the consultation process frustrating; it became evident, for example, that he would need to set up two prices advisory structures, one for each Congress. Employers were alarmed. And when the bill lapsed once Fianna Fáil went into opposition in 1948, employer resistance deterred a revival by later governments.

Lemass's corporatist initiatives failed for lack of political support, and because none of the protagonists was willing to make the necessary concessions. Fianna Fáil wanted a statutory mode in which the essential compromise would be between employers and unions. Employers wanted more influence over government policy without conceding their managerial prerogatives. Trade unions wanted price control, statutory support for the lower paid – and Irish unions wanted rationalisation – but not an incomes policy. The legacy of the period was the creation of national structures that generated a tempo for centralisation. There were lessons too. Fianna Fáil never again tried to impose extensive reform of industrial relations, while trade unions began a slow adjustment of attitudes towards cooperation with government.

The Revival of Corporatist Thinking, 1958–87

The Republic's economy stagnated in the 1950s. Against the backdrop of rapid Western European economic growth, soaring unemployment and emigration generated a crisis of national self-confidence. In the depths of gloom, Fianna Fáil returned to power for another sixteen- year stretch in 1957, with Lemass succeeding de Valera as Taoiseach [Prime Minister] in 1959. Lemass met the malaise with a historic U-turn; adopting an 'open-door' policy towards foreign investment, endorsing 'freer trade', and applying for Ireland to join the European Economic Community (EEC) in 1961. Membership of the EEC followed in 1973. The evident exhaustion of protectionism meant that there was little opposition to the new departure. Although trade unions later opposed entry into the EEC, they were supportive of 'freer trade' at this time. Moreover, Lemass's strategy led to fifteen years of economic expansion, net immigration and near full employment.

Preparing a highly protected economy for free trade prompted state initiatives in four areas: the adoption of an outline form of planning in three Programmes for Economic Expansion, launched between 1958 and 1969, the creation of tripartite consultative bodies on productivity and planning, reform of pay determination and reform of industrial relations.[22] In addition to the tripartite structures, trade unions and employers formed the Employer–Labour Conference (ELC). Lemass hoped that economic planning and consultation would entice unions into a voluntary incomes policy. Reform of pay determination and of industrial relations were also connected. Lemass had long held that free collective bargaining by a multiplicity of unions encouraged rank-and-file militancy, and that the answer lay in centralising authority, within unions, and within the industrial relations system: 'one of the main weaknesses in our present situation is the lack of cohesion and authority in the Trade Union movement', he told Jack Lynch, his successor as Taoiseach.[23] Ideally, he wanted voluntary reform. If necessary, he would resort to legislation. Either way, the industrial relations mode was to remain bipartite. Yet the mild bipartism of the 1960s functioned only with the support of a discreet tripartism, and deeper bipartism in the 1970s eventually gave way to open tripartism.

Lemass's strategy enjoyed limited success, facilitated by the consolidation of the FUE and ICTU during the 1960s. As the decade progressed, the FUE became openly favourable, and Congress leaders more sympathetic, towards centralised bargaining, and the tripartite National Industrial and Economic Council (NIEC) discussed linking economic planning and pay regulation. Workers' traditional suspicion of class collaboration was beginning to soften too. In 1960, Jim Larkin, Jr, secretary of the Workers' Union of Ireland, bemoaned the narrowness of the prevailing wage militant mentality. 'But what do we do about our backward economy? Get more wages! What do we do about the insecurity of jobs, and about unemployment and the under-employed? Get more wages! We can go on with rounds of wages increases [but] we will still have all these problems'.[24] Three years later he could tell his union's annual conference:

> I recall that some years ago if you mentioned the question of increased productivity in a trade union meeting, you would probably be expelled out of the union. Now we have not merely Productivity Committees but we have got the trade unions demanding the right to be represented on Productivity Committees, because the feeling has been developed at least on a limited scale that the efficient running of industry is not just the concern of the employer, or solely his responsibility.[25]

However, for most trade unionists, this budding bipartism stopped short at centralised wage bargaining. Threats of a statutory incomes policy, and legislation to restrict strikes all failed to deliver any substantial reform.

The maintenance men's dispute in 1969 finally created the climate for change. This six-week stoppage of some 3,000 industrial craftsmen in eighteen unions generated widespread disruption, resentment among general workers, and an embarrassing challenge to the authority of Congress. The strike also led to a 20 percent pay rise, inviting comparable claims from other workers.[26] The NIEC now took the view that the 'round' system, wherein pay increases had a 'knock-on' effect, was inherently unmanageable. In 1970 it recommended a bipartite body to set guidelines for wage determination. The government reconvened the ELC, and when the ICTU annual conference rejected a centralised pay agreement, introduced a bill for a statutory incomes policy. Congress then backed down and concluded the first National Wage Agreement (NWA). In return, the government offered some concessions to Congress and withdrew its bill.

Seven NWAs were concluded through the ELC between 1970 and 1978. Unlike previous national agreements, which merely set guidelines for decentralised bargaining, the NWAs marked a real departure. While the first five were bipartite, those concluded in 1977 and 1978 were tripartite. Even before 1977, the distinction between bipartism and tripartism was blurred by the Fine Gael–Labour Party coalition of 1973–7, which displaced statutory threats with budgetary inducements to sustain bipartism. By the mid-

1970s, the NWAs were generating a momentum towards social partnership. Employers were strongly in favour of central agreements, while both Congress and government sought to surmount trade union dissent through deepening tripartism. On returning to power in 1977 with an ambitious economic programme, to which pay restraint was integral, Fianna Fáil overcame mounting trade union misgivings about the NWAs by concluding the 'National Understandings for Social and Economic Development'. The two National Understandings of 1979 and 1980 were novel in that they involved the government directly in pay determination, and introduced two-tier agreements, the first relating to pay, and the second to public policy.

The collapse of tripartism in 1981, and its readoption in 1987, was due primarily to government policy. The political climate underwent a sea change in 1981–2, as concern with rising unemployment yielded to alarm at the escalation of public borrowing. The failure of successive governments to control exchequer spending, coupled with the political instability of 1981–2, when there were three general elections, created a sense of crisis. The Fine Gael-Labour coalitions of 1981–7 prioritised inflation and fiscal rectitude, and when talks on a third National Understanding reached an impasse on the pay element in 1981, the government did not intervene. None of the social partners were happy with the results of centralised bargaining, which had not brought lower inflation, industrial peace, wage moderation, or tax equity for workers in the Pay As You Earn sector.

Free collective bargaining in recessionary conditions did not restore the 'round' system in anything but name, and generally worked to the advantage of employers. While the macro-economic problems persisted in sufficient measure to entice employers into a new social partnership in 1987, the Programme for National Recovery was another example of Fianna Fáil seeking a special relationship with labour to cover an electoral flank. Crucial to the deal was the determination of Fianna Fáil leader Charles J. Haughey to neutralise trade union opposition to the swingeing cuts in public spending introduced by his minority government in 1987. This time, social partnership was judged to be a success, and vital to the economic transformation that followed. Only since that success have employers and Congress leaders come to join the political elite in espousing an ideological, as distinct from a tactical, proclivity for concertation.

Conclusion

Social partnership is not normally associated with a dependent economy, a sectionalist, decentralised trade unionism, and a political system dominated by 'catch-all' parties. Yet these factors explain both the tardy, ad hoc evolution of social partnership, and its eventual adoption. Reducing dependency legitimated strong state direction of the economy after 1932. After 1958, the dismantling of state controls on other areas of economic activity made the regulation of wage determination more important to public policy. Revision of pay bargaining was also integral to a wider, long-standing ambition to reform industrial relations by restructuring trade unionism. For government, employers and labour leaders, decentralised trade unionism acted as an incentive for concertation, even if trade union members did not always share that view.

Finally, the 'catch-all' nature of Fianna Fáil politics conceals the party's dependence on working-class support. Fianna Fáil's abandonment of the Sinn Féin ideal in 1958 weakened its capacity to rule through hegemony. The party's espousal of a more conventional centrist politics, and the growing institutional strength of the FUE and trade unions, required the adoption of a more co-equal relationship with employers and labour. Fianna Fáil was still slow to circumscribe its prerogatives, preferring to press for bipartite change through threats of legislative intervention, with occasional, and ineffective, appeals to patriotism or social responsibility; the 1973–7 Fine Gael–Labour coalition was the first to make real concessions to tripartism. Fianna Fáil's continuation of the process reflected an acceptance that it could no longer guide industrial relations 'from above', using the old weapons of threats and cajolery. The emergent concept of social partnership required more proximate, and material, state engagement if it were to mature. Haughey's inability to secure a parliamentary majority, together with the deteriorating condition of the economy and the public finances, convinced the great survivor to take the process across the Rubicon in 1987.

Notes

1. Unless otherwise stated, sources for the evolution of labour are based on Emmet O Connor, *A Labour History of Ireland, 1824–1960*, Dublin, 1992.
2. Donal Nevin, ed,. *Trade Union Century*, Dublin, 1994: 371.
3. Quoted in Emmet O Connor, *Syndicalism in Ireland, 1917–23*, Cork, 1988: 91.
4. For the political background see J.J. Lee, *Ireland, 1912–1985: Politics and Society*, Cambridge, 1989.
5. Mary E. Daly, *Industrial Development and Irish National Identity, 1922–39*, Dublin, 1992: 15.
6. Michael Gallagher, *Political Parties in the Republic of Ireland*, Manchester, 1985: 158.
7. The share of trade unionists in British unions declined in the south, to about 30 percent by 1930, and 14 percent in the 1980s. William K. Roche, 'Industrialisation and the development of industrial relations', in *Irish Industrial Relations in Practice*, ed. Thomas V. Murphy and William K. Roche, Dublin, 1994: 31. However, Congress retained its all-Ireland remit after partition in 1920–2, and British unions consolidated in Northern Ireland, where they accounted for 77 percent of trade unionists in 1987. Emmet O Connor, 'Labour and left politics', in *Northern Ireland Politics*, ed. Arthur Aughey and Duncan Morrow, London, 1996: 49. As Northern Ireland is largely an adjunct of the British industrial relations system, and has not developed social partnership, this account will be restricted to the Republic.
8. W.K. Roche and Joe Larragy, 'The trend of unionisation in the Irish Republic', in *Industrial Relations in Ireland: Contemporary Issues and Developments*, University College, Dublin, Dublin, 1989: 24–5.
9. Brendan MacPartlin, 'The development of trade union organisation', in *Irish Industrial Relations*, ed. Murphy and Roche: 103–4.

10. William K. Roche, 'The trend of unionisation', in *Irish Industrial Relations*, ed. Murphy and Roche: 61.
11. Nevin, *Trade Union Century*: 435.
12. Patrick Gunnigle, Gerry McMahon and Gerry Fitzgerald, *Industrial Relations in Ireland: Theory and Practice*, Dublin, 1995: 136.
13. Basil Chubb, ed., *FIE: Federation of Irish Employers, 1942–1992*, Dublin, 1992: 3–47.
14. Gunnigle et al., *Industrial Relations*: 136–7.
15. Maurice Manning, *The Blueshirts*, Dublin, 1970: 211–31.
16. See J.J. Lee, 'Aspects of corporatist thought in Ireland: the Commission on Vocational Organisation, 1939–43', in *Studies in Irish History*, ed. Art Cosgrove and Donal McCartney, Dublin, 1979: 324–46.
17. The leading biography is John Horgan, *Seán Lemass: The Enigmatic Patriot*, Dublin, 1997.
18. Daly, *Industrial Development*: 128–30.
19. Brian Farrell, *Seán Lemass*, Dublin, 1983: 26, 72.
20. Ibid., 72; O' Connor, *A Labour History*: 139.
21. On Lemass's corporatism see William K. Roche, 'Pay determination, the state, and the politics of industrial relations', in *Irish Industrial Relations,* ed. Murphy and Roche, 144–8.
22. In contrast with the earlier years, the post-1958 period is reasonably well covered in industrial relations studies. For the corporatist theme, see especially Roche, 'Pay determination', in *Irish Industrial Relations*, ed. Murphy and Roche, 126–205; 'Industrial relations', in *Trade Union Century*, Nevin, 133–46; and Niamh Hardiman, *Pay, Politics, and Economic Performance in Ireland, 1970–1987*, Oxford, 1988; and 'Pay bargaining; confrontation and consensus', in *Trade Union Century*, Nevin, 147–58.
23. Horgan, *Lemass*, 229.
24. Manus O Riordan, 'James Larkin Junior and the forging of a thinking intelligent movement', *Saothar* 19 (1994): 60.
25. Ibid., 62–3.
26. For an account of the strike see Charles McCarthy, *The Decade of Upheaval: Irish Trade Unions in the Nineteen Sixties*, Dublin, 1973.

CHAPTER 12

IRELAND IN THE 1990S: POLICY CONCERTATION TRIUMPHANT

Rory O'Donnell and Damian Thomas

Introduction

This paper describes and explains the remarkable revival and evolution of social partnership in Ireland in the period 1987–97. We begin by identifying the key organisations and institutions of the social partnership, outlining the policy content of the four national partnership agreements, and describing the processes of deliberation and bargaining. Next, the ideas, arguments and values relating to the Irish social partnership are discussed, emphasising the development of a shared understanding of the key mechanisms in the Irish economy. Finally, we outline our explanation of the evolution and maintenance of the Irish Social Partnership since 1987.

Policy Concertation since 1987: Institutions and Participants

The participants in the first three national partnership agreements since 1987 were the traditional social partners: the peak federations representing capital and labour, the principal farming organisations and the government (Table 12.1).

The most recent national agreement, Partnership 2000, (see Table 12.2) witnessed a significant widening of participation, with the inclusion of the community and voluntary sector (referred to as the Social Pillar).

Table 12.1. *Participants in Irish Policy Concertation 1987–96*

National Agreement	Government	Trade Unions	Employers	Farming Organisations*
PNR 1987–90	Fianna Fáil minority government	ICTU	Federation of Irish Employers (FIE), Confederation of Irish Industry (CII), Construction Industry Federation (CIF)	IFA, ICOS, Macra na Feirme
PESP 1991–3	Fianna Fáil–Progressive Democrat coalition government	ICTU	FIE, CII, CIF	IFA, ICOS, Macra na Feirme, ICMSA[1]
PCW 1994–96	Fianna Fáil–Labour coalition government	ICTU	IBEC[2], CIF	IFA, ICOS, Macra na Feirme, ICMSA

Source: see text.
*See Table 12.2 for full names of farming organisations.

Table 12.2. *Participants in Irish Policy Concertation 1997–2000 (Partnership 2000)*

Type	Organisation
Government	The Rainbow Coalition (Centre Left) Fine Gael; Labour Party; Democratic Left
Farming Organisations	IFA : Irish Farming Association ICMSA: Irish Creamery and Milk Suppliers Association Macra Na Feirme ICOS: Irish Co-operative Society
Trade Unions	ICTU : Irish Congress of Trade Unions
Employer and Business Organisations	IBEC: Irish Business and Employers Confederation CIF: Construction Industry Federation CCI: Chambers of Commerce of Ireland ITIC: Irish Tourist Industry Confederation IEA: Irish Exporters Association SFA: Small Firms Association
The Social Pillar: Community and Voluntary Organisations	INOU : Irish National organisation for the Unemployed NWCI: National Women's Council of Ireland NYCI: National Youth Council of Ireland CORI: Committee of Religious Superiors Centres for the Unemployed Society of St. Vincent de Paul Protestant Aid Community Platform[3]

Source: see text.

Trade Unions

ICTU (the Irish Congress of Trade Unions) is the peak labour association, representing some 435,000 workers and accounting for approximately 90 percent of all trade unionists in the country. Earlier studies of neo-corporatist concertation in Ireland highlighted the lack of a concentrated and centralised labour movement in explaining the instability and ineffectiveness of earlier social partnership style arrangements.[4] While trade union merger activity has intensified since 1980, ICTU remains a relatively fragmented movement. However, as Roche stresses, despite a fragmented organisational structure the Irish trade union movement has displayed a capacity to act in a concerted manner and to pursue policies that are in significant respects class oriented.[5] Similarly, while ICTU's influence and authority within the labour movement has been enhanced during the period of social partnership, this reflects both its success at operating within the national political domain since 1987 and its moral authority premised on internal democratic mechanisms, rather than any formal centralisation of decision-making power.

Employers

Irish employers were traditionally represented by two national organisations, the Federation of Irish Employers (FIE) and Confederation of Irish Industry (CII).[6] However, they had considerable overlap in membership and closely coordinated their activities. Their amalgamation in 1993 to form the Irish Business and Employers Confederation (IBEC) was a significant development as it meant that there was now a more unified 'voice' for business in social partnership. In the leadership's view, this has increased their capacity to formulate and pursue a longer-term, more strategically focused, business agenda.[7] It is important to recognise that, as with ICTU, there has been no formal change in the authority of the central leadership to ensure membership compliance with IBEC policy and that acceptance of national agreements remains dependent on an internal vote.[8]

Political Parties

The role of Fianna Fáil in engineering the return to social partnership in 1987, the initial opposition of other political parties, the fact that it resonated so strongly with the party's traditional promulgation of social solidarity,[9] and their electoral dependency on the 'working class' constituency,[10] all tend to suggest that partnership is dependent on this centrist catch-all party.[11] However, since 1987 the party composition of Irish government has undergone rapid change. Indeed, party politics has moved towards a system of permanent, but frequently renegotiated, coalition. Social partnership has not only survived this increasing volatility, but has been virtually institutionalised within the Irish political landscape (see Tables 12.1 and 12.2). There now exists an identifiable cross-party consensus that this represents a viable and appropriate approach to the formulation of economic and social policy.[12]

Agricultural Interests

Irish national farming organisations have, since the mid-1960s, enjoyed a close working relationship with the Department of Agriculture.[13] This has been characterised as both a policy network[14] and a closed policy community.[15] It is generally recognised that outside of their own sectional concerns the farming bodies' role in recent social partnership is somewhat limited and largely parallels an existing meso or sectoral corporatist relationship.

NESC

The National Economic and Social Council (NESC) was established in 1973 as the successor to the National Industrial and Economic Council. Its membership is drawn from the traditional social partners, senior civil servants and government nominees. The remit of the Council is to seek consensus on economic and social issues and to advise the government through the Taoiseach (Prime Minister). The Council's work was important in the re-establishment of social partnership arrangements in 1987 and, since then, has played a key role in shaping the direction of economic and social policy within the state.

Central Review Committee

Under the PNR (Programme for National Recovery), a tripartite Central Review Committee (CRC) was established to oversee and monitor the implementation of the national agreement and in particular to ensure that commitments were being met and that each of the parties was acting in accordance with the terms of the agreement. Some consider that this body was to develop into one of the key institutions of the social partnership as its role evolved beyond formal monitoring. During the first three years the CRC was central to the smooth functioning of the partnership process, and one senior figure described it as 'the oil in the gearbox'.[16] The CRC has subsequently been replaced by the Partnership 2000 monitoring committee on which all the social partners are represented, but the current opinion is that the rather unwieldy structure of this new committee has prevented it from developing an effective role.

NESF

In 1993, the government established a new partnership body, the National Economic and Social Forum (NESF).[17] Its membership encompasses the 'traditional social partners' plus representatives from both the community and voluntary sector and opposition political parties. The role of the NESF is to develop economic and social policy initiatives, especially to combat unemployment and inequality, and to contribute to the formation of a national consensus on social and economic matters. Since its establishment, and subsequent re-appointment in 1995, the Forum has published sixteen reports and eight opinions.

The Policy Content of the National Agreement Programmes

The Programme for National Recovery re-established centralised wage bargaining in Ireland as the social partners and government brokered an agreement that set wage levels in both the private and public sectors for an unprecedented three-year period (Table 12.3). While ICTU's willingness to assent to a relatively moderate and restrictive pay deal surprised commentators and participants alike,[18] it clearly reflected their desire to 'make consensus work' and the extreme difficulties faced by Irish workers. Over the period 1981–7 real take-home pay had been eroded by 7 percent and a principal concern was to 'halt this decline'.[19]

Additionally, moderate wage growth was recognised by the social partners as essential to international competitiveness and control of public expenditure. While pay was and probably remains the 'glue' of the process, PNR and subsequent partnership programmes involved agreement on a wide range of economic and social policies, including tax reform, the evolution of welfare payments, health spending, structural adjustments and Ireland's adherence to the narrow band of the ERM (Exchange Rate Mechanism) and the Maastricht criteria (Table 12.3). PNR saw the adoption of a coordinated response to economic difficulties with a strong emphasis on establishing a stable macroeconomic framework and ensuring the reduction of the debt /GDP ratio. In this context, each partner agreed not to generate inflationary pressures that would warrant devaluation or to seek devaluation when external problems arose. Significantly, the negotiation of PNR signalled the trade unions' willingness to support the radical correction of public finances in return for a commitment to maintain the level and value of social welfare payments. The document also contained a relatively extensive section on employment generation. However, this effectively amounted to a list of rather vague policy aspirations and PNR certainly was not a 'wages for jobs' trade-off.

The three subsequent agreements, the Programme for Economic and Social Progress (PESP), the Programme for Competitiveness and Work (PCW) and Partnership 2000 have displayed a similar form and policy content (Table 12.3). Through the (re)negotiation of these successive national agreements, the social partners have aligned themselves to a consistent and coherent consensus-based strategic framework focused on macroeconomic policy, income distribution and structural adjustment.[20] The setting of pay increases over three years for the public and private sectors has continued, although both PESP and Partnership 2000 included an element of local bargaining. Critically, the pay moderation that has characterised all four agreements has become dependent on a combination of low inflation and fiscal compensation.[21]

A macroeconomic strategy based on the ERM and EMU (Economic and Monetary Union) and the reduction of the national debt burden has remained constant throughout all four agreements. Within this policy continuity there have been, however, key policy innovations. The PESP estab-

Table 12.3. Content of Policy Concertation in Ireland

Programme for National Recovery 1987–90	
Pay Terms	Pay moderation with prospect of fiscal compensation (tax reform); floor for low- paid workers; phasing in of special awards in the public service; no cost- increasing claims allowable; inability to pay clause
Key Policies	Integrated strategy for economic and social development; stable macroeconomic framework (low interest and low inflation regime, non- accommodating exchange rate); reaffirmation of ERM membership; maintenance of social welfare transfer payments; control of public expenditure
Institutions	Central Review Committee established
Programme for Economic and Social Progress 1991–4	
Pay Terms	Pay moderation and fiscal compensation; floor for the low-paid; local bargaining increases of up to 3 percent allowable
Key Policies	Continuation of policy framework established by PNR; targets set for reduction of debt/GNP ratio; responsible, consensus-based income policies at the national level within the framework of macroeconomic stability affirmed as the optimum route to employment growth; establishment of Area- Based Partnerships (PESP Partnerships) to address economic and social deprivation
Institutions	Central Review Committee
Programme for Competitiveness and Work 1994–6	
Pay Terms	Continuation of pay moderation, fiscal compensation; no local bargaining clause
Key Policies	Renewed focus on employment generation; further development of active labour market policies; targets set for reduction of debt/GNP ratio
Institutions	Central Review Committee
Partnership 2000 1997–2000	
Pay Terms	Explicit wage moderation /tax concession trade- off; local bargaining increases linked to productivity and adoption of modernisation programme in public sector
Key Policies	Commitment to deepen and widen participation in social partnership; tackling social exclusion established as a strategic objective; recognition of need to extend partnership to the level of the firm; targets set for reduction of debt/GNP ratio
Institutions	Partnership 2000 Monitoring Committee established to replace CRC with representatives from all four pillars of the partnership; National Centre for Partnership established to promote and facilitate enterprise- level partnership; High Level Expert Group (tripartite) formed to examine trade union recognition

Source: see text.

lished twelve area-based local partnerships to tackle unemployment and social exclusion and this has subsequently been extended to thirty-three such bodies. A recent OECD evaluation of Ireland's local economic development policies considered that the local partnership approach constituted an experiment in economic regeneration and participative democracy of potentially international significance.[22] The latest agreement, Partnership 2000, seeks to address the limited diffusion of enterprise-level partnership through the establishment of the National Centre for Partnership. The agreement also seeks to modernise the public service by enlisting social partner support for the implementation of the Strategic Management Initiative and linking the additional payments under the local bargaining clause to organisational change. The agreement also established the alleviation of social exclusion as a strategic objective and additional funding was assigned for this task.

The Process of Deliberation, Bargaining and Monitoring

NESC's 1986 *Strategy* outlined the social partners' 'common analysis' of the economic and fiscal malaise and their consensus-based policy prescription for addressing this crisis, and each national agreement has been preceded by a NESC Strategy document.[23] The Council's1986 *Strategy* and subsequent strategy reports (1990, 1993, 1996) provided both the impetus and the theoretical framework for a return to centralised concertation. Indeed, this informal process has become institutionalised over the course of the social partnership. NESC performs a function of 'attitudinal structuring' in which the key actors seek to establish a common agenda through intensive debate and negotiation. A number of participants highlight the importance of the deliberative process, as this not only facilitates the forging of a shared understanding but also fosters trust, mutual respect and a better understanding of other parties' interests and identity.[24] Over the last decade NESC has played a pivotal role in social partnership by building and maintaining consensus among the key actors and by shaping the policy repertoire of the agreements. While there is a strong emphasis on fostering a shared understanding, it is also recognised that the formulation of the *Strategy* document represents the first stage in the 'bargaining process' for a national agreement.

While the CRC was established to perform a monitoring role, it also served as an important arena of interaction in which participants could continue to negotiate and bargain over the direction of social partnership. The CRC was particularly important for the trade union movement as it offered them institutionalised access to government ministers and key civil servants.[25] The CRC was also a forum in which issues could be resolved informally before they became 'problematic' and, indeed, any issue that was considered to impinge on the 'atmosphere' of the social partnership could be raised in this forum.[26]

The fact that the traditional social partners negotiated the first three agreements (Table 12.1) and that the pay element was central to all four (Table 12.3) highlights the role of functional economic interdependence in the evolution of the Irish social partnership. While the traditional 'social partners' have long enjoyed a relatively high, if variable, degree of political access, social partnership has resulted in a more institutionalised, structured and regularised mode of interest- group participation.[27]

The establishment of NESF represented an attempt to broaden participation in the deliberative process beyond the traditional social partners, and has been described as an important innovation in public consultation through partnership.[28] The Forum has exerted some influence over policy design, in particular through its Report No. 4, *Ending Long Term Unemployment*, which played a strategic role in the development of an active labour market policy.[29] Despite these achievements, it was recognised that participation in the partnership process remained unevenly developed.[30] Groups such as INOU, The Community Workers' Co-operative and CORI argued that the 'third strand's' involvement through NESF and ad hoc task forces was effectively 'participation without power', and their relative inability to exert any discernible influence on public policy was institutionalised and perpetuated by their lack of full social partner status.[31] The decision to significantly widen participation by fully incorporating the 'third strand' into the negotiation and ratification of Partnership 2000, and to accord full partner status to the social pillar, represented a potentially innovative development in the evolution of economic and social governance (Tables 12.1 and 12.2).[32]

The widening of participation certainly changed the dynamics and mechanics of the negotiating process. Figure 12.1 illustrates the model that was adopted for Partnership 2000. Apart from an initial multilateral session,[33] discussions were conducted bilaterally between the 'rooms' and the government's negotiating team.[34] ICTU and IBEC / CIF were thus conceptualised as constituting one 'room', given their responsibility for the negotiation of the pay and tax elements of the agreement.[35] Subsequently the 'business room' comprised those business organisations who were not directly involved in the pay negotiations, namely the SFA, ITIC, IEA and CCI (see Table 12.2).[36] The social pillar was critical of the fact that this precluded any substantive three-way negotiation of the distribution of resources between pay, tax and social exclusion measures. From the perspective of the trade unions and employers, it was indicative of the fact that pay is 'the glue' of the national agreements and that this rationale must be reflected in the negotiations. While the social pillar was clearly a 'junior partner' within Partnership 2000, it did partake in substantive negotiations and has been afforded an equal role in the monitoring the development of social partnership.[37]

The discourse, bargaining and trade-offs that were channelled through this formal mode of negotiation were reinforced and paralleled by extensive informal interaction between the participants. The consensus among the participants was that the skill and acumen of the negotiators from the Department of the Taoiseach were critical to the success of this complex discursive process.[38] It was they who had the pivotal role of formulating the views, concerns and objectives of all the 'rooms' into a final document that all the participants could 'live' with.

Figure 12.1. *The Four Room Negotiating Model in Ireland*

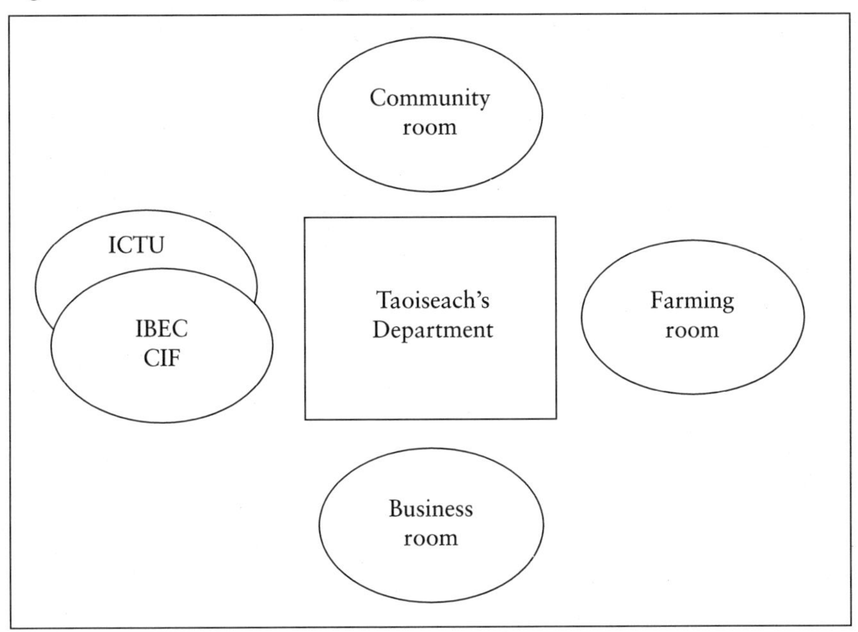

The content, process and participation in the recent Irish agreements suggests that the conceptualisation of social partnership as a model of tripartite functional economic interdependence is increasingly insufficient, as there is a nascent 'corporate pluralism' emerging in which there is regularised, compartmentalised and structured co-option into the public policy process for a diverse network of interest groups.[39] These developments at national level, in conjunction with partnership initiatives at the local level, are indicative of the innovative attempts to reconfigure the relationship between representative and participative democracy, which are fostering new forms of deliberative democracy. This emerging post- corporatist governance in its tripartite or more heterogeneous forms has not replaced but coexists and overlaps with pluralist modes of policy in a shifting and dynamic relationship,[40] effectively generating hybrid forms of governance both within and between policy spheres.

Ideas of Social Partnership

The terms used to refer to Irish social partnership since 1987, which are summarised in Table 12.4, reflect the conditions of its emergence and its evolution over the past decade. The conditions of its emergence have shaped terminology and description in two ways. First, its emergence as a response to deep economic and social crisis meant that it was described and defended primarily in economic terms. Second, it emerged in a country that seemed to lack the institutional, political and structural conditions considered necessary for effective corporatist concertation.[41] These made participants and observers reluctant to characterise the new experiment in conventional corporatist terms, in which the structural and institutional characteristics of organisations are highlighted as the major conditions for success. In this sense, the conceptualisation of the current Irish experiment is in tune with an important emergent stand in the international literature on corporatism that also rejects the emphasis on structural considerations.[42]

The terms of reference for this study distinguish between economic arguments for social partnership, on the one hand, and ideas and norms, such as social harmony, on the other. In order to explain the re-emergence and suc-

Table 12.4. *Key Terms in Ireland*

Term	Usage	Meaning
Negotiated consensus	Core idea in recent partnership	Refers both to the policy-making process which underpins the social partnership and to the policies of the national agreements.
Centralised pay agreement	Common among journalists and some economists	The setting of pay terms for the public and private sectors through negotiations between the government and peak associations representing capital and labour
Social partnership	Most common term among participants	All-encompassing phrase to describe the process whereby the government and the social partners have cooperated in the formulation of economic and social policy since 1987.
Political exchange	Used in a small number of academic commentaries	The principal participants engage in negotiations and bargaining in which they 'exchange'resources. The important characteristic of this process is that the labour market parties transfer bargaining from the labour market to the political arena.
National programme	Refers to triennial agreements since 1987	The three-year programmes which establish both pay terms and the broad strategy for economic and social policy
Corporatism / neo-corporatism	Seldom used in Irish discourse	Institutionalised bargaining between peak associations of labour and capital and the government in which the state becomes a partner in collective bargaining and in return assigns a role in the policy-making process to the social partners. Consequently collective bargaining over pay is tied to broader decision making over economic and social policy.

Source: see text.

cess of Irish social partnership, we propose to extend the framework somewhat. We strongly support the implicit rejection of organisational structure as the key condition for, and explanation of, social partnership. However, the Irish case suggests that we do not face a straight choice between organisational structure and values in seeking to explain partnership. An important factor in recent Irish social partnership is the emergence of a shared picture of the Irish economy and, to a lesser extent, a shared picture of Irish politics and society. This involved a macroeconomic strategy based on ERM, EMU and debt reduction, negotiated consensus on wages, taxation, welfare and public provision, and particular emphasis on the role of structural adjustment and supply-side improvements in enhancing institutional competitiveness.[43]

Arguments for Social Partnership

The arguments for social partnership are summarised in Table 12.5. Here we briefly comment on the shared reasons for partnership, and the logic of trade union, employer and government support and opposition.

Shared reasons

It is clear from Table 12.5 that the shared perspective on the Irish economy, outlined above, is strongly reflected in the arguments advanced collectively by the social partners in successive NESC *Strategy* reports. The common theme in all these arguments is that given the structure of the economy, industrial relations and politics, cooperative approaches to policy making and implementation are superior. The urgency of the issues and the achievement of a new, problem-solving form of cooperation has not only assuaged fears regarding a rehash of earlier failed experiments in concertation but has also generated a commitment to addressing issues through dialogue and cooperation.

The emphasis on structural adjustment and programmes to combat exclusion yielded a second kind of rationale for the partnership approach. As noted above, the PESP initiated an area-based partnership approach to long-term unemployment and local regeneration. This complemented the EC's approach to regional and urban development. The design of these approaches, and reflection on their successes and failures, led the social partners, government and public agencies to articulate the view that the diversity and complexity of social and economic conditions makes it impossible to solve problems with traditional policy-making and administrative systems. State policy, government departments and administrative agencies require the active involvement of affected groups if they are to formulate and organise effective policy approaches. Thus, a part of the emerging Irish system has been the attempt to find a partnership approach in training, active labour market policy, education, anti-poverty work, local development and policy to combat drug abuse. In evaluating these efforts and articulating this approach, the partnership bodies have drawn on the international discussion of new forms of governance, including ideas of 'associative democracy',

Table 12.5. *Key Arguments in Ireland*

Proponent	Argument
For	
NESC	Delivers modest and predictable wage growth which has enhanced competitiveness Supports the correction of public finances Facilitates tax reform Removes inflation/exchange rates from industrial relations and political conflict Assists adherence to, and secures benefits of EMU and ERM Reduces industrial conflict Assists restructuring and reform of public sector Protects distributive policies Improves the quality and effectiveness of public policy
ICTU	Delivers real income growth through modest pay increases in conjunction with tax reductions, lower inflation and lower interest rates Offers organised labour a political voice Provides institutional support and legitimisation for the trade union movement Concertative approach to collective bargaining necessary to secure members interests
IBEC	Delivers modest and predictable wage increases Secures and maintains a low inflation, low interest rate regime Compatible with the pursuit of firm-based strategies for flexibilisation
Government	Economic success Political legitimisation and credibility
Against	
Liberal Economists	'Politicisation of industrial relations adds to the bargaining power of trade unions on an ongoing basis' Protects 'insiders' against 'outsiders who would work for less', so 'raising the level of unemployment and emigration' Increases rigidity of the labour market Inconsistent with ERM and EMU
Some politicians and political observers	By-passes parliament Multi-annual agreement ties the hands of newly elected government Undemocratic and stifles debate 'Consensus' is harmful to policy choice
Industrial relations scholars	Not 'social' corporatism or 'egalitarian' wage policy National partnership not reflected at enterprise level
Trade unionists	Institutionalises pay restraint Ties unions into supporting an overtly business agenda Restricts the development of alternative strategies

Table 12.5. *Continued*

Proponent	Argument
Community and voluntary sector	Not sufficiently inclusive Inclusion constitutes responsibility without power Social exclusion and poverty remain unacceptably high despite growth
ISME (small business)	Barrier to labour market deregulation Exclusionary process Designed specifically to meet the needs of larger firms

Source: see text.

'negotiated governance' and 'private-interest governance'.[44] This is reflected in the arguments for partnership summarised in Table 12.5.

Union Support

For ICTU's leadership, the re-establishment of institutionalised political exchange represented an opportunity to undo the marginalisation of the labour movement that had occurred during the 1980s and to avoid the even worse fate of trade unionism in Britain.[45] Indeed the partnership approach precluded any attempt to address Ireland's problems with a neo-liberal and exclusionary approach.

Having acquired political influence, ICTU is eager to retain this institutionalised role, which has enabled it to function as the quasi-political voice of 'workers'. Although the pay terms in the agreements have been moderate they have, in conjunction with fiscal compensation, low inflation and reduced interest rates, delivered real increases in take- home pay, which contrasts starkly with the period 1981–7. While embracing the shared understanding of the economic realties and principles that underpin the social partnership, ICTU's support remains conditional. This conditional and pragmatic approach means that criticisms of social partnership, such as inadequate workplace partnership, are conceptualised not as reasons to end social partnership, but rather as objectives to be pursued further within the context of it.

Trade Union Opposition

British-based and many Irish craft unions have retained their traditional ideological opposition to any form of centralised agreement that curtails unions' rights to engage in free collective bargaining.[46] In addition there is a growing perception among trade unionists that recent agreements have been unduly restrictive given the unprecedented levels of economic growth. Finally, there is concern that social partnership offers the labour movement only an illusion of power and is a form of political incorporation in which it is tied to a business agenda. The failure to adequately address the issues of trade union recognition or to translate the national consensus into firm-level partnership is considered indicative of the power imbalance inherent within social partnership.

Employer Support

The employer bodies entered the 1987 agreement due to their acute fear of the macroeconomic situation, seeing it as a way to stabilise public finances. Over the course of the past decade their attachment to the partnership approach has widened and deepened and their initial concerns about centralised bargaining have dissipated. IBEC and its affiliates value highly the predictable and moderate wage environment, low interest and low inflation regime, and macroeconomic stability. While the national partnership has improved employer-union relations, at the national level it has not prevented the pursuit of flexibilisation strategies at the level of the firm.[47] Indeed, it is arguable that the national consensus has impinged only marginally on managerial prerogative within individual enterprises.[48]

Employer Opposition

The Irish Small and Medium Enterprise (ISME) federation has offered the most sustained attack on social partnership from the business community. The often vitriolic nature of their comments on social partnership is partially ideologically motivated, as they remain strong advocates of extensive labour market deregulation and resent what they see as the undue influence of ICTU over government policy. They are also critical of the role played by IBEC which, they argue, pursues an agenda designed to meet the needs of larger firms and foreign- owned companies to the detriment of indigenous SMEs. Ironically, however, their stance also reflects their resentment at not being offered a role in the negotiation of the pay terms of the national agreement.[49] While IBEC remains a strong advocate of the partnership process, it has been consistently critical of the failure of successive governments to reform public sector industrial relations and to control public service pay.

Nothing Succeeds Like Success

Social partnership arrangements were re-established in Ireland as a response to a deep and protracted fiscal, economic and political crisis. The role of social partnership in contributing to the turn-around in Irish economic performance has greatly increased the salience of many of the shared arguments for the partnership approach. Moreover, it has ensured that there is an inevitable reluctance among the participants to dismantle a process that is seen as one of the foundations of Ireland's recent success. Of course, economic success can weaken some of the sectional arguments for continuation of partnership, as is evident in the growing concern among trade unionists that they are receiving an inadequate share in the economic boom.

Arguments Against and Criticisms of Social Partnership

In reporting arguments against social partnership, we include criticisms that do not lead to opposition to the partnership approach. The arguments and criticisms are summarised in Table 12.5.

The main arguments against social partnership come from liberal economists who reject significant parts of the social partners' shared understanding of the mechanisms and relationships in the Irish economy. Some have objected to the politicisation of industrial relations because it 'adds to the bargaining power of trade unionism on an ongoing basis.[50] Others have argued that the social partners are 'insiders' whose pay and conditions have been protected at the expense of 'outsiders who would work for less', and that social partnership has had the effect of 'raising the level of unemployment and emigration.[51] An aspect of the strategy that has particularly provoked orthodox and neo-liberal economists is EMU. A preference for the British model of economic and social policy (of the 1980s) is combined with a preference for sterling rather than the Euro.[52] Having failed to shake the consensus on EMU, they argued that EMU (without the UK) requires the abandonment of centralised wage bargaining.

Related arguments against the social partnership derive from the idea that social partnership represents a challenge to representative democracy by giving power to unelected interest groups, by-passing Parliament, stifling debate and tying the hands of newly-elected governments.[53] A few senior politicians have argued that the approach is positively harmful, since the need to achieve a wide consensus prevents clear policy choices.

Other criticisms of social partnership have come from students of industrial relations. Teague disputes that the current Irish experiment can be viewed as *social* corporatism, arguing that it represents the trade union elite consenting to a programme of severe measures to adjust the Irish economy first to fiscal crisis and then to European integration.[54] In addition, it was pointed out by both trade unionists and industrial relations scholars that social partnership at national level is weakly reflected in workplace industrial relations.[55]

Organisations such as the Irish National Organisation for the Unemployed (INOU) and CORI were originally critical of the exclusionary nature of the social partnership process prior to Partnership 2000 (see Table 12.1). While the Social Pillar perceived their involvement in Partnership 2000 as representing a step towards full partner status, they remained concerned over their continued exclusion from the negotiations over pay and taxation.[56] Although they accepted Partnership 2000, they consider the resources allocated to fighting social exclusion to be insufficient and continue to question the other partners' commitment to this objective.

Values in Revent Irish Social Partnership

It is clear from the above that the re-emergence and development of Irish social partnership has been primarily supported by a particular outlook on the Irish economy. As noted above, an outlook on the weakness of Ireland's political system might be seen as implicit, but is seldom articulated explicitly. What about the value or normative dimension? In our view, identification of the nature and role of values in recent partnership is a difficult exercise, and is one to which we return towards the end of the paper. In this section we set out some of the obvious ways in which values have figured in the formulation and discussion of social partnership.

Evidence of Social Solidarity in the Partnership Programmes

A significant element of social solidarity was implicit in the first of the four agreements, with the principle that welfare recipients should not bear the burden of the sharp fiscal correction (Table 12.3). This element of social solidarity is more explicit in subsequent agreements, in which active policy approaches to address long-term unemployment and social exclusion played a central role. ICTU, in particular, drove the adoption of the area-based partnership approach to tackling spatially concentrated economic and social deprivation, and consistently claims to articulate the interests of a broader social constituency.[57] While we should not exaggerate the degree of solidarity shown by trade unions and others, the partnership approach has eventually yielded a situation in which fast economic growth is translating into dramatic growth of employment, rather than strong wage growth.

Social Partnership, Participation and Irish Society

In its 1996 *Strategy* report, NESC outlined its general orientation as one that begins from the belief that 'the widest participation in social life, economic activity and policy-making are inseparable and fundamental requirements for the well-being of Irish society' (p. 63). In setting out an action programme for social inclusion, the Council added:

> The inclusiveness and quality of relationships in social life, communities, economic life and public governance are goals in themselves. These are desirable, quite apart from the fact that inclusive and co-operative participation is productive – economically, socially and in public policy terms. (p. 175).

This is clearly both a functional and normative argument for partnership as a route to participation. Indeed, the Council went somewhat further, tentatively arguing that the partnership 'model of policy-making, business and industrial relations is also consistent with some enduring features of Irish society'.[58] 'Consequently, in the Irish case, social partnership can be more than an industrial relations system' (p. 65). The Council added, however, that 'this apparent fit between the emerging model of policy-making, business and industrial relations, on the one hand, and the characteristics of Irish society, on the other, is hugely qualified by the continuing problem of long-term unemployment and social exclusion'.

Widening Partnership Beyond the Traditional Social Partners

As noted above, an important feature of recent development has been the attempt to widen partnership beyond the traditional social partners. This widening is undoubtedly evidence of an element of social solidarity. There was initial resistance on the part of both trade unions and employers to the inclusion of the voluntary and community sector in national bodies such as NESC and the CRC but, over time, both unions and employers have come to accept the involvement of the community and voluntary sector as a fact of life, although some retain strong reservations about their modus operandi and ability to play the role of social partners.

If the widening of social partnership is evidence of a particular kind of social solidarity, there is a second sense in which it has brought normative issues to the surface. In comparison with trade unions, employers or farm organisations, the voluntary and community sectors tend to make their case in a far more normative manner. This is partly because they see themselves as having fewer power resources or bargaining chips. In part, it is because moral commitments play a prominent role in motivating the involvement of individuals in the voluntary and community sector. Many in that sector see the elements of solidarity in the first three partnership programmes as very limited, and entirely inadequate given the extent of social inequality and disadvantage. As a result, discussion in the National Economic and Social Forum has included debate on alternative visions of society and alternative 'models of development'. This has sometimes strained relations between 'old' and 'new' social partners, and has recently led to sustained reflection on how a wide model of social partnership can be made to work more effectively.[59]

Summary: Four Sets of Values in Evidence

In summary, it is possible to make an initial statement of the value dimension of recent partnership. It is clear that an old-fashioned notion of social solidarity – in the sense of a commitment to social stability through plural representation of different class or occupational groups within a liberal economic and political order – has played some role in supporting recent developments. Some version of that idea of social solidarity has been a feature not only of Irish trade unions, employers' associations and farm organisations, but also of Irish political parties.

A second notion of solidarity is also evident: class solidarity. The ICTU has emerged as the voice of Irish workers across a wide occupational and income range, largely because the issue of income tax has re-aggregated interests even when economic change is dis-aggregating them. While this intra-class solidarity is not generally articulated in traditional class terms its relevance is confirmed by the fact that trade union leaders have to defend social partnership in class solidarity terms against left-wing critics and craft-based adversaries within the union movement. Having said that, it is clear that solidaristic wage policy – in the sense of evening up wages across the economy – is a less important part of Irish partnership than it was in certain Scandinavian cases.

A third form of social solidarity is that between the employed and the unemployed/marginalised. This has been an important aspect of the new partnership model. It is expressed in several ways: modest wage growth, innovation in and extension of anti-exclusion policies, and widening of the partnership process. The widening of the partnership process has in turn brought a fourth value dimension into the picture: a critique of the Irish model of development as inherently unjust, and the argument that partnership is merely about 'distribution' within that model of development rather than a route to an alternative model.[60]

While the role of these values must be recognised, we do not consider that they are the main rationale or explanation for the emerging Irish model of social partnership. Indeed, it would appear that it was the return to tripartite concertation that has actually facilitated the re-articulation and reaffirmation of these values within the policy arena. Moreover, it is arguable that these values have, to some extent, been redefined during this era of social partnership.

Explaining Irish Social Partnership, 1987–98

The editors of this volume pose two related questions. First, what kinds of factors explain social partnership: organisational structures, economic advantages or ideas/values? Second, are the explanatory factors conjunctural, cyclical or long-term?

Since Hardiman's important work, few believe that organisational structures of a conventionally neo-corporatist kind can be found in Ireland. A case can be made for the continuity of the new social partnership with earlier Irish patterns of tripartite negotiation. One is that Irish society and politics displays an organic element that attaches high value to a certain kind of social solidarity, perhaps reflecting Catholic social thought.[61] In a sense, the sceptical view in Hardiman's 1988 book is also a continuity argument, suggesting that temporary success is likely to be undone by underlying structural weaknesses. In the historical chapter in this volume, Emmet O'Connor presents an interpretation which combines both continuity and change. The continuous factor is Fianna Fáil's strategy of 'seeking a special relationship with labour to cover an electoral flank'; the change is the willingness of employers and unions, after the success of 1987–90, to 'join the political elite in espousing an ideological, as distinct from a tactical, proclivity for concertation'.

We are sceptical of any argument that explains Irish social partnership since 1987 by reference to a continuity of values, norms or ideas. The two most obvious values – the Catholic idea of social solidarity and the union idea of class solidarity – have been roughly constant during the twentieth century. Yet social concertation has had a fitful existence. We find it hard to see how these values can explain the absence, then the failure, and finally the success of social partnership. We see these values as background features, and wonder whether they are sufficiently distinct to constitute an explanation of social partnership in one society rather than another.

This does not imply that we reject entirely an explanation in which values play some role. The relevant values in the recent period are those implicit in the combination of bargaining, solidarity, deliberation and problem solving, outlined above. We are in no doubt that there is a value dimension to this approach or orientation. However, it is not easily identified or described. This is partly because the relevant values are not discernible 'values' in the conventional sense of that term. Moreover, as already suggested, these values are constantly being renegotiated and redefined, especially where authority has been devolved to the social partners to formulate and implement appropriate policy responses to specific problems. Implicit in our interpretation is an alternative view of the relation between values and interests, between ideas and the material. It is interesting that the discussion among the social partners on the nature of the new partnership model has, at least initially, played down the value dimension, in order to get a clear look at the procedural and cognitive dimensions.[62] In addition, to date, the explicit discussion of values has been associated with the least successful aspect of the partnership system. One important implication of our argument is that the foundation of the new social partnership is not distinctively Irish – since even the Irish dare not claim 'the problem- solving approach' as an Irish invention.

O'Connor is undoubtedly correct in identifying the importance of successive government attempts to reform and restructure industrial relations since independence. However, we are not convinced that the re-adoption of social partnership in 1987 was 'primarily due to government policy', and that its development since then represents a belated union and employer adoption of the political elite's 'ideological, as distinct from tactical, proclivity for concertation'. First, can political parties still be put in centre stage? The story from independence to the 1980s was certainly one in which government, especially Fianna Fáil, *acted on* trade unions and industrial relations, with varying degrees of success. However, from 1987 to 1997, it seems more true to say that the social partners *acted on* government. The PNR, was, after all, a response to a growing crisis in governance. Second, it is not clear what 'ideological' notion of concertation the Irish political elite had in the past, or has at present. Third, in the past decade the social partners have shown some reluctance to elaborate an ideological idea of social partnership – with the exception of faint, and short- lived, reference to a German-style 'social market economy' by one or two union leaders.

We would explain the emergence and maintenance of the recent Irish social partnership by reference to the following mutually reinforcing factors:

- the deep economic, social and political crisis of the 1980s acted as a catalyst
- the new economic context 'reinforced the need to co-ordinate and the rewards to be gained from co-ordination'[63]

- there was a shared understanding of the key economic mechanisms in the Irish economy
- the partners found a new deliberative, problem-solving, approach
- support is conditional and is renegotiated both between and within associations
- Ireland had a set of supply-side characteristics which has facilitated economic growth
- economic success provides a powerful legitimisation of social partnership and encourages a reluctance to dispense with the process
- the development of an institutional framework for social partnership
- for all of the participants, the process has delivered gains and met specific objectives.[64]

Normatively, there was a certain continuity with earlier efforts at concertation, but we believe this has limited explanatory power. Procedurally, there was a superficial continuity (unions, employers and government in negotiation), but at a finer level of detail the partnership *process* was significantly different. Substantively, the content of Irish partnership differs significantly from the classical postwar models of corporatism and earlier Irish efforts at concertation. A remaining analytical challenge is to explore the normative and cognitive dimension of the new procedure and the new content. In this respect, study of the Irish case might have a role in shaping a new view of post-corporatist concertation.

Notes

1. The ICMSA were involved in the PNR negotiations but, after raising an objection to the final agreement, were effectively excluded from the social partnership. They regained social partnership status in 1990 when they signed up to the PESP.
2. IBEC was formed in 1993 following a merger of the FIE and the CII.
3. The Community Platform was set up by the Community Workers Co-Operative, the INOU, the NWCI, Irish Rural Link, Irish Traveller Movement, Focus on Children, Gay and Lesbian Equality Network, One Parent Exchange Network, CORI, Forum for People with Disabilities, Pavee Point, Community Action Network, European Anti-Poverty Network and Irish Commission for Prisoners Overseas as a mechanism to organise the future participation of this sector in the Partnership. Platform will coordinate third-strand participation with regards to the monitoring function.
4. Niamh Hardiman, *Pay, Politics and Economic Performance in Ireland 1970–1987*, Oxford, Clarendon Press, 1988.
5. William Roche,'Industrialisation and the Development of Industrial Relations' in *Irish Industrial Relations in Practice*, ed. T. Murphy and W. Roche, Oak Tree Press, Dublin, 1997.
6. FIE was the employers' association with responsibility for industrial relations issues whilst the CII could be considered a trade association in that it focused on a broader economic and social remit.
7. Damian Thomas, interview with IBEC leadership, 1997.
8. Ibid.
9. Fianna Fáil's the concept of 'social solidarity' was seen as preventing political mobilisation of social conflict such as between capital and labour or urban and rural interests.

10. Emmet O' Connor, this volume; B. Sheehan, 'Crisis, Strategic Re-evaluation and the Re-emergence of Tripartism in Ireland', M Comm. dissertation., University College Dublin, 1996; Peter Mair, 'Explaining the absence of class politics in Ireland', in *The Development of Industrial Society in Ireland*, ed. John Goldthorpe and C.T. Whelan, Oxford University Press, 1992.
11. The catch-all nature of both Fianna Fáil and Fine Gael means that categorising Irish political parties in terms of a left-to-right spectrum has always been difficult and the emergence of permanent and renegotiated coalition government has added a further dynamic.
12. Rory O'Donnell and Damian Thomas, 'Partnership and the Policy Making Process', in *Social Policy in Ireland: Principles, Practice and Problems*, ed. Sean Healy and Brigid Reynolds, Dublin, Oak Tree Press, 1998.
13. Gary Murphy, 'Towards a Corporate State? Sean Lemass and the Realignment of Interest Groups in the Policy Process 1948–64', Dublin City University Business School Research Paper no.23, 1997; Sean Dooney, 'Irish Agriculture: An Organisational Profile', Dublin, Institute of Public Administration, 1988.
14. Neil Collins, 'Agricultural Policy Networks: The Republic of Ireland and Northern Ireland', in *Political Studies*, vol. 43 (1995): 664–82.
15. Maura Adshead, 'Beyond Clientelism: Agricultural Networks in Ireland and the EU', in *West European Politics*, vol. 19, no. 2 (1996): 583–608.
16. Interview by Damian Thomas, 1997.
17. NESF effectively replaced the Oireachtas Standing Committee on Employment.
18. Damian Thomas, interview with senior civil servant involved in PNR negotiations 1997.
19. Damian Thomas, Interview with Bill Attley (SIPTU), May 1997.
20. Rory O'Donnell, *Ireland and Europe: Challenges for a New Century*, Dublin, Economic and Social Research Institute, 1993; NESC, *Strategy into the 21st Century*, Dublin, National Economic and Social Council, 1996.
21. Jelle Visser notes that this 'exchange' of pay moderation for fiscal compensation has become an integral characteristic of Dutch Corporatist agreements in recent years; see J. Visser 'Two Cheers for Corporatism and One for the Market; Industrial Relations, Unions, Wages and Labour Market Reform in the Netherlands', *British Journal of Industrial Relations*, vol. 36, 1997.
22. Charles Sabel, *Ireland, Local Partnerships and Social Innovation*, Paris, OECD, 1996.
23. NESC, *Strategy for Recovery*, Dublin, National Economic and Social Council, 1986.
24. Authors' interviews with past and present members of NESC, 1997. This aspect of the social partnership is discussed in more detail below.
25. Authors' interviews with CRC members.
26. Authors' interviews with senior trade union leaders. Interestingly IBEC, whilst stressing the importance of the CRC, indicated that it focused on broader economic and social policy issues and that issues relating to pay and industrial relations were not raised in this forum. The trade unionists, however, implied that it was used informally to address concerns relating to these very issues.
27. See O' Donnell and Thomas, 'Partnership and the Policy Making Process'.
28. Gerald Davis, 'Rethinking Policy Making: A New Role for Consultation', in *Administration,* vol. 45, no. 3 (1997): 347–633.
29. This report is widely seen as prompting the development of the Local Employment Service, which aims to actively assist the transition from welfare to work.
30. NESC, *Strategy for the 21st Century*; NESF, *Negotiations on a Successor to PESP*, Forum Report No.1, Dublin, National Economic and Social Forum, 1994; NESF, *Post PCW-Negotiations – A New Deal?*, Opinion No. 4, Dublin, National Economic and Social Forum.
31. Damian Thomas, interview with Social Pillar Representatives, 1997.
32. O'Donnell and Thomas, 'Partnership and the Policy Making Process'. This view was confirmed in interviews with the social pillar bodies. Moreover there was a prevailing perception amongst participants that having decided to afford some groups social partner status, this process effectively snowballed to include a number of organisations who had not sought 'social partner' status and who were surprised at their elevation.

33. At this session all of the participants were given the opportunity to present position papers in the context of the NESF document 'Post PCW Negotiations –A New Deal?' and the NESC Report 'Strategy for the 21st Century'.
34. Top ranking officials from the Department of the Taoiseach constituted the core of this team, and were supplemented by ministers and senior civil servants from various departments depending on the issues which were being addressed.
35. On the employers side IBEC are the dominant organisation given that their membership encompasses all sectors of the economy whilst the CIF represent the construction sector only.
36. The relationship between IBEC and the other business organisations is discussed in Rory O' Donnell and Damian Thomas, *Partnership*, 1998, p. 129.
37. NESF (1996) had postulated three options for third strand involvement in the social partnership consultation, participation and negotiation. The view from the Social Pillar was that their role in Partnership 2000 went beyond the first two options and was closest to full negotiative status (Community Platform 1996: Interviews with Social Pillar representatives).
38. The participants interviewed highlighted in particular the cycle of drafts and reworked sections that were circulated between the rooms and the fact that, at times, changes could be made and one would not have a clear view who was responsible for them.
39. Ash Amin and Damian Thomas, 'The Negotiated Economy: State and Civic Institutions in Denmark', in *Economy and Society*, vol. 25, no. 2 (1996): 255–81; Grant Jordan, 'Pluralistic Corporatisms and Corporate Pluralism', in *Scandinavian Political Studies*, vol. 7, no. 3 (1984): 137–53.
40. Colin Crouch, 'Pluralism and the New Corporatism: A Rejoinder' in *Political Studies*, vol. 31 (1983): 452–60; Ron Martin, 'Pluralism and the New Corporatism', in *Political Studies*, vol. 31 (1983): 86–102.
41. Hardiman, *Pay, Politics and Economic Performance.*
42. Klaus Armingeon, 'Formation and Stability of Neo-Corporatist Incomes Policies: A Comparative Analysis', in *European Sociological Review* 2 (1986): 138–47: Marino Regini, 'The Conditions for Political Exchange : How Corporatist Concertation Emerged and Collapsed in Great Britain and Italy', in *Order and Conflict in Contemporary Capitalism*, ed. J. Goldthorpe, Oxford, Clarendon Press, 1984; 'Still Engaging in Corporatism? Recent Italian Experience in Comparative Perspective', in *Industrial Relations Journal*, vol. 3, no. 3 (1998): 259–78; Martin Bull, 'The Corporatist Ideal Type and Political Exchange', in *Political Studies*, vol. 40 (1992): 255–72.
43. See NESC, *A Strategy for Development*, Dublin, National Economic and Social Council, 1990; NESC, *A Strategy into the 21st Century*, NESC, *Ireland in the European Community: Performance, Prospects and Strategy*, Dublin, National Economic and Social Council, 1989; NESC, *Ireland in the European Community: Performance, Prospects and Strategy*, Dublin, National Economic and Social Council, 1989; Rory O'Donnell, 'European Integration', in *Economics for an Open Economy*, ed. Desmond Norton, Dublin, Oak Tree Press, 1994: 599–608; *Economics for an Open Economy*, Dublin, Oak Tree Press, 1994: 599–608.

??. Rory O' Donnell and Colm O'Reardon, Ireland's Experiment in Social Partnership 1987–96, *Social Pacts in Europe*, ed. Giuseppe Fajertag and Philippe Pochet, Brussels, European Trade Union Institute, 1997.

44. NESC, *New Approaches to Rural Development*, 1994.
45. William Roche, Pay Determination, 1997; Ruari Quinn, 'How Others Saw Us; Political Views', in *Federation of Irish Employers, 1942–1992*, ed. Basil Chubb, Dublin, Gill and Macmillan, 1992.
46. Hardiman, *Pay, Politics and Economic Performance;* William Roche, British Unions in Ireland: Aspects of Growth Performance' Business Research Programme, UCD, Working Paper No. 8, 1995; William Roche 'Industrialisation and the Development of Industrial Relations', 1997. The influential white-collar Manufacturing and Science Union (MSF) broke with this trend and voted in favour of Partnership 2000.
47. George Taylor, 'Labour Market Rigidities. Institutional Impediments and Managerial Constraints: Some Reflections on the Recent Experience of Macro Political Bargaining in Ireland', in *Economic and Social Review*, vol. 25, no. 3 (1996): 253–77.

48. William Roche,'Between Regime Fragmentation and Realignment : Irish Industrial Relations in the 1990s', in *Industrial Relations Journal*, vol. 29, no. 2 (1998): 112–14.
49. ISME were to be included in the negotiations for Partnership 2000 but they withdrew in protest at their exclusion from the negotiations on private sector pay, which were conducted by IBEC and CIF in conjunction with ICTU.
50. Joseph Durkan, 'Social Consensus and Incomes Policy', *Economic and Social Review*, vol. 23 no. 3 (1992): 347–63, but see Joseph Durkan and Colm Harmon, 'Social Consensus, Incomes Policy and Unemployment', University College Dublin, Centre for Economic Research, Working Paper 96/11, 1996.
51. Brendan Walsh and Anthony Leddin, *The Macroeconomy of Ireland*, Dublin, Gill and Macmillan, 1992.
52. Jim O'Leary and Anthony Leddin, 'Monetary and Exchange Rate Policy', in *The Economy of Ireland*, ed. John O'Hagan, Dublin:, Gill and Macmillan, 1996; see also J. Peter Neary and Rodney Thom, 'Punts, Pounds and Euros: in Search of an Optimum Currency Area', mimeo, University College Dublin, 1997.
53. Padraig Yeates, 'The Fifth Estate', *Irish Times*, 5 January 1991: Joseph Lee, 'Partnership 2000 and its Hold on the Next Government', *Sunday Tribune,* 19 January 1997.
54. Paul Teague, 'Pay Determination in the Republic of Ireland: Towards Social Corporatism?', *British Journal of Industrial Relations*, 33(2), June 1995.
55. Roche, 'Between Regime Fragmentation and Realignment'.
56. Community Platform, *Achieving Social Partnership: The Strategy and Proposals of the Community Platform at the Partnership 2000 Negotiations*, Dublin, Community Platform, 1997; Damian Thomas, interviews with social pillar representatives, 1997.
57. The legitimacy of ICTU's claim to represent the unemployed was challenged by the INOU and certainly this caused tension between organisations. In recent years, however, a closer working relationship has developed and it is recognised that ICTU advocated INOU's elevation to social partners status (source: Damian Thomas, interviews with INOU, 1997. See also Manus O'Riordan, 'Towards a European Social Pact – The Irish Experience', paper presented to the *European Observatory – Hans Böckler Stiftung – European Trade Union Institute Conference*, ETUC House, 1 October 1996.
58. 'It places a high value on voluntary participation in social, economic and public life. It seeks accommodation through plural representation and accommodation of diverse interests. It is market-led but social. It is non-dogmatic, informal and co-operative. It reflects an underlying sense of social solidarity and a strong national identity. The country is small enough to actively use these characteristics in an informal policy process which encourages various interest groups to address problems jointly. In recent years this has been reflected in a conscious experimentalism in several public policy, business and industrial relations spheres' (p. 65).
59. NESF; *A Framework for Partnership: Enhancing Strategic Consensus Through Participation*, Report No. 17, Dublin, NESF.
60. Community Platform, *Achieving Social Partnership*, 1997.
61. Ferdinand von Prodzynski, 'Ireland Between Centralisation and Decentralisation', in *Industrial Relations in the New Europe*, ed. A. Ferner and R. Hyman, Oxford, Blackwells, 1992.
62. NESC, *Strategy for the 21st Century*, 1997; NESF, A Framework for Enriching Partnership, Report no, Dublin, NESF.
63. Colin Crouch, 'Incomes Policies, institutions and market: an overview of recent developments' in *The Return to Incomes Policy*, ed. R. Dore, R. Boyer and Z. Mars, London, Pinter Publishers, 1992.
64. Whilst this might seem an obvious point it is important to highlight it especially as it was the gap between the participants' objectives and the outcomes of the process which led to the collapse of the previous tripartite experiments in Ireland. See Hardiman, *Pay, Politics Economic Performance* and Roche, *Pay Determination*.

Chapter 13

Italy in Historical Perspective: The Legacies of Fascism and Anti-Fascism

Gino Bedani

Before the First World War

For most of the twentieth century labour, government and employers in Italy have operated outside a culture of social partnership. This article will highlight the major reasons for this, but will also draw attention to elements of cultural and ideological traditions from which it has not been absent. Towards the end of the century, some of these elements have combined with other developments to steer the main social actors towards a more positive appraisal of the benefits of social concertation.

During the final decades of the nineteenth century Italian industry, particularly in the north, entered a phase of accelerated expansion, which left the unions that emerged in this period with a decisively conflictual and anticapitalist orientation. During the first decade of the twentieth century the liberal statesman Giovanni Giolitti and the socialist leader Filippo Turati together attempted to create a measure of social stability. Giolitti defeated attempts on the right to outlaw strikes and even unions, while Turati managed to strengthen the reformist wing of both the PSI (Italian Socialist Party) and the union confederation CGL, created in 1906. Although their ideas never stretched to the concept of social partnership, they both felt that the legal recognition of unions could help to create a social climate conducive to the country's economic development.

But neither leader was able to keep total control of his side for long. The requirements of monopoly development in industry, and the need to respond to worker militancy, propelled the employers into authoritarian postures that undermined the Giolittian strategy, denying any mediating role to the state. Between 1909 and 1913, with the creation of the employers' association, the Confindustria (1910), the entire edifice of the fragile collective bargaining structures that had been constructed earlier in the decade was destroyed by an employer offensive. The yearly reports prepared by the Confindustria repeatedly rejected Giolittian mediation, arguing that conflict could be brought to an end only by suppressing the worker agitations that had accompanied the whole investment cycle from 1896 to 1907.[1]

On the union side, deep divisions led to the breakaway of revolutionary elements from the CGL to form their own confederation (USI) in 1912. Under the influence of the revolutionary syndicalists, the USI programme kept the movement divided and opposed any form of social partnership. Many of them, moreover, argued for Italian entry into the First World War, thus leaving the working- class movement with no capacity to mount effective opposition to Italy's eventual entry into the conflict.

The First World War and After

Understandably, historians have stressed the importance of the factory council movement, which from 1917 grew out of the radicalised anti-war positions of the workers led by Antonio Gramsci and the revolutionary wing of the PSI in Turin.

There was, however, a sizeable reformist tendency within the PSI, even larger within the CGL, but incapable of effective opposition to the conservative restoration which had been in train since the resignation of Giolitti in 1914. One of the features of this development was the way in which industrial finance capital emerged as the major force refashioning the definition of national interests, eventually taking Italy into the war against Germany and Austria in 1915. The socialist reformists lacked the conceptual and ideological substance to resist the industrialists' view that participation in the war was essential to develop Italy's economic independence. Given the employers' sympathies towards the authoritarian tendencies of the Salandra government, and the shared view of both about the desirability of robust social control, it is not surprising that the reformist socialists' acquiescence within the CGL should find the unions transformed into a disciplinary and organisational organ for the conduct of the war effort in industry.

During the course of the war the industrialists became centrally involved in planning production and war provisions, strengthening their relations with the state to the point of feeling themselves to be 'invested with public duties'.[2] The unions thus found themselves caught up in a tripartitism in reality driven by the other partners. It operated by means of a national Committee for Industrial Mobilisation with its headquarters in Rome, supported by seven- and eventually eleven- regional committees in different parts of the country. These committees, invested with authority by the government, and consisting of representatives from workers' organisations and the employers (although controlled by the latter), ran the whole 'industrial mobilisation' system, coordinating wartime production of supplies and munitions, and making all decisions on matters relating to wages, employment, dismissals, transfer of personnel between plants, and all issues relating to youth and female labour.[3] The system depended on strict control of the workforce, with the prohibition of strikes and the imposition of military-style discipline in the factories.

This experience of mobilisation of national energies generated elements of corporatist thinking in quarters that cannot be suspected of having previously harboured sympathies for the nascent fascist movement. The radical liberal deputy Eduardo Pantano, for instance, spokesman for the parliamentary postwar committee on 'Urgent economic problems' recommended, in 1919, the setting up of bodies 'in which worker and employer organisations are recognised or registered' to take over from parliament 'administrative and legislative functions'.[4] The CGL reformist leadership, favourable to Pantano's idea, successfully proposed a similar resolution at the organisation's convention in May 1919.[5]

A Small Catholic Movement

Although it had a very minor role in pre-fascist Italy, it is worth drawing attention to the small Catholic component of the workers'movement, since some of its principles would inform later developments following the Second World War.

The origins of Catholic social thinking in the modern era lay in the encyclical *Rerum Novarum* (1891) of Leo XIII. An important feature of the document's defence of the working class was its openness to the idea of working-class organisations, within a harmonious social framework: 'It is a great mistake to imagine that class is spontaneously hostile to class ... there can be no capital without labour, nor labour without capital. Concord begets order and beauty, whereas a continuation of conflict leads inevitably to barbarity and wild confusion'.[6]

Catholic social movements built on this formulation in different directions. One tradition, strong outside Italy, developed the call for harmony into a revived medieval corporatism which saw all classes organised into a tightly ordered institutional fabric with the purpose of expunging all forms of social conflict.[7] The small Italian Catholic workers' confederation (CIL) looked to the intellectual leadership of figures like Giuseppe Toniolo, whose more flexible corporatism perceived the proletariat not only as an 'ordered class, through the corporations', but also as a class responding to the risks of industrialised fragmentation by being reconstituted 'through permanent collective representation'.[8]

This Catholic sense of the working class as an identifiable and autonomous social category would survive both the fascist attempt at total integration, and the support given to this by the encyclical *Quadragesimo Anno* (1931) of Pius XI. The Catholic world in Italy was far from sharing a homogenised response to fascism. The leaders of the catholic CIL were to prove more resistant to compromise with fascist syndicates, for example, than their reformist socialist colleagues.[9] After the Second World War, soon after his return from exile, the former leader of the pre-fascist Catholic *Partito popolare italiano*, Luigi Sturzo, polemicising against the fascist experience of corporatism, wrote that 'for the corporation to exist state intervention must fix it by law, and abolish freedom of organisation and initiative'.[10] Sturzo and other Italian Catholics based their more 'democratic' corporatism on the notion of 'Corpi intermedi' (intermediate entities): bodies, categories, or communities whose right to existence and autonomous means of expression could not, in natural law, be surrendered to the state. Such groupings were the family, religious communities, political parties and, to some Catholics, unions. It is to this strain of Catholic thinking that the notion of the *sindacato* (unions) as a *soggetto politico* (political actor or agent), which would later be strongly promoted by the Catholic component from the late 1960s, can be related.

Under Fascism

We have already alluded to elements of corporatist thinking among reformist socialists. But there were other forces on the left which for a while had a stronger input into Italian corporatism. Before creating their own syndicates in October 1920, Mussolini's fascists had given support to the revolutionary syndicalist confederation UIL. By 1921, however, many of the latter's leaders had joined the ranks of the fascists. The authoritarian model of social partnership developed under Italian fascism thus accommodated a popular, revolutionary element within it, in competition with the right-wing nationalist one which eventually defeated and supplanted it.

The leading exponent of fascist syndicalism, Edmondo Rossoni, had spent his early career in the revolutionary syndicalist movement, rising to the rank of general secretary of the UIL in 1918. After abandoning the latter, he became general secretary of the fascist *Confederazione dei Sindacati Nazionali* (CSN), created in January 1922. Rossoni's idea of workers and employers collaborating on the basis of joint decision making, however, immediately began to be undermined. In two agreements involving the fascist unions, the Confindustria, and the state as mediator, the Palazzo Chigi pact (1923) and the Palazzo Vidoni pact (1925), the employers recognised the fascist syndicate members as the sole representatives of labour. But contrary to Rossoni's wishes, the fascist syndicates were not allowed to have their own fiduciary or 'trustees' in the factories, so that union representation had no link with any broader movement beyond the workplace. The first step in securing managerial authority in the workplace under any future corporatist arrangements had been taken.

There then followed further defeats for Rossoni. The Rocco law of April 1926 created special labour courts for compulsory arbitration in unresolved labour disputes. There were numerous references to the corporate state, but the Ministry of Corporations, created in 1926, continued its existence until 1934 with 'no actual corporations to direct'.[11] This would have to wait until the threat of genuine union power within the corporatist arrangements had been removed. A further step in this direction was taken with the promulgation of the *carta del lavoro* (labour charter) in 1927. In the discussions leading up to its drafting, the industrialists' view that it should avoid any reference to minimum pay – or other concessions likely to have a restraining effect on profits – prevailed. It also recognised private enterprise in the field of production as the most effective means of protecting the national interest.[12]

A further blow to Rossoni's ambitions came in 1928, when his *Confederazione Nazionale dei Sindacati fascisti*, which had replaced the CSN, was broken up into a number of separate confederations based on different productive sectors of the economy (industry, agriculture, transport, etc.). The official line was that the creation of workers' associations that paralleled employers' organisations in each economic sector would facilitate interclass collaboration, under state guidance. What this achieved in practice was the further weakening of the workers' syndicates, since they had no unitary confederation to support them in settling contracts and disputes. This last concession to the employers spelt the defeat of Rossoni's syndicalist movement.

Mussolini used the threat, and finally the destruction, of Rossoni's 'integral syndicalism' to obtain the support of the employers, who were initially suspicious of fascism. Its destruction guaranteed the strengthening of management, the restoration of 'order' in the workplace, and was further garnished with fiscal concessions to the industrialists and the assurance of wage reductions in the future.

This did not mean, however, that corporatism was meant to become simply a cover for capitalist hegemony. It was at least the original intention of Mussolini and Rocco to bring the nation's productive forces under the authority and control of the state, but without state ownership. Already, by 1933, with the creation of the public corporation IRI (Institute for Industrial Reconstruction) to salvage the major banks and take possession of the stock in industrial, agricultural and real estate companies owned by the banks, Italian fascism controlled a higher proportion of national industry than any European power except the Soviet Union. Understandably, the employers were nervous about corporatist legislation.

The latter had a number of important consequences for the employers. With the establishment of the corporations in 1934, each employer sector was represented by only one association, and of these only those with membership of the Confindustria received recognition. Agreements were binding on all employers, whether members of the associations or not. Thus Confindustria was boosted at national level, while room for manoeuvre for associations and individual employers at local level was diminished.

The corporations were organised into three major productive sectors (agricultural, industrial and commercial, and services), with eight sub-sectors in agriculture, eight in industry and commerce, and six in the services. All twenty- two corporations were headed by a government official, and the representatives on the corporations nominated by the fascist unions and employers' associations, but approved by the government.[13]

The ideological basis of fascist corporatism in Italy contained strands too numerous to discuss. But once, to the relief of the employers, both Rossoni's 'integral syndicalism' and Ugo Spirito's 'property corporatism' were defeated, the one which was established as the basis of the 1934 legislation was Rocco's nationalist corporatism, in which increasing the nation's wealth and productive capacity took priority over the question of distribution. Private ownership, moreover, was seen as a spur to this activity. In his speech sealing the legislation, Rocco made it clear that 'production, except in special cases where the state intervenes directly for political reasons, remains, as is made clear in the labour charter, in the hands of the private sector'.[14]

The effects of the IRI salvage operation had been to increase the contacts between industrialists and government offices. From the early 1930s the government and Confindustria were turning their attention to the development of large industrial groups, and to the creation of obligatory consortia in numerous branches of industry, thereby increasing large-scale concentrations. Each side could see advantages to itself in these developments. Thus a pattern of collusion, rather than collaboration, developed, in which both government and employers paid lip service to the corporate state, while pursuing their own advantages where there existed common ground, for example in an increased dynamism in foreign dealings, particularly after Ethiopia in 1935. While industry was thus forced to operate within a political framework not of its own choosing, it nevertheless remained true that the centres of economic decision making were in the hands of a 'restricted capitalist oligarchy closely associated with political and party levers of power'.[15] Fascist corporatism in Italy was thus a mixture of authoritarian control of the workforce and employer decision making, but with the latter constrained within a more *dirigiste* framework in areas such as foreign policy.

After the Second World War: From Unitary Confederation to Three-Way Split

After the collapse of the fascist regime, the CGIL *unitaria,* which was formed in 1944, was a new beginning. The most significant feature of the new confederation was that it was a mirror image of the anti-fascist coalitions which governed the country until 1947. The signatories to the CGIL's founding document were leading figures within the Communist (PCI), Christian Democrat (DC) and Socialist (PSI) parties. This fact impressed on the Italian *sindacato* three features, which were to be of major importance in its subsequent development. In the first place, it was firmly politically aligned. The second important feature was that the Cold War splits that would follow would soon polarise around Catholics and communists. The third important characteristic of the CGIL at its foundation was that communist dominance ensured that its major orientation would be 'confederate' and not 'trade-' or industry-based, a feature that survived the subsequent split in the movement, and which, much later, would facilitate developments in the direction of social partnership.

Following the collapse of the anti-fascist coalition and the onset of the Cold War, the CGIL split, so that by 1950 there were three separate confederations: the CGIL (about two-thirds communist and one-third socialist in composition), the CISL (Catholic) and the UIL (republicans, social democrats and the remainder of the socialists). The relative strengths of the confederations at this stage were reflected in membership figures of about 4,640,000 for the CGIL, and 1,190,000 in the case of the CISL. There are no figures available for the smaller UIL but its membership will not have exceeded about 500,000.

Labour historians have tended to over-stress the 'transmission belt' theory in relation to communist union party dealings, according to which the union obeyed party instructions. Yet the orientation of the CGIL, from its beginning, was profoundly influenced by the sturdy independence of its first leader, Giuseppe Di Vittorio, whose early formation in pre-fascist Italy had been in the ranks of the revolutionary syndicalists. At the first congress of the CGIL unitaria, in 1945, he had argued for a role for the confederation in the programme of national reconstruction. Why, he asked, should 'the programme of reconstruction be formulated in government ministries, in the banks and in the headquarters of joint stock companies? It must satisfy in the first place the needs of the people ... It should be worked out with the participation of the people'.[16]

Di Vittorio launched the CGIL's *Piano del lavoro* (Labour Plan) in 1949, a programme of electrification for the south, land reclamation, agrarian reform, including plans for public works, and a construction programme ranging from schools and hospitals to aqueducts, drainage systems and lighting. With the Cold War in full swing, the proposal, seen by the government and by employers as coming from the PCI, was ignored. But in reality not only did it not originate in the party, but the party leadership had considerable reservations about it.[17] The CGIL was adopting a policy-making role, and proposing a form of social partnership not in line with traditional communist conceptions about the role of unions, and their relationship of subordination to the party. It is thus not surprising that Di Vittorio should have led an attack, at the PCI congress in 1956, on the 'transmission belt' theory:

> It is necessary to destroy completely the famous 'transmission belt' theory ... Unions, if they are to be united, cannot be the 'transmission belts' of any party. I propose that this principle be clearly affirmed in the resolution concluding the work of the congress, and that all Italian communists should commit themselves to observing it scrupulously.[18]

In reality, the pressures of Cold War hostility ensured that conflictual perspectives would dominate the practice of the confederation for many years. But although it would take time to resurface, the concept of social partnership was not alien to the historical memory of the CGIL.

Employer Ascendancy and Weak and Divided Unions in the 1950s

For most of the 1950s the confederations were weak and divided, strongly aligned with their parties, and at opposite extremes of cold-war postures.

The CISL, in search of a new identity, and influenced by the 'social harmony' drive of Catholic social teaching, was more disposed to collaborate with the employers. At this stage the more accommodating stance of the CISL, alongside that of the equally anti-communist UIL, led to numerous plant and company-level consultations from which the CGILwas excluded.[19] However, the collaborationism of the CISL led to what its critics called a 'disarmed productivism', in which the profits that were fuelling the 'economic miracle' taking place were dependent on cheap labour, a feature which showed up consistently in the analyses of the government-sponsored Central Institute for Statistics.

An authoritarian model of industrial relations, backed by the government, and of which Fiat was the symbol, had prevailed during the Cold War years. But pressure from sections of the DC and of the CISL managed to secure legislation in 1956 to bring about the secession of all the industries controlled by the state-holding corporations IRI and ENI from the Confindustria. With the creation of the state-holding employers' confederations Intersind and ASAP, the DC of Fanfani controlled major sectors of industry and aimed to give strategic direction to the nation's economy. From this point the private employers became nervous about Fanfani's intentions and, lacking a natural party of government of their own, began trying to strengthen their contacts on the right of the DC and with the centre parties, particularly as the prospect of a centre-left government with the socialists approached towards the end of the decade.

But the tensions between the private employers and sections of political Catholicism increased in March 1958 when the CISL's list of candidates for the union elections was prepared by Valletta, the Fiat manager. This time management had gone too far. It had inflicted a humiliation the CISL could not allow to pass. In the autumn of the same year communists and Catholics joined forces in condemning employer interference in union elections at the Om factories in Brescia. The decade ended with the major confederations having learned the lessons of a deeply divided movement. This was the beginning of a long period of rapprochement.

The 1960s: Rapprochement Between the Unions, the Emergency of a *Soggetto Politico* and the 'Hot Autumn' of 1969

A development of some significance in our considerations was that of the *sindacato* as a *soggetto politico* (political actor). This idea emerged particularly strongly within the CISL, as Catholic workers became increasingly disillusioned with the centre-left's inability to carry out badly needed social reforms. We saw earlier that an element of Catholic social teaching which protected some Catholics from the allure of fascist corporatism was the notion of *corpi intermedi*, structures within society having a self-determining basis in 'natural law'. By extending this notion into the field of labour it was possible to see the union as an organisation with a natural right to represent the 'community of workers' in the social and political fields. This idea could be supported by statements made in Pope John XXIII's encyclical *Mater et Magistra*: 'We cannot fail to emphasise how imperative it is or at least highly opportune that the workers should be able freely to make their voices heard, and listened to, beyond the confines of their individual productive units and at every level of society'.[20]

The sindacato first emerged in real terms as a political actor in its negotiations with the government over pension reforms in 1968. These were brought to completion in February of the following year after a national general strike, the first to be called by the three confederations since 1948. In the wake of this success, the confederations were able to ride the tiger of widespread protest and win back control of negotiations with the employers from the rank-and-file committees (Comitati Unitari di Base, CUB) which had emerged all over the country, in the turbulent 'Hot Autumn' of 1969.[21]

The period of protest surrounding the 'Hot Autumn' shook the employers, the government, and even the confederations themselves, so profoundly that the Italian industrial relations landscape was permanently transformed. By 1970, the country had a workers' charter (*Statuto dei lavoratori*), which gave the unions wide-ranging rights in the workplace and swept away previous repressive employer practices. In a short space of time, wages of Italian workers leaped from among the lowest to among the highest in Europe, and the confederations had taken on board a range of social problems (housing, transport, health) as campaigning issues, with widespread public support.[22] The unions' reform strategies were bolstered by the claim to be treated as a *soggetto politico*. As the Catholic Guido Baglioni claimed, 'the *sindacato* in our country finds itself in a situation which has no parallel in any other capitalist nation ... it is in a position to pressurise, to "bargain" with the government, with which it has become an important bargaining partner'.[23]

The 1970s: A Decade of Union Ascendancy

An attempt was made, after the turbulent events of 1969, to create a single confederation for all workers. The factory councils, which emerged from the late 1960s as the unitary workplace organs of representation, remained, but political affiliations higher up the confederate organisations, particularly those of the CISL and UIL, undermined full, organic unity. The outcome was a tripartite CGIL–CISL–UIL Federation, formed in July 1972, with separate organisations and congresses, but with formalised mechanisms for producing agreed policies and bargaining positions.

Throughout the 1970s the CGIL–CISL–UIL Federation mobilised the workers on a range of social issues, ranging from transport to health, frequently linking them with more traditional union demands. At company level, where traditional divisions and separate identities had weakened, there was a high level of militancy and a strong conflictual approach, which diminished progressively higher up the confederate hierarchies. For the whole decade, the strong egalitarian vein in the Catholic CISL prevailed, forcing down differentials between skilled and unskilled workers, and white- and blue-collar workers, with the weaker-paid reaping the major gains. The agreement secured between government, employers and unions in 1975 over the *scala mobile* (index-linked wage scale), with automatic three-monthly wage rises, led to high labour costs which industry found difficult to sustain.

A threat to incomes and employment came in the wake of the recession in 1974–5, with a slowdown in growth and soaring inflation. The CGIL–CISL–UIL Federation, in order to protect wages, began to engage in regulatory practices in the socio-economic system at the higher levels. As Negrelli and Santi have pointed out, much of the industrial action in the late 1970s became less rooted in rank-and-file demands, was principally demonstrative, and had political aims.[24] This new role of the confederations, together with their exercise of a restraining function, led to a centralisation of collective bargaining at national level, although the diversified bargaining structure at lower levels remained in place.

The EUR programme, agreed by the CGIL–CISL–UIL Federation in February 1978, was the first comprehensive attempt at concertation involving unions, employers and government. The unions accepted wage restraint and the flexible use of labour in return for the promise of a voice in industrial restructuring and new investments. The EUR initiative, originally inspired by the secretary of the CGIL, Luciano Lama, was bolstered by moves afoot to bring the communists into the 'parliamentary majority' at the end of the period of national solidarity, which had begun in 1976. The experiment in concertation was thus tied into a seemingly parallel development of a consociational democracy.

It should be stressed that the programme was not supported by institutional arrangements for union participation in government decisions, although it was anticipated that legislation would form part of the government's approach to keeping its own part of the bargain. The bulk of the agreement, involving both private employers and the state-holding sector, would take the form of the usual negotiated contractual arrangements.

EUR consisted of three basic elements. The first of these was an agreement that firms should provide the unions, every year, with figures on projected employment, production and investment levels, together with plans for restructuring, so that agreements could be reached on patterns and locations of investment. Wage restraint, and even redeployment and the shedding of labour, would be accepted in return. The second aspect of the programme came from the union demand that the government should reorganise and restructure the state-holding sector, with particular attention to modernisation, and to investment in underdeveloped regions. Such action, moreover, was to be decentralised, with greater autonomy granted to regional and local governments. The third proposal, also concerned with government, consisted of the latter's efforts to reform the public administration and produce a more equitable system of social services.[25]

The EUR agreement failed for a variety of reasons: within the unions, difficulties lower down the hierarchy with abandoning the conflictual model, and widespread dissent among the rank-and-file over the proposals;[26] employer resistance to union 'interference'; and government inability to fulfil its own part of the bargain. By the end of 1978, union leaders were becoming increasingly worried about losing touch with the base, and the PCI suspected that its new place in the 'parliamentary majority' was being used to justify non-action by the DC. Its return to opposition on 31 January 1979 brought an end to its own consociational experiment and confirmed the collapse of the EUR agreement.

The 1980s: Redefining the Bargaining Terrain

Political Parties and Employers

Even though it was increasingly felt by the end of the 1970s that a predominantly conflictual approach could not deal with the major problems of the Italian economy (over-manning in industry, high inflation, massive public spending), the first attempt at concertation ended in failure. But a return to the militancy of the 1970s was no longer an option after an important defeat of the unions at Fiat in October 1980.

For many years the private employers had been waiting patiently for such an opportunity. A government that could not afford to alienate labour, and that during the second half of the 1970s could make few important decisions without the approval of the PCI, had put pressure on the employers to reach agreements, such as the one on the *scala mobile* in 1975, which they secretly considered extremely ill-advised and disadvantageous. The EUR programme was itself part of a broadly political settlement, and to them unworkable. They thus shed few tears over its demise. Legislation which had been passed in 1977 and 1978 (laws 675 and 787), geared towards the restructuring of Italian industry, was aimed almost exclusively at large-sized companies, 'but during the first five years of implementation, these policies also concentrated intervention on the "great losers", first and foremost the state-controlled companies',[27] namely the friends of the parties that controlled the state-holding corporations. When, therefore, in January 1979 the PCI left the great 'consociational' experiment which had been going on for three years and returned to opposition, both the DC and Craxi's PSI were determined to show that decisions could be taken without the need for communist approval in either the PCI or the CGIL. The country's political settlement was being refashioned. The Fiat manager Cesare Romiti saw the opportunity to bring to an end a long period of union ascendancy.

The confrontation, triggered by the company's announcement in September that it intended to make 24,000 workers redundant, resulted in a strike, broken by a march of 30,000–40,000 protesters on 10 October wishing to return to work. Many of the protesters, white-collar workers and technicians, were the victims of the egalitarian demands of the unions during the 1970s. The confederations had alienated important sections of their own membership.

Following this defeat, two opposing tendencies emerged in the confederations. There was a strong feeling in the communist component of the CGIL against concertation. Since this component's political ally, the PCI, had abandoned the government of national solidarity, the revamping of old government formulas that followed lacked credibility as providing plausible interlocutors. The CISL, however, and by 1982 the UIL, together with the socialist component of the CGIL, all looked more favourably at the prospect of 'political exchange' since their parties were part of the reshaped coalition (*pentapartito*). Thus in the early 1980s the CGIL–CISL–UIL Federation was under strain.

Tensions over the 'scala mobile' – a case of staggered concertation

What made matters worse was the decision in February 1984 of the country's first ever socialist prime minister Bettino Craxi to reduce the protective cover of the *scala mobile* in February 1984. The CGIL refused to sign up to the agreement supported by the other confederations and the employers. The PCI promoted a referendum on the issue in 1985 that split the confederations and brought an end to the unitary federation and its formal arrangements. Nevertheless, the leaders of the CISL and the UIL knew that despite the political advantages alliances with the parties of government could offer, a sustained attempt to marginalise the communist element within the CGIL was not only unlikely to succeed but also certain to weaken the movement as a whole in the process. But neither did the CGIL wish to remain out in the cold. Consequently, in May 1986 the lengthy arguments were brought to an end with the help of government intervention, and agreement on the *scala mobile* was reached between the parties, this time with the CGIL as signatory.

But caution over measures to marginalise the CGIL was also was shared by many employers. The defeat of the unions at Fiat in 1980 had been used by the Federmeccanica (metalworkers employers' federations) as the point of departure for an attempt to bring about a huge curtailment of collective bargaining.[28] But the hawkish, anti-communist, attitude of the Federmeccanica was not typical of Italian employers as a whole. One of the most successful models for capitalist development in Italy, particularly for small and medium industry, had emerged in the red regions, with the support and cooperation of the unions. Thus even at the height of divisions over Craxi's decree on the '*scala mobile*', a member of Confindustria's Executive Council could be found arguing that it was ill-judged to take a course 'which inevitably frustrated the communist element within the CGIL, for this element remained one of the most judicious and sensible components of the sindacato'.[29]

Developments in Bargaining Methods

The tripartite agreement, which had earlier been signed by government, unions and employers in January 1983, was perhaps the last of those in which 'political' bargaining acted as the catalyst. It broke the impasse in contract renewals between unions and employers, it modified the *scala mobile* to reduce inflation, and employers were given greater freedom in filling job vacancies. Their contributions to pensions were lowered, special programmes for job creation in the south and for youth employment were set up, and there was provision for legislation granting greater protection for part-time and other flexible forms of labour. Finally it was agreed that interconfederate bargaining would act as the chief regulator of lower-level negotiations, fixing ceilings on wages. Despite this agreement, however, both unions and employers proved reluctant to weaken national bargaining at industry level, or even, for that matter, at company level. In effect these two levels remained as the mainstay of the Italian system of bargaining throughout the 1980s.

Ideological conflict over the management of restructuring and technical innovation was more marked at the higher level than at plant level. From the mid- 1980s a high level of bargained change existed throughout the country and in a variety of industries. Labour flexibility, improvement of quality, increased productivity, introduction of new technology, greater utilisation of plant, the linking of earnings to performance, and even management strategy and industrial policy became objects of bargaining at local level.

One of the interesting features of this bargaining was the high level of local government involvement in the central and north-eastern parts of the country, often offering valuable assistance in the restructuring of small companies, retraining programmes for workers, and providing a framework for monitoring and coordinating the activities of small firms involved in the unusual forms of 'collaborative' competition that became a feature of the economy of the 'third Italy'.

A great deal of flexible collaborative bargaining at local level developed throughout the decade. Alongside the added use of local tripartite negotiating structures and local government agencies, these features of the Italian system of bargaining contributed to what Negrelli and Santi have described as 'a significant degree of union control of the deregulation requests made by employers', so that 'the sort of utterly unilateral management control of the process that has occurred in other countries was avoided'.[30]

The Challenge of the Autonomous Unions

One particular development, which probably brought the confederations closer together and closer also to government and employers, was the explosion of industrial action promoted by the 'autonomous' unions in the latter part of the 1980s. The latter operated in sectors which were highly disruptive, creating the misleading impression among the public, between 1986 and 1989, that conflict was out of control, and that the confederations were losing their grip on the workers' movement.[31] What eventually defeated the autonomous unions was the legislation passed in June 1990, after agreement with the confederations and employers, regulating industrial conflict in essential services. But the significance of the legislation went beyond its curtailment of the capacity of the *autonomi* to disrupt and to grow in membership. It was a step closer to the creation of a sense of social partnership between the confederations, the employers and the government.

Breaking Down the Barriers

This inching on all sides towards a more favourable view of social partnership was supported by a series of negotiations on vocational training between the labour and employers' confederations between 1987 and 1990, which received support and encouragement by the government. The agreements reached covered such matters as the length and nature of such training, pay and conditions of service.

In general, however, the private employers in Italy had traditionally been unfavourable towards government involvement at either a formal or informal level. The principal reason for this was that the main party of government, the DC, had a flanking labour organisation (the CISL) which it could not afford to alienate. But so did the DC's coalition partners, the PSDI and the PSI. Thus ever since the watershed period of 1969, whenever the government was involved in negotiations, the private employers always felt the weight of a political agenda tilting towards the other side.

But following the demolition of the Berlin Wall in 1989, the new decade began with moves deliberately aimed at weakening union ties with political parties. The continuation of this trend into the 1990s has thus removed one of the employers' major obstacles to forms of social partnership. Within two years of the collapse of the Berlin Wall, the organised socialist and communist 'components' within the CGIL had disappeared, and the PDS (the reformed and reconstituted PCI) leader, Achille Occhetto, speaking as a guest at the CGIL congress, abandoned the concept of a 'special relationship' between party and union, a step shortly before unthinkable for a communist.[32] Nearly all of the political obstacles to increasing union unity had been removed. By drawing closer together, the confederations could be expected to have fewer problems than ever before in their history in defining a common terrain from which to approach government and employers. At the same time, the abandonment of a special party/union relationship also made it possible for the government itself to function with a greater degree of independence. Subsequent developments in the 1990s should be seen within the context of this scope for greater clarity and independence on the part of the participants in any future social partnership.

Notes

1. For a perceptive account of developments during this period, see A. Pepe, *Movimento operaio e lotte sindacali 1880–1922*, Turin, 1979: 75–84, 145–50.
2. G. Abrate, *La lotta sindacale nella industrializzazione in Italia: 1906–1926*, Milan, 1967: 151. This, and all subsequent Italian quotations, have been translated by the author.
3. See L. Lanzalaco, *Dall'impresa all' associazione. Le organizzazioni degli imprenditori: la Confindustria inprospettiva comparata*, Milan, 1990: 103–4.
4. Cited in A. Lay and M.L. *Pesante, Produttori senza democrazia. Lotte operaie, ideologie corporative e sviluppo economico da Giolitti al fascismo*, Bologna, 1981: 221.
5. See Ibid., 222.
6. *Rerum Novarum*. Encyclical letter of Pope Leo XIII on the condition of the working classes, London, 1991: 10.
7. See G. Pirzio Ammassari, *Teorie del sindacalismo e delle relazioni industriali*, Naples, 1979: 46–8
8. G. Toniolo, *Indirizzi e concetti sociali all'esordire del secolo XX*, Pisa, 1900: 27.
9. See E. Santarelli, *Storia del fascismo*, 3 vols, Rome, 1973, vol. 2: 47.
10. L. Sturzo, *Politica di questi anni, 1950–51*, Bologna, 1957: 309.
11. P. Morgan, *Italian fascism, 1919–1945*, London, 1995: 90.
12. For a summary of the ideological battles in the run-up to the charter, see Santarelli, *Storia del fascismo*, vol. 2: 48–54.
13. For a detailed account of the structures of the corporations, see Ibid., 269–70.
14. Cited in Ibid., 269.
15. Ibid., 54.
16. *La CGIL dal Patto di Roma al Congresso di Genova. Atti e documenti*, 6 vols, Rome, vol. 1: 116.
17. See G. Bedani, *Politics and Ideology in the Italian Workers' Movement*, Oxford, 1995: 81–4.
18. *Ottavo congresso del Partito comunista italiano. Atti e risoluzioni*, Rome, 1957: 437.
19. Daniel Horowitz, in *The Italian Labour Movement*, Cambridge, Mass., 1963: 243, estimated that between 1953 and 1957, out of 748 such agreements, no more than 41 percent included the CGIL.
20. Cited from *The Christian Faith in the Doctrinal Documents of the Catholic Church*, ed J. Dupuis, SJ. Bangalore, 1996: 842.
21. The CUB had emerged in numerous industries as rank-and-file committees of worker delegates with no affiliation to the confederations, and frequently in partial protest against their moderate demands. They were frequently influenced by the ultra-left groups which developed in the period.
22. For an extended discussion in English of this period, see J. Barkan, *Visions of Emancipation: The Italian Workers' Movement since 1945*, New York, 1984: 73ff.
23. G. Baglioni, *Il sindacato dell'autonomia: l'evoluzione della CISL nella pratica e nella cultura*, Bari, 1977: 167–8
24. See S. Negrelli and E. Santi, 'Industrial Relations in Italy', in *European Industrial Relations*, ed. G. Baglioni and C. Crouch, London, 1990: 154–98, 156ff.
25. For a more detailed discussion of the contents of the EUR proposals, see P. Lange and M. Vannicelli, 'Strategy under Stress: The Italian Union Movement and the Italian Crisis in Developmental Perspective', in *Unions, Change and Crisis: French and Italian Union Strategy and the Political Economy 1945–80*, ed. P. Lange, G. Ross and M. Vannicelli, London, 1982: 95–206, 166–79.
26. For a detailed study of this dissent, see M. Golden, *Labor Divided. Austerity and Working-Class Politics in Contemporary Italy*, Ithaca and London, 1988: 89ff.
27. G.M. Gros-Pietro, 'The Restructuring of Large-Sized Industrial Groups', in *Industrial Policy in Italy 1945–90*, ed. M. Baldassarri, London and New York, 1993: 141–59, 153.

28. For a discussion of the Federmeccanica's proposals, see Bedani, *Politics and Ideology in the Italian Workers' Movement*: 254–7.
29. G. Caldarola, 'Due voti di fiducia non fanno una maggioranza', *Rinascita*, 20 April 1984: 4–5, 5.
30. Negrelli and Santi, 'Industrial Relations in Italy': 179.
31. For more detail see *Politics and Ideology in the Italian Workers' Movement*: 278–87.
32. See R. D'Agostini, 'L'unità più vicina', *Nuova rassegna sindacale*, no. 40, 11 November 1991: 9–12, 11.

CHAPTER 14

ITALY IN THE 1990S: POLICY CONCERTATION RESURGENT

Bruce Haddock

Introduction

My concern in this paper is to explain the remarkable resurgence of concertation in Italy in the 1990s in the wake of the acute political and economic crisis which shattered the consensus that had governed public life since 1948. Unions and employers both had to extricate themselves from political relationships that had become deeply compromising. And formal political institutions and practices, always weak in relation to the web of relationships that constituted civil society, had to be refashioned in the light of the unprecedented collapse of the principal governing parties, *Democrazie christiana* (DC) and *Partito socialista italiano* (PSI). The working relationship that emerged may be seen as an adaptation of traditions of social solidarity on both left and right to the challenge of European integration in a hostile global economic environment. The chapter focuses on three principal agreements (the protocol on incomes policy and inflation of July 1992, the Ciampi protocol of July 1993, and the pension reform of May 1995), highlighting the factors that led political, business and union elites to fashion wide-ranging agreements in the face of economic and political crisis.

Context

The 1990s have proved to be a remarkable decade in Italian politics, not least for the trade union movement. The *sindacato* (unions) began the decade in a position of weakness and confusion. Technological developments and the emergence of new patterns of employment had undermined the traditional constituency of the unions among the industrial working class. With small and medium-sized enterprises clearly outperforming heavy industry in the 1980s, levels of unionisation fell and new associations emerged beyond the traditional core of the three peak trade union confederations: *Confederazione generale del lavoro* (CGIL), *Confederazione italiana sindacati lavoratori* (CISL) and *Unione italiana dei lavoratori* (UIL).[1] The conventional wisdom in political economy had also challenged the theoretical assumptions that had been central to union strategy throughout the postwar period. The idea of the state as employer and provider was deeply entrenched, especially in the south, where the private sector was weak. It was assumed that the role of the *sindacato* was either to force concessions from the state (as had been the pattern following the 'hot autumn' of 1969) or to defend concessions already made regarding employment rights and levels of income as the economic climate made the position of employees more vulnerable. At the level of rhetoric, at least, the language of industrial confrontation made sustained tripartite concertation very difficult to attain.

The scope for concertation was further complicated by the clear political divisions between the principal union confederations. The communist-dominated CGIL had always been happier with the language of class conflict than either the CISL (DC-dominated) or the UIL (PSI-dominated). Where the CGIL saw itself representing the interests of a class, both the CISL and the UIL tended to focus on the interests of members. Given the governmental involvement of the DC and PSI throughout the 1980s, it was not easy for the confederations as a whole to present a united oppositional front to the government, even in the face of a consistent squeeze on incomes and entitlements. But neither could the CGIL risk getting out of line with a union membership that had grown more cautious and moderate in response to precarious employment conditions. The lesson of the union defeat in the 1980 FIAT strike still haunted the leadership. And, if anything, structural changes in the Italian economy had made the union position weaker by 1990.[2]

Crisis

The position of the unions was transformed by the political crisis which rocked Italy between 1990 and 1994 in ways that could not have been anticipated.[3] Disaffection with mainstream politics, symbolised by the emergence of the *Lega nord*, seriously weakened the established parties in the 1992 elections. By 1994 the crisis had deepened, with both the DC and the PSI being disbanded following revelations of systemic corruption. The *Partito communista italiano* (PCI), too, had metamorphosed into the *Partito democratico della sinistra* (PDS) in 1991, with a significant rump (*Rifondazione communista*) remaining faithful to the class-based rhetoric and ideology of the left wing of the PCI. Significantly, however, the PCI had remained more or less untainted by the drama of *tangentopoli* (Bribesville).[4] And though the end of the Cold War had made life very difficult for old-style communist parties in Western Europe, the earlier dominance of the reformist leadership of the PCI made the transition to a left-of-centre social democratic identity easily manageable. What is more remarkable, perhaps, is that the collapse of the political authority of the leadership of the CISL and the UIL should have done so little to impair the effectiveness of the trade union confederations.

The role of the CGIL was crucial in this development. Though it had always been difficult to maintain a united front among the confederations, the numerical predominance of the CGIL, together with the emergence of autonomous unions and professional associations and the problems all the confederations had in controlling their grass-roots support, obliged the *sindacato* as a group to be wary of identifying unreservedly with the party-political affiliation of their leaderships. There was thus a clear sense in which the unions could act as a *soggetto politico* (political actor) independently of the established political parties.

A measure of independence was crucial as the political crisis came to a head in 1992–4. What many commentators at the time heralded as the end of the 'First Republic' turned out, on closer inspection and with the advantage of hindsight, to be the collapse of a style of governance. It was not the republican constitution, difficult to manage though that was in certain respects, but the dominant role of the political parties in their 'colonisation' of the institutions of state and the principal organs of civil society that had undermined the legitimacy of the established ruling class in Italy. Throughout the 1980s *partitocrazia* (party-ocracy) was identified as the bane of the republic, distorting the proper functioning of both political institutions and the economy. The fact that the unions were able to carve out a clear niche as a *soggetto politico* thus enabled them to survive the tribulations of their (erstwhile) political masters.

Nor were the unions alone in seeking to distance themselves from the parties. From the late 1980s the peak employer confederation *Confindustria* had been anxious not to identify itself too closely with the position of the DC. The cosy relationship between the political elite and Italy's economic oligarchy actually excluded the small and medium-sized enterprises that had been most successful in the 1980s. *Confindustria* was thus under pressure from its own members to campaign against the economic costs of ill-judged political patronage. *Confindustria* became a principal advocate of institutional reform, especially after the appointment of Luigi Abete to the presidency in 1992.[5] An effective market was seen by many business interests to be incompatible with the kind of clientelistic regime that the DC had created.

Concertation in these circumstances was thus deeply problematic. The usual tripartite relationship between unions, employers and government was distorted by the role of the parties in all three spheres. This, coupled with weak cabinet control in the Italian system, made the formulation and implementation of policy a contorted and inefficient process.[6] Strategic planning was effectively reduced to factional brokerage. Economic management amounted to a series of crisis responses, orchestrated largely by the Bank of

Italy. The situation was recognised to be unsustainable, even by the parties themselves. Yet the system was such that well-placed vested interests could easily block painful structural and institutional reform.

The situation was brought to a head by the double-edged crisis that hit Italy in 1992. The corruption scandals had begun to undermine the legitimacy of *partitocrazia*, yet a concatenation of economic circumstances made decisive political leadership imperative. The terms of the Maastricht Treaty had set targets for the budget deficit, public-sector debt, inflation and exchange-rate stability which few international observers expected Italy to meet. Italy was thus facing a crisis of economic confidence in a state of political paralysis. The fine line separating crisis from catastrophe seemed to have been crossed, exposing Italy to speculative pressure on the international financial markets which even a solidly based government would have found difficult to resist. The lire was in fact forced out of the exchange-rate mechanism in September 1992, leading to a series of devaluations which would see the lire losing about a third of its external value by 1995.[7] What pundits described as a 'Latin American scenario' seemed to be beckoning, with the economy veering out of control.

The restoration of international confidence in Italian financial management was clearly a high priority. Evidence from 1972–6, when there was a comparably acute devaluation of the lire, suggests that containing the cost of labour was likely to be a crucial dimension of any half-way plausible remedial strategy. The notorious *scala mobile* system of automatic wage indexation was established in 1975, following agreement between the union confederations and *Confindustria*. This marked the high point of the conflictual strategy of the CGIL. The government had reluctantly agreed to an arrangement that would only work from the perspective of employers if costs could be passed on to consumers. In the event, the nominal cost of labour increased by 94 percent between 1972 and 1976.[8] Industrial peace had been bought at the price of domestic inflation. That option was simply not available in 1992. The exposure of the major European economies to international competition was such that prospects for growth and employment could not be secured simply by allowing a currency to devalue. Long-term competitive gains from controlled devaluation would only accrue if domestic costs could be contained. It was feared in 1992 that Italy lacked both the political will and the appropriate institutional structures.

Response

Policy concertation effectively (and rather remarkably) filled the void that had been left by the political parties. The first requirement was to secure broad agreement on a framework for formulating incomes policy. It was widely accepted, even on the left, that the *scala mobile* functioned as a structural ratchet on inflation, restricting the scope for a bargaining strategy that accorded a high priority to the protection of employment. Efforts to reduce its inflationary impact had been prominent in the 1980s. Craxi secured agreement in 1983 and 1984 to measures that traded percentage increases against wider concessions on employment and welfare policy.[9] But the *scala mobile* as a framework for incomes policy continued to be regarded as 'untouchable', especially by the CGIL.[10] Economic and political crisis, however, coupled with the stringent requirements of the Maastricht Treaty, focused minds wonderfully. Realism on the union side, which had been evident in negotiations begun in 1990, was suddenly brought to a head. The choice for the unions was essentially between the disruption and uncertainty of a market solution, with all the implications that would have for membership figures that had declined significantly since the 1970s, and negotiated concessions. In the event, a consensual agreement (arguably) proved to be the best market solution.

The symbolic breakthrough was sealed with the signing of the 'Protocol on Incomes Policy, the Struggle against Inflation, and the Cost of Labour'on 31 July 1992. As Richard Locke has noted, the protocol 'was not strictly speaking a collective agreement but rather a document in which the Italian government outlined its future economic policies'.[11] The headline commitment was the definitive abolition of the *scala mobile*, together with a freeze on wages and salaries for the rest of the year and a temporary suspension of firm- or plant-level wage negotiations. At first glance, it might appear that the unions had been forced by circumstances to surrender nearly all the ground won in the 1970s in return for little more than help in maintaining grass-roots discipline. But the agreement must be seen in the wider context of a range of policies designed to reduce government expenditure, especially in relation to public-sector pensions, and to introduce a more equitable system of taxation. The unions had been concerned, in particular, to see Italy's flourishing and varied self-employed sector shouldering a fair share of a tax burden which had previously fallen disproportionately on waged and salaried employees. The introduction of the so-called 'minimum tax' was a signal of the Amato government's resolve to address the chronic problem of tax evasion, something that DC-dominated governments had tacitly avoided for fear of antagonising an important group of their 'natural' supporters.

What might have appeared to be an admission of union weakness was actually a part of a painful process of repositioning in relation to the governmental process as a whole. The CGIL, in particular, had been engaged in a complex and vitriolic internal debate about the appropriate role for a union in a modern capitalist economy. The leadership had committed itself to the principle of 'codetermination' in 1991 as part of a wider programme focused on the extension of democratic control to the economy and workplace. But this had never been accepted by a left wing that continued to think in class terms. Grass-roots opposition to the abandonment of the *scala mobile* led to stormy protest meetings. Bruno Trentin, the Secretary General of the CGIL, clearly felt that he had reached the limit of his discretion and at one point offered to resign.[12]

Abolition of the *scala mobile* alone would not have been acceptable to large sections of the workforce. The difficulties the established union confederations had experienced in controlling their own (declining) memberships and halting the proliferation of autonomous associations would have been exacerbated and could have heralded a renewed period of industrial unrest, as had occurred in the early 1960s.[13] Of more significance was the tripartite accord of July 1993, agreed with the incoming Ciampi government (the Ciampi Protocol). The Protocol confirmed the abolition of the *scala mobile* but went on to elaborate a formal contractual structure for the conduct of industrial relations. Crucially, it was now accepted that salary and wage negotiations would be tripartite affairs, pursued within parameters set by the government's macroeconomic expectations as specified in the budget. Clauses relating specifically to wages would be renewed every two years. Broader matters relating to conditions of work would be settled every four years. *Confindustria* had argued that agreements should be exclusively at the national level, but (following union pressure) company-level negotiations were retained for productivity deals. Important changes were also introduced to the plant-level representation of workers, opening up two-thirds of the positions of shop stewards to election by the entire workforce. It was widely expected that this would significantly weaken the plant-level control of the three principal union confederations. But, in fact, plant-level elections seem to have reinvigorated the confederations themselves, leading them to consolidate their positions and at the same time to enhance their legitimacy.[14]

It was difficult at the time to estimate the likely impact of the Ciampi Protocol. Clearly each of the partners to the agreement had different interests to secure. Ciampi himself described 'the agreement on the cost of labour' as the most significant achievement of his government.[15] Though the Protocol itself was only one among a number of variables, including high unemployment, low expectations for growth, and intense exposure to international competition, it proved more effective in delivering wage restraint than any other policy initiative since the 1960s. Between November 1994 and November 1995, for example, salaries and wages rose by only 3.9 percent, while the cost of living rose by 6 percent.[16] Over a slightly longer period, the nominal cost of labour per unit of industrial production rose by only 8 percent between 1991 and 1995, compared with 94 percent between 1972 and 1976.[17] From the perspective of the government and *Confindustria*, too, the modification to the *Cassa integrazione guadagni* (the government-financed redundancy fund) began to reduce disincentives to employee flexibility.

The advantages of wage restraint and flexibility are, of course, less obvious from a union perspective. What the unions faced, however, was marginalisation from the strategic centres of political and economic life. Many on the right argued that the global integration of markets had rendered neo-corporatist or consociational models of decision making redundant. In these quarters, the Anglo-American model of a minimally regulated market is seen as the most effective response to international competition. Incomes policy in any of its guises smacks of *dirigisme*, brokerage and compromise, yielding sub-optimal outcomes in distorted markets. Even though the model of the pure market may be regarded as unworkable, the rhetoric of laissez-faire clearly serves to delegitimise union influence and involvement. The fact that the unions were able to reposition themselves at the centre of politics in these circumstances was a considerable achievement.

Towards a New Politics?

The political capacity of the unions was very soon put to the test with the victory of the *Polo delle libertà* (the Freedom Alliance), an alliance of parties led by Silvio Berlusconi, in the elections of May 1994. In ideological terms the government was a curious mixture of the consumerism of Berlusconi's *Forza Italia*, the state-centred rhetoric of *Alleanza nazionale*, and the federalism (sometimes verging on separatism) of the *Lega nord*. None of the parties or movements could be said to be sympathetic to the unions. The predominant emphasis in economic policy, especially from Berlusconi, was on market reform as the key to economic renewal in Italy. If Berlusconi had a political model, it was very much Margaret Thatcher. The prospects for constructive concertation in these circumstances were not good.

Berlusconi began by assuring the unions that the procedures of the Ciampi Protocol would continue to be respected. But it was clear from the outset that the involvement of the unions in the formulation of macroeconomic policy would be marginal. And even on issues directly affecting conditions of work, such as pensions reform, union reservations were not taken seriously. For Berlusconi, structural reform of public-sector finances was crucial to the restoration of international confidence in the Italian economy. He felt that the credibility of his government would be undermined if the unions were seen to exercise any kind of veto. In these circumstances, he committed himself to pressing ahead with reform, without union agreement if need be.[18]

Here was a challenge that would really test the capacity of the unions to act as a *soggetto politico*, much as unions in Britain in the 1980s were confronted by uncongenial policy and legislation designed to marginalise them from the political mainstream. Berlusconi had presumably calculated that structural changes to the Italian economy since the 1970s made it unlikely that the unions would be able to orchestrate a sustained campaign of mass protest. Certainly the unions themselves recognised that times had changed and had little appetite for a return to the ideologically charged conflictual strategies of the 1970s. But at the same time grass-roots feeling was so strong that their credibility as the organised representatives of employees was at stake. In the event, Berlusconi's virtual exclusion of the unions from policy making forced them to take to the streets, though with profound misgivings. A general strike and mass demonstrations in October and November of 1994 were among the largest and best organised of the postwar period. Berlusconi was forced to back down, seriously weakening his authority. It is important to stress that the unions were not challenging the authority of the government so much as protesting about their exclusion from the decision-making process. Even on the narrow question of pensions reform, as Michael Braun has pointed out, they accepted that far-reaching changes were necessary. Reforms, however, could not simply be imposed upon a passive workforce. The demonstrations of autumn 1994 can thus be seen as a 'conflict in the name of concertation'.[19]

The important point from the union perspective is that a clear line was drawn between opposition to specific policy and continued endorsement of the Ciampi Protocol. Thus despite the highly charged and confrontational atmosphere between government and unions, important new national wage contracts were agreed harmoniously. The unions had thus effectively cast Berlusconi in the role of *agent provocateur*, precipitating a conflict which could easily have been avoided had the spirit of the Ciampi Protocol been observed.

Whether 'concertation as usual' could be restored very much depended on the attitude of the incoming Dini government in January 1995. The unions had made public their support for Dini and were clearly relieved to be dealing with a 'technocratic' government which studiously avoided confrontational rhetoric. Discussions between government and unions on pensions reform were resumed immediately, leading to far-reaching proposals which tackled both the technical management of pensions and the excessively generous entitlements that parties controlling public funds had been happy to dispense. Employee expectations had to be radically adjusted. In conjunction with the government, the unions were prepared to defend measures that would oblige individuals to revise their life plans fundamentally. They went so far as to organise a referendum of their members on the proposals, effectively promoting a 'vote of confidence' in the Dini government.[20] As Michael Braun has noted, 'the savings achieved by the Dini reform were only slightly lower than would have been achieved by Berlusconi's proposal'.[21] The crucial lesson, however, was political. The unions had shown that they could accept tough decisions and deliver the support of their members if they were treated as partners in a cooperative enterprise.

Cooperation continued in broader areas of economic policy. The 1996 budget was discussed extensively with the unions. It was recognised by all partners (though not by all political parties) that tight control of incomes was a *conditio sine qua non* of economic renewal. Any slippage on that front would simply have allowed domestic inflation to erode the competitive advantage that stemmed from the 1992 devaluation. In the light of continuing efforts to meet the Maastricht criteria, and lingering German suspicions that Italian economic reforms had been cosmetic rather than structural, any concessions on public spending were likely to be construed as a failure of political will among the Italian elite to make hard choices. The unions had no doubt that the interests of their members were best served by sustaining international confidence in the Italian economy. In this sense, the formal decision on 25 March 1998 to admit Italy to the first wave of Euro-membership must be seen as a triumph for concertation. Whether the framework that had emerged following the Ciampi Protocol would prove sufficient to manage the rigours of competition once the single currency was functioning remained, of course, another question.

Concertation had proved its effectiveness as a means of managing economic crisis (see Tables 14.1 and 14.2).[22] The years 1992–8, however, cannot be regarded as typical. A period in which both employers and employees had lost confidence in the political elite could not serve as an ideal model for tripartite partnership. The achievement of these years should not be underestimated. A political elite that could not manage a modern economy was quietly and peacefully replaced. It is important to note, however, that the realism that has been a feature of industrial relations in the 1990s has not always prevailed at the political level. The widely held belief that economic renewal depended upon constitutional reform has not been vindicated. References to the emergence of a 'Second Republic' since 1994 have clearly been premature. Indeed it is surely significant that the restoration of economic stability has enabled tortuous consideration of constitutional reform to be abandoned without agreement, at least for the moment. Prospects for con-

Table 14.1. *Key Arguments in Italy*

Proponent	Argument
For	
Most political actors	Economic stability.
Union confederations	Avoidance of economic marginalisation in an increasingly hostile market context
PDS	Social solidarity.
Confindustria	Wage moderation; control of inflation; meeting EMU convergence criteria.
Government	Control of inflation; reduction of public-sector debt; meeting EMU convergence criteria; enhancing legitimacy in a period of political crisis.
Against	
Most political actors	Fear of corporatism, in fascist sense.
Small business	Fear of marginalisation from national negotiations.
Liberal economists	Fear of creating further obstacles to economic flexibility; fear of continued consolidation of an excessive role for the state in economic management.

Source: see text.

Table 14.2. *Social Pacts in Italy During the 1990s*

Date	Nature
July 1992	Protocol on incomes policy, the struggle against inflation, and the cost of labour
July 1993	Ciampi protocol
May 1995	Pension reform

Source: see text.

structive tripartite partnership are thus still hampered by weakness in the structure of Italian government.

The problem has been highlighted by recent efforts, again led by Ciampi, this time as Treasury Minister, to agree a new social pact following the pattern of the 1993 accord. In an interview in *Il sole 24 ore* Ciampi has argued that the 1993 Protocol gave Italy stability. He sees an effective incomes policy as the key to both counter-inflation strategy and the Italian 'entry into Europe'.[23] The next step, according to Ciampi, is an 'agreement on growth, investment and employment'.[24] He wanted a commitment from the unions to further market flexibility, especially in relation to labour, in return for a commitment from employers to increase investment. How government might facilitate such an agreement was not clear in initial proposals presented in August 1998. Ciampi wanted entrepreneurs to accept that domestic profit levels would be maintained at current levels, with gains from productivity being used to finance further investment and a more aggressive pursuit of markets overseas. In this scheme of things, 'the government indicates the priorities of the system, the rest is left to the market'.[25]

But while government is clearly justified in setting target levels for investment, or at least creating market conditions that favour investment, focus on actual profit levels is unlikely to be effective. The General Secretary of *Confindustria*, Innocenzo Cipolletta, argues that 'increased investment is not a function of current profit levels but of anticipated increases in the level of profit in the future'.[26] The best tactic for the government, on this view, is to reduce the fiscal burden on business and industry. To fix levels of profit is effectively to reduce incentives for investment.

Economists have also been critical. Nicola Rossi, an adviser to Massimo D'Alema (leader of the PDS), has argued that while it is perfectly possible to use legislative means to reduce the rigidities of the labour market, the government simply does not have effective means of securing levels of private investment, short of reintroducing economic controls that would automatically reduce flexibility.[27] For Renato Brunetta, insistence on tripartite agreement would shift Italy back towards neo-corporativism, with all the problems that entails. 'The logic of the grand pact ended with inflation, it no longer works and ought to be abandoned'.[28] For a neo-liberal such as Antonio Martino the whole thing smacks of *dirigisme* and is only intelligible as a political concession to *Rifondazione communista*.[29]

Fausto Bertinotti himself, however, leader of *Rifondazione communista*, could see nothing in the pact beyond a projection of hopes. He had pressed the government to change direction and return to active government intervention rather than another framework for the consideration of possibilities.[30] And though union leaders welcomed the government's commitment to development and growth, the call for labour market flexibility was met with some perplexity. The leader of the UIL, Pietro Larizza, was at a loss to know what kind of flexibility was currently lacking in Italy. He argues that to speak in 'generic terms' about flexibility is actually to evade concrete consideration of real problems.[31] Walter Cerfeda of the CGIL claims that 'all the imaginable instruments of labour market flexibility are already in place'.[32] The unions, in other words, claim to have delivered their side of the bargain already; it remains for *Confindustria* and the government to take concrete steps to increase levels of investment.

Ciampi's new social pact was not finally accepted. This should not be regarded as a reverse for the principle of concertation. The fact that discussions had gone ahead on the basis of a proposal is actually a part of the process. The government had issued a statement of intent, which set the parameters for discussion even in the absence of agreement. And, unlike the situation in 1992–3, failure to seal an accord has no implications whatever for international confidence. In ordinary circumstances, social partners will have different views on the desirability of specific policy initiatives. What we have is consultation on a broad agenda rather than 'codetermination' in the strict sense; but the principle of consensual economic management has been respected.

Concertation Italian Style

Concertation was never an appropriate focus for fine-tuning at the macroeconomic level. Where it has proved to be invaluable is as a vehicle for fostering agreement to broad measures in a factionally divided polity. The stark divisions between the political parties, especially before 1992, concealed a more fundamental trait in Italian political culture. The view of society as a scheme of social cooperation has deep roots in the dominant political traditions.[33] How social solidarity should be mobilised is, of course, a divisive issue. But where orthodox political institutions have failed to sustain social consensus effectively, other organs of civil society have rescued a political class that has often been paralysed by the demands of short-term tactical adjustment.

While there is much agreement among the new political establishment regarding the benefits of concertation as a policy style, it remains problematic among fringe groups. The comfortable consensus was shaken in May 1999 by the assassination of Massimo D'Antona, an academic who had served as under-secretary and adviser to the government in drawing up working details of schemes of concertation. The group claiming responsibility, ominously called *Brigate rosse* (Red Brigade), published a 28-page document on the internet denouncing all forms of concertation and social pacts as species of neo-corporatism. Whether the new-style *Brigate rosse* had genuine links with the group active in the 1970s and 1980s remains unclear. The rhetorical language, however, suggests that the theoretical identification of neo-corporatism with neo-fascism on the extreme left is still resonant.

The hope and expectation of political commentators is that the assassination is an aberration in the process of building a pragmatic and sustainable working political culture. Commentators are more concerned about the capacity of the Italian economy, with its relatively inflexible formal structure, to modernise in the face of international competition. Concertation has so far proved to be an effective means of maintaining solidarity in the context of potentially divisive reforms. But it also puts a severe restraint on the scope of those reforms. The fear is that concertation may be compromised, just as the *compromesso storico* was in the late 1970s, as political initiatives fail to respond to complex and intractable circumstances.

For the moment, concertation yields positive benefits, especially at local level. The mayor of Naples, Antonio Bassolino, announced a programme of measures in May 1999 which he described as 'concertazione tutta napoletana', financed jointly from public and private sources, with a reasonable expectation of 10,000 new jobs being created over four years.[34] It is unlikely that such measures could be replicated nationally, and even less likely that the formal institutional structure of Italian government would enable effective organisation and leadership to be exercised from the centre. Concertation Italian-style fills a gap left by weak central control. Whether it will continue to prove effective in the absence of structural political reform remains an open question.

Notes

1. Gino Bedani, *Politics and Ideology in the Italian Workers' Movement: Union Development and the Changing Role of the Catholic and Communist Subcultures in Postwar Italy*, Oxford, 1995: 326–31.
2. Paul Ginsborg, *L'Italia del tempo presente: Famiglia, società civile, stato, 1980–1996*, Turin, 1998.
3. For background see Patrick McCarthy, *The Crisis of the Italian State: From the Origins of the Cold War to the Fall of Berlusconi*, New York, 1995; and Bruce Haddock, 'The Crisis of the Italian State', in *European Integration and Disintegration: East and West*, ed. Robert Bideleux and Richard Taylor, London, 1996: 111–26. For the specific impact on the trade union movement see Carl Levy, 'Italian Trade Unionism in the 1990s: The Persistence of Corporatism?', *Journal of Area Studies* 5 (1994): 63–70.
4. Sarah Waters, 'Tangentopoli and the Emergence of a New Political Order in Italy', *West European Politics* 17 (1994): 169–82.
5. Liborio Mattina, 'La Confindustria di Abete: dall'alleanza con la DC all'appello multipartitico', in *Politica in Italia: i fatti dell'anno e le interpretazioni*, ed. Stephen Hellman and Gianfranco Pasquino, Bologna, 1993: 265–83.
6. David Hine, *Governing Italy: The Politics of Bargained Pluralism*, Oxford, 1993; and Paul Furlong, *Modern Italy: Representation and Reform*, London, 1994.
7. Salvatore Rossi, *La politica economica italiana 1968–1998*, Bari, 1998: 107.
8. Ibid., 109.
9. Hugh Compston, 'Union Participation in Economic Policy Making in France, Italy, Germany and Britain, 1970–1993', *West European Politics* 18 (1995): 321–2.
10. Richard Locke, '*Eppure si tocca*: The Abolition of the *scala mobile*', in *Italian Politics: Ending the First Republic*, ed. Carol Mershon and Gianfranco Pasquino, Boulder, 1995: 185–95.
11. Ibid., 190.
12. Ibid., 191.
13. Ibid., 193.
14. Mimmo Carrieri, *Seconda Repubblica senza sindacati? Il futuro della concertazione in Italia*, Rome, 1997: 46–51.
15. Paul Ginsborg, *L'Italia del tempo presente*, 520.

16. Michael Braun, 'I sindacati confederali e il governo Dini: il grande ritorno del neo-corporativismo?', in *Politica in Italia: I fatti dell'anno e le interpretazioni*, ed. Mario Caciagli and David I. Kertzer, Bologna, 1996: 229.
17. Rossi, *La politica economica italiana*, 109.
18. Braun, 'I sindacati confederali e il governo Dini', 224–5.
19. Ibid., 225.
20. Ibid., 227.
21. Ibid., 228.
22. Marino Regini and Ida Regalia, 'Employers, Unions and the State: The Resurgence of Concertation in Italy?', *Crisis and Transition in Italian Politics*, ed. Martin Bull and Martin Rhodes, London, 1997: 210–30.
23. *Il sole 24 ore*, 21 August 1998: 3.
24. Ibid., 3.
25. Ibid., 1.
26. *Il sole 24 ore*, 22 August 1998: 5.
27. Ibid., 5.
28. Ibid., 5.
29. Ibid., 5.
30. *La Repubblica*, 23 August 1998: 19.
31. *Il sole 24 ore*, 22 August 1998: 5.
32. Ibid., 5.
33. For broad discussion in relation to the labour movement see Bedani, *Politics and Ideology.*
34. *Il sole 24 ore*, 23 May 1999: 1.

CHAPTER 15

THE NETHERLANDS IN HISTORICAL PERSPECTIVE: THE RISE AND FALL OF DUTCH POLICY CONCERTATION

Anton Hemerijck

Introduction

Over the past few years, the resurgence and proficiency of Dutch social partnership has become the wonder and sometimes envy of foreign commentators. The key to international acclaim has been the miraculous recovery from the 'Dutch disease' in the 1970s by way of modernising the welfare state through a lengthy process of negotiated social policy reform from the early 1980s through to the 1990s.[1] The focus of this chapter is historical. It offers a reminder that contemporary policies and institutions have deep historical roots. The argument is divided into two parts. The first part contains a brief description of the (prewar) origins of Dutch corporatism.[2] This is followed by an analysis of the postwar transformation of the Dutch 'harmony model' in the 1950s and 1960s up to the experience of immobile policy corporatism in the 1970s and early 1980s.[3] I stop just short of the miraculous recovery of policy concertation in the Netherlands in the 1980s and 1990s.

The Origins of Dutch Corporatism

In the following paragraphs, I will examine the Dutch evolution of state formation, its impact on subsequent processes of cleavage mobilisation, and consider their implications for the development of the institutional structures and the ideational dimension of social partnership in the Netherlands.

With the adoption of the quasi-constitution of the *Unie van Utrecht* of 1579, the Dutch established a culturally pluralistic and regionally decentralised polity known as the Republic of the Seven United Provinces. The Dutch Republic emerged from the revolt against Spain.[4] The Dutch revolt has its origins in two rival conceptions of the state; the modern unitary absolutist state and the ancient dual order of the *Ständestaat*.[5] The Dutch nobility responded to a perceived infringement of their traditional corporate rights and ancient liberties by the legal sovereign Philip II of Spain. With the Edict of Nantes of 1581, the States-General renounced their allegiance to Philip II. After having failed to find a new princely sovereign, the Dutch turned to a republican form of government. The emerging political structure of the Republic became a loosely-knit oligarchical confederacy of seven sovereign polities with the States-General at its centre, which allowed *Ständestaat* traditions and institutions to be maintained throughout the Golden Age of the Republic in the seventeenth century. The Dutch Republic was fraught with opportunities for disagreement, obstruction and stalemates in policy making.[6] As regional, religious and national factionalism all became well-understood facts of life, this fostered a political style of constantly accommodating conflict and antagonism through practices of *schikken* and *plooien* – compromising and negotiating mutual concessions – between the many corporate offices and authorities of the Republic.

A number of unifying factors supporting the stability and success of the Dutch Republic in the seventeenth century can be listed. First of all, unity was considered nesessary in order to resist the absolutist ambitions of Spain. Second, the States-General remained small. It comprised only twenty-four men, who knew each other intimately. Much political decision making was prepared in the corridors of the provincial estates and the States-General. Politically divisive issues were often delegated to so-called 'besognes', special committees working behind closed doors, bent on depoliticising problems and accommodating divergent interests. Third, there was the integrating force of the wealthy province of Holland, which contributed almost 60 percent of the budget of the Republic. Economic and political interdependency between Holland and Zeeland and the other provinces strengthened the union. Finally, there was the existence of a para-monarchical office of *stadhouder*, which represented the princely sovereign in the estates. After the revolt, the Princes of the House of Orange held the office of *stadhouder* in more than one province at a time.[7]

The state–church settlement reached in the Dutch Republic involved a compromise between ardent Calvinism and religious tolerance.[8] The revolt against Spain bore a Calvinist stamp, but it did not encourage Calvinist supremacy. The *Unie van Utrecht* stipulated the doctrine of provincial sovereignty, which implied that each province maintained its freedom in religious affairs. As the Republic never developed into a 'unitary state', the Dutch Reformed Church could not become an 'established church'. The absence of a state church and the decentralised character of the Republic thus encouraged the practice of toleration in religious affairs. Also the pervasiveness of bourgeois values among the upper middle classes saved the Republic from bitter antagonisms between state and church. Jews, Mennonites, Remonstrants, Lutherans and Quakers, all succeeded in leading a tolerable existence. And while Roman Catholics, who remained a strong minority, were banned from public worship, they were allowed to conduct services in private.

By the middle of the eighteenth century the splendour of the Dutch Republic was withering away. The failure to resolve basic internal conflicts made it powerless in the face of mounting external pressures. During the French occupation (1803–13) a unitary administrative framework was established.[9] This, however, did not destroy the impact of the earlier legacy of regional diversity and traditions of collegiate decision making. Most important, the unitary state changed the site of political opposition from the provincial to the national political arena.[10]

Cleavage Mobilisation

In the revolutionary year of 1848, King William II agreed to a drastic constitutional revision, introducing direct elections for the Second Chamber, and full ministerial responsibility to the States-General.[11] Two contentious issues came to dominate Dutch politics in the second half of the nineteenth century. These were the 'school issue', the prolonged conflict over public secular and private religious education, and the 'social question', the problem of working-class protest in the face of industrialisation. The school issue evolved around the conflict between the liberal state on the one hand, and Orthodox Calvinists and Roman Catholics on the other. The restoration of Catholic episcopal hierarchy in 1853 finally formalised the separation of the church from the state. During the 1850s animosity arose in Calvinist circles against the liberal government over the status of primary schools. The liberal education bill of 1857 advocated a school system in which broader, rather general, Christian and humanist values were to be taught. Orthodox Protestants demanded of the government the right to establish their own private or *bijzondere* (special) schools. After the publication of the papal encyclical letter *Syllabus Errorum* in 1868, which declared neutral public education unfit for Catholics, Dutch Catholics also turned against the liberal government. At the elections of 1888, the anti-revolutionaries and Catholics were able to achieve a narrow majority in parliament, which brought the liberal hegemony of nineteenth-century Dutch political life to an end. With the School Law of 1889, the coalition introduced a limited degree of public funding for private denominational Orthodox Protestant and Roman Catholic schools. In 1904 and 1908 public aid was also extended to private secondary schools and universities.

The outcome of the 1913 election revealed that stable majoritarian rule had become increasingly precarious. Out of the ensuing political impasse, a process of constitutional revision took place. In the final settlement, which made history as the Great Pacification of 1917, the political parties involved, including the Social Democrats, decided on universal male suffrage and agreed over proportional representation within the frame of a single national constituency and compulsory attendance at the polls. In 1922 suffrage was extended to women. As proportional representation would directly reveal the relative strength of each minority cleavage in Parliament, Parliament came to represent a perfect mirror of the core cleavages of Dutch society. Moreover, Dutch politics came to bear the seal of confessionalism, as Christian Democratic parties held a majority in both Parliament and government throughout the interwar years.[12]

The interwar period became the era of pillarisation in the Netherlands. Each cleavage embarked on the development of detailed networks of social organisations, including schools, universities, political parties, trade unions, employers' organisations, and welfare and health organisations for their adherents. The formation of separate subcultures proceeded at a rather different pace for different ideological groupings. The Catholics organised the most 'total' institution of the pillars of Dutch society. The Social Democrats, when they entered the political arena, found the potential organisational space had already been restricted by the early mobilisation of Calvinists and Catholic workers. The liberal establishment, finally, the most influential grouping for the greater part of the nineteenth century, failed to achieve some form of organisational unity. Their individualist outlook stood in the way of collective organisation.

The policy significance of the Great Pacification lies in the institutionalisation of sharing of political space as a rule of procedure in Dutch policy making. Major public responsibilities in the areas of health care, culture, social housing, unemployment benefits, and even government employment, came to be compartmentalised and run separately by and for different pillars, supported by expert advice from a series of advisory bodies and committees, run on basis of 'parity' representation.

Because the school issue, and thereby the subcultural emancipation of Orthodox Calvinist and Roman Catholic religious groups, preceded the advent of the social question, the politics of industrial relations came to be shaped along denominational divisions in the early decades of the twentieth century. This led to the establishment of pillarised, subculturally segmented, patterns of industrial relations of separate Calvinist, Catholic and Socialist trade unions, and Calvinist, Catholic and Liberal employers' organisations. By means of interlocking directorates, confessional unions and employers' organisations came to be closely connected with like-minded political parties. By absorbing large segments of the working class, confessional pillars circumscribed the development of social democratic class organisation. The emerging twofold-divided Calvinist-Catholic and religious-secular subcultural geography of the Netherlands had two additional consequences for the evolution of the Dutch system of industrial relations. In terms of the organisational capacities of capital and labour, the dynamic of pillarisation encouraged, first, the formation of coherent, vertically integrated, centralised 'peak' trade union and employers' confederations. Second, pillarisation fostered an exceptionally divided pattern of industrial relations and thus forestalled the formation of a unified labour movement.[13]

Corporatist Programme Competition

The impact of the Great Depression on ideological developments within the Calvinist, Catholic and socialist pillars, is of special interest. Over the 1920s and 1930s their respective ideas and ideals of economic order gradually converged. Already in 1891, the leader of the orthodox Calvinists, Abraham Kuyper, proposed to redesign the relationship between the state and civil society over the issue of the 'social question'. In 1897, he proposed a Bill on the Chambers of Labour, which should represent workers' interests, alongside the already existing Chambers of Commerce, which embodied employers' interests, arguing that working and living conditions were first and foremost the joint responsibility of employers and workers. Kuyper's proposal was consistent with the central Calvinist principle of 'sovereignty in private circles' (*soevereiniteit in eigen kring*), which stipulates that both state and civil society hold their own independent spheres of sovereignty.[14]

The Roman Catholic revival of corporatist social thought dates back to the publication of the encyclical letter *Rerum Novarum* in 1891. *Rerum Novarum* advocated a Thomist conception of the relationship between state and civil society. Neo-thomism envisioned a picture of class harmony, a general solidarity between the naturally formed estates of employers, employees, shopkeepers and farmers. The more the economic estates cooperated, the greater moral unity and harmony, and the more enterprise and society would prosper. The guiding principle for the proper relation between the state and civil society was the 'principle of subsidiarity', implying that higher-level organs should not take on tasks that are best served by lower layers in the hierarchy of the social order. With respect to the role of the state, the Catholic vision of social order departs from Calvinist doctrine. In Catholic social thought the state is granted an overriding authority. By contrast, in the Calvinist doctrine of sovereign circles all social spheres are fully sovereign so as to protect them from hierarchical or state interference.

The economist and legal theorist J.A. Veraart is undoubtedly the most important Catholic advocate of a corporatist organisation of Dutch economic life. His ideas on statutory legal industrial organisation, the so-called *Publiekrechtelijke Bedrijfsorganisatie* (PBO) have had a profound impact on the evolution of Dutch social and economic policy making.[15] Veraart believed that a correction to the principle of individualistic competition was best served through the introduction of industrial boards with parity representation for workers and employers in the different branches of industry. The boards were to be granted a large degree of autonomous legislative power and jurisdiction under public law and authorised to take binding decisions on working conditions, prices, wages and the organisation of enterprises. And at the apex of the many separate sectoral councils stood a General Industrial Council (*Algemene Bedrijfsraad*) coordinating the various branches of industry in accordance with the public interest.

In 1919 the progressive Catholic minister of labour, Aalberse, founded the Supreme Labour Council, a national tripartite advisory body. The Supreme Labour Council included employers, trade union leaders, higher civil servants and independent experts. With the introduction of the Supreme Labour Council, organised labour became, for the first time, a 'social partner' in the Dutch political economy. The Supreme Labour Council fostered a climate of mutual understanding between employers' representatives and trade union officials.

In the face of high levels of unemployment during the early 1930s, the Catholic minister of Economic Affairs, Verschuur, proposed the establishment of an Economic Council that moved beyond the Supreme Labour Council of 1919. The Economic Council was to provide a legal basis for the formation of consultative bodies for different branches of industry, with advisory competencies in the field of labour relations and equal representation for the representatives of labour and capital. Verschuur's initiative caused a clear break with the principle of non-interference of the state in the sphere of industrial relations.

After 1918, a highly original reconsideration of the socialist ideal of socialisation took place. The 1920 'socialization report' contained a proposal for a system of regulatory Industrial Boards with public legal status, similar to Veraart's PBO construction of statutory industrial organisation. The 1923 report on industrial organisation and workers' participation introduced the social democratic concept of 'functional decentralisation, according to which Industrial Boards, while formally state organs, would be granted self-governing capabilities independent of the central government. By the mid-1930s the Social Democratic corporatist drive reached its apotheosis. In 1931, the social democratic party (SDAP) and its allied trade union federation (NVV) jointly issued the report on 'New Organs', which was followed in 1935 by the 'Plan of Labour', which marked the completion of the Social Democratic conversion to class compromise and policy concertation. In an attempt to reform rather than overturn capitalism, the Plan of Labour (*Plan van de Arbeid*) involved an ambitious strategy to combat the Depression through structural economic reform. As it made no reference to class struggle, the Plan buried Marxian dogma, and stressed the need to fight the crisis in order to save the Dutch traditions of intellectual freedom and toleration. The Plan also embraced the Keynesian idea of combating unemployment by means of public works.[16]

Before the outbreak of the Second World War, the idea of corporatist industrial organisation was no longer exclusively Catholic. Gradually, the Social Democrats came to abandon their Marxian ideal of socialisation. Although Protestant trade unionists showed sympathy for the Roman Catholic ideal of corporatism, the Catholic and Social Democratic notions of public legal industrial organisation through state initiative remained unacceptable to ardent Calvinists.

The 'Harmony Model' of Political Economy

During the occupation, the 'Nazis reorganised the Dutch political economy into a tightly controlled autocratic regime. After the functional interest organisations of capital and labour were dismantled, employers and trade union leaders began to meet covertly. In secret talks they drafted and designed new structures for the postwar political economy. Both trade unionists and employers agreed that a return to the allegedly decentralised bargaining structure of the interwar period was untenable. These underground meetings were instructive for the establishment of the Foundation of Labour.[17]

One of the few structures created under Nazi rule that was to survive the occupation, was the reorganisation of trade and industry by the Woltersom Commission, named after its chairman, the Rotterdam banker Henry Louis Woltersom. With the support of the Ministry of Economic Affairs, the Woltersom Commission set out to revise economic organisation in the Netherlands in 1940. In an attempt to avert increased intervention in the economy, the Woltersom Commission remodelled economic life horizontally into six representative industrial sectors. The lasting effect of the Woltersom wartime structure for the postwar corporatist reorganisation of the Dutch political economy, is that it eased the transition to government intervention after 1945. At Liberation, the Woltersom organisation was considered an important institution which was able to endorse the necessary cooperation between government and the business community. The Woltersom structure remained in place until the adoption of the Organisation of Industry Act of 1950.[18]

After Liberation, a deeply felt consensus over the urgency of social and economic reconstruction materialised in a virtual explosion of corporatist institution building. Within half a decade, a wide range of tripartite and bipartite boards were built into the Dutch political economy. Dutch social partnership, with its distinct roots in prewar traditions of public administration and societal organisation, was established under the legal framework of the 'Extraordinary Decree on Industrial Relations' in 1945. The measure, drafted by the government exiled in London, installed the Board of Government Mediators (*College van Rijksbemiddelaars*), which granted government far-reaching authority in industrial relations, especially wage determination. Despite the autocratic design of the decree, the formal representatives of the producer groups of capital and labour were exceptionally eager to join with government in the newly created bipartite Foundation of Labour (*Stichting van de Arbeid*). The Foundation, secretly prepared during the occupation, was founded on the shared belief that cooperative industrial relations were indispensable for Dutch reconstruction. The Foundation was soon recognised as 'a principal advisory body' to the government and came to be closely involved in social and economic policy formation through a panoply of consultative committees.[19]

Corporatist Institution Building

Corporatist institution building was completed in 1950 with the establishment of the tripartite Social and Economic Council (*Sociaal Economische Raad*). The Council, unequivocally the pinnacle of Dutch corporatism, was formally established under the Industrial Organisation Act (*Wet op de Bedrijfsorganisatie*), which provided the legal framework for the Statutory Trade Organisation (*Publiekrechtelijke Bedrijfsorganisatie*).

At the level of ideas, the establishment of the Social and Economic Council concluded the debate over industrial organisation and government regulation of economic life of the 1920s and 1930s surveyed above. Eventually the philosophy of the Social and Economic Council formed a synthesis of Catholic and socialist doctrine, combining the Catholic idea of an organic corporatist society and the socialist belief in economic planning and enforceable social and economic policies. In 1945, the Social Democratic Minister of Trade and Industry, Vos, founded the Central Planning Bureau (*Centraal Planbureau*) and appointed the economist Tinbergen as its first director. Tinbergen and Vos had been the keynote writers of the 1935 Plan of Labour. Following the Plan's recommendations, Vos claimed that economic policy should be set out by a national economic blueprint, authorised by Parliament. In December 1945, Vos issued a Green Paper on the creation of industrial boards under public law. The proposal envisaged a vertically integrated system of tripartite boards with far-reaching authorities in production and wage determination, supervised by a national General Economic Council. After a Catholic victory in the 1946 elections, Vos's proposal was swiftly removed from the policy agenda. Eventually, the Catholic Minister of Economic Affairs, Huysmans, issued a compromise, which formed the basis for the 1950 Industrial Organisation legislation and the establishment of the Social and Economic Council.

The principal task of the Social and Economic Council was to coordinate and supervise the self-regulating vertical commodity boards (*produktschappen*), engaged in producing and distributing similar commodities, and administer the horizontal industrial boards (*bedrijfsschappen*) of the enterprises within particular sectoral branches of the economy. The subsidiary function of the Council was to advise the government, which is by law obliged to obtain Council advice before introducing new social and economic legislation to Parliament. While the proposed reorganisation of Dutch trade and industry into an encompassing system of commodity and industrial boards failed, the Social and Economic Council came to receive much acclaim for its role as the paramount government advisory council in social and economic policy formation. The board of the Council consisted of thirty (today twenty-two) official representatives of organised labour and business, and fifteen so-called 'crown members' – (today eleven). The Council is headed by an independent chairman and two vice-chairmen representing business and labour. The crown members are selected by the government on the basis of independent expertise. Routinely, they are professors in economics and law of the major Dutch universities. The president of the Dutch Central Bank and the director of the Central Planning Bureau, 'qualitate qua', hold crown seats. After its establishment, the tripartite Council immediately took over a number of advisory functions from the bipartite Foundation of Labour. Although no formal division of labour between the two corporatist bodies was decided upon, in practice a compromise materialised, whereby the Foundation retained its statutory role as the primary consultant over wage matters and employment conditions, while the Council came to focus more on the structural and longer-term social and economic policy concerns of the Netherlands.

Under the aegis of the Ministry of Social Affairs and the Board of Government Mediators, the bipartite Foundation and tripartite Council, assisted by the Central Planning Bureau and the Central Bank, Dutch corporatism presided over a very successful postwar reconstruction. The corporatist institutional format not only encouraged extreme moderation in industrial relations from the end of the Second World War until the late1960s, it also fostered an exceptionally small and coalescent Dutch economic policy elite. In the many 'interlocking directorates' between the Foundation and the Council, the peak organisations of capital and labour, the ministries of Social Affairs, Economic Affairs and Finance, a small number of selected insiders gained critical authority over the goals and direction of Dutch economic policy. This rather extreme centralisation within the Dutch corporatist format went together with a virtual lack of participatory structures at the level of businesses.

Remarkable was the overall consent of functional organised interests to state-led wage regulation. Bipartite cooperation was based on the shared perception that low wage costs were essential to Dutch reconstruction. For labour, low wages guaranteed future employment of a growing population and the development of social welfare programmes, which came to be tightly connected to wage developments. For employers, low wage costs encouraged export-led growth, industrial investment and helped to foreclose strong economic sectors from squeezing weaker ones by offering higher wages. Prewar legislation provided for additional ministerial authorities in universally binding collective agreements. In accordance with the 1927 Collective Agreement Act and the 1937 Collective Agreement Extension Act, the Minister of Social Affairs could declare the collective bargaining results legally binding for all workers and firms within different branches of industry. This meant that firms and workers not organised by the contracting parties were bound by collective agreements reached.

While the Dutch pattern of wage determination was extremely autocratic in design, in actual practice the social partners were closely involved in wage-setting procedures through their representation in corporatist institutions. Throughout the era of stringent wage regulation, the Ministry of

Social Affairs sought to establish so-called 'economically permissible' wages, in close cooperation with the Foundation, on the basis of Council advice and Central Planning Bureau economic forecasts.[20]

Under the conditions of the expanding world economy, the low wage strategy gave the Netherlands a competitive edge over neighbouring economies. Between 1945 and 1949 real wages were successfully kept below the 1938 level. Dutch wages were an estimated 20 to 25 percent below those in Germany or Belgium between 1950 and 1960.

Concertation Without Consensus

Corporatist wage control came under threat as labour markets tightened in the late 1950s. Employers, confronted with acute labor shortages, actually sidestepped central wage guidelines by offering so-called 'black wages', in excess of nationally negotiated agreements. In 1963, government decided to hand over the task of approving collective bargaining agreements from the Board directly to the Foundation. Wage determination finally came to revolve around free negotiations between independent functional interests. The new practice prompted a dramatic wage drift.[21] In an attempt to recapture lost control, the government turned to the Foundation for advice on a new system of wage regulation, to be formalised under a new Wage Law, which was to replace the 1945 Decree.

In 1968 the government introduced the new Wage Determination Law (*Wet op de Loonvorming*) to Parliament, which allowed for continued government intervention in wage determination by way of the crude measure of a universal wage freeze. The Bill prompted the most disruptive episode in Dutch postwar industrial relations. The introduction of the new wage bill went together with the emergence of a marked divergence in political outlook among the social partners. Both came to reject, for altogether different reasons, the state-led incorporation of functional interests in 'responsible' income policies. Organised labour, pressed by militant rank and file, took on a more assertive posture in its demand for industrial democracy, while employers adopted a distinctive neo-liberal 'laissez-faire' tone in opposition to industrial reform.[22] From the late 1960s until the early 1980s, as a result of the wage explosion (including non-wage social security contributions, together with the increases in the oil price) inflation accelerated and the economy weakened, while the welfare system expanded. At first, this expansion could be financed through growing gas revenues but eventually it led to a vicious cycle, called the 'Dutch disease'. Real labour costs increased sharply, exceeding productivity gains, the profit position of international firms deteriorated, unemployment rose dramatically and the economy went into a pronounced recession in 1981. Short of sidetracking the corporatist institutional format completely, only two uncomfortable policy strategies for continued government leverage over wage matters remained. Policy makers either had to persuade the centrally weakened and politically radicalising trade union movement to join a traditional corporatist social contract, or they could impose restraint through the tactless and plausibly deficient measure of a universal wage freeze. This peculiarly Dutch corporatist policy dilemma, arising from the 'path-dependent' historical choice of an extremely stringent low wage adjustment strategy at the heart of Dutch social partnership, set the stage for corporatist immobilism in the 1970s. From 1973 to 1982 the government continually intervened in wage setting as the social partners were unable to reach agreement. During this period the Social and Economic Council was scarcely in a position to produce meaningful unanimous opinions.

The second oil crisis of 1979 hit the Netherlands much harder than the first oil price shock of 1973. Unemployment figures kept exceeding levels nobody had ever thought possible. Under this predicament, a marked shift in outlook surfaced in the Dutch political economy. In June 1980, the Scientific Council of Government Policy issued an alarming report on the state of Dutch manufacturing, which contained a biting critique of Dutch corporatism and its single-minded focus on incomes policy.[23]

The experience of a decade of immobile corporatism opened the way for the formation of an austerity coalition in the Netherlands. The Lubbers administration which came to office in November of 1982 decisively broke with the accumulated frustrations of a decade of failed attempts at 'concertation without consensus' by authoritatively pursuing its austerity programme without consulting the social partners in the Foundation of Labour and the Social and Economic Council.[24] Continued internal union strife, consistent failures to arrive at responsible collective agreements in the Foundation, together with the inability of the Council to issue unanimous policy recommendations, led the 'no-nonsense' government to take up the advice of more technocratic expert commissions, a trend already evident in the 1970s.

At the inauguration of the new coalition, the stage was set for a tough confrontation between the government and organised labour. However, with unemployment at a postwar record and persistent decline in membership, the trade union movement was in no position to wage industrial conflict.[25] After a decade of failed tripartite efforts, the centre-right coalition's entry into office was crowned by a bipartite social accord on 24 November. Coming together in the Foundation, trade unions and employers agreed to reopen already concluded collective agreements and repeal automatic price compensation clauses in exchange for opening discussions over working-time reduction and the creation of part-time jobs, in a concerted effort to halt the rise in unemployment, enhance labour market flexibility, and restore the profitability of Dutch industry. The Wassenaar Accord was not a conventional corporatist social contract, stipulating binding wage guidelines and working conditions. The agreement contained a rather ambiguous bipartite appeal to sectoral contracting parties to renegotiate 'wage-claims already incorporated in collective agreements' for 'a better allocation of existing employment', without increasing wage costs.[26] Both Wim Kok and Chris Van Veen, the leaders of the largest trade union federation and employers' organisation, put much energy into getting their newly found bipartite agreement in Dutch industrial relations accepted by their respective affiliates and rank-and-file membership. In short, the Lubbers administration, despite its neo-liberal posture, ironically, channelled and presided over the resurgence of social partnership in the Netherlands. Between 1983 and1993, a new, less ambitious pattern of social partnership emerged on the basis of the new-found consensus over the goals, methods and constraints of social and economic policy concertation. In terms of policy content, the new string of accords returned to prioritise voluntary wage restraint in the pursuit of business profitability, investment growth and employment growth, job redistribution, and welfare reform.

Ironically, the deliberate and untried by-passing of ineffective corporatist institutions by the 'no-nonsense' Lubbers administration in 1982, resulted in the marked resurgence of social partnership in the Dutch political economy for most of the 1980s and 1990s. This goes to show that left-over institutions, even faltering policy legacies, continue to shape the choices and behaviour of contemporary policy actors.

Notes

1. J. Visser and A. Hemerijck, *'A Dutch Miracle': Job Growth, Welfare Reform and Corporatism in the Netherlands*, Amsterdam, Amsterdam University Press, 1997.
2. A.C. Hemerijck, The Historical Contingencies of Dutch Corporatism, (Dissertation, Oxford, Balliol College, 1993).
3. A.C. Hemerijck, 'Corporatist Immobility in the Netherlands', in C. Crouch and F. Traxler (eds), *Organized Industrial Relations: What Future?,* Aldershot, Averbury, 1995: 183–226.
4. J.I. Israel, *The Dutch Republic; its Rise, Greatness, and Fall 1477–1806*, Oxford, Oxford University Press, 1995.
5. E.H. Kossmann, 'Popular sovereignty at the beginning of the Dutch Ancien Régime', in I. Schöffer et al. (eds), *The low countries history yearbook*, ed. I. Schöffer et al., Acta Historiae Neerlandicae (vol. 14), Den Haag,Martinus Nijhoff, 1981: 1–28
6. J.L. Price, *Holland and the Dutch Republic in the Seventeenth Century*, Oxford, Clarendon Press, 1994.
7. H.H. Rowen, Political ideas and institutions in the Dutch Republic, papers presented at the Clark Library Seminar, 27 March 1982 (Los Angeles: University of California).
8. J.A. Bornewasser, 'The Authority of the Dutch State over the Churches, 1795–1853', in: A.C. Duke and C.A. Tamse (eds), *Britain and the Netherlands: Church and State since the Reformation,* Den Haag, Nijhoff, 1981.
9. S. Schama, *Patriots and Liberators: Revolution in the Netherlands 1780–1813,* London, Fontana, 1977.
10. H. Daalder, Ancient and Modern Pluralism in the Netherlands, the 1989 Erasmus Lectures at Harvard University, working paper no. 22, Minda de Gunzburg Center for European Studies, Harvard University, Cambridge, Mass., 1990.
11. E.H Kossmann, *The Low Countries 1780–1940*, Oxford, Oxford University Press, 1978: 259, 310.
12. A. Lijphart,*The Politics of Accommodation: Pluralism and Democracy in the Netherlands*, Berkeley, University of California Press, 1968; J.A.A. van Doorn, 'De onvermijdelijke presentie van de confessionelen' in: J.W. de Beus, J.A.A. van Doorn, Percy. B. Lehning (eds),

De Ideologische driehoek: Nederlandse politiek in historisch perspectief, Meppel/Amsterdam, 1989.

13. J.P. Windmuller, *Labor Relations in the Netherlands*, Ithaca, NY, Cornell University Press, 1969.
14. R.S. Zwart, *God's Wil in Nederland*, Kampen, Kok, 1996; H.J. van Streek, H.-M.Th.D. ten Napel and R.S. Zwart, *Christelijke Politiek en Democratie*, The Hague, SDU, 1995.
15. F. Van Waarden, 'Corporatisme als probleemstelling', in: H.J.G. Verhallen, R. Fernhout and P.E. Visser, *Corporatism in Nederland,* Samsom, Alphen a/d Rijn, 1980: 17–69.
16. P.W Klein, 'Depression and Policy in the Thirties', in: *Acta Historitiae Neerlandicae,* Studies in the history of the Netherlands, 1975.
17. Windmuller, *Labor Relations in the Netherlands.*
18. G. Hirschfeld, *Nazi Rule and Dutch Collaboration; the Netherlands under German Occupation 1940–1945*, Oxford, Berg, 1989.
19. W.J. Dercksen, *Industrialisatiepolitiek rondom de jaren vijftig*, Assen, Van Gorcum, 1986.
20. W.J.P.M. Fase, *Vijfendertig jaar loonbeleid in Nederland: terugblik en perspectief*, Alphen a/d Rijn, Samsom, 1980.
21. W. Van Drimmelen and N. Hulst, *Loonvorming en loonpolitiek in Nederland*, Groningen, Wolters-Noordhoff, 1987.
22. T.Akkermans and P. Grootings, 'From corporatism to polarisation: Elements in the development of the Dutch industrial relations' in C. Crouch and A. Pizzorno (eds), *The Resurgence of Class Conflict in Western Europe since 1968*, vol. I, London, 1978.
23. H. van Dellen, (ed.), *Een nieuw elan, de marktsector van de jaren tachtig*, Deventer: Kluwer, 1985.
24. J. Toirkens, *Schijn en werkelijkheid van het bezuinigingsbeleid 1975–1986*, Deventer, Kluwer, 1988.
25. D. Braun (1987), 'Political immobilism and labour market performance: The Dutch road to mass unemployment'. *Journal of Public Policy* 7/3: 307–35; J. Visser, 'Continuity and change in Dutch industrial relations', in G. Baglioni and C. Crouch (eds), *European Industrial Relations: the challenge of flexibility*, London, Sage, 1990: 199–240; J. Visser, 'The Netherlands, the end of an era and the end of a system', in R. Hyman and A. Fenner (eds), *Industrial Relations in Europe*, Oxford, Blackwell: 323–56.
26. J. Visser and A. Hemerijck, *'Dutch Miracle'* Amsterdam, Amsterdam UP, 1997: 81–116.

CHAPTER 16

THE NETHERLANDS IN THE 1990S: TOWARDS 'FLEXIBLE CORPORATISM' IN THE POLDER MODEL

Hans Slomp

Introduction

The second half of the 1990s has been the best of times for Dutch social partnership. International admiration for the 'Dutch model' or 'Polder model' acclaims its fast-growing flexibility, active labour market policies, wage moderation, cuts in social security spending, and most of all the rapid decrease in unemployment. All of these accomplishments were reached in an atmosphere of compromise, or '*overleg*', as the Dutch say when they refer to their system of compromise-oriented and cooperative negotiations. This chapter traces the developments in social partnership from disappointing concertation in the early 1990s to successful consultation in later years, as well as the ideas and ideals that motivate social partnership and its transformation.

Core features of Dutch *centraal overleg* are its institutionalisation, the interplay of tripartite and bipartite contacts, and the heavy state monitoring of collective bargaining. This makes it necessary to include tripartite control of policy fields and wage policies in any survey of Dutch social partnership.

Frequent nation-wide tripartite and bipartite contacts take place in two institutions: the *Sociaal-Economische Raad*, SER (Social and Economic Council) and the *Stichting van de Arbeid* (Foundation of Labour).[1] The SER is composed of trade unions, employers' confederations and independent outside experts, in equal numbers. Trade unions and employers are represented by three confederations each, but the largest trade union confederation FNV and the general employers' confederation VNO-NCW are the main participants. The eleven outside experts (*Kroonleden*), including the

SER president, are appointed by the *Kroon* (the government). Most of them are university professors in economics or law and they are representative of the major ideological currents in Dutch society. Among them are the president of the national bank, *Nederlandse Bank,* and the president of the *Centraal Planbureau* (CPB), which issues authoritative reports on economic conditions as well as forecasts that take into account various scenarios of collective bargaining. The *Stichting van de Arbeid* is an employer/trade union council in which the confederations meet not only to establish a framework for sector bargaining but also to give advice to the government. Government ministers sometimes assist at committee meetings within the SER and at least twice a year they engage in *overleg* with the *Stichting* about economic and social conditions.

Policy Concertation in the Netherlands during the 1990s

The decade opened with disillusionment. In December 1989 the government, employers and trade union confederations had agreed upon an informal 'Common Policy Framework' which included increasing social security expenditure and a series of tax measures designed in part to compensate wage moderation. However, sectoral unions then demanded higher wages, while the employers became more and more disappointed about the government's failure to reduce the *wig* (wedge) between gross and net wages, which mainly consists of social security contributions and income tax. Soon the agreement was a dead letter. Consultation continued, however, focusing in particular on labour market participation, social security costs and wage policies.

In 1992 the SER issued a report, '*Convergentie en Overlegeconomie*', about the conditions that had to be met in order to join the Economic and Monetary Union. Two weaknesses of the Dutch economy had to be addressed most of all: the low rate of labour participation and the large size of the public sector. The SER recommended wage moderation, reduction of the *wig*, more incentives in the social security system to get people back to work, and an activating labour market policy. '*Convergentie en Overlegeconomie*' echoed the concerns that had been expressed in 1990 by the WRR (the Scientific Council for Government Policy).[2] This WRR report had rejected the long-standing Dutch focus on compensating exit from the labour market by means of social security benefits for a new priority: labour market participation. In addition to the long-term unemployed, the report argued that the almost one million disability benefit (WAO) claimants, out of a total labour force of six million, and the many women without paid jobs, should (re)enter the labour market – a long overdue recognition of the low female participation rate.

Although the SER adopted the new priorities, it was divided with respect to the resolution of the WAO problem. Under pressure from its members, the FNV rejected any cuts in this part of social security despite growing criticism of the use of disability benefits as a form of higher unemployment benefit (in order to facilitate lay-offs, many employers complied with the trade union demand to classify redundant workers as disabled). Ignoring the divided SER and a large protest demonstration organised by the trade unions, the government implemented stern politics of austerity. At the same time the abuse of the WAO as unemployment pay became an issue in Parliament. A parliamentary committee investigated employer/trade union control of social security – a heavy parliamentary weapon that is not used frequently. The committee condemned both social partners for their total control of social security spending and the abuse of the WAO, and, despite the social partners' opposition, the government introduced a new form of supervision by independent outsiders.

Meanwhile, the *Stichting* mainly responded to repeated government threats to impose wage control. In 1993 it issued an agreed report: 'A New Course'. This 'basic agenda' for collective bargaining was far more pessimistic than the 1992 SER report. The country faced 'extremely alarming' economic conditions and would 'have to cope with an ever-increasing and permanent unemployment issue and all this against the background of an already low rate of labour participation'.[3]

After the WAO débâcle, the SER was rehabilitated a bit in 1994 when it published 'Social and Economic Policies for the Medium Term 1994–1998'. This echoed the pessimism of 'A New Course' and recommended the forceful promotion of labour market participation, large savings in state expenditure, and wage moderation. During the preparation of this SER advice, the FNV met with opposition within its own ranks to wage moderation without any compensation. In the mid-1990s the FNV leader had a hard job in explaining its lack of internal agreement to the other SER members.[4]

Tripartism and bipartism were not only concerned with social security and wage policies, but also with works councils, labour conditions and state employment agencies. Worker participation was extended and the minimum enterprise size for the establishment of works councils was lowered along the lines indicated by the SER. SER recommendations also contributed to changes in other policy fields, including 'Arbo'-policy, concerned with workplace labour conditions, the tax system and research policies. One of the Arbo priorities was to reduce sickness leave. The change in the tax system simplified the system and lowered income taxes as a means of reducing the *wig* between gross and net wages. In research policies, financing was shifted from the universities to national research councils in order to improve research quality.

A short-lived accomplishment which employers and trade unions could point to in the first half of the decade was the 'tripartisation' of the state employment service. In addition to deregulation, one of the arguments in favour of a tripartite employment service was that the involvement of local government, regional employers and union officials would improve contacts with business and make the system more sensitive to the labour market, but as early as 1994 the failure of the newly created tripartite system was revealed in yet another parliamentary report, in particular its inability to get the long-term unemployed and unemployed migrant workers back to work. While employers and trade unions continued to defend tripartite control, the government narrowed the functions of the regional employment offices to assisting the vulnerable groups they had so far helped the least.[5]

The second half of the decade was quite different. In the mid-1990s economic conditions improved, economic prospects brightened and there was a significant change in politics. After the 1994 elections, which were dominated by the cuts in social security (including the WAO), a 'purple' (red-blue) coalition assumed office under Prime Minister Wim Kok, a former FNV president, consisting of social democrats, conservative liberals and social liberals – the first Dutch cabinet without Christian Democrats for almost a century. The two liberal parties were less rooted in the old pillarisation networks than the social democrats or the Christian Democrats and lacked strong links with the organisations represented in the SER. In the new coalition they saw their chance and pressed successfully for the abolition of the government obligation to ask SER advice on all major social and economic measures.

The purple coalition displayed greater initiative than its predecessor. More market and less government was its first priority, more government (initiative) and less concertation its second one. The SER preference for lower (income) taxes was honoured even more than before, but in anticipation of a radical tax overhaul. The government enforced an extension of shop opening hours and a relaxation of working-time rules, in order to increase flexibility. In neither area did it wait for SER reports. Without much discussion it also privatised the sickness insurance programme and bypassed the tripartite employment service in its job-creating programme. *Overleg* in the *Stichting* on the state of the economy became more general in coverage and long-term in perspective, without much room for an immediate 'swap' of interests.[6]

The trend of government initiative in favour of the free market was continued under the second purple government. By then, the 'Dutch Model', namely a peaceful shift towards more working-time flexibility, wage moderation and lower social security costs, had become a source of national pride. Immediately after being formed in 1998, this government announced plans to abolish the tripartite employment service altogether and integrate it with municipal social security offices.

Under the purple governments, the SER published its reports on medium term socioeconomic policy with more modesty than before. In 1996, employers and trade unions elaborated a major theme from 'A New Course' in 'Flexibility and Security'. The agreement stressed the need to strike a balance between flexibility (more part-time work) and security (the legal protection of part-timers).[7] The agreement marked the definite trade union break with overall working-time reduction as a compensation for wage moderation in favour of part-time work. Wage moderation and flexibility remained the catchwords of the *Stichting*-report 'Agenda 2002', published in 1997.

The Debate on Concertation

At the celebration of the SER's fortieth anniversary in 1990, the tone was one of praise but even more one of criticism and defence. The most widely used terms to legitimise the continuation of the SER were consensus, cooperation, *overleg* and social *draagvlak* (see Table 16.1). The latter denotes a wide base of support among employers and employees both for government measures and for joint agreements. It prevents exclusion of affected groups and guarantees general compliance. *Overleg* is considered to be an expression of cooperation; its aim is to create a wider *draagvlak* and it should result in consensus. The four concepts figured in almost every speech by government ministers, employers' and trade union leaders as well as in SER reports and newspaper comments. Consensus, cooperation, *overleg* and social *draagvlak* have two traits in common: they refer to the representation and integration of as many interests as possible in social and economic decision making, and to the prevention of conflict. Both principles, no-exclusion and no-conflict, have their roots in Dutch (religious) pillarisation and in early efforts to introduce corporatism.

As a former Minister of Social Affairs and Employment stated: 'The citizens can be sure that any SER advice expresses the interests of both employees and employers. That is of great importance in a social democracy like ours. It is a safety guard, a guarantee against political arbitrariness.'[8] A former trade union leader added: 'the SER is responsible for the fact that problems do not directly result in labour conflicts.'[9] The arguments for and against policy concertation are summarised in Table 16.2.

Table 16.1. *Key Terms in the Netherlands*

Term	Meaning
Centraal accoord	Central level agreement
Centraal overleg	Central level bargaining
Drieledig overleg	Tripartite consultation
Kroonleden	Government-appointed SER members
Koppeling	Linkage between wages and social security benefits
Onderhandelen	Bargaining
Overleg	Cooperative bargaining, always to result in an agreement. The keyword of Dutch social partnership
Polder Model	The Dutch Model of successful *centraal overleg* that results in state budget cuts, wage moderation and low unemployment
SER	Social and Economic Council
Sociaal draagvlak	Wide social support for policies
Sociaal overleg	Tripartite or bipartite *centraal overleg*
Sociale partners	Employers' and trade union confederations
Stichting van de Arbeid	Bipartite Foundation of Labour

Source: see text.

Table 16.2. Key Arguments in the Netherlands

Proponent	Argument
For	
All parties and organisations involved	Consensus
All parties, but less so after government change in 1994	Social *draagvlak* in order to prevent exclusion and guarantee compliance
Government, trade unions	Against lobbying and fighting culture in which the strong prevail
Employers	Favours decentralisation of collective bargaining
Against	
Government	Time-consuming
Government, political parties	Reduces the primacy of politics

Source: see text.

The no-exclusion and no-conflict principles are juxtaposed to two other types of political and social culture: a pluralist open market of lobbying for influence, in which representation is unequal and a matter of secrecy, and a fighting culture in which sheer force counts. The SER president defended his institution as a counter-force against the lobbying culture. In the SER 'employers and employees give accounts of their viewpoints in public. If the SER did not exist, they would continue to seek contact with politics but in that case it would be by means of lobby activities behind closed doors'.[10]

In particular the FNV president frequently spoke about the negative side of a fighting culture, and not merely to appease radical opponents within the trade union movement. He contrasted the *overleg* culture with social policy making in the United States, 'where you keep falling over beggars and homeless people'.[11] Although leaders of the employers' associations warned about creeping centralism, they also defended consensus building and central-level *overleg* as a precondition of fruitful collective bargaining at sector and enterprise levels: '*Centraal overleg* is the legitimisation of a pluriform and many-faceted decentralised *overleg*'.[12]

The most widely heard criticism of the SER was its lack of speed. Prime Minister Ruud Lubbers called it 'a bale of hay which slows down everything and produces a lot of nuances but does not sufficiently bring forth the sharp focus you need when you want to change something.'[13] In the early 1990s the interplay between government politics and advisory councils became a topic of broad public debate. Politics had left too many decisions to civil servants and to advisory bodies and should resume its responsibilities rather than hiding behind the network of advisers.[14] At first this appeal for a 'rehabilitation' of politics, as a constituent element of democracy, implied an attack upon bodies like the SER. It was not until a couple of years later that the focus of attack shifted towards politicians who attempted to hide behind non-political institutions. The appeal was related to the increasing number of alarmed voices about the general lack of interest in politics. The call for more politics did not refer to the traditional objection against corporatism as undermining parliamentary prerogatives and therefore being undemocratic. It focused on the initiating role of government in society, not on the national government's responsibility before Parliament.

The SER defence against the criticism that it spoiled politics was to blame the government for its use of the SER as a means of covering up divisions in the government or lack of political initiative. As a *Kroonlid* stated: 'The SER should not allow the government to abuse it in order to mask the failure of politics.'[15] Many comments admitted this point, yet it was generally regarded as a minor issue besides the lack of speed and agreement in the SER.

Despite the criticisms, the neglect of SER advice in the WAO affair was regretted by all SER members, and was not appreciated by public opinion either. Newspapers spoke about '*overleg-economie* in a deadlock', 'government like a bull at the gate in WAO-policy'.[16] In 1994 almost all organisations represented in the SER expressed their disappointment about the abolition of compulsory SER consultation. The FNV president predicted that the erosion of the SER would bring the 'fighting economy' closer.[17] However this time the tone in the newspapers was not in favour of the SER. They referred to the measure as marking the overdue end of an era ('one more shovel of sand on the grave of pillarization').[18] The growing distance between the government and the social partners was generally appreciated.[19] At the time the Polder Model was internationally acclaimed, the social liberal Minister of Economic Affairs continued to wonder if social partnership did not take too long and was too rigid.[20] The praise of the Polder Model concentrated most of all on bipartite *sociaal overleg*, with the government taking the initiative, facilitating trade-offs, and promising labour law changes in accordance with the central agreements. When the Dutch social partners were awarded the German Bertelsmann prize in 1996, it was a high state official who explained the system while the employers' and trade union leaders posed as old friends. However it was the *Stichting*, not the SER, that triumphed. While consensus and *overleg* continued to be basic values of social partnership, the term cooperation, which implied too much harmony, was replaced by 'mutual understanding' or 'mutual trust'. An employers' report on the Dutch economy published in 1997 mentioned as advantages of the *overleg-economie* the medium-term rather than short-term orientation, mutual trust as a basis for changes in policy, and the opportunities for decentralisation in combination with national concerns.[21] The concept of social *draagvlak* had also lost part of its magic, being considered to imply too much employer and trade union involvement in government policies, and was less and less referred to in public debate. However, as before, the terms consensus and *overleg* still pointed to the basic principles of no-exclusion and no-conflict.

Analysis: The Road to 'Flexible Corporatism' in the Polder Model

Dutch social partnership is a combination of three forms of *sociaal overleg*: first, consultation on social and economic policies; second, joint control and monitoring of social security and regional employment agencies; and third, joint monitoring of collective bargaining. The SER mainly serves the first activity (consultation), while the *Stichting* is active in all forms. Since the government is heavily involved in monitoring wage bargaining, all three forms are variations of tripartism. *Centraal overleg* without any government involvement at all hardly exists. The government is not an outside 'third party' but a 'third partner' in various forms of social partnership. Monitoring collective bargaining is implicitly considered to be a regular ingredient of social policy making.

It was the first form of social partnership that was at stake in the critical voices about the SER early in the decade. It was the second form that was the target of criticism about the role of employers and trade unions in social security control. Finally, it was the third form that was meant when the Polder Model got international fame during later years.

The three forms had been mixed up completely in the 1989 tripartite 'Common Policy Framework'. Although it was no more than an informal declaration of intent, it was the ultimate example of tripartite policy concertation, in which the social partners shared responsibility for national economic and social policies, and the government for wage bargaining. The failure of these efforts prompted the disappointed employers to speak of a breach of mutual trust and to refuse any new tripartite agreement. From that time on, the first form of *sociaal overleg* (tripartite consultation) was reduced from concertation (co-determination) to consultation, and even that was not very successful in the first half of the decade. Although SER reports influenced government policy in a number of fields, the SER was more important in encouraging employer–trade union consensus on economic and social conditions than in its impact on the government. Moreover, the general attitude towards social and economic conditions was one of urgent need for remedial measures, for which government initiative was better suited than time-consuming consultation.

The employer and trade union role in the second form of social partnership (social security administration and employment services) also came under attack. Their role in social security control was reduced and tripartite control of the employment service was introduced but soon weakened again. What remained was bipartite control under state supervision, with increasing room for market forces and declining opportunities for control.

In the third form of social partnership the government pressed for wage restraint and was not left empty-handed. The social partners complied and expressed the urgency of the situation themselves in the 1993 appeal for wage moderation and differentiation. This agreement also looked like bipartite control under state supervision.

The continued large numbers of inactive people and the state deficit, even under conditions of economic growth, constituted the major concerns of all three parties involved, but strategies differed. While the government encouraged or even tried to impose wage moderation – the usual formula since 1945 – employers favoured a differentiation of wages, including lower wage costs for unskilled workers. In their demand for severe cuts in the state budget, they could point to the 3 percent EMU limit on the state deficit. The trade union strategy consisted of wage moderation and overall working time reduction but, under pressure from persistent high unemployment, their aim shifted from reducing unemployment to fighting inactivity through the new combination of wage moderation and part-time work. It was the trade union recognition of the state of emergency that re-established bipartite bargaining in the *Stichting* in 1993.

In the mid-1990s a number of developments reinforced the radical change in the Dutch economic, political and social climate. They also affected the culture of, and attitude to, social partnership, leading to a reappraisal of the *overleg-economie*.

Unemployment had declined from 11 percent in 1983 to 5.4 percent in 1992 but increased again to 7.6 percent in 1994.[22] In combination with the low overall participation rate and the high state deficit, this rise occasioned the gloomy visions of the SER and the *Stichting*. The decline of unemployment that started in 1994 seemed the start of a longer trend and occasioned more optimistic visions, in spite of the precarious nature of many new jobs.[23] In social security, the expectation that WAO numbers would drop, for the first time in two decades, materialised. From a nation living off its social security benefits, the country seemed well under way to a bright future as a nation at work. This change was due even more to increasing flexibility and a growing female participation rate, most of all in part-time work. However this issue did not reach the agenda of the social partners until 1992, when women were already entering the labour market in great numbers. The female participation rate reached an almost normal European level of 50 percent in 1996. Voluntary wage restraint, as laid down in 'A New Course', was also complied with. Sector union protests were mainly aimed at cuts in social security.

In addition to the bright economic perspectives, the purple coalition meant a radical change in politics. The two liberal parties claimed 'more responsibility for politics' and 'politics first', in order to strengthen the free market. The Social Democratic Party now enjoyed more room for unpopular measures, including definite decisions on the WAO, because the WAO affair had weakened its links with the trade unions.

The new government approach to social partnership stressed the distinction between the three forms of *sociaal overleg*. The government made it clear that as a matter of principle it abandoned any pretension of policy concertation in favour of consultation. The SER came to occupy a less prominent niche in social partnership, without slowing down government initiative. The second form of social partnership stabilised as bipartite control under state supervision, and the third one changed towards bipartism without supervision. The employers were no longer merely involved in social *overleg* – they even initiated it. Their disappointment with the government failure to cut the budget and the lack of trade union efforts to moderate wages had made way for a more positive stance based on the new union commitment and the purple coalition's savings. The trade unions had wholeheartedly accepted the protection of part-time workers and they could 'moderate' their moderation, in view of the changing economic conditions.

The appearance of new protagonists in 1995 and 1996 contributed to the changes in *sociaal overleg*. The major employers' and trade union leaders were succeeded by presidents of sector organisations who were more attached to bipartite bargaining than to tripartite consultation. The new primacy of politics was also visible in the gradual shift from university professors to ex-politicians as outside experts (*kroonleden*) in the SER.

The new outlook has reinforced the demarcation line between government responsibilities and employer–trade union bargaining in the three forms of social partnership. The government pursues policies and supervises social security and employment agencies. Employers and trade unions advise on state policies, administer social security and the employment service under state supervision, and monitor collective bargaining without state involvement. The demarcation line between government responsibility for state policies and the social partners' responsibility for collective bargaining is reflected in the declining popularity of the term social *draagvlak*, which is now considered to focus too much on employer and trade union involvement in government policy making.

The demarcation is a flexible one, and can be overstepped if conditions require and all parties agree. As in the old days, the 1996 bipartite agreement 'Flexibility and Security' was a response to a government request to the *Stichting* for advice, since the government itself was divided. The agreement became known as the 'kitchen table accord' because one meeting took place at the FNV negotiator's home, since he was unable to find a babysitter for that evening. The government gratefully welcomed the accord as the basis of changes in social legislation. This agreement helped to bridge the different opinions within the purple coalition and was the finest example of policy concertation during the 1990s. It also shows the conditions of success of social partnership in the Polder Model: first, a demarcation line between the government's and the social partners' responsibilities; second, the possibility of shifting from one form of social partnership to another, especially between the first and the third forms; and, third, selectivity in the possibilities of changing from consultation to government initiative-without-consultation. This combination of pragmatic shifts, flexibility and selectivity might be called 'flexible corporatism', in which the degree of flexibility is based on mutual consent but with a final say for the government. Changing the forum of the talks was learnt at the beginning of the decade. Growing understanding between employers and trade unions had not been forged in the *Stichting* but in the difficult SER talks, and government initiative was assured by handing over contentious matters to bipartite talks in the *Stichting*.

Summarising, despite occasional attempts to refer tricky subjects to employers and trade unions, the purple government has substituted policy consultation for policy concertation and has given up interfering in collective bargaining. Consequently, employers and trade unions prefer bipartite *Stichting* agreements to SER debate as a means of influencing the government and of stating their own priorities in bipartite activities such as wage bargaining. In their fine survey of the Polder Model, Visser and Hemerijck write about different forms of corporatism in the various policy fields (social security, employment, wages).[24] The stricter distinction between government responsibilities on the one hand and bipartite control of wage negotiations on the other has in fact resulted in 'flexible corporatism'. Employers and trade unions are less involved in government policies, while the government merely monitors wage bargaining, but both the social partners (for advice) and the government (for legalisation of bargaining results) are available if assistance is needed.

Conclusion

From a country suffering from very stringent wage policies during the 1950s, 'wage explosions' during the 1960s, overspending (the 'Dutch disease') during the 1970s, two-digit unemployment rates during the 1980s, and almost one-sixth of the total labour force receiving disability benefits, the Netherlands have at last got international fame as a model of successful social partnership.

Under the pressure of economic problems, including high unemployment, a low participation rate and a high state deficit, the national government has redrawn the boundaries within the system of Dutch social partnership. Concertation has become consultation, and a clear distinction is made between tripartite consultation on government policies and bipartite collective bargaining. This 're-politicisation' of state policies is compensated by a 'depoliticisation' of collective bargaining, although the reduced role of government in wage bargaining is actually more a change towards less government than one of less politics, since government interference was hardly ever a political issue. The new kind of social partnership was forged under the pressure of the commonly felt need to bring about two epochal changes in labour market conditions: the shift from compensating lack of work by means of social security to creating jobs through more flexibility, and the adaptation to women's demands for more flexibility in the form of part-time jobs. The trade unions not only pursued wage restraint but also came to approve these changes, neither of which was in line with their previous policies. The agenda was not set by employers, however, but by the government, the EMU, and most of all by the large numbers of women who entered the labour market.

In summary, there is both change and continuity, as the social partners have embraced the changed form of social partnership as a new way to realise its basic principles: no exclusion and no conflict.

Bibliography

Borstlap, Hans. 'Konsensorientierte Politik der kleinen Schritte – das Beispiel Niederlande', in: Stefan Empter and Andreas Esche, eds. *Radikalkur oder Evolution*, Gütersloh, 1997, 118–28.

Bottenburg, Maarten van. *Aan den Arbeid: In de wandelgangen van de Stichting van de Arbeid 1945–1995*. Amsterdam, 1995.

Empel, Frank van. *The Dutch Model: The power of consultation in the Netherlands*. Den Haag, 1997.

Empter, Stefan and Andreas Esche, eds. *Individual Responsibility and Solidarity: New Approaches in Social and Collective Bargaining Policy*. Gütersloh, 1997.

Hofstra, N.A. and P.W.M. Nobelen, eds. *Toekomst van de overlegeconomie*. Assen, 1993.

Klamer, Arjo. *Verzuilde dromen: 40 jaar SER*. Amsterdam, 1990.

Leijnse, Frans. Overlegmodel nadert eind. *Zeggenschap*, vol. 7, no. 5, 8–10.

Ministerie SZW. *Social Policy and Economic Performance*. Den Haag, 1997.

SCP. *Sociale en Culturele Verkenningen*. Rijswijk, 1992–1998

SER. *SER Bulletin* 1990–1998.

SER. *The Dutch road to EMU: convergence in concert*. Den Haag, 1992.

SER. *Dutch medium-term socio-economic policy (1994–1998)*. Den Haag, 1994.

SER. *Sociaal-economisch beleid 1996–2000*. Den Haag, 1996.

SER. *Sociaal-economisch beleid 1998–2002*. Den Haag, 1998.

Schmid, Günther. 'The Dutch Employment Miracle? A Comparison of Employment Systems in the Netherlands and Germany', in: Lei Delsen and Eelke de Jong, eds. *The German and Dutch Economies*. Berlin, 1998, 52–85.

Soskice, David, Bob Hancke, Gunnar Trumbull and Anne Wren. 'Wage Bargaining, Labour Markets and Macroeconomic Performance in Germany and the Netherlands', in: Lei Delsen and Eelke de Jong, eds. *The German and Dutch Economies*. Berlin,1998, 39–51.

Stichting van de Arbeid. *A New Course: Agenda for the 1994 Negotiations on Collective Agreements in a Medium-term Perspective*. Den Haag, 1993.

Visser, Jelle and Anton Hemerijck.*'A Dutch Miracle': Job growth, Welfare Reform and Corporatism in the Netherlands*. Amsterdam, 1997.

VNO-NCW. *De Nederlandse economie: van moeras naar succesvol poldermodel?* Den Haag, 1997.

Notes

The author wishes to thank Hugh Compston, Kees Kok and Erik van Merrienboer for their comments.

1. M. van Bottenburg, *Aan den Arbeid*, Amsterdam, 1995.
2. SER, 1992.
3. Stichting van de Arbeid, *A New Course: Agenda for the 1994 Negotiations on Collective Agreements in a Medium-term Perspective*, Den Haag, 1993.
4. *SER bulletin* 1994, no. 4/5.
5. J. Visser and A. Hemerijck, *A Dutch Miracle: Job Growth, Welfare Reform and Corporatism in the Netherlands*, Amsterdam, 1997: 155 ff.
6. F. van Empel, *The Dutch Model: The Power of Consultation in the Netherlands,* Den Haag, 1977: 11.

7. Stichting, *A New Course.*
8. *Gelderlander*, 29 February 1990.
9. Ibid.
10. *Trouw*, 4 October 1990.
11. *Nederlands Dagblad*, 5 October 1990.
12. *Staatscourant*, 4 October 1990.
13. A. Klamer, 1990.
14. *Trouw*, 4 October 1990.
15. *Vrije Volk*, 3 October 1990.
16. *NRC*, 6 October 1991; *Financieel Dagblad*, 31 July 1991.
17. *Telegraaf*, 25 March 1995.
18. *NRC*, 22 February 1995.
19. F. Leijnse, 1996.
20. *SER bulletin*, 1997, 2.
21. VNO-NCW, 1997, 20.
22. *OECD Economic Outlook*, 1997, A24.
23. Schmid 1998, 52–85.
24. J. Visser and A Hemerijck, 1997.

Chapter 17

Spain in Historical Perspective: Fascist Corporatism and Social Pacts

Robert A. Robinson

It is commonplace to explain the present-day Spanish political system as the result of a democratisation process characterised by elite strategies of negotiation and agreement 'from above' and the pressures and demands of mobilised social movements 'from below'.[1] The success of the transition towards, and consolidation of, liberal democracy in Spain is said to have depended heavily on the dynamics of consensus, conciliation and compromise, a context in which neo-corporatism, or more particularly, social partnership played a crucial role.[2]

Concertation, defined as the participation of organised interests, normally trade unions and employers' associations, in the formation and implementation processes of economic and social policy, emerged in Spain under specific circumstances and for a limited time period. The experience of tripartite concertation at the national level in Spain has not been a persistent, recurrent policy-making style but rather one with a short, truncated history. Recent discussions have tended to focus on the absence or crisis of social concertation and the reasons explaining the unstable and precarious nature of such arrangements: changes in economic cycles, the indifference or antipathy of social democratic governments, economic policies aimed at improving the efficiency of market mechanisms and, in particular, the weakness and division of organised labour.[3] From this perspective tripartite consultation and negotiation have not been outstanding features of the Spanish political and administrative tradition. Nevertheless, throughout the nineteenth and twentieth centuries ideas, values, practices and institutions developed under different political systems – parliamentary monarchy, authoritarian dictatorship and liberal democracy – which have clearly influenced the prevailing conditions and character of social concertation in Spain. This chapter seeks, through an analysis of the relations between economic interests, labour and the state, to identify the historical institutional, ideological and cultural features that have impeded or sustained the development of social partnership and policy concertation in Spain.

Economic Interests, Labour Organisations and the Spanish State: From Early Beginnings to the Eve of the First World War

The associative traditions of economic organisations in Spain constitute an important legacy influencing the nature of contemporary relations between interest groups and the state. The origins of the associative behaviour of business and labour can be traced back to the latter half of the nineteenth century. The first associations of workers, based on pre-industrial craft guilds, were organised initially for insurance and mutual assistance purposes, although increasingly they assumed a role in the defence and promotion of workers' interests, with the right to associate forming their key political demand.

The General Workers' Union, (Unión General de Trabajadores – UGT) founded in 1888, represented relative moderation and pragmatism in the articulation of workers' interests; its strategy was a combination of the use of the strike weapon and legal political action, with the support of the Spanish Socialist Workers' Party (Partido Socialista Obrero Español – PSOE) seeking to pressure public authorities to introduce legislation improving the working conditions of labour – the eight-hour day, a minimum salary and equal pay for men and women. From the outset the Socialist trade union opted for a reformist strategy which complemented the PSOE's aim to secure, via parliamentary means, state power in order to transform society. The ideology of Spanish socialism regarded pressure politics as a practical method for securing economic and social advances for workers. In stark contrast to the Socialists, the anarcho-syndicalists declared their apoliticism, their contempt for political parties and bourgeois democracy and their principal aim as the annihilation of the state. The National Confederation of Labour (*Confederación Nacional del Trabajo*, CNT), founded in 1911, advocated direct action and violence as instruments in order to weaken the bourgeois state, contribute to its disappearance, and finally achieve a social revolution. The anarcho-syndicalist belief in the revolutionary general strike and class war hardly constituted a sound basis for the institutionalisation of peaceful, cooperative industrial relations; rather, the anti-system CNT was openly hostile to capitalism and the state, rejecting legal political action and the parliamentary game.

The degree of fragmentation of interest representation was exacerbated by the presence of secular–religious conflicts, a rural–urban cleavage and regional–nationalistic sentiments.[4] In a way similar to the experiences of other European countries, the publication of Leo XIII's encyclical *Rerum*

Novarum in 1891 provided a stimulus for the creation of workers' associations under the tutelage of the Catholic Church. In Spain the most notable organisational development came in the shape of the Catholic Workers' Circles founded by the Jesuit priest Antonio Vicent.

The Catholic Workers' Circles was a movement of agricultural cooperatives, savings banks, insurance schemes and recreational clubs. Vicent was inspired by corporatist philosophy based on the harmony of interests between workers and employers and the notion of the unity of distinct social classes through the corporation. In his written reflections on the *Rerum Novarum*, Vicent invoked nostalgically and glorified the pre-industrial guild system as the organisational model to be followed in order to create a corporatist regime that would secure social peace and harmony.[5] Vicent, in his role as publicist of Catholic social doctrine and the idea of social partnership and corporatist organisation in Spain, was helped by the aristocratic figure of the Marqués de Comillas who provided the financial backing for numerous activities and initiatives. At the turn of the century, however, the Catholic Workers' Circles went into organisational decline.

The origins of the associative activity of employers in Spain are to be found initially in the articulation of business interests to encourage protectionism rather than as a response to the rise of organised labour. The protectionist debate came to dominate public discussions of economic policy from the 1870s onwards, and business representatives sought to persuade government of the desirability of pursuing a high tariff policy. Such was the fundamental tenet of the Promotion of National Production (*Fomento de la Producción Nacional*) founded in 1868, and the organisational forerunner of the Promotion of National Manufacturing (*Fomento del Trabajo Nacional*). The Promotion of National Production, despite its determination to forge a national-level organisation, had its principal membership base in Catalonia and defended the sectoral interests, essentially textiles, of the Catalan bourgeoisie. In a similar fashion the National League of Producers (*Liga Nacional de Productores*) founded in Bilbao in 1893, was unable to uphold its national calling and was succeeded by the Biscayan League of Producers (*Liga Vizcaína de Productores*), which concentrated its organisational efforts in the Basque province and represented heavy industry, particularly iron and steel.[6] Sectoral and regional differences apart, such trade associations held the common aim of protecting national industry from the competitive forces which resulted from low tariff barriers. Largely in response to such calls, the country's commercial policy experienced a U-turn after 1891, adopting a determinedly protectionist stance.[7] According to one interpretation, this sea change in economic policy reflected the influence wielded by business associations in the political system at the time.[8]

The development and pattern of the representation of business interests during this period offered a clear symmetry with the organisations of labour: the existence of weak, divided, competitive rival organisations with regional strongholds. Indeed, the regional, rather than national, complexion of economic interest groups owed much to the nature of Spanish economic development. Undeniably the pace and direction of economic development shaped the evolution of economic interest organisations. The slowness of industrialisation was a marked characteristic of Spanish economic development for the nineteenth and much of the twentieth century.[9]

The Spanish government, by the early 1880s, showed signs of growing concern over social questions and the complex problems of industrialisation. The Commission of Social Reforms (*Comisión de Reformas Sociales*), established in 1883, was charged with the task of preparing reports on working conditions and presenting proposals and initiatives to the Spanish Parliament with the aim of elaborating legislation to improve social and working conditions. The Commission was appointed by the Minister of the Interior with the Conservative Cánovas del Castillo named as its first President. Apart from the permanent central Commission, a decentralised network of temporary provincial and local commissions was organised with the specific task of reporting on the circumstances and needs of the working class across the country. The provincial commissions had a membership of fifty-two, made up of the civil governor, the mayor and an assorted group of representatives of employers, workers, the liberal professions, clerics, the military, the judiciary, councillors and provincial deputies, all designated by their respective organisations or elected by a free vote. The workers' representatives were limited to ten seats. The local commissions had a membership of twenty-three with only five worker participants and a structure and representation like the provincial bodies. Certainly no significant legislative measures were produced as a result of the Commission's deliberations. Nevertheless, the Commission of Social Reforms was remarkable for it constituted the formal incorporation and acceptance of organised labour in policy-making processes.

It was not until the country experienced a significant increase in industrial unrest at the start of the twentieth century and the concomitant growth of labour organisations that the state opted for an explicit interventionist strategy in social policy. The Liberal politician Canalejas presented a project to create an Institute of Labour (*Instituto de Trabajo*), based on an ambition to improve the condition of the working class and mitigate the social and political consequences of conflict between employers and workers.[10] The project ultimately failed to be implemented although its importance resided in the fact that it was to be a formal body of government, with research, information and consultative functions, and with equal representation for workers and employers.

In 1903 the Institute of Social Reforms (*Instituto de Reformas Sociales*) was created as a permanent organisation for the study of the conditions of the working class and as a 'think tank' to propose legislative measures to improve the welfare of labourers and their families. Like its predecessor, the Commission of Social Reforms, as well as having a central governing body it was also characterised by a decentralised structure made up of provincial and local boards. Membership of the national body comprised thirty members, eighteen chosen by government and six representatives each chosen by workers and employers. Representation in the various subcommittees followed a similar pattern with the government maintaining a majority of seats. The Institute counted on the participation of labour and business representatives for consultative purposes that affected particularly the tasks of the Ministries of the Interior, and Agriculture, Industry, Trade and Public Works. The Institute was charged with the responsibility of preparing legislative proposals in various fields and of ensuring compliance with policy measures. To this extent, the activities of the Institute can be recognised as an important step towards social concertation in policy making and implementation. It was significant in that it provided a permanent environment and favourable milieu promoting cooperation and understanding between the representatives of capital and labour.

The Institute of Social Reforms, through its information and advisory activities, and as a representational channel for the social interlocutors, stimulated the government to introduce an assortment of legislative measures dealing with health and safety, the rights of children and women in the workplace, working hours and insurance schemes, as well as the creation of organisational frameworks for the institutionalisation of industrial conflict. In 1908 legislation was passed establishing Councils for Industrial Conciliation and Arbitration, although the industrial relations system continued to present a model based more on contestation than on bargaining. In this sense, the attitudes, behaviour and pattern of organised business and labour, together with disposition of government, provided the opportunities and constraints for processes of social concertation. It is important to recall that the anarchist movement at the time remained firmly outside any embryonic concertative policy community. Instead of piecemeal reform the anarcho-syndicalists sought revolution. Moreover, Spanish employers rejected state intervention in the industrial and social sphere, claiming it limited freedom and the 'natural harmony' of participants in the labour contract.[11] In any case, despite the state's declared concern for social affairs, legislative measures were limited, insufficient and incomplete.[12]

At the time of the First World War, the scope for the institutionalisation of industrial relations and the development of concertative practices appeared extremely limited as an explosion of industrial unrest and social agitation swept the country. In the context of union mobilisation and increasing state intervention in the social and industrial spheres, Spanish employers in 1914 resolved to create a strong, centralised business organisation in the shape of the Spanish Employers' Confederation (*Confederación Patronal Española*), in order to contest organised labour and secure economic privileges from government. The endeavours to establish a single, encompassing peak association were undermined, however, by the existence of fissures based on regional and sectoral differences, and alternative expressions of business representation. Indeed, the overwhelming presence of small enterprises in the industrial and commercial fabric of the country provided the basis for the formation of a distinct organisation representing such interests, the Spanish Guild Confederation (*Confederación Gremial Española*).[13]

Business, Labour and the State: From the Crisis of the Parliamentary Monarchy to the Civil War

The decline of the parliamentary monarchy, which had been established in 1875, was due to the enormity and seriousness of the challenges it faced and the incapacity of the regime to adapt and resolve them. The atmosphere of crisis and system breakdown worsened as Spain, after 1917, and between 1919 and 1920 in particular, experienced levels of industrial unrest hitherto unknown; a tremendous explosion of union membership accompanied intense strike activity. Employers responded to worker militancy with lock-outs and called for tough repressive measures against trade union organisations. The culture of fear and the language of class war dominated the atmosphere, leaving little, if any room for social dialogue and negotiation.

The Institute of Social Reforms, the most concertative institution up to that date, had become overshadowed and made inoperative by the gravity of the social conflict, street violence and police and military repression. The political appeals of employers' organisations at the time were essentially limited to calls for the restoration of public order through the intervention of the military and protests at the weakness of the regime. To this extent, employers did not lament the ending of the parliamentary monarchy; in fact, their discontent contributed to the ambience that encouraged Primo de Rivera's coup d'état in 1923.[14]

The dictatorship of Primo de Rivera provoked significant changes for the organisations of business and labour and their interactions with the state. Primo de Rivera saw little need for a plurality of political parties and a 'degenerated' parliamentary democracy; he suspended the Constitution and the Parliament and aimed to replace them with a new corporatist order based on an ideology of class harmony.[15] This authoritarian corporatist model sought to structure industrial and economic relations on the basis of professions or 'corporations'. The National Corporatist Organisation (*Organización Corporativa Nacional*), established in 1926, had classified twenty-seven distinct economic sections, although the system only became truly operative for industry and commerce (agriculture being somewhat neglected). The basic institutions of this pyramidal system were the Joint Committees (*Comités Paritarios*) which at local, provincial and national levels brought together the representatives of business and labour, on an apparent equal footing, to negotiate industrial relations issues such as wages, labour contracts and work regulations.

The Joint Committees represented, however, an extension of earlier patterns of industrial relations behaviour and a reflection of previously held values and pertinent ideologies in Spain, a point recognised by Eduardo Aunós, who, as Minister of Labour, was the principal ideologue behind the establishment of the corporatist regime. Aunós was certainly influenced by other corporatist experiments at the time. In April 1926 he travelled to Italy to investigate the nature of the Italian corporate state and he met with Mussolini and Bottai, the Minister of Corporations. However, Aunós was keen to emphasise the existence of preceding corporatist practices in Spain, the legacy of the guild system and influence of Catholic social teaching as forming the basis for his corporatist model.[16]

Under the dictatorship the local Joint Committees constituted the basic pillar of the whole corporatist edifice. The local Joint Committees in each industry were comprised of five representatives for the employers and an equal number of representatives for labour with the president and vice-president named by the Minister of Labour. The Joint Committees were responsible for the regulation of the working conditions in the industry or profession, the avoidance and resolution of industrial conflicts and the administration of job opportunities for the unemployed. In addition, a grouping of Joint Committees from different localities, the Comités Paritarios Interlocales, was charged with the task of making proposals to government concerning professional and technical measures deemed necessary for the industry.

The next level in the corporatist organisational hierarchy, the Mixed Commissions of Labour (*Comisiones Mixtas del Trabajo*) represented voluntary groupings of Comités from various industries united under the organisation of a single Council whose president and vice-president were appointed by the Ministry. In addition to the functions and obligations assigned to the Joint Committees, the Mixed Commissions of Labour were responsible for the development of institutions involved in education, culture, training, and research into social issues. The Councils of Corporations (*Consejos de Corporaciones*) at a higher level represented the Joint Committees from each of the twenty-seven Corporations, with the president and vice-president named by the government, and employers and workers with eight representatives each. It was incumbent upon this institution to regulate labour contracts throughout the industry, to inform government of opportunities to improve legislation and to 'invigorate associational life'.[17] The highest level of organisation in the corporatist structure was the Delegated Commission of Councils (*Comisión delegada de Consejos*), comprising of seven representatives each for employers and workers and a president, the Director General of Labour. This supreme body represented all the Corporation Councils and constituted the maximum level of arbitration and conciliation and acted as the consultative organ for the Ministry of Labour, Commerce and Industry.

The National Corporatist Organisation was based on the principles of state intervention in social problems and the need to organise the economic life of the country. However, despite the corporatist rhetoric, the corporatist structure of the Primo de Rivera regime was organised as an instrument to control social conflicts rather than develop a particular economic policy with the equal participation of both sides of industry.[18] In this way the corporativisation of organised interests did not extend to all groups. The Primo de Rivera regime discriminated between 'insiders' and 'outsiders': the UGT and the Free Trade Unions (*Sindicatos Libres*) were recognised as legitimate participants while anarchist and communist organisations were repressed. The

Free Trade Unions had been formed in 1919 with the specific aim of combating the spread of CNT influence among the working class, particularly in Barcelona.[19] They were the sort of 'professional', non-revolutionary organisation the dictatorship preferred, particularly when they assumed the regime's corporatist ideology as part of their own. The CNT, in contrast, was considered an illegal organisation and ceased to be operational during this period.

Nevertheless, those elements of organised labour embraced by the dictatorship welcomed many features of the corporatist regime. The fortunes of the Socialist trade union under the dictatorship were certainly better than those of their anarchist counterparts. Primo de Rivera sought to incorporate the UGT into the political system rather exclude it, an approach which in large part reflected his concern to reinforce moderate currents within the Spanish trade union movement. At the same time, the ascendancy of the more reformist elements in the UGT and PSOE facilitated Socialist acceptance of the corporatist policies of the Primo de Rivera regime. Moderate Socialist leaders such as Besteiro had been receptive to, and influenced by, diverse ideological currents such as Regenerationism and Krausism, which defended the idea of an organic system of political representation. The opportunity to participate as an autonomous organisation in the corporatist system was accepted by the UGT leader, Largo Caballero. He regarded incorporation into state institutions as a chance to maintain the Socialist organisation intact, gain an advantage over its principal competitor, the CNT, and secure social improvements for workers.

As a result, the participation of the Socialist trade union was not limited to the labour machinery of the National Corporatist Organisation, but rather UGT representatives occupied positions in a plethora of technical, administrative and consultative agencies. The 1926 Labour Code, for example, had been elaborated with the collaboration of UGT representatives. The pragmatic UGT leader Largo Caballero agreed to occupy a seat in the Council of Labour (*Consejo de Trabajo*) and became the workers' representative in the Council of State (*Consejo del Estado*) a consultative body in which business was also represented.

By the end of the 1920s the Socialists came to distance themselves from the Primo de Rivera regime as it descended into crisis. In 1929 UGT representatives did not accept their nominations to the National Consultative Assembly (*Asamblea Nacional Consultativa*), the key corporatist consultative institution consisting of representatives from the Administration, the official regime party – *Unión Patriótica* – and functional interests. By the time of its creation it was widely recognised that the National Assembly was simply an irrelevant, flimsy façade for the regime with no real weight in the policy making process of the dictatorship.

Business groups generally welcomed the advent of the dictatorship due to its promises of social peace and public order and an interventionist, protectionist approach to spur national economic development. The incorporation of business representatives into a variety of corporative bodies, such as the Council of the National Economy (*Consejo de Economía Nacional*) and regulatory commissions governing markets and prices, was well received. Indeed, prior to the 1923 coup, significant sections of the business community, frustrated with the operation of the parliamentary monarchy, had developed ideas supportive of corporatist structures and policies. A variety of business organisations had called for the creation of institutions in which organised interests and professions could secure representation in order to influence policy decisions.[20]

However, as time passed the dictatorship increasingly had to confront opposition to its policies from business quarters. Criticism focused specifically on fiscal policy reform, the pace and efficiency of works projects, and corruption and favouritism in public contracts. Business organisations such as the Federation of National Industries (*Federación de Industrias Nacionales*), representative of large-sized enterprises linked to the major banks, expressed concern over the soundness of public finances. Other organisations such as the Association of Social and Economic Studies (*Asociación de Estudios Sociales y Económicos*), which had played an instrumental role in provoking the withdrawal of employers' representatives from the Institute of Social Reforms, were particularly critical about the social features of the regime's corporatist policy. Employers condemned excessive state regulation in the social sphere and the obligatory participation of employers in the Joint Committees. The incorporation of business into the corporativisation process, which so defined the political, economic and social systems established by Primo de Rivera, was considered a threat to the economic and political freedoms of employers. It was this feature of the regime that, perhaps more than any other aspect, progressively distanced the majority of employers from the new corporate order. The fall of the Primo de Rivera dictatorship, followed subsequently by the fall of the monarchy, was the result of an accumulation of problems and conflicts with a variety of discontented groups: intellectuals, university students, the military, trade unions and employers.

The climate of anticipation and desire for change was confirmed by the proclamation of the Second Republic in 1931. The ambitious programme of the Azaña government, in which Largo Caballero, the UGT leader, held the post of Minister of Labour, sought to resolve the fundamental problems faced by society, the economy and the polity: agrarian reform, army reform, the religious question and regionalism. The enormity of these issues overshadowed the more mundane question of the adequacy of policy responses to the economic recession, something of particular interest to business. Indeed, business organisations soon became disenchanted with the new democratic regime as government was increasingly distracted from confronting the negative consequences for industry of the economic downturn during this period.

Certainly the recession affected different sectors and activities in an uneven way that made the presentation to government of a united, coherent view a difficult task for the representatives of business. A new venture in business organisation, the Economic Union (*Unión Económica*) was established in 1931 to develop itself as the single, encompassing peak association able to articulate the demands of business in a coherent and consistent fashion. Such a movement was once again weakened by the fragmentation of business: differences in enterprise size, sectoral and regional interests continued to undermine the capacity of business to speak with one voice. However, the articulation of business interests was made even more complicated as business organisations had to establish linkages with a new political class, and adapt to new mechanisms and channels of influence in decision-making processes.[21] It is not surprising then that some business leaders suggested the formation of a Second Chamber representing economic interests.[22]

Business was most concerned with the government's reformist programme of social and labour relations policy measures, designed by Largo Caballero to improve the working conditions of labour and reinforce the role of trade unions: the eight-hour day, health and safety legislation, maternity leave, sickness benefits and holidays with pay. In 1931 Mixed Boards (*Jurados Mixtos*), made up of trade union and employers' representatives, were established and charged with the tasks of conciliation and arbitration in industrial disputes and the development of work regulations concerning salaries, contracts, hours of work, overtime and dismissal procedures. In addition, the Mixed Boards were responsible for the supervision of the implementation of social policy and could, if necessary, make proposals to government concerning improvements in legislation. In many ways the Mixed Boards were an extension of the Joint Committees of the Primo de Rivera dictatorship but with a wider range of functions and increased powers for workers' representatives. Certainly in terms of structure there were clear similarities with the Comités, with each Jurado consisting of an equal number of members representing workers and employers and with the president and vice-president appointed by the Minister of Labour. They were also organised according to sectoral activity or professions although not all professions were subject to regulation by a Jurado Mixto.

From the perspective of organised business the Jurados were simply a mechanism of Socialist control giving workers' representatives effective instruments to improve wages and conditions to the detriment of business profitability. Business organisations mounted an aggressive campaign against the Jurados Mixtos; however, disputes remained over the question of whether to reform or eliminate the Jurados.[23] The reticence and distrust of business was a feature that undermined the potentiality of the Jurados as a framework for concertative practices and policies. Indeed, business considered the Jurados as biased and partial. In particular, the UGT was regarded as the principal beneficiary of Socialist participation in government and seen as enjoying direct influence in the design and implementation of public policy, especially social policy. The CNT opposed the Jurados Mixtos outright. The atmosphere was hardly conducive to the stabilisation and institutionalisation of industrial relations or the development of concertative practices in policy making.

The triumph of the Right in the elections of 1933 simply served to raise the temperature of social tensions and conflicts as the new government planned to reverse previous policies, and in particular, the advances secured by the labour movement. For example, in 1935 the Mixed Boards were reformed, limiting the power of the trade unions and essentially undermining their position in the industrial relations system. With the entrance of members of the Catholic Spanish Confederation of the Autonomous Right (*Confederación Española de Derechas Autónomas*, CEDA) into government the majority of Socialists believed that the period of collaboration with the bourgeois democracy had come to an end. The CEDA had as its ultimate aim the creation of a Catholic corporate state, an idea that Pius XI had defended in his 1931 encyclical *Quadragesimo Anno* and which represented a continuation of earlier themes in Catholic social doctrine.

The elections of February 1936, won by the Popular Front, illustrated the extent to which Spain had become divided into two antagonistic and belligerent camps. The degree of mobilisation and polarisation of society and politics was exacerbated by a wave of industrial unrest, public disorder, and 'direct actions' immediately after the elections. In such a setting it is difficult to conceive how organised business and labour could accomplish the bargaining and compromises with government that define the concertative style of policy making. The highly charged political and social climate characteristic of Spain at this time was inimical for the development of a routine and robust concertative mode of policy formulation and implementation. The military uprising in July 1936 and the ensuing civil war left little room for consensus and accord.

Business and Labour under Franco's Dictatorship and the Transition Towards Democracy

Franco's dictatorship declared the creation of a New State, which, among other things, abolished democratic liberties, prohibited trade unions and established a corporatist institutional system to take their place. The Spanish Syndical Organisation (*Organización Sindical Española*, OSE) was considered part of a corporatist tradition based on a belief in the harmony of economic and social interests and class collaboration. The Falange, whose corporatist doctrine, heavily influenced by Catholic social thought, had provided the initial ideological gloss for the regime, was formally charged with the intricate organisation of the national syndicates. From the outset, the OSE's political dependence and limited autonomy was clear.

In 1940 two laws established the legal basis for the OSE.[24] The OSE represented an extremely complex, hierarchical and unitary organisational form based on the obligatory membership of employers and workers in vertical syndicates, classified according to economic sectors, under the direction and discipline of the state. The National Syndicates *(Sindicatos Nacionales)* were organised in over twenty productive sectors at two distinct levels, national and provincial. At the national level the maximum political authority was the figure of the National Delegate, named by Franco, and in charge of the

National Syndical Centre *(Central Sindical Nacional*) made up of the presidents of the worker and employer sections of each national syndicate. The position of the National Delegate later disappeared, to be replaced by the Minister for Syndical Relations who presided over the Syndical Congress, elected by the councils of employers and workers. At the provincial level, the same arrangement was repeated with the Provincial Delegate, who was named directly by the National Delegate and who presided over a provincial council made up of the presidents of local syndicates, elected by employer and worker sections. It is right to say that in this early period the representativeness of these institutions was extremely limited; rather, they were considered principally as mechanisms to control labour conflicts.[25] Even when syndical elections were held in the late 1950s which allowed for the growth of alternative expressions of worker representation, the OSE remained essentially an instrument of worker control at the disposal of the regime.

Although employers were obliged to integrate into the vertical syndicates, business interests enjoyed a certain degree of autonomy by having a variety of channels that they could use to influence policy. First, the traditional organisations representing business interests, such as the *Fomento de Trabajo Nacional*, continued to operate independently from the vertical syndicates by changing their legal status. Second, certain sectoral business associations, although formally part of the OSE, managed to preserve their independence and expand their activities. Third, business made use of the same vertical structures that would eventually be infiltrated by workers' representatives; in this case, business exploited the official corporatist set-up to express its concerns and be heard by policy makers. Lastly, informal clientelistic traditions also continued to persist through personal contacts between business leaders and the political class.[26]

The absence of autonomous organisations representing labour highlighted the politics of exclusion applied by the regime to those unprepared to accept the principles of the movement. From the perspective of organised labour three distinct periods can be identified with respect to the nature of its interactions with the Francoist regime.[27] During the first phase, from the early 1940s to the end of the 1950s, there was a virtual absence of organised trade union activity, apart from isolated instances of worker protest in Barcelona and Vizcaya in the late 1940s and early 1950s, which were essentially a reaction to the harsh conditions of the autarkic model of economic development implemented by the dictatorship throughout this period.

The second phase, beginning at the end of the 1950s and early 1960s, coincided with the liberalisation of the economy and an accelerated industrialisation process, precipitating a period of vigorous strike activity in regions such as Catalonia, the Basque Country, and Asturias; the wave of strikes increasingly combined purely economic demands, such as wage rises and working conditions, with political demands, calling for democratic freedoms and genuine labour representation, particularly once workers' leaders linked to political parties such as the Spanish Communist Party started to steer the movement. The emergence of a spontaneous, decentralised, encompassing workers' movement, the Workers' Commissions (*Comisiones Obreras*, CC.OO) and a more traditional style of union organisation, with a strong Catholic tendency, the Workers' Syndical Union (*Unión Sindical Obrera*, USO) challenged the historical predominance of the CNT and UGT among the Spanish workforce. These new movements had decided to use 'Trojan horse' tactics to occupy positions of influence within the structures of the official vertical syndicates. The opportunities to do this came as institutional room for action opened up once collective bargaining was allowed after 1958 through the Law on Collective Bargaining and after elections for shop stewards and shop stewards' committees were held. The 'historic unions' had rejected the infiltration of the official syndicates; they argued that such tactics would give the OSE an air of legitimacy. In fact, the progressive substitution of official representatives by authentic worker delegates served to discredit the official syndicates. In addition, CC.OO played an increasingly important role in the opposition to the regime, displacing the CNT and UGT, who rejected the tactics of infiltration. These historic unions had suffered the brunt of the repression after the civil war and their exiled leaderships appeared to lose touch with the dynamics and pulse of the new generation of workers. The lack of real presence inhibited the UGT and CNT in their capacity to influence and control worker opposition to the regime.

The third phase began in the early 1970s and continued until the democratic transition process. The CC.OO during this period assumed a central role in the wave of strikes that affected a variety of sectors across different areas of the country. The CC.OO had secured a dominant position in the workers' movement and the Communists were the ascendant group within CC.OO.[28] In 1971, the UGT experienced a change of leadership with the transfer of the organisation's executive from outside Spain to inside the country; this allowed the Socialist trade union to reorganise, extend its influence and recover its historic role in the Spanish labour movement. The CNT, in contrast, appeared to lose out to the CC.OO who were particularly strong in the anarcho-syndicalist union's traditional fiefdoms, Catalonia, Aragon and Andalusia. The refusal of the CNT to infiltrate the official syndicates, although logical and coherent from the standpoint of the union's ideological traditions, clearly hindered the organisational revival and ascendancy of anarcho-syndicalism in post-Franco Spain. The USO during this period continued to occupy positions in the structure of the OSE though not on the same scale as CC.OO, while fighting to maintain its independence from party political influence. It was precisely the activities of such trade unions which constituted the 'pressure from below', influencing decisively the nature of the transition to democracy after the death of Franco in 1975.

The experiences of the various elements of the Spanish trade union movement during the Francoist dictatorship had a decisive influence on the development of trade unionism after the death of the dictator. Under liberal democracy the Spanish labour movement continued to be divided, competitive and relatively weak. Indeed things had changed little in terms of the organisational characteristics of Spanish labour since its origins. However, significant changes had taken place in terms of trade union ideologies, strategies, tactics, attitudes and values. The labour movement under democracy has been consistently supportive of institutions and processes, moderate and restrained.

Social concertation was able to develop in recent years because at last Spain has established the democratic institutions and political culture necessary for such arrangements to succeed. The changes experienced by the trade union movement have been an important conditioning factor but equally business has been able to create a single, encompassing peak association, which has greatly facilitated concertative policy practices. However, even more relevant has been the willingness on the part of employers to design and implement economic and social policies through concertation.

Conclusion

It would be erroneous to argue that Spain has had a long tradition of social partnership and policy concertation. Indeed the concept of 'social partner' is very much an imported product from those countries regarded as benefiting from a modern, European industrial relations system and policy process. Unfortunately, for the greatest part of the last hundred years Spanish historical development has been characterised predominantly by deep, violent social antagonisms and hostilities. As we have seen, conflict and confrontation rather than the cooperation and compromise characteristic of social concertation have distinguished industrial relations and politics in twentieth-century Spain. The inability of Spaniards to resolve conflict through stable, peaceful mechanisms has been highlighted by the experiences of authoritarian dictatorships, fragile democratic episodes and the tragedy of civil war.

The practices of political exchange – compromises, trade-offs, give and take, concessions and agreements to disagree – so characteristic of social concertation and social partnership have had difficulty taking root. However, this is not to say that the recent experience of social concertation has been without precedents or precursors. The institutional arrangements, which, under different political systems, brought organised interests together during the last century, represented a useful collaborative exercise. The vitality of ideas and attitudes from diverse quarters promoting social harmony and class collaboration certainly also left their mark. However, it is only in recent years that Spain has established a system of institutionalised norms of tolerance.[29] It is the consolidation of this system that, perhaps more than any other factor, has conditioned the opportunities for social concertation in post-Franco Spain.

Notes

1. J. M. Maravall, *La política de la transición*, 2nd edn, Madrid, 1984.
2. V. Peréz Díaz, *El retorno de la sociedad civil*, Madrid, 1987.
3. J.Roca, *Pactos sociales y política de rentas: el debate internacional y la experiencia española (1977–1988)*, Madrid, 1993.

4. J.J. Linz, 'Política e intereses a lo largo de un siglo en España, 1880–1980', in *El corporatismo en España*, ed. M. Pérez Yruela and S. Giner, Barcelona, 1988: 67–123.
5. A. Vicent, *Socialismo y anarquismo*, Valencia, 1895: 567–613.
6. M. Cabrera and F. del Rey, 'Los intereses económicos organizados en España. Un siglo en la historia del asociacionismo empresarial', in *La empresa en la historia de España*, ed. F. Comín and P. Martín Aceña, Madrid, 1996: 441–56.
7. J.M. Serrano, *El viraje proteccionista de la Restauración. La política comercial española, 1875–1895*, Madrid, 1987.
8. J. Palafox, *Atraso económico y democracia. La Segunda República y la economía española, 1892–1936*, Barcelona, 1991: 30.
9. L. Prados de la Escosura, *De Imperio a Nación. Crecimiento y atraso económico en España (1780–1930)*, Madrid, 1988.
10. J.I. Palacio, *La institucionalización de la reforma social en España (1883–1924)*, Madrid, 1988.
11. A. Soto, *El trabajo industrial en la España contemporánea (1874–1924)*, Madrid, 1988.
12. J. P. Fusi and J. Palafox, *España: 1808–1996: el desafío de la modernidad*, 2nd edn, Madrid, 1997: 168.
13. M. Cabrera, *La patronal ante la II República. Organizaciones y estrategia (1931–1936)*, Madrid, 1983.
14. F. del Rey, *Propietarios y patronos. La política de las organizaciones económicas en la España de la Restauración (1914–1923)*, Madrid, 1992.
15. S. Ben Ami, *La dictadura de Primo de Rivera, 1923–1930*, Barcelona, 1983.
16. E. Aunós, *La política social de la dictadura*, Madrid, 1944: 58.
17. Ibid., 68.
18. M. Tuñón de Lara et al., *La crisis del estado: dictadura, república, guerra*, Barcelona, 1985: 64.
19. C. Winston, *La clase trabajadora y la derecha en España, 1900–1936*, Madrid, 1989.
20. J.L Goméz-Navarro, *El Régimen de Primo de Rivera: reyes, dictaduras y dictadores*, Madrid, 1991: 402.
21. Palafox, *Atraso económico*: 175.
22. Cabrera, *La patronal*: 268.
23. Ibid., chap 5.
24. The Ley de Unidad Sindical and the Ley de Bases de la Organización Sindical constituted the legal framework for the OSE. See J. Amsden, *Collective Bargaining and Class Struggle in Spain*, London, 1972.
25. J.Foweraker, *La Democracia Española*, Madrid, 1990: 120–1.
26. Cabrera and del Rey, 'Los intereses económicos': 452.
27. J.A. Sagardoy and D. León, *El poder sindical en España*, Barcelona, 1982.
28. R. Fishman, *Organización obrera y retorno a la democracia en España*, Madrid, 1996.
29. V. Pérez Díaz, *La esfera pública y la sociedad civil*, Madrid, 1997.

CHAPTER 18

SPAIN IN THE 1990S: STRATEGIC CONCERTATION

Miguel Martínez Lucio

Introduction

This chapter will attempt to outline the evolving nature of union and employer strategies and their relation to the state in the context of concertation. It will outline the nature of the political challenge facing union and employer organisations in Spain. It will describe the types of solutions that have emerged since the early 1990s with regard to new types of 'weak-corporatist' relations at the micro and macro level.[1] In the case of Spain, the perceived limitations of the grand pacts of the early 1980s, the increasing political interest in market-based solutions to economic and social problems, and the changing nature of social and economic processes have contributed to a new type of neo-corporatist experience.[2] The author labels this experience 'fragmented corporatism' or 'corporatism from below'. The key social actors have adopted a strategy of trying to operationalise what were previously dysfunctional state roles in employment relations whilst extending the remit of what has been a very narrow system of joint regulation into broader issues within the firm and the workplace – in effect they have been trying to modernise and operationalise regulation. These actors are still 'involved', but within very specific areas of social intervention and in terms of operationalising and modernising the role of the state as 'administrators' and somewhat less as policy makers.[3]

Corporatism in Spain – A Case of Negotiated Corporatism[4]

The history of post-Francoist state-labour relations in Spain is a rich and complex one. Whilst neo-corporatist intermediation has been sporadic in the last twenty years, it has played a vital role. Firstly, at critical moments social pacts proved crucial in the establishment and stabilisation of the liberal democratic process. Second, they contributed, alongside other factors, to the emergence of the socialist UGT union (*Union General de Trabajadores*) as a moderate counter to the more radical CC.OO (*Comisiones Obreras*), given that the UGT was provided with a protagonist role within such processes. Third, they ensured that key developments in sensitive areas such as labour market and employment reform were subject to a degree of political bargaining and negotiation.

Some historical background

The legacy of state corporatism in Spain (see Robinson, this volume) impacts on the nature of state regulation in post-Franco Spain, for example the continuity of labour ordinances which regulate details of the employment relation, the form of workplace politics and representation in terms of works councils (albeit altered since the mid-1970s). However, in terms of the nature of macro-level representation at the level of the state the Francoist years left little, thankfully, although the legacy of dysfunctional state intervention in the employment relation remained. Neither state/authoritarian nor societal/liberal corporatism were ever consistent or representative models of the perceived ideal types.[5] But that is exactly what makes this case so interesting.

The concertation of the first ten years of democracy was based on a series of discontinuous and varied 'grand pacts'. It was also an arena of inter-union rivalry. One significant aspect was the marginalisation of CC.OO, which allowed UGT to establish itself institutionally and politically. This partly reflected the employers' organisations' (CEOE) policy of favouring the UGT. CC.OO was excluded from the Basic Interconfederal Agreement (ABI) of 1979 and the Interconfederal Framework Agreement (AMI) of 1980, which covered issues related to the bargaining process and incomes. But the 1981 National Agreement on Employment (ANE), signed following the attempted military coup d'état of February, was truly tripartite, involving government, employers and both major unions. It offered employment creation and a range of other social measures in return for wage moderation. CC.OO also participated in the Interconfederal Agreement (AI) of 1983, following the Socialists' election victory in 1982. But when the socialist PSOE (*Partido Socialista Obrero Espanol)* invited all the economic actors to discuss a new two-year tripartite agreement in 1984, the AES (Economic and Social Agreement), the CC.OO did not participate, concerned at the failure of the agreement to ensure the implementation of social measures – a recurring theme in Spanish neo-corporatism. Employment and social measures were combined with a commitment to contain incomes. For employers, concertation was a rational response at a time of union strength when no actor wished to see an all-out confrontation in view of the political fragility of democracy.[6]

From the late 1980s, recession and the unions' own organisational difficulties meant that employers (and the government) had less incentive to contain union demands through concertation. Nor were employers keen to pay for wage moderation with improved social provision and possibly expansionist economic policies.[7] The CEOE resisted strong forms of corporatist involvement in order to avoid the institutionalisation of relations between the state and labour, and to prevent the development of a strong social dimension.[8] For government, too, the value of concertation diminished from the mid-1980s. The long period of PSOE government under Felipe González provided political and economic stability and helped entrench democratic institutions (although well before the end of the PSOE era, mounting government corruption was calling political stability into question). The need for tripartite peak bargaining as a political stabiliser therefore diminished. Roca has argued that corporatism was not the only rational response to the requirements of the transition.[9] Rather, it has to be seen more as a 'strategy' for coping with social conflict and generating consensus initiated by government in response to a particular conjuncture. This 'strategic displacement' of decision making has been a central feature of economic policy in democratic Spain.[10]

The latter years of Socialist government

From the general strike of 1988 through to the election of a Conservative government in 1996, dialogue between the unions and the Socialist government was minimal to say the least. Whilst the role of the state had expanded in relative terms under the Socialist government, their engagement with the language of market politics, plus increasingly personal differences with leaders of the socialist UGT and the disdain displayed towards any alternative socialist orientation, made any neo-corporatist dialogue virtually impossible.[11]

Yet by the 1990s the situation was clearly unsatisfactory for all sides. For employers, any reform to what they perceived to be highly rigid labour markets would be impossible without the consent of the unions, in one form or another. The supposed costs of dismissal and its juridical processes has been an obsession for employers since the 1970s.[12] Despite the job destruction that has been extensively facilitated by the role of state institutions in individualising employment termination, and the fact that one-third of the Spanish workforce had been put on temporary contracts, the belief that employers in Spain face a highly rigid regulation of the labour market has not been undermined.[13] From the governmental perspective, both reforms to the welfare state and to labour market regulation would necessitate some type of social dialogue, regardless of the decreasing 'attendance levels' at the general strikes (which were always relatively high to start with). Furthermore, the whole modernisation of industrial relations would seem to be central to future improvements in productivity. This modernisation of industrial relations was becoming fundamental and attractive to the labour movement. A broader union role within the workplace and a more coherent system of collective bargaining could not be achieved solely through the use of symbolic political mobilisation, the results of which had proved to be less than consistent.

In 1994 negotiations emerged between employers and the two main union confederations over the government desire to replace the labour ordinances. This led to an agreement that paralleled the legal changes being made by government – the *Acuerdo Interconfederal en Materia de Ordenanzas Laborales y Reglamentaciones de Trabajo* (Inter-confederal Agreement on the Labour Ordinances and Work Regulations).[14] This was to mark an important development in the reconstitution of some, albeit limited, neo-corporatist type bargaining driven by employers and unions. The old labour ordinances were a series of state regulations that covered a range of issues in the working environment. They had been part of an attempt to circumvent the need for trade unionism but had survived the end of the Francoist dictatorship (1939–75). They provided workers with very detailed sets of regulations regarding, for example, job classifications and seniority structures. In the context of post-Franco Spain they became a central feature of worker rights, alongside independent and democratic collective bargaining. However employers began to question their validity and efficacy in a context of a changing workplace,[15] as they were seen to place limits on the flexible deployment of workers within companies. The unions, whilst generally supporting the ordinances, felt that they would be more effective if modernised and placed within the context of collective bargaining.[16] As for the government, they felt that the ordinances were an unwanted form of state intervention. If anything, the government wanted to distance itself from the internal routines of the employment relation. Many of the main social actors considered the chemical sector's national agreement, which since the 1980s had updated the labour ordinances and tied them into the content of collective bargaining, to be a positive example.

The negotiations concerning the labour ordinances represented a form of neo-corporatist bargaining which was to be more flexible, strategic and agreements driven than the social pacts of the 1980s. Unions and employers were trying to operationalise and respond to the changes taking place in government policy. The 1994 pact was an agreement that was specific and focused; it was not couched in terms of any grand pact covering a range of issues organised around a general exchange between labour and capital. However, regardless of significant developments since the 1994 legal changes, the content of collective agreements at the sectoral level have been unevenly expanded, and in some sectors the new sets of 'ordinances' were still not agreed to. This contributed to an increasing voluntarism within certain industrial sectors. In 1997 a further commitment to try to organise and cover the gaps in micro-level employment regulation left by the withdrawal of the labour ordinances emerged through the agreement *Acuerdo Interconfederal sobre Cobertura de Vacios* (Interconfederal Agreement on the Coverage of 'Vacios'[17]). By late 1998 the trade unions were beginning to realise the costs of formal 'state withdrawal' from areas of employment regulation, as employer interest in developing effective sector-level bargaining was not consistent.

Coupled with this focused model of bipartite and tripartite bargaining was the establishment of the long overdue *Consejo Economico y Social* (CES – Social and Economic Council). The lack of a commitment to a permanent forum for social representation within the state was central to the 'strategic displacement' strategies of the 1970s and 1980s. Whilst, on the one hand, there was a set of unarticulated and separate agreements covering a range of issues, on the other the formalisation of trade union representation at the level of the state was to occur at specific consultative and (as we will see below) operational levels. In this respect the 'corporatism of the 1990s' is not so distant from the 'strategic displacement' of the 1980s.

Flexible corporatism and the Conservative government

The development of this new wave of dialogue must be set within the general political agreement that emerged within Spain in the wake of the decline of the PSOE government and the political uncertainty facing the country in the mid-1990s. The *Pacto de Toledo* (Toledo Agreement) between the main political parties underpinned much of the consensus on the social role of the state with regard to pensions. For some, the pact was ambiguous and did not constitute a firm response to the long-term social challenges facing the Spanish state.[18] This pact was primarily a political pact guaranteeing the basis of one of the most sensitive issues in Spain (i.e. pensions) and establishing a framework for a commitment to maintain a social dimension to the state in areas such as pensions. The Spanish right had developed an ambivalent relationship with its far right and Thatcherite orientation, as witnessed in its increasing interest in the policies of the 1997 British Labour Government's 'Third Way'.

With the election of the *Partido Popular* (PP) Conservative government in 1996 came the irony of a new phase of state-labour relations. The growing distance between the unions and the Socialist Party had encouraged the development of a more coherent set of macroeconomic and industrial relations practices within the socialist government, based around the pursuit of labour market deregulation and the containment of state social programmes, which the 1996 PP government subsequently deepened. The two main unions responded to these political developments through a more consistent union programme of collaboration on matters related to collective bargaining and by opening a dialogue with the new government, which had formally committed itself to maintaining the social role of the state.

A new set of tripartite and bipartite agreements (see Table 18.1) on specific social and industrial relations issues underpinned this new wave of dialogue, which involved the government, trade unions and employers (in some cases the agreements were bipartite but overall it was based on a three-way, albeit complex, relation). Furthermore, a new type of participation within the state was being developed. Together with employers, the unions were to act as overseers of discrete and separate areas of state intervention – for

Table 18.1. *A Selection of the Main Agreements in the 1990s in Spain*

Date	Agreement	Content
1994	*Acuerdo Interconfederal en materia de Ordenanzas Laborales y Reglamentaciones de Trabajo* (Interconfederal Agreement on the Labour Ordinances and Work Regulations)	Industrial relations, production issues and collective bargaining
1996	*Acuerdo sobre Racionalizacion del Sistema de Seguridad Social* (Agreement on the Rationalisation of the System of Social Security)	Social security and pensions
1997	*Acuerdo Interconfederal para la Estabilidad del Empleo* (AIEE – Interconfederal Agreement for Stability in Employment)	Employment contracts and labour market flexibility
1997	*Acuerdo Interconfederal sobre Negociación Colectiva* (AINC – Interconfederal Agreement on Collective Bargaining)	Collective bargaining and coverage
1997	*Acuerdo Interconfederal sobre Cobertura de Vacios* (Interconfederal Agreement on the Coverage of 'Vacios')	Industrial relations, production issues and collective bargaining
1998	*Acuerdo sobre Contratos de Empleo a Tiempo Parcial* (Agreement on Part-time Employment Contracts)	Aimed at improving the condition of part-time employees along with their social security supports

Source: see text.

example, monitoring contracts in public employment agencies. Initially suspicious of such developments, the CEOE and CEPYME (Spanish Confederation for Small and Medium Sized Firms) realised that this would provide unions with a limited, albeit symbolically important, role within areas of the state. Hence the new wave of political bargaining had two dimensions, a strategic one and a structural one, although neither of these could be considered to be institutionally extensive.

Agreements were signed in 1996 between the two main unions and the government on the reform and maintenance of public pension levels until 2001 (*Acuerdo sobre Racionalización del Sistema de Seguridad Social* – Agreement on the Rationalisation of the System of Social Security) along with social employment payments for agrarian workers. These were signed within the political framework of the *Pactos de Toledo*. This agreement developed due to the fact that pensions had become such a central political issue in the 1980s. For the right, it would remove a potential Achilles' heel that could be exploited by the left. The 1996 agreement between these two sides regarding the social and employment protection for agrarian workers followed a similar logic. Like the emerging cohort of pensioners, this group of workers and their families, having seen improvements in their economic position since the early 1980s, were central to the electoral fortunes of the socialists.

The main agreement of the 1990s was the 1997 *Acuerdo Interconfederal para la Estabilidad del Empleo* (AIEE – Interconfederal Agreement for Stability in Employment). This agreement covered issues relating to employment contracts, collective bargaining and the replacement of the labour ordinances. This was paralleled by the *Acuerdo Interconfederal sobre Negociacion Colectiva* (AINC – Interconfederal Agreement on Collective Bargaining) and the *Acuerdo Interconfederal sobre Corbertura de Vacios* (AICV), which has already been discussed. This wave of agreements constituted a major development in the debate on labour market flexibility. Various aspects of the content of these agreements were reproduced and supported through legislation.[19] The background to the agreements was the combination of employers' demands for greater flexibility in relation to redundancy and dismissals, union demands for less temporary contracting, and the social realisation that a key part of the labour market – especially female and younger workers – were beyond the remit of industrial relations regulation.[20] The main neo-corporatist actors had felt that the 1994 labour market reforms had developed in an uneven manner.

The development of a new type of 'permanent contract' was at the heart of the 1997 AIEE agreement. This contract was less stringent than the traditional model in terms of dismissal but much more stable than the short-term contracts that had proliferated since the early 1980s. The contract was aimed at specific groups of unemployed workers who had been relatively excluded from the labour market, and was seen as a hybrid contract that would run for an experimental period of four years. The new laws effectively made it relatively less costly to dismiss people, under certain circumstances. The argument was that this made more stable employment a more attractive option for employers. The assumption was that employers would modify their industrial and employment behaviour. In addition, a systematic approach to training contracts was established. Such contracts would be regulated by the state, as would the temporary contracting agencies that had emerged since the socialist reforms of the early 1990s. Furthermore, the government provided a range of incentives for the use of such contracts. There were other features to the AIEE, but one of the main outcomes was the establishment of mechanisms to oversee these changes and to measure developments, something the previous pacts tended to ignore. The government supported these new initiatives through the development of employment and training programmes. Another agreement that developed the AIEE was the *Acuerdo sobre Contratos de Empleo a Tiempo Parcial* (the Agreement on Part-time Employment Contracts), which aimed at improving the condition of part-time employees along with their social security support. This agreement was signed between the two main unions and the government.[21]

The AINC agreement was aimed at restructuring and extending the remit of collective bargaining in order to establish an articulating role for the national sector level of bargaining. This would provide minimum standards for lower levels and clarify the link between the distinct levels of bargaining.[22] Interestingly, pay was to be structured nationally at the sector level, but detailed pay levels were to be decided locally, an indication of the fact that incomes control is not central to the new corporatism. In fact, in 1999 the unions adopted an assertive strategy for pay increases due to the status of the economy and the growing awareness of the position of Spanish wage levels compared to other West European countries.

The AIEE and the AINC received mixed reports during the initial stages of their implementation. In 1998 the *Insituto Nacional de Empleo* reported that the new 'contratos indefinidos' increased to 9 percent of new contracts in 1997, but this was not a major improvement on previous levels. Concerns have been raised within the unions that the main role of unions was to watch and observe labour market trends but that these trends do not show more than a partial reversal of the trend towards temporary contracting. The overall investment in, and commitment to, training by employers and the state has increased, but according to the tripartite *Consejo Economico y Social* this is not a substantial alteration of Spain's position.[23] The question of employment was still the subject of public demonstrations by unions. Unions criticised the lack of progress on working hours, the social protection of unemployed workers, and the nominal increases in the funding of training in 1998.[24] There was also the perennial concern about whether employers would comply systematically with new reforms regarding the regulation of temporary contracting – although some key firms did set up benchmark strategies to stabilise the conditions of their peripheral workers.

Overall, these new neo-corporatist relations are representative of a new type of political exchange based primarily on labour market and employment issues. First, agreements were not tied to any incomes policy and were not articulated within a broader dialogue on social issues, although a series of dialogues and tripartite 'mesas' were constituted under the PP government. These met regularly but through a dual format, that is, the 'mesas' were constituted in such a manner that the government representatives met with unions and employers separately. After the initial wave of agreements in the first two years of the PP government there was a significant slowdown in the frequency of agreements and the extension of 'social' participation at the level of the state.

The second dimension of the new wave of neo-corporatist dialogue and representation relates to the structural changes taking place at the level of the state. A series of tripartite state institutions were established to oversee and coordinate the role of the state in the regulation of health and safety, and in the support and regulation of training and development programmes. Not only were unions to participate in decision making within these areas of state regulation at the macro level, but at the regional level they were also to actively organise and administer activities such as training. Many of these developments had their origins in the last years of the Socialist government, when the prospect of political change motivated policy makers to deepen the role of the social actors in key areas of employment regulation. The role of the social actors – employers and unions – was developed in terms of their adopting a greater managerial and administrative role within the area of labour regulation both nationally and at the level of the regional autonomous state, where a range of employment agreements had been emerging. However, the primary characteristic of Spanish neo-corporatism remains one of flexibility and agreement-specific negotiation processes. Table 18.2 illustrates this flexibility with some of the terminology used.

Table 18.2. *Key Terms in Spain*

Term	Meaning
Mesa Redonda	Round Table
Concertacíon Social	Social Concertation (consultation)
Interlocutores Sociales	Social Interlocutors
Pacto	Pact
Acuerdo	Agreement
Acuerdo Interconfederal	Interconfederal Agreement
Consejo Económico y Social	Economic and Social Council

Source: see text.

Conceptualising and Evaluating Spanish Corporatism in the 1990s

Much could be written about the 'decline of labour' and the end of its political role in contemporary society through corporatist structures. Kelly has recently outlined the genre of 'decline', looking at its political and social basis in a critical and evaluative manner.[25] Amoroso has argued that capital at the macro level (in the form of new right ideology) and at the micro level (through the evolution of new management practices such as Toyotism) has replaced labour as the main agent of social and political change.[26] Labour was assigned to a corner of history, to be replaced by other groups.[27] For many this role reversal, along with the decline in neo-corporatist relations, was due to the changing nature of the global economic system and the decline of the nation state and the emergence of new international competitive relations.[28] Moreover the new wave of labour representation exists within a context in which since the mid-1980s the role of the state within the economy appears to have been shifting towards supply-side considerations and more indirect influences on economic relations.[29]

However much of the new literature points to the 're-emergence' or 'continuity' of corporatist relations in Europe.[30] The question is, how? In the case of Spain there is no singular motive or rationale underpinning the dynamics of corporatist intermediation. Perhaps this explains its consciously fragmented nature.[31] The competing logics that underpinned the development of the state – the dual transition outlined above – and the competing rationales in terms of the strategies of the social actors have contributed to an uneven system of tripartism within industrial relations. In summary, the main political reasons beyond the broader structural factors outlined above were the perceived limitations of grand pacts and the problems of their implementation, the ongoing interest in market-based policies of deregulation, the ideological and personal tensions between the Socialists and the unions, and the interest in consensual labour market reform. The main normative basis was a concern with unemployment but more importantly a general commitment to democratic dialogue within the employment relationship and its regulation – but this was not such a strong set of commitments that they were universally shared.

Regini argues that it is also essential to understand the predispositions of those actors engaging in neo-corporatist practices and their assessments of the gains and losses (see Table 18.3 below).[32]

Table 18.3. *Key Arguments in Spain*[33]

Proponent	Argument
For	
The Conservative government	Need for social peace and dialogue, given tensions under the Socialist government Labour market flexibility Tackle unemployment through new forms of contracting
Employers	Need for labour market flexibility in terms of easier dismissal and recruitment Draws unions into debates on reform of industrial relations and less reliance on government Limits state role and passes the regulation of employment onto actors
Labour	'Modernise industrial relations' and involve labour in greater issues of employment regulation which have not been very effective Maintain key social 'conquests' of the 1980s through negotiation Involvement in broader employment agendas; enrich collective bargaining and extend the remit of the unions Provide the basis for greater employment and stability in employment
Against	
The Conservative government	May involve unions further in decision-making, flexible negotiations preferred Undermines project of privatisation
Employers	Fear amongst some employers of a deepening of state-labour relations and a greater trade union involvement in managerial prerogative
Labour	Uneven follow-through from employers and the state in terms of implementation Role of mobilisation in the identity of Spanish labour may be undermined – a concern of some radical groups in CC.OO and increasingly in the UGT that such agreements would undermine Socialist prospects for victory and legitimate Spanish right

Source: see text.

The strategic and partial character of Spanish corporatism is conscious; it is not an outcome of corporatist 'failure' even if governments and employers have played a key part in the development of an uneven corporatism. However, unlike the period of 'strategic displacement' of the 1980s, it is clear that the rationale and interest in strategic and partial corporatism has been assimilated, to a certain extent, by organised labour. Firstly, there are the experiences of the 1970s and the 1980s, i.e. the lack of delivery on social aspects of the grand pacts.[34] Secondly, there is the realisation that the modernisation and maturation of the system of industrial relations could not be expected to emerge from the state which had exhibited dysfunctional characteristics in questions of state regulation, for example health and safety, training and development, conflict resolution and labour flexibility. Hence a new model emerged which developed the flexible and strategic character of the neo-corporatism of the early 1980s. This model was based on specific, unarticulated agreements (except, in part, for the AIEE, which assumed a new government commitment to training and job creation) and on shifting the locus of responsibility in the regulation of employment.

These developments represented a 'socialisation' of state functions, that is, their transfer from the state itself to the industrial relations actors.[35] This development of 'strategic displacement' also entailed a fragmentation of the regulation of social policy, which was organised between different agencies and issues. Employers saw in this system a move away from traditional state regulation and intervention: the new forms of bipartite and tripartite control were seen as allowing for a less rigid set of regulations to develop. This was quite different from the view held by the CC.OO and the UGT. For the unions these developments transferred the regulation of employment to employer-labour relations and supposedly extended collective bargaining in terms of its form and content. The attraction of such developments is that they allow unions the chance to operationalise systems of state regulation which have been less than effective and consistent since the 1970s. Increasingly, sectoral, regional and company levels of bargaining were to internalise some of the key features of employment regulation. In this respect, the terms 'fragmented corporatism' and 'corporatism from below' seem appropriate for the description of such a national experience. However the stability of this model will depend on various factors: the actual degree of stability that emerges within the labour market and employment, the internal consensus on this approach that can be generated within the unions, the way in which government and employers comply with agreements, and finally the extent to which the unions feel that they may be legitimating the presence of a Conservative regime. The political factors of Spanish industrial relations and corporatist relations remain significant.[36]

Notes

1. R. Hyman, 'Changing Trade Union Identities and Politics', in *New Frontiers in European Industrial Relations,* ed. R. Hyman and A. Ferner, Oxford, 1994.
2. J. Aragon Medina, 'Crisis economica y reformas laborales', *Economistas* (1993): 22–31; V. Pérez Díaz and J.C. Rodríguez, 'An overview of Spanish human resources, practices and policies', in *Employment Relations in a Changing World Economy*, ed. R. Locke, T. Kochan and M. Piore, Massachussets, 1995.
3. Such a fragmented role at the level of the state, it could be argued, is complemented by a supposedly fragmented role within the ambit of the corporation and the centre of employment (L.E. Alonso, 'Macro y micro corporatismo', *Revista Internacional de Sociologia,* no. 8–9 (1995); M. Regini, *Uncertain Boundaries: The Social and Political Construction of European Economies,* Cambridge and New York, 1995.
4. Certain parts of this section are taken from a piece written by the author on Spanish industrial relations for A. Ferner and R. Hyman, *Changing Industrial Relations in Europe,* Oxford, 1998.
5. P. Schmitter and G. Lehmbruch, eds, *Towards Corporatist Intermediation*, London, 1979.
6. J. Roca Jusmet, 'La concertación social', in, *Las Relaciones Laborales en España,* ed F. Miguélez and C. Prieto, Madrid, 1991.
7. Pardo Avellaneda and J. Fernández Castro, 'Las organizaciones empresariales y la configuraciondel sistema de relaciones industrials en la Espana democratica, 1977–1990', in *Las Relaciones Laborales en España,* ed. F. Miguelez and C. Prieto, Madrid, 1991.
8. M. Martínez Lucio, 'Employer Identity and the Politics of the Labour Market in Spain' *West European Politics*, January 1991; M. Jose Aguar, Alexandre Casademunt and Joaquim M. Molins, 'Las Organizaciones Empresariales en la Etapa de la Consolidacion Democratica (1986–1997)', in Faustino Miguelez and Carlos Prieto, eds, *Las relaciones laborales de empleo en España*, Madrid, 1999.
9. J. Roca Jusmet, 'Economic analysis and neo-corporatism', paper presented at European University Institute, 1983; Roca Jusmet, Jordi, 'La concertación social', *Las Relaciones Laborales en España,* ed F. Miguélez and C. Prieto, Madrid, 1991.
10. M. Martinez Lucio, MA Dissertation, University of Essex, 1983; J. Foweraker, *Making Democracy in Spain,* Cambridge, 1989.
11. W. Rand Smith, *The Left's Dirty Work,* Pittsburgh, 1998.
12. M. Martinez Lucio, 1991, 'Employer Identity'.
13. A. Bilbao, 'Trabajadores, gestión económica y crisis sindical, in F. Miguélez and C. Prieto, eds, *Las Relaciones Laborales en España,* Madrid, 1991.
14. Other agreements, such as the one relating to conflict resolution, followed a similar logic of moving parts of the regulation of the employment relationship to the social actors and away from the state.
15. A. Baylos, 'La Negociacíon Colectiva en el Acuerdo Interconfederal', *Gaceta Sindical,* September 1997.
16. L. Morillo, 'Ordenanzas Laborales: Situación actual y procesos de negociación', *Gaceta Sindical Mayo,* 1996.
17. *Vacios* is the legal vacuum left by the withdrawal of regulations on specific employment issues, for example grading of jobs.
18. V. Pérez Díaz, *El Retorno de la Sociedad Civil,* Madrid, 1990; V. Pérez Díaz, 'El Pacto de Toledo', *Economistas,* 68 (1995).
19. Consejo Economico y Social, *Memoria,* 1997.
20. V. Pérez Díaz and J.C. Rodríguez, 'An overview of Spanish human resources, practices and policies', in R. Locke, T. Kochan and M. Piore, eds, *Employment Relations in a Changing World Economy.* Massachussets, 1995.
21. There were other agreements, such as the changes to the regulation of health and safety, which fitted the logic of passing onto the social actors a key part of the burden of employment regulation, but the chapter has focused on the more transparent ones.

22. M. Martinez Lucio, 'Spain: Regulating Employment and Social Fragmentation', in A. Ferner and R. Hyman, eds, *Changing Industrial Relations in Europe,* Oxford, 1998.
23. Consejo Economico y Social, *Memoria,* 1998.
24. *Gaceta Sindical,* April 1988. In one regional state the government's employment institutions had used this transfer to relieve themselves of 'inefficient' staff, keeping the most able within the national institutions.
25. J. Kelly, *Rethinking Industrial Relations,* London, 1998.
26. B. Amoroso, 'Industrial Relations in the 1990s', *International Journal of Human Resource Management* 3(2) (1992).
27. A. Giddens, *The Consequences of Modernity*, Oxford, 1994.
28. P.C. Schmitter and J.R. Grote, 'The Corporatist Sisyphus: Past, Present and Future', paper presented at conference on Plotting our Future: Technology, Environment, Economy and Society, Florence. European University Institute, 1997; G. Baglioni, 'Introduction' in G. Baglioni and C. Crouch, eds, *European Industrial Relations: The Challenge of Flexibility.* London, 1990; S. Lash and J. Urry, *The End of Organised Capitalism.* London, 1987; L.E. Alonso, 1994, op cit.
29. W. Streeck, *Social Institutions and Economic Performance,* London, 1992.
30. C. Crouch, 'Beyond Corporatism: the impact of company strategy', *New Frontiers in European Industrial Relations*, ed. R. Hyman and A. Ferner, Oxford, 1994.
31. I use fragmented not in a pejorative manner but as a term that explains the form of the neo-corporatist bargaining process. Politically, one could argue, it is in fact quite articulated and strategically structured.
32. M. Regini, 'The conditions for political exchange', *Order and Conflict in Contemporary Capitalism.* ed J. Goldthorpe, Oxford, 1984.
33. These are based on the analysis of the press and specialist/professional journals along with a range of interviews with key individuals within each relevant organisation.
34. A. Moran, 'Auje y Crisis de los grandes acuerdos sociales de los 80', *Cuadernos de Relaciones Laborales,* no. 9 (1995).
35. Consejo Economic y Social, 1997, op cit.
36. F. Miguelez Lobo and C. Prieto, *Las Relaciones Laborales en España*, Madrid, 1991.

CHAPTER 19

SWEDEN IN HISTORICAL PERSPECTIVE: THE RISE AND FALL OF THE SWEDISH MODEL

James Fulcher

Swedish Corporatism?

Policy concertation has been highly developed in Sweden. Exceptionally centralised and encompassing interest organisations have been extensively involved in the formulation and implementation of government policy. Concertation has taken the form not only of top-level consultation and negotiation between governments and interest organisations but also the representation of these organisations on the boards controlling administrative agencies. In some areas policy development and implementation has, at times, been largely delegated to the organisations. This pattern of policy concertation has been widely labelled 'corporatist' and Sweden has indeed been considered one of the most corporatist of European societies.[1]

There has, however, been little corporatist theorising in Swedish political thought. The only nineteenth-century thinker of any consequence to advocate corporatism was Erik Gustav Geijer (1783–1847), who was at one time strongly influenced by Hegel but then recognised that there was no organisational basis for corporatism in Sweden and adopted a liberal perspective.[2] Much later, after there had been considerable organisational development, Gunnar Heckscher used the term 'free corporatism' to describe the relationship between organisations and the state in 1930s Sweden, and argued that Sweden was in fact more genuinely a corporatist country than Germany and Italy, where corporatism was no more than a cover for state control. His use of this term was, nonetheless, criticised for implying that Sweden was in some sense a fascist country.[3]

More recently, foreign academics have widely applied the corporatist label to Sweden. This has, however, been rejected by some 'labour movement theorists', such as Korpi, who took issue with the idea that the Swedish state controlled working-class organisations by incorporating them. Korpi argued that in Sweden it was the labour movement that had taken control of the state and used its political power to advance the interests of labour.[4]

More recently Rothstein has called for a broader and less ideological use of corporatism to describe integrative structures of political coordination that can both *mobilise* and *control* organised groups, without prejudging their consequences for these groups.[5] There can be little doubt that according to this definition Sweden has been highly corporatist.

Pre-Industrial Origins

Corporatism is usually associated with the period of Social Democratic rule that began in the 1930s but Rothstein has shown that the corporatist tendencies in the Swedish state can be traced back to the nineteenth century. In 1888 the Workers Insurance Committee proposed the establishment of a work-accident insurance scheme that would involve worker and employer representatives in its administration. This proposal and others like it failed, and it was not until 1903 that the first corporatist institutions were actually created. These were local labour exchanges controlled by boards consisting of equal numbers of worker and employer representatives, with an impartial chairman.[6] Thus the beginnings of Swedish corporatism can be found in the early development of social policy to deal with the problems generated by industrialisation.

This suggests that there was something in the character of the Swedish state that disposed it to seek corporatist solutions to the emerging problems of an industrial society. According to Rothstein, the key features of the Swedish state were its well-developed administrative capacity and its non-exclusive character. State officials sought to involve those affected by a policy in its implementation, to draw on their knowledge and expertise, and legitimate the policy.[7]

Rothstein argues that this early corporatism has been neglected in studies of Swedish political development, which have focused on its representational aspects. It is well known that democratisation was late in Sweden–the democratic breakthrough in Swedish politics is usually dated to 1917, considerably later than it was in Denmark and Norway.[8] Although it took a long time for labour to gain an effective parliamentary voice, it did, however, early acquire influence over administrative matters. Indeed, Rothstein suggests that it was the early development of an inclusive corporatism that resulted in the labour movement becoming reformist.[9]

How is this early corporatism to be explained? One line of explanation refers to the distinctively dual structure of the historic Swedish state. Ministries were relatively small organisations concerned only with the development and formulation of policy. Ministers have not been responsible for policy implementation, and have indeed been prohibited from interfering in this, for it is the responsibility of semi-autonomous agencies with their own directors and controlling boards. These agencies have enabled the involvement of organisations external to the state in policy implementation.[10]

It is also important to set corporatism in the wider context of Sweden's distinctive pre-industrial society, which was a non-feudal agrarian society with an independent peasantry and a weak bourgeoisie and aristocracy. Their weakness meant that there was little class conflict. The state was not drawn into conflicts between powerful interest groups and did not become identified with a particular class interest. The result was a non-exclusive and relatively non-coercive state with popular legitimacy. As Rojas has put it: 'The National State, which in Western Europe was often both the result of and the mediator among highly differentiated and not so infrequently contraposed interests, was in Sweden the expression of an unusual social cohesion'.[11]

It has been claimed that the cohesive character of pre-industrial society largely explains the spirit of compromise, cooperation and policy concertation regarded as typical of the 'Swedish model'. This cohesion was the result not only of class relationships but also of the ethnic, linguistic and religious homogeneity of the population. The high integration of Swedish society has been linked to Swedish collectivism as well. This, it is argued, stemmed from the isolation of peasant communities and the Lutheran character of the dominant religious tradition, which together strengthened social control, generated conformity and weakened individualism.[12]

Class Conflict and Class Organisation

It is generally agreed that pre-industrial Swedish society was fairly cohesive but any notion that the persistence of this cohesion is sufficient to account for Swedish corporatism is deeply misleading.

Industrialisation led to intense class conflict. Sweden became known later for its 'labour peace' but up until the 1930s it experienced an internationally high level of industrial conflict.[13] It was this conflict that lay behind the development of the centralised and encompassing organisations that became the key players in corporatism. They switched from being organisations that generated conflict to organisations that suppressed it.

This is well demonstrated by the escalating industrial conflict of the period leading up to the first central agreement, the December Compromise of 1906. The national union federation(*Landsorganisationen,* LO), was founded in 1898 but it was initially an uncentralised organisation for mutual assistance with little control over its member unions. The founding of the LO and the political general strike of 1902 then stimulated the formation of the Swedish Employers' Association (*Svenska Arbetsgivareföreningen,* SAF), which rapidly absorbed the other employers' associations. The SAF made aggressive use of the lockout weapon against the unions, driving the LO to take increasing control of its constituent unions and in 1906 force an agreement on them which recognised the 'employer's rights'.[14]

The centralisation of union and employer organisations then provided the basis for the creation of corporatist institutions at national level. The first such institution was the Social Board (*Socialstyrelsen*) of 1912, which was set up to deal, broadly speaking, with the social problems created by the emergence of a working class. The LO and SAF both had two representatives on this body. Other such institutions, the *Försäkringsrådet* and *Arbetsrådet*, councils that dealt with work accident insurance and hours of work issues, were established shortly afterwards on the same basis.

This involvement of the LO and the SAF in the development of social policy meant not only that they were drawn into the administration of public affairs, it also brought their leaders together in regular meetings at a time when they were frequently engaged in industrial conflict. Rothstein emphasises that these meetings were taken seriously and attended by the top leadership of both organisations.[15] Corporatist institutions can therefore be said to have paved the way for the eventual emergence of the joint central regulation of industrial relations by the LO and the SAF.

It was, however, the existence of centralised organisations that made these top-level contacts possible and significant. One of the reasons why these contacts failed to bear fruit in Britain, where governments made many attempts to initiate them, was the absence of organisations of this sort.[16]

The relative absence of class conflict in *pre-industrial* Swedish society resulted in the emergence of a strong but inclusive state, but it was the intense class conflict *after industrialisation* that created the centralised, class-wide organisations that mediated between the corporatist state and the Swedish people. Paradoxically, it was probably the homogeneity of the population that generated such an intense class conflict. The absence of major ethnic, religious or linguistic divisions magnified the salience of class divisions, which were not cut across by other lines of conflict. The significance of pre-industrial homogeneity for corporatism was not that it led directly to a cohesive industrial society but rather that it provided the conditions in which strong class solidarity and class conflict could forge the class organisations that enabled the later development of an integrative corporatism.

Social Democracy and Corporatism

Although the origins of corporatist institutions can clearly be traced further back in Swedish history, it was under Social Democratic rule in the 1930s that the organisational relationships central to Sweden's modern corporatism were established. This can be seen in the Social Democrats' relationships with workers', farmers' and employers' organisations.

Social Democratic government after 1932 led to the greater involvement of trade unions in policy making and strengthened the position of the unions in Swedish society. Thus, in 1934 the LO returned to the Unemployment

Commission, the body responsible for the administration of government labour market policy, which had been formed in 1914 with representatives of both the unions and the employers. The union representatives had left in 1926, because it was dominated by employers and state officials holding 'free market' views.

The unions also became responsible for the administration of the new programme of unemployment insurance set up by the Social Democrats. Rothstein claims that this 'Gent system' accounts for the exceptionally high level of union membership in Sweden, for it gave workers a greater incentive to join unions by overcoming the 'free-rider' problem, that is, that non-members save on membership costs but benefit as much as members from union-negotiated wage increases. He argues that this system was quite deliberately introduced by the Social Democrats in order to help the unions to build up their membership.[17] The government also passed in 1936 a law that recognised labour's right to union membership.

On the other hand, the unions were subjected to greater control. The government was concerned about the impact of strikes on its economic policy and at first proposed regulatory legislation, before leaving the LO and the SAF to work out a joint solution through the Basic Agreement of 1938. Significantly, the government did not repeal the 1928 laws that had made strikes during the course of a collective agreement illegal and had set up a Labour Court, though it had opposed these laws at the time. Greater union influence was matched by greater control of the unions.

The government could not, anyway, simply rely on the strength of the labour movement and required the support of the farmers as well. Although the Social Democrats clearly won the election of 1932 and greatly increased their parliamentary representation, they did not have a majority. This they acquired through their 1933 crisis agreement with the Agrarian Party. Since they did not themselves achieve a parliamentary majority until 1960, this alliance with the Agrarian Party and its successor, the Centre Party, was critical to long-term Social Democratic rule.

Rothstein situates this agreement in the earlier development of agrarian collectivism. Increasing domestic competition and falling international prices resulted in a growing agricultural crisis. Around 1930 the main organisations of Swedish farmers began to campaign for the state regulation of milk prices and the compulsory membership of all milk producers in cooperatives. Before the 1932 election, they secured legislation to this effect from a Parliament dominated by the bourgeois political parties, even though these measures flew in the face of bourgeois principles. Rothstein argues that the main bourgeois party did not dare to risk opposing the farmers in the run-up to an election.

This was, according to Rothstein, the decisive moment when collectivism made its breakthrough. It was a major step away from the market regulation of prices in the interests of consumers to state regulation in the interests of producers. Furthermore, once the principle of collective organisation had been accepted for farmers, it could not be denied to workers, a link made quite explicitly by the Social Democrats and recognised by the bourgeois parties.[18]

The collective organisation of Swedish farmers played, therefore, a key role in the establishment and maintenance of Social Democratic rule and created a new strand in Swedish corporatism. The independent organisation of farmers has been one of the fundamental features of the Swedish political scene, for it has prevented the emergence of a strong, national Conservative Party on the British model. The historic condition for the independent organisation of farmers was the predominantly smallholder character of Swedish agriculture and the ancient conflict between the peasantry and a bureaucratic urban elite.

Social Democratic rule involved close relationships not only with the collective organisations of producers but also with the owners of capital. The employers had been trying for some time to secure legislation that would regulate union behaviour and, as we saw above, such laws were passed in 1928. By the later 1930s, however, the SAF considered that it was dangerous to increase state control under Social Democratic rule, since this might lead to the regulation of capital as well as labour. The SAF began instead to develop its links with the LO in order to substitute their joint regulation of industrial conflict for state regulation. The result was the famous Basic Agreement of 1938, which established an institutional framework for the joint central regulation of industrial relations.

On the other hand, the SAF began to distance itself from the bourgeois parties in order to demonstrate its political neutrality and influence the various commissions and investigations, such as the 1936 Rationalisation Commission, set up by the government to explore policy issues. With the Industry Association the SAF established in 1938 an Industrial Research Institute that would provide the state with apparently 'neutral' advice based on technical expertise. This strategy soon bore fruit, when the government declared a 'reform pause' in 1938 and introduced measures to stimulate investment, in part by reducing the taxation of profits.

Although Sweden was a non-belligerent in the Second World War, it was surrounded by countries that were at war or under occupation. A coalition government was formed and the economy was brought under extensive state regulation. The result was a 'war corporatism' that brought many industrialists on to the bodies that regulated the wartime economy. It is, nonetheless, important to emphasise that the 1930s developments in policy concertation were mainly the result of the earlier changes in the relationships between the state and Sweden's leading interest organisations.

Much of the further development of policy concertation in the 1930s can be explained in terms of the politics of Social Democratic rule. The Social Democrats' close links with the LO brought the unions into policy making. The problem of achieving a parliamentary majority drove the Social Democrats towards an accommodation with the farmers. Stable Social Democratic government pushed the employers towards a corporatist strategy.

The Social Democrats' capacity to enter pragmatic relationships with the major interest groups of Swedish society also depended on ideological change. After presenting a radical programme and losing seats at the 1928 election, the Social Democrats dropped much of the socialist rhetoric from their 1932 manifesto and shelved plans to take industries and resources into public ownership.[19] The government recognised that the achievement of its welfare goals depended on the profitability of industry and the maintenance of the international competitiveness of the Swedish economy.

This ideological shift was encapsulated in the concept of society as a 'people's home' (*folkhem*). An old idea in Swedish politics, this was given new content by Per Albin Hansson, Prime Minister from 1932 to 1946. It used the metaphor of the home to call for a society where people treated each other like members of a household. 'In the good home equality, consideration, co-operation, and helpfulness prevail' (Hansson quoted by Tilton).[20] While retaining radical demands for greater equality, the Social Democratic Party was presenting itself as the party not just of the working class but of the whole people. The new emphasis was on cooperation rather than class conflict. The *folkhem* revived the cooperative and cohesive sentiments of pre-industrial Sweden.

Postwar Corporatism

A wide-ranging corporatism had been established in the 1930s but the struggle between socialism and capitalism continued below the surface and periodically re-emerged. It resurfaced in the postwar conflict over planning. The Social Democrats' 1944 Programme contained state planning proposals that provoked an immediate reaction from the Directors' Club of prominent engineering companies. This led to a campaign against planning that forced the SAF to abandon its policy of cooperating with the Social Democratic state and instead support the bourgeois parties in the 1948 election.[21]

After losing seats in the 1948 election, the Social Democrats reverted to less radical policies that made possible a return to corporatist relationships. In 1948 and 1949 the government negotiated stabilisation agreements with the employers to restrain price and wage increases and in 1949 secured the LO's agreement to a wage freeze. Between 1949 and 1955 business leaders, together with the representatives of the farmers' organisations and the union federations, met weekly with ministers and civil servants at the so-called 'Thursday Club' to discuss economic policy. The government sought the cooperation and trust of business, while in exchange business was given some influence over economic policy.[22] The anti-corporatist Directors' Club folded in 1953.[23]

Greater Social Democrat electoral success in the later 1950s strengthened the government's position and it no longer needed to negotiate policy with business organisations. Consultation continued, however, notably through the annual conferences at the Prime Minister's residence at Harpsund, which gave rise to the term 'Harpsund Democracy'. These highly publicised conferences were regularly attended by invited leaders of the main organisations of business, the farmers, the unions and the cooperative movement. The conferences started in 1955 and ended in 1964.

During the rest of the 1960s consultations continued within the more formal structure of the Economic Planning Council, established in 1962. This was the government's response to criticisms of 'Harpsund Democracy' and calls for a more continuous and long-term planning of the economy. The Council's deliberations were more technocratic and were informed by the investigative and statistical work carried out by a support unit composed of the organisations' experts. Elvander has commented sceptically that these meetings were, nonetheless, purely consultative, that no decisions were made by the Council, and no planning really occurred. He concluded that neither the Harpsund conferences nor the Council gave the organisations any significant influence over government policy.[24]

Does this mean that no real policy concertation was taking place? It is important here to bear in mind the government's shift of policy since the 1940s. It had abandoned planning and adopted policies acceptable to business. For its part, the LO leadership was committed to wage restraint and market-oriented policies of economic growth and rationalisation. There was, in a sense, little need for concertation, since there was little conflict between the government and the main interest organisations over policy. There was at this time a top-level consensus that all would benefit if the size of the 'economic cake' was maximised by allowing a dynamic capitalist economy to operate freely.

Policy concertation was also built into legislative and administrative processes. Legislation routinely involved the consultation of interested parties in an attempt to arrive at generally agreed policies. Typically, an investigative commission, with representatives from the main political parties and interest organisations, would be set up to prepare legislation. The commission's proposals were then formally circulated to interest organisations through the standard *remiss* consultation procedure and their responses were taken into account in the actual drafting of legislation.

Once legislation was passed, detailed regulations were produced by the appropriate administrative agency. As we saw earlier, the administrative wing of the Swedish state consisted of semi-autonomous agencies, which were responsible for policy implementation and were not under direct ministerial control. An agency's governing board could incorporate the representatives of interest organisations and there was in this period a marked increase in their numbers. The proportion of agencies with such representatives rose from 28 percent in 1946 to 64 percent in 1968.[25]

Some areas of policy were largely delegated to the organisations themselves. The central organisations of the unions and the employers took responsibility for dealing with a wide range of economic and industrial relations issues that in other countries became matters of government policy. Policy delegation to these organisations, which could then work out their own compromises, was a functional alternative to policy concertation by the government.

Thus, on the model of the 1938 Basic Agreement, the LO negotiated a series of central agreements with the SAF to settle major industrial relations issues. Incomes policy was, in the 1950s and 1960s, largely left in the hands of the LO and the SAF, which imposed wage restraint through central wage agreements that were virtually economy-wide in scope. This has been called a system of joint central regulation, though it is in some ways a misleading term, for behind the façade of LO-SAF cooperation lay employer economic power, backed by state agencies, such as the Labour Court. Central wage bargaining was, in fact, forced on the LO by the SAF during the 1950s. At local level the employer was dominant, for the LO had accepted the 'employer's rights', under duress, in the December Compromise of 1906.[26]

Labour market policy was developed and administered by the LO itself. LO economists came up with the innovatory ideas at the heart of Sweden's internationally celebrated labour market policy. There were certainly employer representatives on the Labour Market Board but the union representatives were in a majority. This might all seem to run against the pattern of joint central regulation and employer power but the central thrust of the policy, until at least the later 1960s, was to create a dynamic labour market which supplied labour where it was needed, directed labour rather than capital, and kept inflation low. Such a policy was clearly in the interests of the employers, while the LO's heavy involvement legitimated it and committed the unions to it.

Agriculture was another area where policy was largely delegated to an interest organisation, though there is not space here to explore this aspect of Swedish corporatism.[27]

The interest organisations and the state had mutual interests in this apparatus of policy concertation and delegation. The rationale for the heavy involvement of interest organisations in the state's policy-making activities was well established. It enabled them to exercise influence on the ever-widening activities of the state. So far as the state was concerned, it allowed the state to draw on their expertise and resources, secure their support for policy, and legitimate it. Governments could also conveniently wash their hands of responsibility for those aspects of policy making in the hands of independent agencies and organisations. The autonomy of the administrative agencies in many ways suited ministers, since they could not be held responsible for policy implementation, though they could still make their influence felt, through control of the personnel and budgets of these agencies.[28]

Does this mean that Swedish corporatism was motivated solely by considerations of interest? It did have a pragmatic character, emerging out of deals and compromises and practical working arrangements, without any fanfares or programmatic statements or declarations of principle. As we have seen, there was no real theory of Swedish corporatism and, apart from the rather isolated figure of Gunnar Heckscher, no one really advocated it.

Corporatist arrangements did, however, depend on values of compromise. A willingness to compromise has been a widely celebrated feature of modern Swedish culture. The Basic Agreement of 1938 was seen as embodying this willingness and there has been much reference to *Saltsjöbadsanda,* the 'spirit of Saltsjöbaden', the seaside town where the agreement was made.

Another important term is *samhällsintresse*, the interest of society as a whole, which was much used by Per Albin Hansson, and became a standard term in the Swedish political vocabulary. Elvander has emphasised that when making policy proposals interest organisations were expected to argue in terms of the 'interest of society' if they wanted them to be taken seriously. The interest of a particular group had to be legitimated by reference to the notion of an underlying common interest.

Organisations also had to use information and persuasion rather than agitation and pressure, demonstrating how their proposals could be of general benefit through reasoned argument and with the support of evidence gathered from scientific investigations. The experts employed by organisations played a central role in the development of national policy, which emerged mainly from the organisations rather than the political parties. Professional expertise provided a common meeting-ground and policy concertation through expertise was one of the key features of Swedish corporatism. Thus, the highly influential EFO report, which established a framework for calculating the level of wage increase that could be tolerated by the economy, was produced by the chief economists of the LO, the TCO and the SAF.[29]

Corporatist relationships are vulnerable to the criticism that they are undemocratic, bypassing Parliament and encroaching on the territory of political parties. 'Harpsund democracy' came under fire during the early 1960s from both the Left and the Right. It was also argued that Swedish interest organisations were themselves becoming increasingly undemocratic, because of centralisation and their internal reorganisation into larger units. The unions, with their highly centralised bargaining and internal reorganisation into larger branches, were a case in point.

On their own these criticisms had little force, for a corporatist political culture was by this time solidly established. Elvander found that in 1965 an overwhelming majority of members of parliament considered that the existing relationships between the organisations and the government were 'valuable for society'.[30] Union organisations defended themselves by arguing that internal democracy was not an issue, since leaders and members held essentially the same interests. Underneath the consensual surface of Swedish society there were, however, more fundamental conflicts that were generating stresses and strains within corporatist institutions.

Corporatism in Decline

These conflicts can be traced back to the 1950s battle over the form to be taken by supplementary pensions. The LO pressed for legislation and state funding, while the employers sought a negotiated scheme that would keep pension funds in company hands.

On this issue there was no consensus and no easy compromise. It was not just a matter of the most appropriate way of funding pensions. A state-funded scheme would place large amounts of money in the hands of the state, and the investment of these funds could make possible the eventual collectivising of the ownership of industry. This decision over pensions had, therefore, important implications for whether Sweden would have a capitalist or a socialist future and reactivated this question. The government settled the issue, for the time being, by opting for a state-funded scheme but imposed restrictions on the investment of state funds, so that the threat to private capital was removed.[31]

This was a key turning-point in the Social Democrats' political strategy and in Swedish political alignments. The Social Democrats had been losing support in recent elections and had to decide whether to revive their alliance with the Centre Party or gamble on constructing a broader movement by allying with white-collar workers. It opted for the latter strategy and made significant electoral gains as a result. This decision prepared the way for an eventual radicalising of Social Democratic policy and the reconstruction of a 'bourgeois' alliance that included the Centre Party. The scene was set for a polarisation of Swedish politics that would make compromise and joint concertation far harder to achieve.[32]

Polarisation was fuelled by a growing grass-roots discontent in the later 1960s. Although the 'Swedish model' was at this time the envy of the world there were many sources of dissatisfaction in Swedish society. There was a growing sense that Social Democratic rule had failed to achieve greater equality and there were unfulfilled expectations amongst radicals and within the labour movement. Economic growth had generated full employment and rising standards of living and welfare, but this was at the cost of increasing pressure on labour, as work stress increased and the work environment deteriorated. Rising prices and higher taxes anyway brought the growth of real disposable income to a halt at the end of the 1960s. Organisational centralisation left people feeling powerless. A sense of powerlessness was strongly felt in the labour movement and the famous Swedish 'labour peace' came to an end with an explosion of strikes at the end of the 1960s, notably the long strike in the northern iron mines during the winter of 1969–70.

The labour movement responded to internal discontent by paying more attention to its members and developing a programme for greater industrial and economic democracy. This programme mobilised the manual/non-manual labour alliance from the pensions conflict in an 'employee front', which attacked the power of the capitalist employer and ultimately the private ownership of capital. There was a burst of legislation in the 1970s, culminating in the Codetermination Act of 1976, to provide workers with more protection in the workplace and influence over company decisions. Private capital itself was attacked through the Meidner Plan to transfer the ownership of industry to union-controlled funds, a scheme adopted by the LO in 1976.[33]

This radicalisation of the labour movement provoked a radical employer response. In the 1970s the SAF reacted by seeking to integrate workers at plant level and launching an educational and informational campaign to re-establish the employers' ideological dominance.[34] The SAF also supported the Moderate Party, the most right-wing bourgeois party, and tried to bring about a change of government. The consensus on welfare capitalism broke down with the emergence of a bourgeois alternative calling for the reduction of state expenditure, lower taxation and a revival of market forces. Policy making had become less consensual and more ideological.

The decline of corporatist concertation was most evident in the attempt to legislate the Meidner Plan. A Royal Commission was set up to prepare legislation but it ended its work in 1981 without agreement. Opinions on this issue were more polarised than on any other in recent Swedish history. The employers and their political allies were implacable in their opposition. The machinery of concertation totally failed to produce agreement. Legislation to create Employee Investment Funds was eventually imposed in 1983, but these were little more than a pale shadow of the Meidner funds and had no significant effect on industrial ownership.[35]

Employer alienation was reinforced by the 1970s breakdown of the machinery for the joint central regulation of wage bargaining. The central wage agreements of the 1960s appeared to be a distinctively Swedish solution to the intractable problem of how to contain wage increases within full employment economies. The centralisation of bargaining had, however, been sold to the unions as a means of improving the position of the lower paid and during the 1960s their unions put growing pressure on the LO to deliver on this. Meanwhile, the white-collar unions began to create their own centralised bargaining organisations. Their rivalries with each other, and with the LO manual worker unions, increasingly disrupted wage rounds. The centralisation of the LO, together with a growing grass-roots discontent, stimulated local opposition movements and strike waves. By the 1970s the central bargaining machinery was not producing wage restraint and labour peace but strikes, lockouts, sectional rivalries and upwardly spiralling wages.[36]

How did the state respond to this collapse of corporatism during the 1970s? One response was to construct a looser and more decentralised structure of policy concertation. During the 1980s there was an extensive decentralisation of decision making to local authorities. Legislation took a less directive 'framework' form, leaving more discretion to the administrative agencies and local authorities. Discontented groups were incorporated by granting them greater representation in these agencies and authorities. Conflict at the centre was reduced but, as Ruin has pointed out, at the cost of magnifying policy-making problems in other ways. The involvement of more interest groups made it more difficult to reach agreement, while legislation became vaguer and less effective, problems of national coordination emerged, and the government began to lose control of policy making.

Governments responded rather differently to the collapse of central bargaining and began to intervene in a more directive and authoritarian way. During the 1980s the employers were pressing for a decentralisation of bargaining, with the support of some unions, but the LO continued to seek coordinated settlements. Social Democratic governments intervened increasingly to try to bring these about and came close to implementing state incomes policies of the kind introduced in Britain in the 1960s and 1970s. They experimented with price and dividend controls, established wage norms, and at least considered incomes policy legislation. During the extraordinary crisis of 1990, the government tried to push through a package that would freeze wages, prices, dividends, rents and local taxes, while banning strikes and increasing fines for strikers.[37]

By the end of the 1980s Swedish politics was drifting in a state of near paralysis. The corporatist structure of policy concertation and centralised joint central regulation had been collapsing since the late 1960s. The radicalisation of the labour movement did not, however, lead to a socialist transformation, for the Social Democrats backed off from measures that might weaken employer power or challenge the capitalist basis of the Swedish economy. Although a right-wing alternative emerged and Sweden was indeed governed by 'bourgeois' parties between 1976 and 1982, the right was politically divided and unable to make an effective break with the past. When the Social Democrats returned to government, they benefited from the favourable economic conditions which sheltered the Swedish economy during the 1908s. They nonetheless became more and more concerned with the declining competitiveness of Swedish companies and the growth of public expenditure. The Social Democratic leadership drifted to the right and came into conflict with the LO, a conflict which disabled the labour movement as an effective force.

New social movements and new political parties, centred particularly on environmental and religious concerns, emerged to fill the vacuum. The Social Democrats continued to govern but Micheletti argues that 'the 1980s marked the end of Social Democratic hegemony'.[38] Old collectivist loyalties have given way to both new collectivities and a new individualism. Welfare has increasingly become seen as a matter for the individual and new, voluntary, self-help bodies, rather than the state. In the 1980s a 'repluralisation and resurgence of Swedish civil society' had taken place.[39]

Conclusion

Strong class organisations made Swedish corporatism possible. Although certain features of pre-industrial Sweden facilitated the emergence of an inclusive state in a cohesive society, it was above all the driving force of class conflict which created the centralised and unified class organisations that established Swedish corporatism in the 1930s. These organisations then provided the basis of policy concertation and joint central regulation during the 1950s and 1960s.

This same strength of Swedish class organisation then undermined corporatism. Corporatist structures could not in the end contain the tensions and conflicts generated by a dynamic Swedish capitalism. These tensions and conflicts forced the labour movement to mount a powerful, radical challenge to the power of private capital. Sweden's strongly organised employers then counter-attacked and attempted to carry out a new 'bourgeois revolution'. The exceptionally high level of union organisation also resulted in complex rivalries that wrecked central bargaining. By the end of the 1980s the institutions of corporatist concertation were in disarray but neither the Left nor the Right had been able to give Swedish politics a new direction.

Notes

1. P.J. Williamson, *Corporatism in Perspective: an Introductory Guide to Corporatist Theory,* London, 1989: 150.
2. G. Heckscher, *Svensk Konservatism före Representationsreformen,* vol. 1, Stockholm, 1939: 141–61.
3. G. Heckscher, 'Arbetsgivarna och 1960s-talets Samhällsutveckling', in L. Lohse, *Arbetsgivarnas Inställning till Föreningsrätt: Arbetarskydd och Arbetstid I Statsvetenskaplig Belysning,* Stockholm, 1963: 29.
4. W. Korpi, *The Democratic Class Struggle,* London, 1983: 46–50.
5. B. Rothstein, *Den Korporativa Staten: Intresseorganisationer och Statsförvaltning i Svensk Politik,* Stockholm, 1992: 30–1.
6. Ibid., 84ff.
7. Ibid., 100.
8. N. Elvander, *Skandinavisk Arbetarrörelser,* Stockholm, 1980: 29–33.
9. Rothstein, *Den Korporativa Staten,* 82.
10. R. Premfors, 'Den Komplexa Staten', in *Stater som Organisationer,* ed. G. Ahrne, Stockholm, 1998: 42–4.
11. M. Rojas, 'The "Swedish Model" in Historical Perspective', *Scandinavian Economic History Review* 39 (1991): 68.
12. M. Mörner, '"The Swedish Model": Historical Perspectives', *Scandinavian Journal of History* 14 (1989): 255, 263.
13. G. Ingham, *Strikes and Industrial Conflict,* London, 1974: 30.
14. J. Fulcher, *Labour Movements, Employers, and the State: Conflict and Co-operation in Britain and Sweden,* Oxford, 1991: 76–9.
15. Rothstein, *Den Korporativa Staten,* 90.
16. Fulcher, *Labour Movements, Employers, and the State,* 128.
17. Rothstein, *Den Korporativa Staten,* 313–23
18. Ibid., 110–58.
19. H. Tingsten, *Den Svenska Socialdemokratins Idéutveckling* vol. 1, Stockholm, 1967: 289–325.
20. T. Tilton, *The Political Theory of Swedish Social Democracy: Through the Welfare State to Socialism,* Oxford, 1991: 127.
21. Söderpalm, *Direktörsklubben,* 139–44.
22. N. Elvander, *Intresseorganisationer i Dagens Sverige,* 2nd edn, Lund, 1972: 192–9.
23. S.A. Söderpalm, *Direktörsklubben,* 152.
24. Elvander, *Intresseorganisationer,* 204–6.
25. O. Ruin, 'Participatory Democracy and Corporatism: the Case of Sweden', *Scandinavian Political Studies* 9 (1974): 183.
26. Fulcher, *Labour Movements, Employers, and the State,* 191–6.
27. See Micheletti's detailed study of the relationship between farmers' organisations and the state. M. Micheletti, *The Swedish Farmers' Movement and Government Agricultural Policy,* New York, 1990.
28. T. Larsson, *Den Svenska Statskicket,* Lund, 1994: 230.
29. G. Edgren, K.-O. Faxén and C.-E. Odhner, *Wage Formation and the Economy,* London, 1973.
30. Elvander, *Intresseorganisationer,* 308.
31. B. Molin, *Tjänstepensionsfrågan,* Gothenburg, 1965: 130–7, 173, 179.
32. Fulcher, *Labour Movements, Employers, and the State,* 262–4.
33. Ibid., 264–80.

34. T. Bresky, J. Scherman and I. Schmid, I., *Med SAF vid Rödret,* Stockholm, 1981: 153–64.
35. H. Heclo and H. Madsen, *Policy and Politics in Sweden: Principled Pragmatism,* Philadephia, 1987: 268–78.
36. Fulcher, *Labour Movements, Employers, and the State,* 204–21.
37. J. Fulcher, 'The Social Democratic Model in Sweden: Restoration or Termination', *The Political Quarterly* 65 (1994(: 207.
38. M. Micheletti, *Civil Society and State Relations in Sweden,* Aldershot, 1995: 117.
39. Ibid., 116.

CHAPTER 20

SWEDEN DURING THE 1990S: THE DEMISE OF CONCERTATION AND SOCIAL PARTNERSHIP AND ITS SUDDEN REAPPEARANCE IN 1998

Victor A. Pestoff

Introduction

When the 'Swedish Model' collapsed in the early 1990s, and along with it both social partnership and corporatism, most observers were not only surprised but amazed and astonished. How could this happen in a country known for its strong unions and employer organisations and its peaceful industrial relations; moreover, in a country often associated with 'the middle way' and the 'politics of compromise'? After more than a decade of intensive employer campaigns against centralised collective bargaining during the 1980s, and zigzag results of decentralising, in the 1990s Swedish collective bargaining experienced both decentralisation and recentralisation parallel to each other.

After decades of Social Democratic dominance, Sweden experienced a period of non-socialist government in the late 1970s. The Social Democrats returned to power in the 1982 election and 'politics as usual' was the order of the day. However, a decade later, in the early 1990s, Sweden experienced a brief period of neo-liberal ascendancy under the Bildt government. It pursued an active, if not aggressive, policy of decentralisation and deregulation that relied heavily on market solutions to major social and political problems that previously were left to negotiations between the social partners.[1] The central institution of corporatism in Swedish public administration, lay representation, was abolished by the Bildt government in 1992. All organisational representatives were formally removed from the governing bodies of public administration boards and replaced by personal representatives. But a closer examination shows that it is more a question of the emperor's new clothes than corporatism's final checkmate.[2] When the Social Democrats returned to government in 1994 they were preoccupied with the economic situation, due to the economic crisis and huge budget deficit left by the Bildt Government. They were forced to pursue a strict austerity policy, and cut-backs have been particularly severe with respect to social welfare services. Issues like concertation and social partnership have been secondary to the economy and social services.

How could Sweden transform itself into a society dominated by neo-liberal ideas and the politics of conflict in such a brief period? Attempts to explain why and how this happened and discussions of the future of the Swedish Model find different answers in the works of different authors.[3] Many observers are still confused today, unsure of what happened and how it happened. The following three sections contribute to a greater understanding of social partnership in Sweden during the 1990s by exploring the demise of policy concertation in the early 1990s.

Given these conflict-filled and dramatic developments in the 1990s, the renewed interest in social consultation and policy coordination late in 1998 come as a great surprise. Shortly after the *Riksdag* elections in September 1998, SAF (the Swedish Employers' Confederation) and the central trade unions, LO (Swedish Confederation of Trade Unions), TCO (Central Organisation of Salaried and Government Employees) and SACO (Swedish Organisation of Professional Associations), announced the initiation of discussions/consultations, called the 'Alliance for Growth', aimed at promoting long-term conditions for growth and employment and exploring how necessary changes could be reached in agreements between the partners to the labour market and the government, rather than by the government alone. This will be discussed in greater detail in the next to last section.

The Demise of Policy Concertation

The most dramatic event in the breakdown of the spirit of compromise in industrial relations came in 1990, when the Social Democratic government failed to get the support of the Swedish Employers' Confederation (SAF). It simply refused to attend the negotiations called by the Minister of Finance, Kjell-Olof Feldt, to revive centralised collective bargaining. Their refusal started a chain of events that led to his resignation, and then that of the entire government.[4] The subsequent inability or unwillingness of the employers and unions to reach agreements at the central level was met by growing government intervention and coordination of collective bargaining in the 1990s in the name of the nation's economy.[5]

The neo-liberal assault in the early 1990s on institutions of policy concertation, social partnership and corporatism was aimed at removing the last vestiges of such forums for social negotiations and promoting a greater reliance on market solutions. The principal architect of this anti-social partnership and anti-corporatist stance was SAF. But as one of the main social partners itself, it could promote its objective either by extensive opinion formation campaigns, or by *fait accompli* or by a combination of both. SAF spent huge sums on opinion formation in the 1980s and 1990s.[6] However, once SAF decided to withdraw or abstain from participating in institutions of social partnership few other arguments carried much weight. SAF's refusal to participate provided an unequivocal 'last word' against the continuation of such arrangements. It quite simply becomes impossible to continue centralised collective bargaining or lay representation if the employers refuse to participate, as developments during the 1990s demonstrate.

Very few forums for concertation survived the neo-liberal onslaught in the early 1990s. Macro forums for concertation, like the Harpsund, Haga, and later the Rosenbad negotiations, had already fallen into disuse in the late 1970s. A more prevalent form of concertation in the early 1990s was found in the sectoral forum provided by the governing bodies of public administrative boards charged with filling out and implementing broad framework laws. Employer organisations and trade unions, among others, had nominated representatives to these governing bodies, but most of this representation was formally eliminated by the 1992 law replacing organisational representatives with personal ones. The few remaining institutions for formal participation in policy concertation after the de-corporatisation decision in 1992 were found in the field of labour policy, that is, the Labour Court and the Pension Insurance Funds. The Labour Market Board (AMS) now includes one union official each from LO and TCO, two business representatives and two members of the *Riksdag*.

In a few cases the statutes of corporatist administrative boards responsible for labour market matters were changed and organisational representation on the governing body was replaced by representation on one of two separate advisory councils, one for employers' and another for workers' representatives, such as those attached to the Occupational Health and Safety Board (ASS) and the Labour Market Board. In the former case, each advisory council meets separately with the top directors of ASS one week before the meeting of its governing body. They present their arguments on important matters included on the agenda of the governing body. But while LO decried this reform due to the lack of opportunities to meet their counterparts and reach a compromise on various issues, SAF applauded it.[7] Moreover, the trade union representatives on the advisory council stated that they represented general societal interest, while SAF's representatives claimed that they could only represent the narrow, special interests of their own organisations.[8]

However, various ad hoc work groups at ASS that work with specific technical issues or problems are still comprised of the organised representatives of labour and employers. The work of such ad hoc groups has not changed much, thus these representatives feel they have similar influence today compared with previously. Similarly, two-thirds of the representatives on the Regional Work Life Boards felt that the de-corporatisation decision had not changed much.[9] Moreover, 74 percent of the business representatives currently on the County Labour Market Boards were, or had previously been, active in SAF's branch employer organisations. All of them had either remained on as 'personal' representatives, after sitting for years as a SAF representative, or had been recommended to their present post by SAF. All of them had continuous contacts with SAF for example attending two-day meetings arranged by SAF for all the business representatives, and regularly received systematic information provided by SAF.[10]

Key Terms

The signing of a Basic Agreement in 1938, the *Saltsjöbadsavtal*, between the employers and unions ushered in an era of labour peace and cooperation that stood in sharp contrast to the previous high rate of labour market conflicts. It both set down the rules of the game for industrial relations and collective bargaining and made it clear that employers and unions could manage such matters together without state intervention. This both set the stage for bipartite rather than tripartite industrial relations for many decades to follow and paved the way for the development of the politics of compromise, policy concertation and corporatism in Sweden. In spite of the collapse of the politics of compromise in the 1970s and 1980s, and greater state intervention in industrial relations in the 1990s, the concepts of *Saltsjöbadsavtal/ Saltsjöbadsanda* (see Table 20.1) still carry a nearly magic aura of one happy, harmonious family. It is in the context of a lost golden age that the concept reappeared in late 1998. *Saltsjöbadsavtal inom räckhåll,* 'Basic Agreement within reach' was the headline for the lead story on the first page of the nation's largest morning newspaper, *Dagens Nyheter*, on 8 December 1998.

Another main concept used in the Swedish discussion of policy concertation, social partnership and corporatism is *arbetsmarknadsparterna*, the parties/partners to the labour market, sometimes shortened to *parterna* (the parties/partners). Historically this concept bears the connotation of strong central organisations for both employers and workers that demonstrate restraint on the demands of their members and accept responsibility for the good of society as a whole, rather than merely promoting the special interests of their own members. This connotation reflects, of course, the development of the 'Swedish Model' of industrial relations following the historic agreement between SAF and LO, the *Saltsjöbadsavtal.* It also implies self-governance by the parties/partners, or bipartite responsibility by them for industrial relations, without any interference from the state. Developments in recent decades made this specific connotation increasingly out-of-date, starting with the radicalisation of Swedish politics in the late 1960s, then the 'Democratisation of Work-Life' programme passed by the *Riksdag* in the mid-1970s, followed by the bitter struggle over the wage-earner funds in the 1980s, and finally the

Table 20.1. *Key Terms in Sweden.*

Term	Meaning
Saltsjöbadsavtal	The basic agreement between SAF and LO, reached in 1938 at the spa of Saltsjöbaden
Saltsjöbadsanda	A spirit of compromise between the employers and unions
Arbetsmarknadspartnerna	The labour market partners: employers and trade unions
Partnerna	The partners: employers and trade unions
Korporativism and nykorporatism	Corporatism and neo-corporatism
Lekmannastyrelser	Lay boards, the governing bodies of public administrative boards, composed of civil servants, politicians and organisational representatives
Samförstånd	Understanding, agreement or collaboration
Förhandlingsekonomi	The negotiated economy, or the economic part of a negotiated order, where corporatism comprises the political part

Source: see text.

decentralisation of collective bargaining in the 1990s, and ended in greater state intervention in, and regulation of, industrial relations.

The concepts *korporativism* or *nykorporatism* refer to corporatism and neo-corporatism. These are still primarily pejorative concepts in the Swedish language, and the negative connotations were amply exploited by SAF and some non-socialist parties during the 1980s. Corporatism was something that was historically associated with fascism and Mussolini, and Sweden was a democratic country, that is, not subject to corporatism. SAF phrased its campaigns against the nomination of lay representatives to the governing bodies of public administrative boards in terms of eliminating corporatism. It arranged several conferences and seminars, and published books spelling out the ills of corporatism from the mid-1980s onward. Corporatism was depicted as incompatible with a parliamentary democracy and examples of the undemocratic influence gained by the unions or cooperatives were frequently cited. SAF arranged its final conference on this topic in December 1991, just three months after the *Riksdag* election, under the heading 'Farewell to Corporatism', and issued a book with the same title.[11] This was SAF's final word in the debate, and its *fait accompli* of withdrawing its over 6,000 representatives took effect some weeks later.

A fourth key concept is *lekmannastyrelser*, which literally means 'lay boards' or lay representatives on the governing bodies of public administrative boards. These boards were designed to promote the democratisation of the public administrations. Rather than allowing the General Director of a public administrative board to make all the important decisions alone, he/she was assisted by a governing body composed of civil servants, members of the *Riksdag* and representatives of 'concerned' parties. In 1960 there were thirty-four public administrative boards with 318 lay representatives. Thirty years later these figures had increased to ninety-one boards with 825 members. About one-fifth of these lay representatives were nominated by interest organisations, the rest being civil servants and politicians. In 1997 there were seventy-four boards with 633 members. The decrease in the 1990s is the result of the decision to de-corporatise them in 1992. However, the major result of this decision has been to replace civil servants with politicians, while the proportion of organisational representatives has remained constant. Moreover, business has actually increased its over-representation on the governing bodies of public administration boards during the 1990s at the expense of trade unions.[12]

A fifth term of importance is *samförstånd*, which means understanding, agreement or collaboration, and refers to the 'politics of compromise' or 'the middle way'. This too became a pejorative term in the neo-liberal assault on social partnership in the 1980s and early 1990s. A final key term is *förhandlingsekonomi*, or 'negotiated economy', which stems from the Norwegian Parliamentary Power Investigation. It refers to the allocation of scarce resources via negotiations between independent actors in business, organisations and the state, rather than through either the market or central planning.[13] It is equated by some with the economic part of a 'negotiated order', while corporatism refers to the political part.

Arguments For and Against Concertation

Following the neo-liberal assault on policy concertation, social partnership and corporatism, which culminated with the Bildt government in 1991 and the decision to de-corporatise the Swedish public administration in 1992, there was very little discussion of such topics. SAF's strategy to gain influence via *fait accompli* provided the final word. Further debate after that point was simply moot. None of the main protagonists – SAF who opposed organisational representation, *Landsorganisationen* (Swedish Trade Union Confederation: LO) and *Tjänstemännens Centralorganisationen* (Salaried Employees Central Organisation: TCO), who supported it – changed their view of the benefits and disadvantages of lay representation in the years that followed the decision to remove organisational representatives and replace them with personal representatives.[14]

SAF's announcement to withdraw its over 6,000 lay representatives from the national, regional and local public administration boards provided a conclusive argument to those who wished to terminate organisational representation on boards. Some even refer to it as the final 'death blow' to corporative representation.[15] Thus the 1992 law that replaced organisational representatives with personal ones states that 'the principle of interest representation, with the need to achieve a balance between the partners, stands and falls with the participation of the concerned organisations in the nomination procedure. SAF, as noted, does not participate any longer in these nominations. The principle of interest representation cannot therefore be upheld any longer'.[16] Moreover, in the *Riksdag* a spokesman for the Bildt government argued that 'it would be a question of one-sided influence from one party' if this situation remained uncorrected.[17] No neo-liberal government with any self-respect would promote greater influence for unions once the employers withdrew their representatives, so *fait accompli* became a decisive argument once again. SAF, the ex-communist Left Party and the New Democratic Party also supported the elimination of organisational representatives in 1992.

In the debate leading to the decision to remove the organisational representatives on the governing body of the public administrative boards in 1992, various arguments were made by the leading actors (see Table 20.2). The five main issues in de-corporatisation debate concerned: a) the independence of the public authorities vis-à-vis the ministries, b) the purpose of the administration, c) the forms for managing public administrative boards, d) the forms for decision making in public administration boards and e) the role and representation of interest organisations on the governing bodies of public administration boards.[18] Various types of conflicts took place behind the scene about the removal of the organisational representatives. In terms of politics, they can be summarised as two main types of conflicts, one as a struggle between two views of democracy and another as a struggle between two interest groups, the employers and unions.[19] Both of these are explored in greater detail below.

Table 20.2. Key Arguments in Sweden

Proponent	Argument
For	
LO, TCO	Promotes the broad, general interest
LO, TCO	Broadens and deepens democracy
SAP, VP	Provides insights into and control of the public administrative boards
SAP, VP	Promotes opinion representativity
SAP	Leads to more effective decision making
Against	
SAF	Promotes narrow, organisational specific interests
SAF	Undemocratic
SAF	Results in corporatism
Non-socialist parties	Results in less political accountability and responsibility
SAF, non-socialist parties	Need for balance impossible once SAF withdrew, expel union representatives
SAF, non-socialist parties	*Fait accompli*
Non-socialist parties	Leads to less effective decision making

Source: see text.
Note: arguments refer to representation of organisations on administrative boards.

The two contrasting views of democracy opposed 'an accountability or responsibility model', against 'an opinion representativity model'. In the former the public administration was held directly responsible to politicians and to Parliament, without the intermediation of various interest groups. In the latter, lay representatives were supposed to gain insights into the public administration and control the activities of civil servants as well as promote general societal interests rather than the special interests of their organisation.

In terms of the struggle between interest organisations, the interests of employers were pitted against those of the unions, but they also had different views of the role of interest organisations. SAF argued that lay representation was both undemocratic and could be equated with corporatism. Moreover, it argued that its representatives could only promote the special interests of its members, not the general interest of society. Both LO and TCO stated that lay representations served to strengthen democracy and provide greater control of the public bureaucracy. In addition they maintained that their representatives promoted the general interest of society rather than the narrow interests of their own members. However, SAF was both the initiator and principal promoter of the de-corporatisation debate in the mid-1980s and decisions to eliminate organisational representatives in the early 1990s. SAF arranged conferences and seminars, financed research and published books, reports, etc., critical of organisational representation and undertook other steps to question the democratic legitimacy of organisational representation. The unions' efforts to defend organisational representation were very meagre by comparison. Thus in the struggle between the employers and unions, the former clearly triumphed in 1992.

A more detailed study of the debate about de-corporatisation between 1987 and 1994 shows that three schools crystallised: a 'rule of law' school, a 'representation school' and an 'effectivity' school'.[20] The non-socialist parties' arguments in favour of boards managed solely by a director general, without a governing body, were often based on the idea of a clearer political responsibility of the public administration to the *Riksdag* and, therefore, it was argued, greater rule of law. Most actors favoured representativity, but they differed on how to achieve it. Many actors accepted the delegation of decision making through 'framelaws', but with differing starting points. The Social Democrats and leftist parties accepted delegation when combined with popular insight and control. The administration could make decisions if it was representative and functioned as a channel of popular will, institutionalised by lay boards with organisational representation. The parties comprising the Bildt coalition felt that representativity could best be guaranteed by reserving political decisions to elected assemblies. If decisions were delegated, it was best to do so to a director general, without a governing body, as he/she could more easily be removed. The same parties together with the Left Party were negative to all form of corporative representation. Finally, effectivity was favoured by all parties, but once again they differed on how to achieve it. The Conservative, Liberal and Centre Parties felt this was best achieved by a clear division between the political and administrative spheres. By contrast, the Social Democrats felt this was best achieved by involving the 'concerned parties' (i.e., the major interest organisations) in the decision-making process.[21]

Not all actors were consistent in their argumentation on the issue of organisational representation during the entire period. Moreover, although some of them took the same stance on organisational representation, they supported their position with arguments from different schools. We find in 1987 that SAF, together with the Conservative, Liberal and Leftist Parties, relied on arguments from the 'Rule of law' school for eliminating organisational representatives. In 1992 and again in 1994 they continued to do so, now together with the Centre and Christian People's Party and New Democracy, but without the Left Party. By contrast, LO, TCO and *Lantbrukarnas Riksförbund* (Federation of Swedish Farmers: LRF) argued in favour of the 'representation school' in 1987 and 1992. But LO and TCO, together with the Social Democratic Party, also argued for the 'effectivity' school in the same years. In 1994 the two unions combined arguments from both schools again, while LRF abstained from taking a stance and the Social Democrats appeared split on the issue.[22]

While SAF's anti-corporatist stance appears consistent over time, subsequent developments suggest that a desire for greater organisational influence outweighed the importance of democracy. The removal of organisational representatives and their replacement by 'personal' ones, the increased proportion of business representation on lay boards, the regularity of their contacts with the 'personal' representatives from business, and the shift to lobbying the leading persons of these same public administrative boards by business interests[23] all suggest that this reform can be considered as 'the emperor's new clothes'.

The Sudden Reappearance of Concertation in Late 1998

After a neo-liberal decade that was hostile to the very idea of social negotiations or any kind of discussions between the central organisations of labour and employers, the announcement at the end of October 1998 of a renewed dialogue between SAF and the central unions LO, TCO and SACO awakens images of a new era of compromise. However the news of the sudden renewal of consultations between the central labour market organisations also illustrates the abrupt re-entry of 'real politics' onto the Swedish scene, just one month after the *Riksdag* elections of September 1998. These consultations have very clear political aims, as a closer look at some of the first reactions to them shows.

The leading liberal morning newspaper, *Dagens Nyheter*, had the following editorial about the news when it broke, under the commentary, 'The new discussions give hope in spite of a political situation that appears hopeless'.

> Neither the unions nor employers rely on what the political system can create/provide concerning shorter working hours and (labour market) conflict

rules. Thus, it's better to take the initiative. Their press release indicated that their discussions will focus on everything that is central for growth: taxes, EMU, the climate for small business, the functioning of the labour market, energy policy, etc. Some (are) purely political questions, others are not … .

Corporatism? Yes, it's not the ideal reform process that is desirable in a democracy. But the political system is paralysed by thinking that the reforms demanded by reality are 'politically impossible'. At the same time unions in Sweden are too strong to be excluded as legitimate social factors by business …[24]

Elsewhere, *Dagens Nyheter* noted that:

Their motives are different. The unions realise that threats to labour market laws by increasing de-regulation are just around the corner if the parties to the labour market can't agree among themselves. The employers realise that the government's collaboration with the Left Party and Greens means that there will not be any easily-won successes at that level. And nobody can be sure that decisions won't be reversed by a new majority in four years.[25]

The Chairman of SAF, Anders Sharp, wrote a debate article in the same issue of this newspaper, where he spells out the preconditions for the success of these discussions.

There are four basic pre-conditions for our 'Alliance for Growth' to succeed. First, Sweden must clearly show that she wants to join the EMU. A reliable plan to decrease taxes and employer taxes is second. Moreover, labour law must be changed and finally possibilities for the development of competence within firms must be improved. If the government and *Riksdag* can't manage to make decisions in these four areas the 'Alliance for Growth', which SAF, together with LO, TCO and SACO, advocates, will remain empty.[26]

Two weeks later the leaders of seven industrial unions wrote a debate article in *Dagens Nyheter*, under the headline: 'We can reconsider collective agreements. Let's develop collaboration with employers to promote growth'.

A rational and competitive production system must be promoted; growth in industry must increase. We are therefore ready to discuss changes in our collective agreements with the employers. We want to develop our collaboration with the employers in industry concerning not only collective agreements but also about education, research and the EMU. Concerning the latter we propose to study Finland's approach with its buffer funds against economic instability, more closely. We also demand that the decision to phase out nuclear energy be reconsidered.[27]

One month later *Dagens Nyheter's* lead story was that a new basic agreement, or *Saltsjöbadsavtal,* was within reach. SAF's tough demands were paired with an invitation that paves the way for its return as a central actor in labour relations. SAF was willing to join LO, TCO and SACO in establishing a bipartite arbitration board to decide in cases of wage conflict. This, in turn, would give LO a new central role in wage negotiations, something it lost when centrally coordinated wage negotiations were terminated in the 1980s.[28] These negotiations have been shrouded in great secrecy, but the government has nevertheless given the negotiators the strongest possible support and has promised not to interfere by proposing new laws if the parties can agree on new rules among themselves. However there is still a threat of legislation (if they fail), as is apparent from the proposals by Öberg's investigation, and this puts extra pressure on the negotiators. Negotiations about a new basic agreement have now reached a decisive point, and what attracts unions about reaching a quick agreement is that this might lead the politicians to promise tax reductions in the parallel 'Consultations about Taxes' that are taking place between all the *Riksdag* parties and the Department of Finance.[29] Furthermore, the Ministers of Finance and Business made public in mid-December their plans to lower taxes if the negotiations between the employers and unions were successful and if they assumed greater responsibility for wage developments and labour peace during collective bargaining.[30]

Negotiators for the employers and unions met twenty-five times in the Alliance for Growth to prepare a draft proposal, but just before the Christmas holidays LO refused to continue to participate. SAF, LO, TCO and SACO all had different explanations for the breakdown of the negotiations. However, the government stated that it would 'call' the partners to renewed discussions after the holidays. In mid-January the Minister of Business, B. Rosengren, announced his intention to meet the leaders of business and trade unions to discuss the business climate in Sweden. This initiative may provide the basis for renewing direct consultations between SAF, LO, TCO and SACO. A 'working group' composed of five business representatives and four unionists, together with staff from the Ministry of Business,[31] are preparing proposals that are similar to those of the 'Alliance for Growth',[32] and the Minister of Finance is continuing discussions concerning tax reductions and reforms.[33]

Conclusions

It should be kept in mind that the Swedish economy continued to globalise rapidly and that the productive capacity of Swedish firms continued to grow faster outside Sweden's borders than at home during the 1990s. In 1965 two-thirds of the staff of Swedish multinational companies worked in Sweden, but by 1997 three-fifths were employed abroad.[34] Increasing internationalisation means that Swedish multinational companies increase their dependency on their host country and similarly decrease it on their home country, as their sales and production expand abroad. Twelve of the twenty-five largest companies on the Stockholm Stock Market had 90 percent or more of their sales abroad in 1997, eight of them had more than three-fourths of their employees abroad, while another seven had more than half of their employees abroad.[35] Swedish multinational companies operate in several national settings simultaneously, and must do so astutely if they are going to survive and succeed, while labour often has a more limited, national perspective.

Both domestic developments and changes in Europe help explain the sudden change of heart by Swedish employers. This sudden about-turn also demonstrates the importance of politics. There has not been a renewed debate in recent years about the virtues or vices of policy concertation, social partnership, nor corporatism. What has changed, however, is the political climate and reality after the recent *Riksdag* elections in September 1998. The Social Democrats are at the lowest level of support and representation in the *Riksdag* since the 1930s, the Leftist Party is now the third largest party, with more votes and seats than ever before, and two of the non-socialist middle parties, the Centre Party and the Liberal Party, are hovering just above the 4 percent lower limit for representation in the *Riksdag*. In such a situation it is impossible for the non-socialists to form a coalition government and the Social Democrats must find permanent allies if they are going to continue to rule Sweden. Given the election results, their allies are now the Greens and the Left Party, while earlier during the previous *Riksdag* the Social Democrats had ruled in alliance with the Centre Party. Politics counts, and SAF is very much aware of it.

Moreover, the election results one week later in Germany only helped to reinforce the business analysis of the hopelessness of the current political situation. From a business perspective the Red/Green coalition in Germany proved even worse than the weakened Social Democrats in Sweden. The policies enunciated by the new German coalition government, in particular in relation to new environmental taxes, negotiations to voluntarily close nuclear plants, and the reduction of the retirement age to sixty years, could only aggravate SAF's fear of the whims of electoral politics and increase its willingness to find a compromise at home.

While this may initially appear to qualify as a short-term, nation-specific explanation for this dramatic turn of events, the fact that social democratic, labour or socialist parties participate in eleven of thirteen governments in the European Union, and that they have prepared a common election manifesto[36] for the EU Parliament elections in June 1999, provides added impetus to the conciliatory attitude of SAF. Under present circumstances not only do politics look dismal at home in Sweden, and even more so in nearby Germany, but with the strong leftist dominance in most EU countries there is simply nowhere else to turn, nowhere else to invest that can provide better political prospects, no more business-friendly climate close to home. The unique degree of internationalisation of the Swedish economy means that Swedish business may become more interested in seeking social compromises and accepting policy concertation again, in order to stave off something worse.

Notes

1. V. Pestoff, 'The Demise of Concerted Practices and the Negotiated Economy', in *Participation in Public Policy-Making. The Role of Trade Unions and Employer Organizations*, ed. T. Treu, Berlin and New York: de Gruyter, 1992; V. Pestoff, 'Towards a new Swedish model of collective bargaining and politics', in *Organized Industrial Relations in Europe: What Future?*, ed. C. Crouch and F. Traxler, Aldershot: Avebury, 1995.

2. P.-O. Öberg, 'Medborgarnas inflytande och särintressenas makt: Korporatism och lobbying i statsförvltning'/Citizen influence and group interest power: Corporatism and lobbying in the public administration, Uppsala: PISA rap. no. 17, 1997, 105pp.; P.O., Öberg, 'Intresserepressentation i verkstyrelser/the Representation of Organized Interest in Swedish on Administrative Boards', Uppsala: uppsats för Statsvet. förb. Årsmötet, 1997; C. Nyqvist, 'Organisationernas inflytande efter avkorporatiseringen/Organizational influence and de-corporatization', Uppsala: PISA:, rap. no. 4, 1996.
3. See Pestoff, 'Towards a new Swedish model'; J. Pontusson, 'Between Neo-Liberalism and the German Model: Swedish Capital in Transition', in *The Political Economy of Modern Capitalism*, ed. C. Crouch and W. Streeck, London and New Delhi: Sage, 1997; J. Fulcher, 'The Social Democratic model in Sweden: Restoration or Termination?', *The Political Quarterly* (1994): 203–13; A. Kjellberg, 'Sweden: Restoring the Model?', in *Changing Industrial Relations in Europe*, ed. A. Ferner and R. Hyman, Oxford: Blackwell, 1988.
4. This is the first and only time that a Social Democratic government has resigned in Sweden. It reconstituted itself a week later, but without its dynamic Minister of Finance, K.-O. Feldt, and was greatly weakened by this episode. Pestoff, 'Towards a new Swedish model'.
5. Kjellberg, 'Sweden: Restoring the Model?'.
6. Pestoff, 'Towards a new Swedish model'.
7. Nyqvist, 'Organisationernas inflytande'.
8. Ibid.
9. Öberg, 'Medborgarnas inflytande'.
10. Öberg, 'Intresserepressentation i verkstyrelser'.
11. SAF, *Farväl till korporatism!*, Stockholm: SAF, 1991. The cover of the book depicts a broom sweeping the letters of the word c-o-r-p-o-r-a-t-i-s-m from the Swedish mainland into the Baltic Sea.
12. Öberg, 'Medborgarnas inflytande'; Öberg, 'Intresserepressentation i verkstyrelser'.
13. K. Nielson and O.K. Pedersen, 'The Negotiated Economy: Ideal and History', *Scandinavian Political Studies* 11/2 (1988): 79–101. K. Nielson and O.K. Pedersen, *Forhandlingsökomomi i Norden*, Copenhagen and Oslo: DJÖF & Tano forlag, 1989; V. Pestoff, 'Organisationers medverkan och förhandlingar i svensk konsumerntpolitik' in *Forhandlingsökomomi i Norden*, ed. K. Nielson and O.K. Pedersen, Copenhagen and Oslo: DJÖF & Tano forlag, 1989.
14. Ibid.
15. Öberg, 'Medborgarnas inflytande'.
16. Law prohibiting representatives of organisations from sitting on the lay councils of public administrative boards (Prop. 1992/93:123) p. 15.
17. Ibid., 17.
18. H. Wockelberg, *Verksledningsdbatten. En analys av partiers och intreseorganisationers förvaltningspolitiska idéer*, Uppsala, PISA rap. no. 11, 1996.
19. Öberg, 'Medborgarnas inflytande'.
20. Wockelberg, *Verksledningsdbatten.*
21. Ibid., 58–9.
22. Ibid., 62.
23. Pestoff, 'Towards a new Swedish model'; Öberg, 'Medborgarnas inflytande'; Öberg, 'Intresserepressentation i verkstyrelser'.
24. *Dagens Nyheter*, Editorial, 24 October 1998, p. 2.
25. *Dagens Nyheter*, Labour Market Section, 24 October 1998.
26. *Dagens Nyheter*'s synopsis of A. Sharp's debate article, 24 October 1998, p. 4.
27. *Dagens Nyheter*'s, synopsis of the debate article by eight trade union chairmen, 8 November 1998, p. 4.
28. *Dagens Nyheter*, 8 December 1998, 'Basic agreement within reach', pp. 1 and 10.
29. Ibid.
30. *Dagens Nyheter*, 15 December1998; debate article by E. Åsbrink, B. Rosengren and M. Sahlin, p. 4.
31. Sometimes referred to as the 'Super Ministry'.

32. *Dagens Nyheter*, Labour Market Section, 26 January 1999.
33. *Dagens Nyheter*, Politics Section, 26 January 1999.
34. *Dagens Nyheter*, 24 May 1997.
35. *Svenska Dagbladet*, 17 May 1997, sNL (commercial section), p. 1.
36. *Dagens Nyheter*, Politics Section, 30 January 1999.

PART II

COMPARISONS AND CONCLUSIONS

CHAPTER 21

THE POLITICS OF POLICY CONCERTATION IN THE 1990S: THE ROLE OF IDEAS

Hugh Compston

Introduction

In this book we have collected together matched political and historical analyses of the dynamics of policy concertation in ten West European countries, defined as the codetermination of public policy by the government, employer groups and trade unions.[1] The reason for choosing this particular phenomenon to study is that whether final decisions on state policies are made solely by the state or are codetermined with employers and trade unions is an important political question because giving employers and unions the right of co-decision changes the very nature of governance in the country concerned. Furthermore, it also changes the nature of the ensuing policy decisions by restricting them to within parameters set by employers and unions. While employers and unions may also have influence where the government retains the final word, policy concertation institutionalises this state of affairs.

One important explanatory focus of the study is the extent to which the nature and incidence of policy concertation can be explained in terms of ideas, values and arguments. This is an angle that has not been explored before in any systematic manner in relation to policy concertation or related phenomena. Another reason for examining the role of ideas and arguments is the failure of the major institutional theory in this area, neo-corporatism, to explain not only why policy concertation is surviving the weakening of the large, powerful employer and union organisations that neo-corporatist theory sees as being crucial to its existence, but also why policy concertation is coming into existence in countries, such as Ireland, that lack these institutional 'prerequisites'.

The purpose of this chapter is to draw together some of the main findings of the political country chapters and carry out an exploratory comparative analysis of the role of ideas and arguments in explaining the scope of policy concertation in Western Europe in the 1990s.

The first step is to map the policy scope and institutional nature of policy concertation between 1990 and 1997 in the ten West European countries covered – Austria, Britain, Denmark, France, Germany, Ireland, Italy, the Netherlands, Spain and Sweden – using data from the political country chapters. This reveals that concertation on employment policy and social policy is the norm in Western Europe, and that significantly wider policy concertation occurred during the period under review only in Austria, Ireland and Italy. Policy concertation was absent only in Britain.

This mapping exercise is succeeded by a brief discussion of the extremely diverse concepts used in national political discourses about policy concertation, followed by an account of the nature and incidence of the most prominent arguments for and against policy concertation. This shows that the most widespread arguments in favour of policy concertation are that it reduces conflict and brings economic benefits, while the most common argument against policy concertation is that it is undemocratic.

Finally, the role of these arguments in explaining why policy concertation is wider in scope in some countries than others is examined by means of a comparative configurational analysis. This suggests that the prominence of arguments relating to representativeness and popular support explains the continued existence of very wide and pervasive policy concertation only in Austria, and the fact that policy concertation in Austria, Ireland and Italy as a group is wider than elsewhere can be explained by the prominence of arguments relating to national economic benefit.

The Scope and Nature of Policy Concertation in Western Europe

Table 21.1 summarises the policy areas covered by concertation between 1990 and 1997 in the ten countries under consideration.[2] Within categories defined by policy scope a distinction is made between countries in which policy concertation is normal and frequent and countries in which it is more sporadic, episodic and superficial.

It is evident from this table that the European norm is for at least some components of employment policy and social policy to be codetermined by means of agreements struck between the state, business and trade unions. Only in Austria, Ireland and Italy was the scope of policy concertation significantly wider than this, and in only one country, Britain, was policy concertation absent altogether.

The patterns of policy concertation in the three *wide-concertation countries* are rather different.

In Austria the Social Partnership established in the 1950s continues to provide multiple forums for policy concertation. Austria is the archetypal

Table 21.1. *Policy Content and Frequency Of Concertation in Western Europe, 1990–1997*

Country	Policy areas covered
Wide-concertation countries with frequent concertation	
Austria	Social policy, fiscal policy, monetary policy, investment policy, industrial policy, social welfare, labour law, job creation and training, employment, EU issues
Wide-concertation countries with sporadic concertation	
Ireland	Overall macroeconomic policy strategy; social welfare; government spending in general; employment policy, including active labour market policy; regional policy
Medium-concertation countries with sporadic concertation	
Italy	Taxation, expenditure (especially pensions), labour law
Narrow-concertation countries with frequent concertation	
Denmark	Labour market policy, work environment policy
Netherlands	Social security, employment policy
Sweden	Many sectors until 1992, then restricted to labour market policy and pensions
Germany	Social insurance, labour law, health, reconstruction of the East
Narrow-concertation countries with sporadic concertation	
Spain	Employment law and social security
France	Employment law and social security
Non-concertation countries	
Britain	None

Source: chapters on the politics of policy concertation in the 1990s in Austria (Emmerich Tálos and Bernhard Kittel), Britain (Peter Dorey), Denmark (Mikkel Mailand), France (Nick Parsons), Germany (Jeremy Leaman), Ireland (Rory O'Donnell and Damian Thomas), Italy (Bruce Haddock), the Netherlands (Hans Slomp), Spain (Miguel Martinez Lucio) and Sweden (Victor Pestoff).

corporatist country, with its compulsory Chamber system and a long tradition of policy concertation overseen by the informal but influential Parity Commission. Although the Parity Commission has been downgraded in importance in recent years, and in general the relevance of the Social Partnership has declined somewhat, policy concertation nevertheless remains well established in the form of formal and informal advisory councils to ministries and public institutions, bargaining between coalition parties (which are interlocked with the functional Chambers and the peak trade union confederation ÖGB), and informal meetings between government officials and representatives of trade unions and employers. The legitimacy of the Social Partnership, which has been questioned in recent years by opposition parties, was reinforced when referenda in 1995 and 1996 produced strong majorities in favour of the continuing existence of Chambers with compulsory membership, and recent opinion polls demonstrate continuing strong popular support.

Policy concertation is a much more recent development in Ireland, having commenced only in 1987 when the first of a series of three-yearly tripartite incomes policy based social pacts was signed. These have included provisions relating to a wide range of policy areas, including economic, social, labour and regional policy. Despite the fact that Ireland lacks a corporatist structure of interest intermediation based on large and centralised interest groups, policy concertation has become well established in a variety of different forums.

In Italy, policy concertation has not been as wide as in Austria or Ireland, nor as regular, but social pacts were agreed in 1992, 1993 and 1995 during the period of economic and political crisis of the early 1990s. The 1993 Solidarity Pact, which covered taxation and government spending as well as employment policy and social policy, was an especially significant event in Italy's political economy.

Six of the ten countries have been classified as *narrow-concertation countries*, on the grounds that policy concertation was restricted essentially to employment policy and social policy. The term employment policy encompasses state regulation of conditions of employment, industrial relations law, labour market policy and work environment policy. Within social policy, areas such as pension policy are especially relevant. However it should be noted that the table indicates the policy areas within which concertation takes place but not the scope of policy within these areas that is decided by concertation.

Narrow policy concertation as defined has taken a number of different forms.

In Denmark, concertation on labour market policy and work environment policy takes place in temporary pre-legislative committees and permanent national tripartite committees, although this mode of policy making appears to be in decline and does not apply to social policy.

Cooperation between the government, employers and trade unions has been a feature of Dutch political economy for decades but has focused primarily on wage setting rather than the determination of public policy. In fact the state has been involved in wage setting for so long that to some extent it is seen as a branch of public policy. For the purposes of this study, however, we have defined public policy specifically to exclude wage concertation (see Introduction). Since the failed tripartite agreement of 1989, policy concertation as distinct from wage concertation has been restricted to some areas of employment policy and social policy since, unlike in other countries, policy concertation has not been granted as a tradeoff for the wage concertation that has been a feature of the 1990s. Despite the continuation of extensive dialogue on public policy between the state, employers and trade unions, Dutch governments of the 1990s have kept the final decision in most important areas of public policy firmly in their own hands. Indeed a process of de-concertation has taken place, in the sense of a growing separation of the spheres of government and industrial relations: the government has intervened less in industrial relations, while the social partners have been less involved in policy making.

In Germany, policy concertation normally covers only certain areas of social insurance, labour law and health, mainly as a consequence of the involvement of employers and unions in the administration of these areas of public policy, but in 1993 a one-off Solidarity Pact was concluded as a means of facilitating reconstruction of the East. However an Employment Pact agreed in 1996 was not implemented. At the time of writing, negotiations were under way to conclude a new Employment Pact, but this falls outside the period under examination.

In Sweden, decades of policy concertation in the form of the participation of organisational representatives in the decision making of the governing boards of public administrative agencies came to an end in 1992 when the centre-right Bildt government replaced group representatives with lay members selected, at least officially, for their expertise. This followed the unilateral withdrawal of employer representatives in 1991. The only significant policy-making institutions in which this de-concertation process did not occur were pension funds and the Labour Market Board.

In Spain, major reforms to labour law and social security were accomplished by means of negotiations leading to the conclusion of a number of social pacts between 1994 and 1997 that included the government either as a formal participant or as the author of legislation needed to implement the contents of bipartite agreements between employers and unions.

While France lacks the tradition of cooperation between the state and social partners that has characterised most of the above countries, labour law and social provisions in France are often determined, as in Spain, by means of legislation based on the content of bipartite agreements between employers and trade unions, although it should be borne in mind that not all of France's competing trade union confederations are necessarily signatories to these agreements.

There is just one country in which policy concertation was non-existent: Britain, where all forms of policy concertation were extinguished by the 1979–97 Conservative government.

Table 21.2 lists the forums in which relevant discussions took place during the 1990s. Entries in brackets refer to forums in which policy concertation might have taken place during the time period under consideration, but in fact didn't.

It can be seen that formal institutions designed to promote cooperation between the government, employer organisations and trade unions exist everywhere but in Britain, and even here such an institution, the National Economic Development Council (NEDC), existed up to 1992.

The main forums in which policy concertation did take place between 1990 and 1997 can be classified into five main categories:

1. tripartite negotiations for social pacts (Ireland, Italy, Germany and Spain);
2. tripartite negotiations in committees designed specifically as forums for policy concertation (Austria, Ireland, Denmark);

Table 21.2. *Forums for Policy Concertation, 1990–1997*

Country	Forum
Austria	Parity Commission and its subcommittees on wages and prices, economic and social affairs and, since 1992, international affairs Government mediation (tripartism): ministers invite representatives from all social partners to discuss and decide controversial issues on both a regular and ad hoc basis Bipartite negotiations: social partners are regularly asked by the government to work out a joint proposal for a specific regulation Parliamentary commissions: (a) top representatives of interest organisations have a seat in Parliament on Socialist or People's Party ticket and thus consult within Parliament, (b) parliamentary commissions invite experts from social partners to discuss issues Informal negotiations between social partners, frequent at all organisational levels
Britain	[Past potential forum: National Economic Development Council until 1992]
Denmark	Temporary pre-legislative committees Permanent tripartite committees
France	Bipartite negotiations the results of which are translated into law [Potential forums: Economic and Social Council, Planning Commissions, social summits] Social insurance agencies
Germany	Social security funds Negotiations for 1993 Solidarity Pact
Ireland	Negotiations for three-year tripartite national agreements National Economic and Social Council Central Review Committee, Partnership 2000 monitoring committee, National Economic and Social Forum Informal negotiations
Italy	Negotiations for social pacts Social insurance agencies
Netherlands	Informal negotiations [Past forums: Social and Economic Council, government negotiations with bipartite Foundation of Labour] Employment and social security agencies
Spain	Tripartite negotiations Bipartite negotiations with government enacting supportive legislation [Potential forum: Social and Economic Council]
Sweden	Lay boards of public agencies until 1992, then pension funds, Labour Market Board [Past forums: non-institutionalised negotiations]

Source: chapters on the politics of policy concertation in the 1990s in Austria, Britain, Denmark, France, Germany, Ireland, Italy, the Netherlands, Spain and Sweden.

3. tripartite negotiations within the regular state policy-making apparatus, for example in committees attached to ministries (Austria);
4. tripartite negotiations within the governing boards of executive agencies (most countries);
5. bipartite business-union negotiations, the results of which are implemented unchanged by the state, for example on employment law (Denmark, France, Spain).

The Language of Policy Concertation

One of the aims of this study was to examine the ways in which policy concertation and related phenomena are conceptualised in the ten countries covered. For this reason contributors were asked to identify the key characteristic terms used in their country's discourse about policy concertation. In the main, these referred to four types of phenomena: cooperative modes of decision making, employers and unions as social actors, concertative and consultative institutions, and particular programmes. These terms are too numerous to be summarised easily, but a list of them and their meanings is given in the Appendix to this chapter.

The most striking feature of this list is its sheer diversity. No one term is prominent in all the countries surveyed. The most widespread were 'social partnership' (Austria, Britain, Denmark, Germany and Ireland), with the term 'social partner' but *not* 'social partnership' being reported for a further two countries (France and the Netherlands); and 'concertation', which was prominent in five countries (Austria, France, Germany, Italy and Spain), although generally used in a weaker, less binding sense than the one defined for this book.

In addition, the language used to refer to policy concertation and associated ideas and practices is largely nation-specific. In numerous cases, key terms were unique to individual countries.

Finally, it was noticeable that the word 'corporatism' had distinctly negative connotations in all four countries in which it is listed as being prominent in political discourse (Britain, France, Italy and Sweden). The term 'social partnership', on the other hand, appears to lack these negative connotations.

Arguments For and Against Policy Concertation

Another of the main aims of this study was to discover the types of arguments that are being employed either to advocate policy concertation or to attack it. To this end, contributors were asked to identify the arguments that were prominent in their countries for and against policy concertation. Given their expertise, we are confident that all the most prominent arguments have been identified, although the degree to which less prominent arguments are identified may vary from country to country due to variations in contributors' orientation and thoroughness. Conclusions are therefore drawn cautiously from only the most striking features of the comparisons.

The most prominent arguments for and against policy concertation are summarised in Tables 21.3 and 21.4 respectively. These are aggregated into rows according to whether their meanings are identical, and then grouped into two more general categories: arguments that are clearly and directly oriented to institutional self-interest, and arguments that are not so clearly related to self-interest but instead argue that policy concertation is good for society in some way. Arguments relating both to policy concertation as a process and to the outcomes of policy concertation are included. While the arguments as reported do not generally refer precisely to what we call policy concertation, care has been taken to ensure that their content does apply to policy concertation, and this is the term used in the analysis instead of the terms actually employed in each country.

Once again, the diversity of items in this list is striking: twenty-four distinct arguments in favour of policy concertation and twenty-nine arguments against, although a number of these arguments are closely related. A significant number of arguments are prominent in just one country.

The most widely shared arguments in favour of policy concertation relate to notions of social peace and economic benefit.

The exact wording of the *social peace argument* varies, but it is clear that there is a widely shared view in Western Europe that policy concertation is desirable as a means of minimising conflict and promoting social peace. In Austria, peak employer and union groups argued that policy concertation leads to low levels of social conflict, while in Ireland the reduction of industrial conflict was specified as an advantage by the tripartite National Economic and Social Council. In the Netherlands, all parties and organisations agreed that policy concertation enabled conflict to be avoided, and in Germany the employer peak organisation BDA declared that social policy should be made via consensus and compromise rather than by conflict and struggle. Alternatively, the value of social peace was mentioned: the German BDA also argued that social peace is indispensable and the result of dialogue that directs divergent interests to compromises capable of securing majority support, and the conservative government in Spain saw a need for social peace and dialogue in view of the tensions that had arisen under the previous socialist government.

A closely related argument is the normative proposition that public policy ought to be made by consensus, as the reason for this is often the avoidance of conflict. In Denmark the key concept is conflict-based consensus, the argument being that it is desirable to resolve conflicts in a rule-governed way that leads to agreement rather than to imposed solutions. In the Netherlands all parties and organisations agreed on the desirability of reaching consensus, and in Germany both employers and unions saw value in consensus.

The other main argument in favour of policy concertation is the *economic benefit argument*. In Austria all parties and groups agreed that policy concertation has a positive effect on unemployment and inflation, while in

Ireland it was argued that social pacts yield modest and predictable wage increases that reduce inflation and interest rates and thereby enhance competitiveness. Policy concertation was also perceived as enabling Ireland to adhere to, and benefit from, European Economic and Monetary Union (EMU). In Italy all three policy actors saw policy concertation as enhancing economic stability. The government and employers stressed in particular control of inflation and the role of social pacts in enabling Italy to become eligible for membership of EMU by meeting the required convergence criteria. In Germany the peak union confederation DGB argued that the rapid reduction of mass unemployment is most likely to be achieved by the cooperation of the state, business and trade unions. In Spain the government and employers advocated policy concertation as a means of securing greater labour flexibility, while the unions argued that it provides the basis for greater employment and stability in employment. In Britain the peak union confederation TUC advocated policy agreement as being important for the achievement of low inflation, new jobs, sustainable economic growth, improved living standards and the eradication of poverty.

The main argument deployed across Western Europe *against* policy concertation (Table 21.4) was that it is undemocratic in that it usurps the governing role of political democracy through parliamentary elections. This is also a direct implication of the separate argument that policy concertation leads to fascist corporatism.

The argument that policy concertation is undemocratic was one put by opposition parties in Austria, while in Ireland a number of politicians and political observers argued that policy concertation is undemocratic in that it bypasses Parliament and ties the hands of newly-elected governments. In France, political parties agreed that the state should take decisions alone because it alone embodies the 'general will', as distinct from sectional interests, and British Conservatives considered that policy concertation undermines parliamentary sovereignty. In Italy there was a widely shared fear that policy concertation would lead to fascist corporatism, and this was also an argument put in Sweden by employers. In addition, Swedish employers and political parties (apart from the Social Democrats) agreed that policy concertation results in less political accountability and responsibility to Parliament.

Related to this is the argument made by opposition parties in Austria that participants lack representational legitimacy and do not represent minority interests. Small business and community groups in Ireland also criticised policy concertation as excluding many groups, while in Sweden employers put the closely related argument that policy concertation promotes only narrow organisationally specific interests, a view shared by British Conservatives.

Aggregation of categories can be risky, but it is worth mentioning that arguments relating to the slowness, inefficiency and resistance to innovation of policy concertation were put by a variety of policy actors in a number of different countries, as were various arguments to the effect that policy concertation is economically harmful.

Table 21.3. *Arguments For Policy Concertation*

Arguments	**Scope of policy concertation**									
	Wide, freq	Wide, sporadic	Medium	Narrow, frequent				Narrow, sporadic		None
	Austria	Ireland	Italy	Denmark	Netherlands	Sweden	Germany	Spain	France	Britain
Overtly self-interested Increases union legitimacy and influence		U						U	U	
Directly helps union members (services for members, real income growth)	U	U								U
Promotes greater union involvement in employment regulation								U		
Directly helps business (wage moderation)		E	E							
Enhances government legitimacy and credibility		G	G							
Supported by group members/population	EU									
NOT so overtly self-interested Social peace/reduces conflict (including industrial conflict)	EU	O			GEU		E	G		
Preference for consensus				GEU	GEU		EU			
Economic benefit for country (stability, inflation, employment, interest rates, EMU criteria, public debt, training)	GEU	GEUO	GEU				UO	U		UO
Need for labour market flexibility								GE		
Promotes solidarity			G		GU					
Protects distributive policies		O								
Promotes social justice							U			
Helps eradicate poverty										U

Table 21.3. *Continued*

Arguments	Scope of policy concertation									
	Wide, freq	Wide, sporadic	Medium	Narrow, frequent				Narrow, sporadic		None
	Austria	Ireland	Italy	Denmark	Netherlands	Sweden	Germany	Spain	France	Britain
Improves quality and effectiveness of public policy		O		U	GEU					
Assists reform of public sector		O								
Provides insight into, and control of, executive agencies						U				
Representativeness of social partners	GEU									
Promotes general interest and opinion representativity						U				
Prevention of exclusion					GEU					
Draws unions into debates on industrial relations and less reliance on government								E		
Limits role of state								E		
Maintains social conquests of 1980s								U		
Enables negotiated modernisation of social structures									U	

G = Government, E = Employers, U = Unions, O = Other (Ireland: tripartite council; Denmark: opposition parties; Germany: tripartite council; Britain: One-Nation Conservatives). Entries for Sweden refer to participation of interest representatives on boards of executive agencies.

Source: chapters on the politics of policy concertation 1990–7 in Austria, Britain, Denmark, France, Germany, Ireland, Italy, the Netherlands, Spain and Sweden.

Note: The categories utilised in this table (and Table 21.4) are defined rigorously in terms of identity of meaning. This means that the distribution of arguments has not been affected by aggregation decisions by me.

Table 21.4. *Arguments Against Policy Concertation*

Arguments	**Scope of policy concertation**									
	Wide, freq	Wide, sporadic	Medium	Narrow, frequent				Narrow, sporadic		None
	Austria	Ireland	Italy	Denmark	Nether-lands	Sweden	Germany	Spain	France	Britain
Overtly self-interested										
Groups lose autonomy					x				U	EU
Restrains pay rises		U								U
Excludes small business		E	E							
Reduces state autonomy					G					G
Costly for business	E					e				
Community sector included but powerless		O								
Association with unions an electoral liability/desire to cultivate business										G
NOT so overtly self-interested										
Undemocratic (bypasses parliament; ties hands of newly-elected governments; undermines universal suffrage, popular sovereignty, general will of people)	O	O				GE			G	G
Fear of corporatism understood as fascism			GEU			E				
Promotes narrow interests						E				G
Excludes some interests	O	EO								
Participants unrepresentative of constituents	O									
Reduces primacy of politics					GO					

Table 21.4. *Continued*

Arguments	Wide, freq	Wide, sporadic	Medium	Narrow, frequent				Narrow, sporadic		None
	Austria	Ireland	Italy	Denmark	Netherlands	Sweden	Germany	Spain	France	Britain
Commitments not kept								U		G
Conservative (impedes innovation, stifles debate, restricts policy choice)	GO	O		O	G		E			
Slow, inefficient	GO	O			G					
Restricts alternative union strategies		U								
Harms economy (EMU, employment, emigration, flexibility, management)		O							E	GE
Increases union power		O						G		E
Labour markets: increases rigidity/blocks deregulation		EO								
Interferes with free market						e				G
Excessive state role in economic management			O							G
Commits unions to business agenda		U								
Not social or egalitarian; poverty, social exclusion stay high		O								
Rejection of co-management of state/capitalism									U	
Promotes state-union relations, union involvement in managerial prerogative								E		

Table 21.4. *Continued*

Arguments	Scope of policy concertation									
	Wide, freq	Wide, sporadic	Medium	Narrow, frequent				Narrow, sporadic		None
	Austria	Ireland	Italy	Denmark	Netherlands	Sweden	Germany	Spain	France	Britain
Out of date										G
Undermines privatisation								G		
Impedes labour mobilisation								U		

G = Government, E = Employers, U = Unions, O = Other (Austria: opposition parties; Ireland: liberal economists, some politicians and political observers, industrial relations scholars, community sector; Denmark: some civil servants). Lower-case entries represent second opinions of authors or others (Sweden: James Fulcher). Entries for Sweden refer to participation of interest representatives on boards of executive agencies.
Source: chapters on the politics of policy concertation 1990–7 in Austria, Britain, Denmark, France, Germany, Ireland, Italy, the Netherlands, Spain and Sweden.

Policy Concertation: Rhetoric and Reality

What, if anything, do the nature and incidence of arguments prominent in political discourse have to do with the scope of policy concertation in each country?

As mentioned earlier, the data on the distribution of prominent arguments has to be considered to be somewhat soft due to the impossibility of being sure that all contributors used exactly the same yardstick when they identified 'prominent arguments'. This comparability problem is an unavoidable consequence of using different people to collect a type of qualitative data that cannot be measured in any technical manner. Even content analysis of documents would not solve this problem because the incidence, nature and importance of any defined set of types of documents – election manifestos, press releases, conference reports, media coverage etc. – varies greatly between countries.

Nevertheless, the expertise of our contributors means that it is reasonable to suppose that the tables are largely accurate, and a cautious, inductive approach does make it possible to derive some limited but plausible conclusions about why the policy scope of concertation between 1990 and 1997 in the ten West European countries covered was wider in some countries than in others.

There are at least two reasons why arguments prominent in political discourse might be expected to affect policy concertation. First, such arguments are often the means through which other potential causal factors impinge on the minds of policy elites, organisation members and the population at large. For example, an expert belief that policy concertation is good for the economy can only become a causal factor in creating or sustaining policy concertation if it is transmitted in the form of an argument to policy makers and others.

Second, prominent arguments may express ideas and values that independently affect support for policy concertation. For example, the social peace argument may express a widely shared norm that leads people to shun conflict and therefore welcome cooperative decision making. In this case the prominence of the relevant argument is an indicator of the assumed real causal factor rather than a causal factor itself, but it may also become a causal factor itself insofar as the expression of this norm strengthens its hold on people's minds.

If a factor is a necessary (but not sufficient) condition for relatively wide policy concertation to occur, this means that this factor occurs not only in all countries in which wide policy concertation does take place but also in one or more other countries. That is, its occurrence does not guarantee wide policy concertation, and for this reason one may doubt whether it is an actual causal factor. If it is a causal factor, one or more other factors also need to be cited before the causal explanation can be completed. On the other hand, if a factor is a sufficient (but not necessary) condition for relatively wide policy concertation to occur, this means that it is found only in countries in which wide policy concertation takes place, but not in all of these countries. In other words, wide policy concertation can occur even when this condition is not present, meaning that its presence is not crucial to the existence of wide policy concertation. Again, if it is an actual causal factor, one or more other factors also need to be cited before the causal explanation can be completed. If a factor is a necessary *and* sufficient condition for wide policy concertation to occur, however, this means that it is found in all the countries in which wide policy concertation occurs and in no other countries. It is these factors that are the prime candidates to be key causal factors.

For policy concertation to occur at all, governments, employers and trade unions must all agree to participate, because this is the nature of policy concertation as defined. This means that all three policy actors have leverage over whether policy concertation takes place. For this reason we need to consider why, on the basis of the arguments that they put forward, each of the three policy actors participate in wide policy concertation.

Table 21.5 displays the arguments put by governments, employers and unions that constitute necessary and/or sufficient conditions for relatively wide policy concertation to take place, based on the distribution of positive arguments for policy concertation set out in Table 21.3. Because the pervasive nature of policy concertation in Austria is qualitatively different from the social pact based policy concertation of Ireland and Italy, necessary and/or sufficient conditions are identified separately for Austria and for all three wide-concertation countries together.

Table 21.5. *Necessary and Sufficient Conditions for Wide Policy Concertation*

Prominent Arguments	**Austria**		**Austria, Ireland and Italy**	
	Necessary	Sufficient	Necessary	Sufficient
Representativeness of social partners	GEU	GEU		GEU
Economic benefit for country	GEU		GEU	GE
Enhances government legitimacy and credibility				G
Supported by group members/population	EU	EU		EU
Directly helps business				E
Social peace/reduces conflict	EU			U
Directly helps union members	U			

G = Government, E = Employers, U = Unions.
Source: Table 21.3.
Note: To be a necessary condition, an argument must be prominent in Austria or in all three wide-concertation countries whether or not it is also prominent elsewhere. To be a sufficient condition, an argument must be prominent *only* in one or more of the wide-concertation countries, but not necessarily in all of them. Arguments that are both necessary and sufficient conditions are therefore those that are prominent in Austria or in all three wide-concertation countries but not elsewhere.

Austria: representative legitimacy and popular support

The fact that policy concertation is wider and deeper in Austria than elsewhere can be explained in terms of political rhetoric by the prominence of arguments relating to representative legitimacy and popular support.

First, only in Austria do the government, employers and trade unions all argue that the participation of the social partners in policy concertation is legitimated by their representativeness. Moreover, there seems little reason to consider that this argument could be made as powerfully anywhere else, as only in Austria do the social partners (Chambers) have 100 percent membership as a result of membership being compulsory. For this reason the validity of the data on which this part of the explanation is based are not affected by comparability problems.

Second, only in Austria do both employers and unions argue that the Social Partnership, of which wide policy concertation is an integral part, is supported both by their constituents and by the general population. It is possible that the members of employer organisations and trade unions as well as the population in general are equally supportive of policy concertation in other countries such as in Ireland, where the social pacts are associated with a dramatic improvement in the economy, but only in Austria was this argument supported by the results of referenda of organisation members and widely publicised opinion polls. For this reason it seems reasonable to accept that even if this argument was prominent elsewhere, it was most prominent in Austria.

As these two arguments are closely related, it seems reasonable to consider them as being two aspects of a single *gestalt*, rather than to attempt to choose between them as rival explanations. For this reason I conclude that the simplest explanation of why policy concertation remains wider and deeper in Austria than elsewhere is the prominence of the representative legitimacy and popular support arguments. Although there are a number of other arguments that could be considered to be necessary conditions for the existence of relatively wide policy concertation in Austria, namely that policy concertation directly helps business and union members, is economically beneficial and reduces open social conflict, these arguments are also found in other countries and cannot explain why Austrian policy concertation is wider in Austria than elsewhere.

Austria, Ireland and Italy: national economic benefit

From the perspective of political rhetoric, the critical factor explaining why policy concertation is wider in Austria, Ireland and Italy as a group than elsewhere is the prominence of the argument that policy concertation is economically beneficial. While this economic benefit argument was also used by trade unions in three countries in which wide policy concertation does not occur, namely the Netherlands, Germany and Spain, it was only prominent as an argument put by governments and employers in Austria, Ireland and Italy. This implies that it was the views of governments and employers, not unions, that were decisive.

The economic benefit argument is secure against comparability problems in that the relevant country chapters leave no doubt that it was in fact prominent in all three wide-concertation countries. The possibility that this argument should also have been listed for other countries in Table 21.3 can also be discounted as a problem.

First, the possible omission of the economic benefit argument as a union argument from the entries for other countries does not affect the analysis because we have already taken into account the fact that union arguments to this end occurred in a number of countries in which wide policy concertation does not take place: it alone was not the decisive factor.

Second, there appears little chance that contributors are missing prominent arguments on the part of governments that policy concertation is economically beneficial. In Britain, not only the former Conservative government but also the current Labour government display no economic interest in policy concertation whatsoever. In France the government often initiates social summits, but in relation to public policy these deal only with employment policy and social security. In Spain the government's principal interest is in reform of the Franco-era labour laws. In Denmark the government displays no economic interest in wide policy concertation, while in Sweden it was the 1991–4 conservative government that terminated official interest group participation in executive agencies, and the current Social Democratic government shows no sign of using economic arguments to press for a return to wider policy concertation. In the Netherlands the government's economic enthusiasm is for wage concertation, not concertation on public policy. While to some degree this is true of governments in Austria, Ireland and Italy too, in these countries policy commitments by government are part of explicit or implicit tradeoffs for wage restraint. Policy concertation is therefore an integral part of the package that is considered to be economically beneficial. In the Netherlands, on the other hand, policy commitments are not made by government in exchange for wage restraint. The only country apart from Austria, Ireland and Italy in which the government does appear to see policy concertation as being economically beneficial is Germany, where the new Social Democrat-Green coalition is, at the time of writing, attempting to negotiate a Pact for Employment, Training and Competitiveness. If negotiations do produce an agreement in which wide policy concertation takes place, this will strengthen the explanation being proposed.

Third, it appears unlikely that contributors are missing prominent arguments by employers that policy concertation is economically beneficial, as it seems clear that employers outside Austria, Ireland and Italy remain unconvinced that policy concertation is good for the economy. This is especially true of Britain, France and Sweden, where employers take a strong free-market line. In Spain employers see little economic benefit in policy concertation beyond the reform of labour law, in the Netherlands again it is wage concertation that is of interest rather than policy concertation, in Denmark employers display no interest in wide policy concertation, and in Germany employers are participating in the current negotiations but in a spirit of considerable scepticism.[3]

Summing up, the simplest causal explanation of why policy concertation is wider in Austria, Ireland and Italy than elsewhere is that the government, employers and unions all agree that policy concertation is economically beneficial, the attitudes of the government and employers in this respect being the decisive factor.

Conclusions

Comparative analysis of policy concertation and its associated ideas and values in ten West European countries over the period 1990–7 enables a number of major conclusions to be drawn.

First, the West European norm is for at least some components of employment and social policy to be determined by agreements struck between governments, employers and trade unions. The scope of policy concertation is significantly wider only in Austria, Ireland and Italy. Only in Britain is policy concertation absent altogether.

Second, the key concepts in political discourse about policy concertation and related phenomena are extremely diverse and mainly nation-specific.

Third, prominent arguments for and against policy concertation are also extremely diverse, but advocates of policy concertation most commonly seek to legitimate it through arguing that it reduces conflict and brings economic benefits, while opponents argue most commonly that it is undemocratic.

Fourth, identification of those arguments that were prominent only in Austria suggests that the simplest explanation in terms of political rhetoric of why policy concertation is wider and deeper there than elsewhere is the prominence of (a) the argument that the participation of the social partners in policy making is legitimised by their representativeness, and (b) the argument that the Social Partnership, to which policy concertation is integral, has the support not only of most organisational members but also of the population in general.

Finally, identification of those arguments and combinations of arguments that were unique to Austria, Ireland and Italy as a group suggests that the simplest explanation in terms of political rhetoric of why policy concertation was wider in these three countries than elsewhere was that only in these countries did governments, employers and unions agree that policy concertation is economically beneficial, the attitudes of the government and employers in this respect being the decisive factor. This means that although the other factors cited in the relevant country studies may be important as contributory influences, tripartite agreement on the economic benefits of policy concertation appears to have been the critical factor in determining whether broad policy concertation actually took place.

Appendix: Key Terms Used in Relation to Policy Concertation in Western Europe

This list is based on the chapters on the politics of policy concertation in the 1990s in Austria (Emmerich Tálos and Bernhard Kittel), Britain (Peter Dorey), Denmark (Mikkel Mailand), France (Nick Parsons), Germany

(Jeremy Leaman), Ireland (Rory O'Donnell and Damian Thomas), Italy (Bruce Haddock), the Netherlands (Hans Slomp), Spain (Miguel Martinez Lucio) and Sweden (Victor Pestoff).

Austria

Sozialpartnerschaft: Network of close interactions and concertation among the ÖGB, the Chamber of Labour, the Economic Chamber, the Chamber of Agriculture and government agencies aimed at a long-run consolidation of interests by means of (1) autonomous interaction of unions and employer organisations in incomes policy, and (2) participation of interest groups in political decision-making processes, including preparation of government bills.

Sozialpartner: Term referring to all agents of social partnership except government agencies, although often only the ÖGB and the Economic Chamber are meant.

Konzertierung: Participation of interest associations in policy formulation and policy making.

Akkordierung: Participation of interest associations in policy making with the explicit search for, and realisation of, tri- or bipartite compromises.

Kooperativ-konzertierte Politik (Konsenspolitik): Policy style based on cooperation and concertation between the government and all major interest organisations in which political decisions stem from bargained compromises between the actors.

Beiräte/Kommissionen: Advisory councils charged with strategic and evaluative concerns attached to public institutions in which the social partners, among others but often dominantly, have a seat, often allocated to them by law.

Britain

Social partnership (trade unions): Unions (TUC), employers (CBI) and government jointly pursuing common economic and social policies.

Corporatism/tripartism (trade unions and political parties): Pejorative term referring to the incorporation of the CBI and TUC into economic policy making in the 1960s and 1970s.

Sectional interests (Conservatives): Pejorative term referring to producer groups, especially trade unions, pursuing sectional interests to the detriment of the national interest.

National Economic Assessment (Labour in 1980s and early 1990s): Proposed exchange of information and views between ministers, trade union leaders and employers' representatives in order to facilitate agreement on economic policies, but without reverting to corporatism.

National interest (political parties): Subordination of sectional interests to the interests of the British people or the economy.

Denmark

Trepartsforhandlinger: Temporary tripartite concertation designed to lead to government commitment to adopt certain policies.

Treparts-drøftelser: Temporary tripartite consultation, not necessarily aiming for government commitments.

Treparts-samarbejdet: Tripartite cooperation, refers to the work of the permanent tri- and quadrapartite boards, committees and councils at national as well as regional/local level.

Firparts-drøftelser: Quadrapartite consultation in social policy, where the national federation of the municipalities is a powerful actor.

Socialt partnerskab: Social partnership, refers to various kinds of bipartite (employer-employee) or tripartite cooperation inside or outside the state apparatus at national as well as regional/local level.

France

Social partners (state, media): Unions, employer organisations and the state in their roles of representative institutions for the purposes of social regulation.

Social actors (unions, employers): Term used in opposition to 'social partners' to reject the idea of partnership and joint interests.

Corporatism (all actors): Defence of sectoral interests (from the restrictive *corporations* of feudal France).

Corporatism (unions): Implication in the co-management of the state/capitalism.

Concertation (all actors): Non-binding consultation, with the connotation on the part of unions that their views should be taken into account.

Defence of wage-earner interests (unions): The sole responsibility of unions; often used as an argument against concertation.

General will/interest (political parties): Popular sovereignty as expressed and delegated to political representatives through the ballot box.

Intermediary bodies (political parties): Pressure groups, including unions, seen as undermining the 'general will', especially by the Right.

Germany

'Bungalow-Gespräche': Informal 'bungalow discussions' equivalent to the British 'beer and sandwiches' tradition: bi- and trilateral consultations between the federal government, employers' and trade union leaders, originating under Helmut Schmidt in the 1970s and actively maintained by Helmut Kohl, forming the basis for a temporary 'alliance for jobs' in 1996.

Bündnis für Arbeit: 'Alliance for work' or 'alliance for jobs' deployed to achieve a coordinated, tripartite approach to macro policy, notably on wages, investment and working-time. In the electoral propaganda of both Greens and Social Democrats it was synonymous with 'Concerted Action' (see below).

Konzertierte Aktion: 'Concerted action': non-binding discussions inaugurated by the Grand Coalition in 1967 and surviving until 1977, involving the peak organisations of labour (DGB, IG-Metall) and capital (BDI, BDA) as well as the federal government and federal bank, which produced a brief voluntary agreement on wage restraint in 1967 and 1968. Plans promoted by trade unions to develop the institution into a formalised system of macro-political concertation were never taken seriously by either of the two other parties. The term has also been used to describe successful cooperative arrangements within specific sectors, such as health, which involve a plurality of interested parties.

Mitbestimmung: 'Co-determination' is used both to describe the specific institutions of labour representation within German private companies and to denote the inclusion of a plurality of interest groups, above all of organised labour, in macro-political affairs.

Mitspracherechte: The right to inclusion in political and other discussions.

Soziale Symmetrie: 'Social symmetry': term employed by trade unions in relation to an assumed balance of social distribution ratios; employers and government ministers (including Social Democrats) present the term as meaning merely social progress which ensures real income increases for all.

Sozialpartner: The 'social partners' – employers and trade unions – were established as part of common political currency after the Second World War in the wake of the disastrous labour-capital polarities of the years up to 1945.

Sozialpartnerschaft: 'Social partnership' is shorthand for the consensual system of labour-capital relations that developed in the 1950s within a complex and juridified framework and with the active support of state institutions, notably the labour courts.

Ireland

Negotiated consensus (core idea in recent partnership): This refers both to the policy-making process which underpins the social partnership and to the policies of the national agreements.

Centralised pay agreement (journalists, economists): The setting of pay terms for the public and private sectors through negotiations between the government and the peak associations representing capital and labour.

Social partnership (most common term among participants): An all-encompassing phrase to describe the process whereby the government and the social partners have cooperated in the formulation of economic and social policy since 1987.

Political exchange (academic observers): The principal participants engage in negotiations and bargaining in which they 'exchange' resources, which has the effect that the labour market parties transfer bargaining from the labour market to the political arena.

National programme: The three-year programmes that establish pay terms and the broad strategy for economic and social policy.

Italy

Concertazione (concertation): Practice aimed at reaching agreement between unions, employers and the state on the control of economic and social variables. This can operate between two or three of the social partners, and can be conducted at national, regional, industrial or company level.

Consociativismo (consociationalism): A political arrangement whereby government and opposition collaborate.

Neo-corporativismo (neo-corporatism): System for the regulation and negotiation of competing economic interests represented by unions, employer associations and the state. The social categories are explicitly recognised by the state as representative of the major confederations of employers and unions. In Italy the term has been used in a variety of ways, not always consistently. The experience of fascist corporatism has made many groups wary of using the term in a positive sense.

Scambio politico (political exchange): Bargaining in which unions and employers seek to reach agreement in exchange for public resources from the state, frequently with the aim of achieving social stability.

Scala mobile (index-linked wage scale): Formalised scheme introduced in 1975 according to which wages nationally were increased in line with the cost-of-living index. Finally abolished by agreement in July 1992.

Solidarismo (solidarism): Tendency to base political, economic and social policy on consensus and collaboration between parties and interests. This is a value deeply entrenched in both Catholic and lay traditions in Italy.

The Netherlands

Sociale partners: Employer and trade union confederations.

Overleg: Cooperative negotiations designed to lead to agreement (in contrast to bargaining, which lacks this connotation). It is the keyword of Dutch social partnership in relation to negotiations between the government, employers and trade unions and between employers and unions alone. Its aim is to create a wider base of support for policies, achieve consensus and prevent conflict and exclusion, so it implies the representation and integration of as many interests as possible into social and economic decision making.

Sociaal draagvlak: Wide social support for policies, in particular among employers and employees, in order to prevent exclusion of groups that are affected and to guarantee compliance with policies. Becoming less popular due to the connotation of too much employer and union involvement in government policy making.

Consensus: The aim of *overleg*.

Cooperation: Implies harmony.

Mutual understanding, mutual trust: Terms replacing 'cooperation' as aims of *overleg*.

Polder model: the Dutch model of successful *centraal overleg* that results in state budget cuts, wage moderation and low unemployment.

Spain

Concertacíon Social: Social concertation (consultation).

Interlocutores Sociales: Social interlocutors.

Pacto: Pact.

Acuerdo: Agreement.

Acuerdo Interconfederal: Interconfederal Agreement.
Consejo Económico y Social: Economic and Social Council.

Sweden

Saltsjöbadsanda: Spirit of compromise between employers and unions, named after the basic agreement between SAF and LO reached in 1938 at the spa of Saltsjöbaden, with the connotation of one happy harmonious family.

Arbetsmarknads-partnerna or *partnerna*: The parties to the labour market, with the connotation of strong central employer and worker organisations that demonstrate restraint on members' demands and accept responsibility for the good of society as a whole rather than just promoting the special interests of their own members.

Korporativism/nykorporatism: Corporatism/neo-corporatism, with pejorative connotations of associations with fascism and Mussolini, implying that it is undemocratic.

Lekmannastyrelser: Lay boards, the governing bodies of public administrative agencies, which are composed of civil servants, politicians and organisational representatives. Originally designed to promote the democratisation of organisations.

Samförstånd: Understanding, agreement or collaboration, referring to the 'politics of compromise', but a pejorative term during the 1980s and early 1990s.

Förhandlings-ekonomi: The negotiated economy, or the economic part of a negotiated order where corporatism comprises the political part.

Notes

1. For a full discussion of the precise definition of policy concertation as the term is used in this book, see the Introduction.
2. The analysis contained in this chapter is based entirely on the case studies in this book on the politics of policy concertation in the 1990s in Austria (Emmerich Tálos and Bernhard Kittel), Britain (Peter Dorey), Denmark (Mikkel Mailand), France (Nick Parsons), Germany (Jeremy Leaman), Ireland (Rory O'Donnell and Damian Thomas), Italy (Bruce Haddock), the Netherlands (Hans Slomp), Spain (Miguel Martinez Lucio) and Sweden (Victor Pestoff).
3. As another check on the possibility that prominent arguments were omitted or non-prominent arguments included, Table 21.3 was re-examined to determine whether any plausible new explanation emerges as a result of omitting any single entry, considering each cell in turn. However no additional plausible explanation emerged. The possibility that another explanation would emerge as a result of *adding* a single entry was then tested. It was found that if it were the case that employers in Austria argued prominently in favour of policy concertation on the grounds of economic self-interest, the prominence of this argument would become a necessary and sufficient condition for relatively wide policy concertation to occur in all three wide-concertation countries (Austria, Ireland and Italy). Given the tendency of organisations to identify national economic benefit with their own economic benefit, however, this is quite close to the economic benefit explanation that emerges from the table as it is.

Chapter 22

Social Partnership 1880–1989: The Deep Historical Roots of Diverse Strategies

Stefan Berger

The historical chapters in this book have demonstrated conclusively for each country that the politics of concertation can look back on ideas and practices of social partnership which, in some cases, have been traced to the nineteenth century. Based on the evidence provided by the individual country studies, I would like to draw out a number of comparative conclusions. For reasons already outlined in Hugh Compston's comparative chapter on the 1990s, they will have to be necessarily tentative and preliminary. First, I would like to compare the development of institutional mechanisms of policy concertation and consultation. Which forums existed at what point in time? The existence of institutions alone, however, is not a good indicator for the extent of policy concertation and consultation actually taking place. Hence, secondly, I would like to establish the scope for policy concertation and consultation that took place over the course of the twentieth century. This should allow us to see whether there is a correlation between a strong tradition of practices of social partnership and wide concertation in the 1990s, and vice versa, whether narrow-concertation countries of the 1990s tend to lack a tradition of institutionalised practices of social partnership. One of the central aims of this chapter is to examine the extent to which explanations of policy concertation in the 1990s need to include reference to historical factors. It should be noted that I will take into account both concertation and consultation.[1] If one wants to find out whether history matters, a long tradition of consultation might obviously facilitate the institutionalisation of concertation in the 1990s. Hence, for the historical analysis, both consultation and concertation need to be taken into account. Finally, the qualitative evidence provided by the country chapters should allow us to draw some careful comparative conclusions about factors that strengthened and/or weakened mechanisms of policy concertation in Western Europe in the twentieth century. This should also provide some indication as to the character of social partnership: what strategies could be legitimated in specific historical circumstances by appealing to the values of social partnership and seeking to set up institutional mechanisms of policy concertation?

Institutional mechanisms for policy concertation and consultation

As we can see from Table 22.1, the origins of social partnership can be found either in the sphere of social policy before 1914 (Germany, Spain and Sweden), and/or in the notion of a state-driven industrialisation process (Germany and Austria prior to 1914; Ireland in the interwar period). Whilst institutionalised forms of bipartite policy concertation between government and industry can be traced back as far as the 1818 *Kommerzdirektorium* in Austria, the first genuinely tripartite chambers appeared in Germany, with the short-lived Prussian Economic Council, established in 1880, and the German Economic Senate, established in 1883. The potentially illiberal and authoritarian side of policy concertation became immediately visible, as both chambers were designed to bypass Parliament on all matters of social and economic policy legislation. It was to set the precedent for authoritarian corporatist experiments popular in the first half of the twentieth century (in Austria, Vichy France, Germany, Italy and Spain, in the latter case until well into the second half the twentieth century). A more liberal variant, which coexisted, albeit it uneasily at times, with parliamentary democracy and a liberal political culture, remained dominant in Britain (post-1945 and pre-1979), Denmark, France, Ireland, the Netherlands and Sweden (from the interwar period onwards with the exception of Sweden, where the process had already started before the First World War).

Bipartite policy concertation and consultation between employers and the state happened earlier than tripartism and remained far more widespread. The interest of the state in developing its economic infrastructure made government turn to the experts, i.e. company managers and employers' organisations. Authoritarian variants of concertation and consultation often saw close collaboration between the state and employers, whereas any representation of labour in tripartite organisations only had a token character.

The labour market parties developed close relationships with political parties in many countries. Where the latter were capable of 'capturing' the state, either trade unions or employers wielded considerable influence over government policies. Trade union power was thus noticeable in Sweden from the early 1930s onwards. In the post-1945 period the empowerment of trade unions was also noticeable in Britain, the Netherlands and in Denmark.

Where there were close contacts between unions and strong political parties which were excluded from government over long periods of time, such as in France and Italy (with strong communist unions and parties), this tended to militate against the successful implementation of mechanisms of concertation.

Occasionally we also find institutions that are set up by the labour market parties in order to exclude the state, as far as possible, from the spheres of collective bargaining and social and economic policy making in the wider sense. Institutions such as the ZAG in Germany and the Industrial Commission in Austria (both set up in the aftermath of the First World War), as well as the Mond–Turner talks in Britain (late 1920s) attempted to find agreement on policy issues and pressure government to adopt their proposals rather than initiate a legislative process of its own. In Britain, Germany and Austria such attempts were short-lived and ended in failure in the interwar period, while in Sweden and Denmark they were more successful.

There is, of course, no necessary correlation between the existence of institutions and the successful practice of policy concertation and consultation. Germany and Britain, for example, have a long history of tripartite institution building, yet it can be described as a history of false starts, failures and disappointed hopes. At the other end of the spectrum Denmark has had no permanent institutional mechanisms for policy concertation, yet, in actual practice, the labour market parties have played an influential role in the legislative process on a wide range of social and economic policies. Overall, only some countries, in particular Sweden and Austria, have a strong correspondence between the existence of permanent institutions of policy concertation and actual policy concertation being carried out successfully.

In the Spanish case permanent institutions were established by authoritarian variants of corporatism between the 1920s and the 1970s. Their replacement by more liberal variants in the 1970s and 1980s raises the question of whether authoritarian concertation can in fact pave the way for liberal concertation, a question equally applicable to the national contexts of Austria, Germany and Italy. At the very least it is striking that countries with a tradition of fascist corporatism developed diverse mechanisms of liberal policy concertation in different post-fascist political systems.

Furthermore, in a clear majority of countries successful policy concertation only really took off after the Second World War. Labour relations before 1914, and often even in the interwar period, remained too antagonistic for ideas of social partnership to make much progress. This is true for Austria, Britain, France, Italy and Spain. The only real exception can be found in the Scandinavian countries of Sweden and Denmark, where more harmonious forms of coexistence and compromise between employers, labour and the state were found often well before 1914. Yet, even a country like Sweden, despite strong notions of social partnership, experienced extremely turbulent industrial relations in much of the interwar period. In Ireland, it was the peculiar colonial legacy that furnished notions of social partnership with a certain appeal, although, here, as in the majority of cases, policy consultation had some weight only after 1945 and concertation was virtually without

Table 22.1. *Forums for Concertation*

	Pre-1914	1914–18	1919–39	1939–45	Post-1945
Austria	*Kommerzdirektorium*; advisory committees and boards advising govt.	Complaints Commission; General Commission for the War and Transitionary Economy; Ministry of Social Welfare	Economics Council; German Labour Front	DAF	Parity Commission; Advisory Committee on Economic and Social Questions
Britain	–	Whitley Councils	National Industrial Conference	National Joint Advisory Council; Joint Consultative Committee; National Production Advisory Council for Industry; Whitley Councils	Council for Prices, Productivity and Incomes; National Economic Development Council; Economic Development Councils for specific industries; Dept. of Economic Affairs
Denmark	–	–	Councils, boards, commissions and ad hoc committees set up by the government, where labour market parties were represented and consulted prior to any legislation being passed.		
France	–	–	National Economic Council; Matignon summit	Ministry of Labour's Labour Charter	Planning Commissions; social summits; Economic and Social Committee; Social Insurance Agency Boards
Germany	Prussian Economic Council; German Economic Senate; advisory boards with ministries	Auxiliary Service Law	Reich Economic Council; advisory boards with ministries; DAF	DAF	Advisory boards set up with particular ministries; Concerted Action

Table 22.1. *Forums for Concertation*

	Pre-1914	1914–18	1919–39	1939–45	Post-1945
Ireland	N/A	N/A	Senate	Commission on Vocational Organisation	Employer-Labour Conference; National Industrial and Economic Council; National Wage Agreements
Italy	–	Committee for Industrial Mobilisation	Fascist Corporations	Fascist Corporations	1970 Workers' Charter; 1978 EUR programme; 1977, 1983, 1985, 1986, 1988 & 1989 tripartite agreements on a wide range of economic and social issues.
Netherlands	–	–	Supreme Labour Council; Economic Council	Woltersom Commission's restructuring of economic organisations	*Stichting van de Arbeid;* Social and Economic Council; Employment and Social Security Agencies
Spain	Institute of Social Reforms; Commission of Social Reforms	–	National Corporatist Org.; Council of National Economy; National Consultative Assembly; Mixed Boards; Spanish Syndical Org.	Spanish Syndical Org.	Spanish Syndical Org.; Social pacts
Sweden	Social Board; Insurance and Works' Councils	Unemployment Commission	Economic Planning Council and joint government–industry committees		Many boards including Labour Market Board and commissions working on a wide range of policy proposals.

Source: chapters on the history of social partnership in the above countries

precedent before 1987. In the Netherlands, the interwar experiments with tripartism were unsuccessful, largely because, in a highly pillarised society, it was closely connected with the Dutch Catholic milieu. Although this perception was beginning to break down before 1939, it was only after 1945 that forms of policy concertation came to the fore of Dutch policy making.

The Scope and Extent of Practices of Social Partnership

The lack of correspondence between institutions and actual practice of concertation and consultation is precisely why we will have to turn to establishing the actual extent to which policy concertation and consultation was taking place (see Table 22.2). For reasons of comparability I will adopt Hugh Compston's differentiation between wide-, medium- and narrow-concertation countries, but will amend them by consultation.

According to this historical analysis, concertation and consultation in some areas of social and economic policy making can indeed be confirmed as the norm in Western Europe. In fact, from a historical perspective, the scope for policies of social partnership was significantly wider before the 1990s. Five countries, Sweden, Denmark, Austria, Spain and the Netherlands qualified as wide-concertation and consultation countries, whereas no country witnessed a complete absence of experiments with forms of social partnership policies. This contrasts favourably with the comparative analysis for the 1990s, when only three countries qualified as wide-concertation countries, whereas one country, Britain, showed no signs of concertation whatsoever.

The diversity of mechanisms and practices of concertation and consultation, already mentioned by Hugh Compston for the 1990s, is even more striking when one looks over the whole of the twentieth century. Each country developed structures and features of social partnership policies that were unique to that country, underlining the importance of the national framework of politics throughout the twentieth century. Furthermore, the authoritarian variants of social partnership need to be differentiated from the liberal democratic ones. Three of the wide-concertation and consultation countries, Sweden, Denmark and the Netherlands, have an unbroken and long tradition of liberal democratic forms of concertation and consultation. The two others, Austria and Spain, experienced high levels of social and economic conflict during the first half of the twentieth century. In both cases, a 'solution' to these problems was eventually found in the authoritarian restructuring of social relations in the interwar period. When the dictatorships gave way to more liberal forms of political government, concertation, for very different reasons, was not abandoned. In Austria, the peculiar invention of the notion that the country had been 'occupied' by German fascists between 1938 and 1945, together with the impact of Soviet occupation post-1945, formed the basis of relatively harmonious mechanisms of conflict resolution by the two main political parties, SPÖ and ÖVP, which were closely allied to the labour market parties. Together they established one of

Table 22.2. *Policy content and frequency of concertation and consultation in Western Europe, c. 1880–1989*

Country	Policy Areas Covered
Wide-concertation and consultation countries with frequent concertation and consultation	
Sweden	wide range of social, economic and labour market policies starting from 1912/14, and continuing from the 1930s to the early 1990s; at its strongest between the 1950s and the 1970s.
Denmark	much less institutionalised and apparent than the Swedish example, the labour market parties have been continuously involved in a wide range of social, economic, education and labour market policies from before 1914 with increasing weight from the 1930s onwards, although the scope was greater in Sweden than in Denmark; arguably, we have been witnessing more consultation than concertation; nevertheless the influence of labour market parties on the formulation of public policy has been both continuous and high.
Austria	starting later than either Sweden or Denmark, with little concertation or consultation taking place before 1945 (apart from short-lived experiments in 1917 and 1918/19); however, since the end of the Second World War, concertation and consultation has been extensive on all areas of social, fiscal, monetary, investment, industrial policy as well as on social welfare, labour law, job creation, training and issues of employment.
Spain	with a long and continuous history of authoritarian mechanisms of concertation and consultation from the 1920s to the 1960s (first under Rivera and then under Franco, with a brief interruption by the Republic), Spain was also in the forefront of liberal corporatist attempts at concertation/consultation in the 1970s and 1980s, when grand social pacts sought to regulate wide areas of social and economic policies.
Wide-concertation and consultation countries with sporadic concertation and consultation	
Netherlands	more intermittent than in the cases of Sweden and Denmark, and less strong than in the case of Austria; consultation for a brief period after 1919 and in the 1930s giving way to more rigid forms of concertation between the 1950s and the 1970s, in particular in the areas of social security, employment policy, labour relations and economic policies; from the 1970s return to more informal variants of policy concertation and consultation.

Table 22.2. *Continued*

Country	Policy Areas Covered
Medium-concertation and consultation countries with sporadic concertation and consultation	
Ireland	hardly any concertation, but a considerable amount of consultation; attempts ranging back to the 1930s, but more successful only from the 1950s onwards; covering issues of productivity, economic planning, reform of pay determination and industrial relations, and public policy issues; some narrow policy concertation in 1970s, e.g. on tax; the Programme for National Recovery of 1987 marked the move from a medium- to a wide-concertation and consultation country.
Germany	one of the earliest countries to develop tripartite institutions of policy concertation and consultation which, theoretically, were to deal with a wide range of economic and social policies; the antagonistic nature of labour relations in the first half of the twentieth century prevented any considerable amount of tripartite concertation and consultation taking place – despite a number of attempts being made; heavy involvement in decision making about diverse aspects of economic and public policy only during the First World War and in its immediate aftermath; from the 1950s onwards sporadic and often rather narrow attempts at concertation and consultation, e.g. Concerted Action in the 1960s/70s; stronger in certain regions and sectors.
Britain	mechanisms of concertation and consultation started in the First World War, but they did not become influential until after 1945; the scope of the attempts, particularly in the 1960s and 1970s, was conceived in far broader terms than in Germany; already attempts in 1917 involved agreements on employment conditions, workforce education and management efficiency; during the Second World War many aspects of government policy were subject to concertation and consultation procedures; from the late 1950s onwards, economic policy, the setting of production targets, general economic planning were all part of regular concertation and consultation procedures; it was only after 1979 that the Conservative Party under the leadership of Margaret Thatcher systematically destroyed all mechanisms of concertation and consultation.
Italy	as in many countries, mechanisms of concertation and consultation were given a boost by the country's involvement in the First World War, when all aspects of the wartime economy became subject to concertation/consultation procedures; however, also as in many other countries, this was short-lived and did not continue much beyond the end of the war; strong antagonisms between the labour market partners quickly resurfaced after 1918, were repressed in yet another authoritarian variant of concertation and superseded post-1947 by Cold War divisions, when the strong Communist presence always made mechanisms of concertation and consultation sporadic, tentative and volatile; major change to successful tripartite agreements in the 1970s and 1980s.

Table 22.2. *Continued*

Country	Policy Areas Covered
Narrow-concertation and consultation countries with sporadic concertation and consultation	
France	intermittent and punctuated by violent antagonistic clashes between the labour market parties, often involving the state, mechanisms of concertation and consultation were not absent in France and can be traced back once again to the First World War and its immediate aftermath; especially after 1945 there was often consultation on a wide range of social and economic policies, but remarkably little agreement.

Source: historical chapters in this book and discussions with the authors of the relevant chapters.

the most extensive systems of policy concertation in Europe. In Spain, the authoritarian mechanisms of social partnership established by Franco tentatively began to allow a limited degree of semi-independent working-class representation in the 1950s and 1960s. This paved the way for the relatively smooth transition to liberal democratic variants of social partnership after 1976. Concertation procedures were scaled down in scope only after the grand social pacts of the 1970s and early 1980s had failed.

Of the medium-concertation and consultation countries, one, Britain, is widely regarded as the very model of a liberal democratic country, while the other, Germany, is often seen as the one West European country where liberal democracy failed to take root to any significant extent before 1945 (the closest parallel would be with Italy). The fourth, Ireland, is the case of a latecomer in state building with a colonial legacy. Germany is the one country that developed the widest range of theories of social partnership, both authoritarian and liberal democratic. In its practice, however, the liberal democratic variant failed during the 1920s, and the authoritarian variant won the upper hand in the 1930s. Once again, the legacy of this for postwar West Germany is ambiguous. On the one hand, the labour market parties were suspicious of the state and state interference in 'their' spheres of interest, but on the other, both unionists (insofar as they had been involved with DAF activities and continued in the DGB post-1945) and employers had experience with policies of concertation and consultation and were not opposed on principle to seek the cooperation of the state over specific policies. However, the postwar attempt to set up a coherent and lasting structure for policy concertation was rather limited in both scope and time.

The levels of social antagonism and conflict in Italy were comparable to the levels we found in Austria, Spain and Germany during the first half of the twentieth century. Once again, 'pacification' came in the form of a fascist dictatorship which institutionalised an authoritarian variant of social partnership. Like in Germany (but unlike in Spain and Austria), there was no easy transition from this to liberal democratic variants of social partnership. On the contrary, under the conditions of the Cold War, and with the strongest Communist Party and trade union movement in Western Europe, politics and labour relations remained antagonistic to a considerable degree, despite attempts by the communist union movement in particular to bridge the divide at certain times. Only after the union movement had become a major political player in the context of the 'hot autumn' of 1969 did tripartite agreements begin to be struck in the 1970s and 1980s. Consolidation of the unions by the government became an almost constant feature of the Italian system of social partnership. Britain was also similar to Germany in that any attempts to develop forms of social partnership in the interwar period failed thoroughly. They succeeded only in the context of the Second World War. After 1945, without the experience of authoritarian forms of policy concertation and consultation, British politicians and representatives of the labour market parties experimented with such forms without having to consider the past as a burden. Yet, it was only really sections of the Labour Party and (to a lesser extent) the unions that championed forms of social partnership between the end of the Second World War and the end of the 1970s. The Conservative Party, the employers' federations and important trade union leaders always took a rather standoffish perspective on the whole undertaking, which contributed to no small extent to the failure of British experiments with social partnership in the late 1970s. Any renaissance of concertation in Britain will face the difficult task of erasing this memory of failure, but supporters of social partnership concepts in Britain can at least look back on a strong indigenous tradition.[2]

In Ireland, the colonial legacy provided fertile soil for attempts to institutionalise mechanisms of social partnership. Furthermore, state-led attempts to transform Ireland from a predominantly agricultural to an industrial society also served as an incentive to develop forms of policy concertation and consultation from the 1930s onwards. The highly successful forms of policy concertation since 1987 have a firm foundation in a healthy and strong tradition of policy consultation in the postwar era.

Finally, in historical perspective only France fits into the category of narrow concertation and consultation countries. In France a short-lived authoritarian variant of social partnership was established with the help of the German occupiers in the Second World War. Before and after, the French experience was characterised by a long history of antagonism and strife between the labour market parties, which were, at different times, allied to the state. Despite the existence of a considerable body of (in particular Catholic) social theory, attempts to develop forms of policy concertation and consultation remained always intermittent and volatile.

With the exception of Spain, all of the wide-concertation and consultation countries were rather small countries, whereas larger countries found it much more difficult to develop equivalent mechanisms.[3] Yet this consideration already leads us into questions of why concertation and consultation worked in some countries at certain times, and why it did not in others.

Reasons for the Relative Success and/or Failure of Policy Concertation and Consultation in Western Europe

The Character of the State

In countries with a strong state tradition, such as Germany and Austria, the administrative capacity for establishing mechanisms of policy consultation was in place already in the nineteenth century. In fact, the strongest supporters of social partnership ideas often came from the more enlightened sections of the vast civil service. Other countries, notably Britain, simply lacked the degree of professionalisation and administrative capacity to facilitate such mechanisms.

Around 1900 most West European states had adopted an antagonistic position towards organised labour. They tended to side with employers in a string of attempts to repress or sideline labour organisations attempting to achieve greater social justice and a more democratic politics. Where state repression was strong, such as in Germany, Austria, Spain, Italy and France, working-class organisations became revolutionary and tripartite consultation procedures stood little chance of success. Levels of repression were obviously very different, but in all those countries the state was unwilling to take positive action to accommodate working-class interest organisations.

States hostile to labour can be juxtaposed to states that showed a greater willingness to devise inclusive policies aimed at integrating the working classes and their interest organisations into the state. The latter became pioneers in the establishment of mechanisms of policy consultation and concertation. The prime example was Sweden, where the state had already taken a proactive stance in facilitating concertation by the early 1930s. The Danish system of conflict-based consensus as well as the Dutch 'enabling state' which facilitated the self-organisation and self-administration of the social actors were also well suited to the early development of processes of social partnership. In Ireland the language of social partnership came to underline the state's attempts to industrialise the country and was aimed to win support among both employers and trade unions.

Political Culture

Mechanisms of consultation and concertation flourished in countries with a cohesive national political culture. Few societies could have been as cohesive as the Swedish, where ethnic, religious or linguistic divisions were not very noticeable. The memory of the cultural homogeneity of the peasant communities of pre-industrial times might even have helped to overcome the high levels of class conflict in the late nineteenth and early twentieth centuries. A spirit of compromise also reigned in Denmark, where a consensus-oriented political culture put a high value on the balancing out of societal interests. In Ireland the traditions of rural peasant communities and the predominance of Catholic social thought also tended to underline the advantages of cooperation over antagonism. Furthermore, Irish political culture was dominated by the memory of colonial exploitation and occupation, a memory which had the power to unite Irishmen around the national issue and facilitated recurrent attempts to pursue a politics of social partnership.

While the Netherlands, throughout much of its twentieth-century history, was characterised by high levels of polarisation into different social milieux, long-standing practices of conflict accommodation, compromise and negotiation (ranging back as far as the sixteenth century), contributed to a climate of mutual tolerance among the social actors in which mechanisms of social partnership could flourish after 1945. In Austria and Germany the cohesiveness of antagonistic social milieux was eroded only in the context of fascism, the Second World War and occupation. Yet, as we have seen above, the lessons learnt by the two countries were very different and consequently their postwar experiences with policies of concertation and consultation were also different.

Where societies and politics remained polarised around antagonistic political cultures, such as, in their very different ways, in Spain, France, Italy and Britain, little headway was made with regard to establishing a lasting practice of social partnership even after 1945. Antagonistic social relations in Spain produced one of the longest-lasting authoritarian variants of social partnership. Attempts by the state and the social actors to unite around a new democratic politics in the 1970s produced attempts at conflict accommodation via policy concertation, but by the late 1980s these had ended in failure. In Italy the strong division between a Catholic and a communist political culture produced tensions, exacerbated by the Cold War, which ultimately did allow only for a belated stab at policies of social partnership in the 1970s and 1980s. In France, the strong revolutionary Jacobin tradition militated against the establishment of intermediary organisations that would have to stand between the state and its citizens. As the political culture in Britain rested to a considerable degree on the belief in parliamentary sovereignty and the traditions of a *laissez-faire* state, any institutions of policy consultation or concertation which could have interfered with this were always regarded with a good deal of mistrust by wide sections of the state and the social actors.

Interest Fragmentation and Pluralisation

There is a well-established relationship between high levels of interest fragmentation and weak social partnership politics. In countries such as France, Italy and Spain, continued organisational divisions in both the union and the employer camps have torpedoed attempts at policy consultation and concertation throughout the twentieth century. Equally, where united peak organisations do not have sufficient authority over their constituent members, such as in Britain, policies of social partnership have been difficult to implement. By contrast, where highly centralised and powerful bodies exist, such as in Sweden, Denmark, Austria (post-1945) and Germany (post-1945), an important precondition for the implementation of mechanisms of policy consultation and concertation has been met. The Netherlands is an exceptional case in this respect, for we have witnessed a considerable degree of interest fragmentation which has not prevented the successful adoption of policies of consultation and concertation. The other obvious exception is Germany, where powerful peak organisations existed post-1945, but concertation never really got off the ground.

A further correlation can be established between the success of policies of social partnership and close relationships between political parties and the social actors (the Netherlands, Denmark, Sweden, Austria and Germany post-1945).[4] Where strong links between unions and parties were either tenuous or where the political parties were not wholly committed to social partnership politics, such as in Spain, France, Italy and Britain, the success rate of mechanisms of policy consultation and concertation remained relatively limited.

The Impact of Ideas, Values and Norms

Highly diverse and even conflicting ideas, values and norms have underpinned policies of social partnership in the twentieth century. They can be categorised into:

a. social conservative, fascist and authoritarian ideas
b. social liberal ideas
c. Catholic social thought
d. social democratic ideas
e. technocratic ideas

Social conservative, fascist and authoritarian ideas have been particularly strong in Germany, Austria, France, Spain and Italy. They tended to formulate policies that aimed at integrating workers into the state without accepting independent working-class organisations. Furthermore they often were defined by an express hostility towards liberalism.

Social liberals, by contrast, were more willing to cooperate with independent working-class organisations within a liberal-democratic framework of politics. Like their social conservative counterparts, they often came from highly educated middle-class backgrounds with some experience in either the civil service or higher education. This tradition was particularly strong in Britain and Germany, but there is hardly a country without any kind of social liberal thought impacting on social partnership politics.

Many of the countries discussed here, i.e. Spain, Italy, France, Ireland, Germany, Austria and the Netherlands have a strong tradition of Catholic social thought, which was one the main protagonists of the idea of social partnership. It stressed both the rights and obligations of private ownership and sought to facilitate a balancing out of interests on the basis of either the organisation of society into estates or the implementation of processes of consultation and concertation between state and social actors. Catholic social thought thus underpinned both authoritarian (estates-based) and liberal variants of social partnership in the twentieth century.

Social Democratic ideas strengthened policies of social partnership in several countries under discussion here. At the beginning of the twentieth century, most Social Democrats were professed Marxists, but their Marxism did not necessarily result in the adoption of an antagonistic policy towards employers and the state. Pre-1914 Second International Marxism was strongly influenced by Kautskyanism. It combined a firm belief in progress with a technocratic vision of an increasingly efficient capitalism being transformed step by step into a socialist economy and society in a peaceful process that would also lead to the eventual capture of the state apparatus through the ballot box. Hilferdingian social thought and Austro-Marxism more generally developed these ideas in the interwar period.[5] The perspective of this policy was still transformatory, but the practice amounted to social partnership politics. Swedish Social Democratic thought in the 1930s, as exemplified in the writings of Ernst Johannes Wigforss or Per Albin Hanson, lay the foundations of the type of welfare capitalism which combined issues of social justice with social patriotism. Reformist Social Democrats were at the forefront of developing ideas that endorsed social partnership in all of the countries discussed in this volume. Particularly strong traditions could be found in Sweden, Germany, Austria, Britain and France.

Technocratic ideas were also prominent in a variety of countries. The notion that policies of social partnership were economically beneficial for the country and hence would also be in the interests of both social actors, is a commonplace argument which can be found in all four of the above ideological traditions. Technocrats such as Robert Schuman in France and Henry Louis Woltersom in the Netherlands exemplify this position after 1945. They often drew from several of the above ideological positions and sometimes, as in the case of the Dutch NVB, consciously attempted to merge some of these ideologies.

The overall strength of an admittedly diverse and even conflicting set of values, norms and ideas connected with social partnership in Europe is also reflected by a brief survey of the language of social partnership (see Appendix in Chapter 21). Thus, the term partnership – or at the very least a cognate term expressing the notion of partnership – appears in all countries under discussion here. On the other hand, many of the terms are country-specific, indicating that each of these European countries has a different and in some ways unique history of social partnership. Many terms refer to specific thinkers, schools of thought or historically contingent events that appeared only in one country. However, as we have noted above, while the developments of mechanisms and ideas of social partnership differed from country to country, there were common arguments and features that connected all of those policies. One would have to look towards trans-European comparisons to establish whether the notion of social partnership is a genuinely European idea (with lots of different versions) or whether there are non-European variants as well.

The Impact of War

Both world wars acted as important catalysts for the development of mechanisms and ideas of policy consultation and concertation. The First World War saw moves towards tripartism in all countries involved directly in the conflict, i.e. Britain, France, Italy, Germany and Austria. Consultation and concertation were perceived as necessary means to ensure the maximisation of effort for the respective war economies. At the same time, the war generated new ideas of directed economies which boosted notions of social partnership. The predominant discourse of national unity proved congenial to the acceptance of such ideas. However, after 1918 no country successfully developed more permanent mechanisms of policy consultation, let alone concertation.

It was only in the context of the Second World War that Europe witnessed a revival of those ideas and practices. Once again, the language of class and sectional interest was abandoned in favour of the language of 'national interest'. In Britain, the Second World War produced the most extensive system of social partnership ever. The war even affected neutral countries: in Sweden the social actors and the state moved closer together, and there was also more enforced cooperation in Ireland. The German occupation of France, the Netherlands and Denmark all had immediate and medium-term consequences for the politics of social partnership.

The war itself with its destruction and dislocation had an important impact on the social structures of the respective national societies. It contributed towards destroying the old social milieux, and old identities were uprooted, allowing the notion of a new beginning to grasp hold over the imagination of the social actors in diverse countries. The rebuilding of Europe at the end of the Second World War also provided an important incentive for policies of social partnership, which were perceived as suitable for overcoming the extraordinary economic and social crisis. In several countries social democratic and christian democratic political parties joined forces and, under the conditions of the Pax Americana, came up with social partnership as the blueprint for economic recovery.

Summary

No single one of the five factors discussed above was sufficient to explain the success or failure of policies of consultation and concertation in Western Europe. Where one did get, first, an accommodationist state, secondly, a more or less homogeneous political culture, thirdly, highly centralised and powerful interest organisations closely linked to political parties (which in turn were favourably inclined to social partnership politics), fourthly, a set of ideas, norms and values conducive to those politics, and finally, wartime experiences which strengthened notions of social partnership, there mechanisms of policy consultation and concertation flourished (see Table 22.3). In the twentieth century, Sweden, Denmark and, perhaps most surprisingly, Ireland came closest to fulfilling all of these preconditions. In Austria also we have identified the existence of a great number of these preconditions, while they tend to be less complete in medium- and narrow-concertation and consultation countries (with the obvious exception of Ireland).

All wide- and medium-concertation and consultation countries, with the exception of Spain, have had an accommodationist state tradition. The

Table 22.3. *Factors positively influencing moves towards concertation and/or consultation in Western Europe, c. 1880–1989*

	Accom. State	Homog. Pol. Cult.	Centr. Interest org.	Links parties – social actors	Ideas	War
Sweden	Y	Y	Y	Y	Y	Y
Denmark	Y	Y	Y	Y	Y	Y
Austria (pre-45)	N	N	N	Y	Y	Y
Austria (post-45)	Y	N	Y	Y	Y	Y
Spain	N	N	N	N	Y	N
NL	Y	N	N	Y	Y	Y
Ireland	Y	Y	Y	Y	Y	Y
Germany (pre-45)	N	N	N	Y	Y	Y
Germany (post-45)	Y	N	Y	Y	Y	Y
Britain	Y	N	N	Y	Y	Y
Italy	N	N	N	Y	Y	Y
France	N	N	N	N	Y	Y

Y= Yes, N=No
Source: historical chapters in this book

Spanish case is an exception because of its long tradition of authoritarian social partnership. France, a narrow-concertation and consultation country, lacked an accommodationist state, while in the case of Austria and Germany, the change after 1945 from an antagonistic to an accommodationist state also proved essential for the development of policies of social partnership. By contrast the link between homogeneous political cultures and social partnership is less firm. Only two of the four wide-concertation and consultation countries, namely Sweden and Denmark, can be described as homogeneous political cultures, while Austria, the Netherlands and the four medium-concertation countries, as well as France, lack any homogeneous political culture. Highly centralised interest organisations were present in all wide-concertation and consultation countries, whereas they were absent in France. With the exception of Germany post-1945 and Ireland, they were, however, also absent in all medium-concertation and consultation countries. Strong links between political parties and interest organisations existed everywhere, with the exceptions of Spain and France. Ideas, values and norms of social partnership were also present everywhere.[6] War seemed to have had no significant impact on labour relations only in Spain.

Strategies of Social Partnership: Pacification of Labour in Times of Crisis or Working-Class Emancipation

Authoritarian variants of social partnership, i.e. the fascist regimes of Germany, Austria, Italy and Spain, were motivated by the explicit aim of 'pacifying' labour. They developed a complex mixture of brutal repression and attempts to integrate workers into their respective 'national communities'. The 'directed economy' of National Socialist Germany saw the strongest subordination of the interests of capital and labour under the state. Yet here, and even more so in other authoritarian versions of social partnership, the restructuring of labour relations went hand in hand with largely informal but nonetheless close bipartite cooperation between state and employers' organisations. While no independent representation of workers' interests was allowed, industrialists exerted an important influence over economic policy decisions. Authoritarian variants of social partnership often left a complex legacy: on the one hand the social actors were wary of the state and state intervention in the social and economic sphere. On the other hand, in particular where there were strong personal and/or institutional continuities that went beyond the breakdown of authoritarian versions of social partnership, the practices, values and mechanisms of authoritarian social partnership could feed into those of liberal-democratic social partnership. Thus, the Nazi idea of the *Volksgemeinschaft* had some links to the West German notion of social partnership, and the Spanish experiments with social pacts in the 1970s owed something to the long tradition of authoritarian social partnership. While Austro-fascism and National Socialism stood discredited in Austria after 1945, the turn towards social partnership in the postwar era again owed something to authoritarian notions of the same idea before 1945.

Employers were likely to turn to policies of social partnership only in times of economic and political crises, when their position was threatened and weak. Hence, the success of social partnership policies depended vitally on the strength of labour and its power in forcing the employers' hand. Where organised labour built successful alliances to other social groups or where it successfully managed to win political power in the state, employers were forced into a series of compromises (Sweden and Denmark in the interwar period; the Netherlands, Austria, Germany after 1945, Spain in the 1970s and early 1980s). However, nowhere did these compromises involve restrictions on the employers' managerial prerogatives and nowhere did they lead to the kind of economic democracy which would have given workers' representatives a decisive say over the running of their companies. Contrary to the hopes and aspirations of interwar social democracy, social partnership policies did not transform traditional forms of capitalist economic management.

After 1945, even in its social democratic disguise, social partnership stopped being an anti-capitalist device. In the context of the Cold War, reformist social democratic parties as well as christian democratic parties adopted various strategies of social partnership as the means to achieve a more just distribution of wealth and greater social equality within the accepted framework of a capitalist economy. While in government, many of these parties institutionalised technocratic decision-making processes based on 'scientific' and 'objective' economic and social data. In the post-Second World War golden age of social democracy, the politics of social partnership promised to labour, first, a say in economic decision making, secondly, participation in the implementation of social policies, thirdly, increased rights at the shop-floor level and fourthly, overall rising living standards for employees. The spoils of unprecedented economic growth did indeed reach workers in Western Europe during the long economic boom from the 1950s to the 1970s, but nowhere did the policies of social partnership contribute to any lasting redistribution of economic power. Even in Sweden, as James Fulcher stresses in his contribution to this volume, 'behind the facade of labour movement dominance ... lay employer power'. When the Swedish labour movement adopted the Meidner plan in 1975 this constituted one of the rare challenges to the economic and managerial powers of the employers. Consequently the Meidner plan threw the Swedish model of social partnership into crisis. In several West European countries employers were not shy about calling for state help, and they came to benefit from social partnership policies in a variety of ways: first, the regulation of labour conflict resulted in fewer strikes, secondly, wage moderation improved economic performance and increased profits, thirdly, at the end of both world wars, when the capitalist system was threatened in a number of countries, the ideology of social partnership helped to stabilise it. By contrast, labour's hopes for a more equal distribution of national wealth, of the implementation of minimum wages and of measures which would create employment were more often disappointed than fulfilled.

By the 1980s, social partnership policies came under increasing attack in most West European countries. Under the impact of globalisation, an aggressive neo-liberalism preached a more antagonistic stance towards labour, and employers' organisations were increasingly unwilling to continue underwriting the social democratic consensus that had emerged at the end of the Second World War. However, the deep historical roots of social partnership policies in twentieth-century West European history will make it difficult to steer Europe towards an American-style neo-liberalism. The resilience of policy concertation and consultation in all but one (Britain) of the countries discussed here demonstrates the continued strength of ideas and practices of social partnership at the beginning of the twenty-first century.

Notes

1. For the important differentiation between the two see the introduction to this book.
2. John Monks, the general secretary of the TUC, championed the concept in his speech to the 1998 TUC conference, and in January 2000 he gave a very favourable account of 'The European Model of Social Partnership' in a special lecture at the London School of Economics which has since been published under the title 'Europe or America?', *New Times* 12 (February 2000): 26–29.
3. And in Spain, of course, such mechanisms were institutionalised only under the conditions of a repressive dictatorship.
4. In Ireland, we have the somewhat peculiar case of one and the same party establishing strong links to both unions and employers.
5. For more details, see in particular chapters on Austria and Germany.
6. For more details, see in particular chapters on Austria and Germany.

CHAPTER 23

POLICY CONCERTATION IN WESTERN EUROPE: A CONFIGURATIONAL APPROACH

Hugh Compston

Introduction

In this book we have analysed the nature and incidence of policy concertation as a mode of authoritative decision making in each of ten West European countries over the course of the twentieth century, with special attention paid to the 1990s. Policy concertation, which we define as the codetermination of public policy by the government, employer associations and trade union confederations, is important because it is an alternative to pluralist policy making in which the government no longer has the last word in the shaping of public policy. This guarantees influence for the other participants – employers and trade unions – and therefore affects the content of public policy by ruling out types of policy decisions that are unacceptable to employers and/or trade unions, introducing policies that the government would not otherwise have instituted (in exchange for employer and union concessions) and, in certain cases, rendering feasible policy options not previously open to the government, such as policies dependent on wage restraint.[1] The matched historical and political chapters on policy concertation in each country were followed by two chapters in which the findings of the political and historical chapters respectively were compared to identify the role of ideas and values in determining the nature and incidence of policy concertation. The purpose of this final chapter is to construct and test an overall theoretical model of the political dynamics of broad policy concertation, by which is meant concertation over a broader range of public policy than the West European norm of employment and/or social policy.[2]

My starting point is the failure of the standard neo-corporatist model adequately to explain the pattern of broad policy concertation in recent years. There are many different variants of neo-corporatist theory, but arguably the most influential argument associated with this school of thought starts with the proposition that the existence of corporatist systems of interest intermediation in Schmitter's original sense, namely large, unified and centralised organisations representing employers and employees,[3] means that the organisations involved can no longer externalise the economic costs of their actions. If a trade union in a single industry makes excessive wage claims, it may be possible for employers in that industry to pass these on in the form of higher prices to the rest of society, but if a union movement that encompasses most of a nation's workforce makes excessive wage claims, the resultant price rises hit everyone, including union members. For this reason encompassing union movements are expected to be more open to negotiating wage restraint than smaller or divided movements, leading governments to enter policy concertation with the intent of offering policy concessions in exchange for wage restraint.[4] Corporatism is also expected to facilitate negotiations by limiting the number of participants and by giving to leaders of trade union confederations and employer peak associations the ability to make the binding commitments on behalf of their members that are essential if political exchange is to take place on a continuing basis.[5]

The problem is that this model fails to account for the incidence of broad policy concertation in Western Europe in the 1990s. Although it can explain the persistence of broad policy concertation in Austria, where the compulsory Chamber system is as close to an ideal-type corporatist system as exists in Western Europe, it cannot explain the rise of broad policy concertation in Ireland, where the distribution of power within employer associations and trade unions is relatively decentralised, or its resurgence in Italy, where employer associations and trade union confederations are institutionally divided.

In this chapter I respond to this explanatory failure by setting out and substantiating an alternative theory that provides a parsimonious yet compelling explanation of the incidence of broad policy concertation over the course of the twentieth century. This new theory explains broad policy concertation in terms of the changing configurations of values of just three variables: the nature of contemporary problems; the degree of pre-existent shared understanding of the aims and mechanisms of economic policy among governments, employers and unions; and the perceived capacity of political actors to implement their side of the agreements that are the essence of policy concertation. The first part of the chapter is devoted to describing this configurational theory and how it works. The second part uses the findings of the country studies to demonstrate that the political dynamics of broad policy concertation can be almost completely accounted for in terms of the shifting configurations of values of the three explanatory variables.

A Configurational Model of Policy Concertation

In his influential book *Agendas, Alternatives and Public Policies*, John Kingdon explains policy making in terms of the interaction of three streams of events: problems, policies and politics. Decisions are made, he argues, when a window of opportunity is opened when simultaneously a compelling problem is recognised, a solution in the form of a technically and politically feasible policy proposal is available, political change such as election of a new government makes politicians receptive, and potential constraints are not too severe.[6] It is this approach to causal explanation that inspires the construction of the configurational model of policy concertation set out below, although the process of applying Kingdon's approach to a different dependent variable has resulted in quite a distinct theory: the idea of a problem stream is kept, but the place in the theory of the policy stream is taken by the evolution of the relationship between the economic views of governments, employers and unions, and the place of the political stream is taken by the evolution of the capacity of the policy actors to implement agreements reached. Nevertheless, the basic logic of the two theories remains much the same.

The essence of the configurational theory of broad policy concertation is that existing modes of policy making tend to persist unless challenged by a serious problem with which they cannot cope. Where this problem is one that arguably can be tackled better by policy concertation, there will be pressure to introduce this new mode of policy making, but broad policy concertation will only occur in practice if at the same time there is a certain degree of pre-existent shared understanding of the aims and mechanisms of economic policy, and the prospective participants are perceived to be able to implement their sides of any agreements reached. This explanatory logic can be extended to identify the conditions under which broad policy concertation is prevented from taking place or, once established, either persists over time or is terminated.

After specifying more precisely the three key explanatory variables and their hypothesised causal relationships with broad policy concertation, this section sets out the predicted outcomes in terms of broad policy concertation of each possible combination of these variables.

1. Problems

The first proposition of the configurational theory is that the spur for governments to consider switching from pluralist policy making, in which they are lobbied by employers and trade unions but keep the final decisions in their own hands, to broad policy concertation, in which policy is made by agreement with employers and trade unions, is the appearance of an intractable problem that the government perceives could be better handled by policy concertation than by unilateral action.

The three main such problems are war, economic difficulties and social unrest.

The reason why *war* motivates moves towards policy concertation is that a serious external threat necessitates a rapid transition to a war economy and then maintenance of maximum production for the needs of the war effort via a system of planning that links demand and supply. This raises the question of how the government can best secure the compliance of private sector employers and workers not previously subject to planning. Command and exhortation may be ineffective, and authoritarian measures may be counter-productive. We would therefore expect government attempts in at least some areas of the economy to secure the cooperation of employers and workers by offering policy concessions in exchange: policy concertation. However this war concertation is strictly short-term: the end of the war removes the incentive for governments to concert on public policy, which means that governments are expected to withdraw from policy concertation once the war is over in order to resume keeping the final decision on public policy in their own hands.

The main *economic difficulty* that leads governments to contemplate policy concertation is inflation where the government sees this as being at least partly fuelled by wage rises, as concern to control wages leads governments to consider offering policy concessions in exchange for wage restraint. Inflation may be perceived as a problem either because it is high in an absolute sense or because it is high relative to other countries even though low in absolute terms. The agreements that result from consequent negotiations may be short-term incomes policy agreements and social pacts that include policy provisions, or long-term continuing processes of exchanging policy concessions for wage restraint. Unlike war concertation, economic concertation may last: if it is perceived to be successful in containing wages, governments (and employers) would be expected to conclude that abandoning it would lead to a resumption of excessive wage rises. For this reason they would be expected to stay with policy concertation, rather than abandoning it once wages were under control.

Social unrest such as strikes, demonstrations, occupations and riots motivate governments to consider offering influence over public policy to the representatives of workers as a means of appeasing them and their constituents, especially where revolution appears to be a real possibility. Like war concertation, however, any policy concertation that results from social unrest would be expected to be short-term: once the social unrest subsides, the incentive for governments (and employers) to participate is removed, and they would be expected to withdraw as soon as they were convinced that this would not lead to a resumption of the disturbances.

In short, the configurational theory holds that broad policy concertation may be motivated by war, economic difficulties or social unrest, but in general would be short-term because governments (and employers) withdraw once the motivating problem is dealt with *unless* they believe that this problem would reappear if policy concertation were discontinued. For this reason the type of broad policy concertation most likely to last is economic concertation insofar as high inflation is expected to reappear if concertation is abandoned.

2. Shared economic understanding

The second proposition of the configurational theory is that broad policy concertation will not take place unless there is a certain degree of shared understanding among the government, employers and trade unions about the aims and mechanisms of economic policy. Although it is difficult to specify all the aspects of economic policy on which this pre-existent shared economic understanding is necessary, from a logical point of view three can be identified.

First, all political actors must accept capitalism. If trade unions or socialist governments are actively trying to overthrow the capitalist system, sustained policy concertation with employers would not be expected to take place.

Second, all political actors must accept the legitimacy of trade unions and collective bargaining. If employers and/or governments do not, then not only is it difficult to obtain the wage restraint often desired by governments and employers in exchange for policy concessions, since the coordination of wage rises via collective bargaining is rendered impossible, but in addition the degree of hostility and distrust between employers and unions is likely to prevent agreement anyway.

Third, in relation to economic concertation in particular, all political actors must agree that wage restraint is desirable for economic reasons, at least in principle. If unions do not accept this, they would be unlikely to agree to the wage restraint desired by governments and employers, which would reduce the incentive for governments to make policy concessions and therefore render broad policy concertation unlikely.

3. Implementation capacity

The final provision of the configurational theory is that potential and actual broad policy concertation may be undermined by implementation problems. If agreements are struck but not implemented by one or more of the signatories, this undermines confidence in the efficacy of these agreements from the point of view of the other signatories. It is here that corporatist theory is relevant, as implementation of promises would be expected to be easier where employer associations and trade union confederations are large, centralised and disciplined. This is also true of governments: implementation of government commitments would be expected to be easier where governments are based on disciplined single-party majorities in the relevant legislature(s) and preside over a disciplined and centralised administration.

4. Predictions

Each of the above three variables can be considered to have two values: a serious relevant problem exists or it doesn't; a significant degree of shared understanding exists or it doesn't, and serious implementation problems exist or they don't. Based on the causal connections described above, each of the eight possible combinations of these values of the three variables can be associated with a specific prediction about the incidence of broad policy concertation. These predictions are set out in Table 23.1.

Table 23.1. *Configurational Theory: Variables and Predictions*

Relevant problem	Economic agreement capacity	Perceived Implementation	Prediction about broad policy concertation
X	X	X	Comes into existence if not already existent; terminated if it is already existent (due to problem not being solved by policy concertation)
	X	X	Persists where it already exists *provided* the problem is expected to reappear if concertation is terminated, otherwise terminated; prevented where it does not already exist
X	X		Prevented or terminated
X		X	Prevented or terminated
	X		Prevented or terminated
		X	Prevented or terminated
X			Prevented or terminated
			Prevented or terminated

Source: see text.

The Configurational Model Applied

We are now in a position to use the information provided in the country chapters to determine the extent to which the incidence of broad policy concertation in Western Europe over the course of the twentieth century is consistent with the predictions of the configurational model.

As detailed in the Introduction to this book, the term 'policy concertation' is defined for analytical purposes as national-level discussions between government representatives and representatives of peak employer and/or trade union confederations that lead to agreements on public policy, that is, to government commitments to adopt particular policies, as opposed to discussions that do not lead to such commitments: codetermination of policy, as opposed to mere consultation. For the purposes of this chapter we are interested in concertation over a broad range of public policy, rather than concertation that is restricted to just a few areas.

Incomes policies are covered insofar as they include government commitments on economic policy, but their wage components are excluded because wage setting is not the exclusive province of the state, apart from the wages of its own employees. Thus concertation over wage levels is considered to be a factor that influences policy concertation rather than a constituent part of policy concertation as such: an independent variable, rather than part of the dependent variable. Fascist corporatism, as practised in countries such as Italy, Germany, Spain and Vichy France, is excluded from consideration on the grounds that free policy concertation between independent political actors did not take place within these systems.

To test the configurational theory, the history of the incidence of broad policy concertation between 1900 and 1997 detailed in the country chapters is examined to determine the extent to which it is consistent with the predictions of the theory concerning the incidence of the causal factors specified by the theory. As the country chapters were completed before the configurational theory was devised, this represents quite a severe test. Although I do not wish to deny the existence of causal variables other than these, the theory to be tested implies that all other causal variables are either relatively unimportant, fit into the model as intervening variables, or operate through the three proximate causal variables specified by the configurational theory, on the basis that the incidence of broad policy concertation can be adequately explained without reference to any of them.

Table 23.1 specified the expectations of policy concertation consequent on each configuration of values of the three variables. Conversely, for each development in the history of broad policy concertation, the predictions of the model in relation to the presence or absence of the hypothesised causal factors can be identified. These are as follows.

1. The *creation* of broad policy concertation is expected to be accompanied by (1) the recognition of a serious relevant problem; (2) considerable preexistent agreement on the aims and mechanisms of economic policy; and (3) the absence of obvious serious obstacles to implementation.
2. The *persistence* of broad policy concertation is expected to be accompanied by (1) the solution or disappearance of the problems it was designed to solve where these are expected to return if concertation is abandoned, plus the non-appearance of any other relevant serious problems; (2) the continuation of a considerable degree of agreement on the aims and mechanisms of economic policy; and (3) the continuing absence of serious implementation problems.
3. The *termination* of broad policy concertation is expected to be accompanied by one or more of the following: (1) the continued existence of the original relevant problem, *or* its solution/disappearance where it is *not* expected to return if policy concertation is terminated, *or* the appearance of another serious relevant problem; (2) the emergence of serious disagreements on the aims and mechanisms of economic policy; and/or (3) the emergence of serious implementation problems.
4. The *non-existence* of broad policy concertation is expected to be accompanied by one or more of the following: (1) the lack of a serious relevant problem; (2) significant disagreement on the aims and mechanisms of economic policy; and/or (3) the existence of obvious serious obstacles to implementation.

Where the hypothesised causal factors are not identified by the authors of country chapters as being causally important, their values (null values) are assumed for the purposes of the analysis to be as follows. Where no problem is mentioned, it is assumed that no serious relevant problem exists.

Where the degree of shared economic understanding between the political actors is not mentioned, it is assumed that this remains unchanged from previous periods. Where implementation problems are not mentioned, it is assumed that no significant such problems are perceived to exist.

The countries to be examined, and the authors of the historical and political country chapters respectively on which the account is based, are Austria (Jill Lewis, and Bernhard Kittel and Emmerich Tálos), Britain (Chris Williams and Peter Dorey), France (Susan Milner and Nick Parsons), Germany (Stefan Berger and Jeremy Leaman), Ireland (Emmet O'Connor, and Damian Thomas and Rory O'Donnell), Italy (Gino Bedani and Bruce Haddock), the Netherlands (Anton Hemerijck and Hans Slomp), Spain (Robert Robinson and Miguel Martinez Lucio), and Sweden (James Fulcher and Victor Pestoff). Denmark, although the subject of two country chapters, has had to be excluded due to insufficiently detailed information on the period prior to the 1990s. Except where otherwise indicated, the account is based solely on these chapters plus subsequent consultations with their authors.

In terms of the frequency, breadth and duration of policy concertation over the twentieth century as a whole, the nine countries surveyed can be classified into three groups: high-concertation countries (Austria, the Netherlands and Sweden), medium-concertation countries (Britain, Ireland, Italy and Spain), and low-concertation countries (France and Germany), as detailed in Table 23.2. However it should be noted that the nature and extent of policy concertation varies widely not only between countries but also within countries over time. Policy concertation was central to policy making in the Netherlands and Sweden for decades, for example, but is now of little importance, while the rise of wide policy concertation in Ireland and Italy recently is something of a surprise from a historical point of view.

The examination of the incidence of broad policy concertation and its correlates begins with the First World War and its aftermath, since little if any significant policy concertation took place prior to this, then considers the 1930s, the Second World War, the long postwar boom up to the late 1960s, the more troubled period between the late 1960s and late 1980s, and the decade since then up to 1997.

1. The First World War and its aftermath

The first occasion on which significant tripartite policy concertation took place in our nine West European countries was during the latter stages of the First World War, in which external threat and the need to overcome economic problems such as deteriorating output and industrial unrest were followed by policy concertation, or moves towards it, in all five of our countries that were combatants: Austria, Italy, Germany, France and Britain. The fact that policy concertation occurred despite the lack of shared economic understanding between governments, employers and trade unions can be explained in terms of the configurational theory by the tendency during wartime for political actors to sink their differences in the common cause. The fact that policy concertation took place despite the relatively small size and decentralised nature

Table 23.2. *Incidence of Policy Concertation 1900–1997*

Country	Episodes of policy concertation
High concertation countries	
Austria	First World War policy concertation; Social Partnership from 1950s
Sweden	Combination of top-level negotiations, representation on executive agencies and participation in policy-making commissions from 1930s to 1992
Netherlands	Postwar policy concertation up to late 1970s/early 1980s; abortive 1989 Common Course Agreement
Medium concertation countries	
Britain	Beginnings of policy concertation in First World War; extensive policy concertation in Second World War; 1960s planning; 1974–9 Social Contract
Ireland	Incomes policy agreements of 1970s; social pacts from 1987
Italy	First World War policy concertation; 1968–78 union-dominated policy concertation; 1978–84 social pacts; social pacts from 1992
Spain	Broad social pacts of late 1970s and early 1980s; narrow social pacts 1994–7
Low concertation countries	
France	1936 Matignon summit; 1968 Grenelle Accords
Germany	First World War policy concertation; 1993 Solidarity Pact

Source: chapters on Austria, Britain, France, Germany, Ireland, Italy, the Netherlands, Spain and Sweden; communications with the authors. Authoritarian corporatism is excluded because this was either a façade for state control (the fascist corporatism of Germany, Austria, Italy, Vichy France and Franco's Spain) or carried no real weight in policy making (Primo de Rivera's Spain).

of many employer organisations and trade unions at this time, which might otherwise have been expected to impede implementation of any agreements reached, can be explained in terms of the theory by three factors. First, implementation would be expected to be facilitated by the sense of common purpose in the face of a common enemy. Second, the relevant organisations may become more centralised in response to the stimulus of a new function, as happened in Britain, for instance. Third, the increased state powers characteristic of wartime not only make it easier for governments to carry out their own commitments, but also may enable them to help the other participants implement their sides of agreements, for instance by legislating to generalise agreed wage rises to all firms and employees. All three of the configurational theory's preconditions for the establishment of broad policy concertation – a relevant problem, a degree of economic agreement and implementation capacity – therefore appear to be met. A further prediction of the theory, that the end of the war would be followed by the termination of this style of policy concertation due to the removal of the motivating problem, is also fulfilled, as war concertation was dismantled everywhere after the war ended.

The failed attempts to establish more permanent broad policy concertation in Austria, Germany, France and Britain in the aftermath of the First World War can also be explained in terms of the configurational theory, as these efforts occurred in the wake of serious problems in the form of war damage and social unrest but were obstructed by the restoration to prominence of the widely differing economic views of employers and trade unions in particular. Where policy concertation did briefly take place, as in Germany, its continuation was undermined by its failure to solve the economic problems it was set up to deal with. In Italy, however, no serious attempts at policy concertation were made despite enormous social upheaval and the currency of pro-concertation views in certain quarters.

2. *The 1930s*

The circumstances of the establishment of the first lasting period of broad policy concertation in our set of nine countries, which occurred in Sweden during the 1930s, are also consistent with the configurational theory. Although the Depression hit Sweden hard, significant policy concertation did not emerge until the area of economic agreement among the political actors was substantially broadened when the Social Democrats, with whom the unions were closely allied, accepted the capitalist economy and the need for international competitiveness following their defeat in the 1928 'Cossack election'. In addition, the Saltsjöbaden Agreement of 1938 demonstrated that employers and unions accepted each other's existence and legitimacy. Implementation of subsequent agreements does not appear to have been a significant problem. The establishment of broad policy concertation in Sweden during the 1930s, based on top-level negotiation between governments and interest organisations as well as the long-standing representation of these organisations on the governing boards of the semi-autonomous administrative agencies that implement most public policy, was followed by several decades of economic success.

The Depression also saw attempts to establish policy concertation in all of the other four non-fascist countries, namely Britain, France, Ireland and the Netherlands, as well as in Spain during the interval between the de Rivera and Franco dictatorships. However in Britain the introduction of broad policy concertation was blocked by economic disagreement, as significant sections of employers were implacably opposed to the prospect of economic intervention by the state or trade unions. In France, social unrest in the form of a wave of strikes and occupations preceded the tripartite Matignon summit of 1936, but there was little if any shared economic understanding among the political actors and this momentary broad policy concertation did not survive the ousting of the left-wing Popular Front government. This is in accord with the prediction of the configurational theory that broad policy concertation caused by social unrest comes to an end when the social unrest subsides, especially when there is little if any shared economic understanding among the participants.

The Netherlands looked as though it was headed for broad policy concertation within an elaborate set of corporatist institutions, with a plethora of plans being put forward as Catholic, Calvinist and social democratic positions converged, but a large gulf remained between the nationalisation-oriented views of the socialist union confederation NVV and the strict conservative economic policy of the government, and no action had been taken by the time war broke out in 1939. Similar proposals were advocated in Ireland, but these were not acted upon apart from making the Senate ostensibly a vocational Chamber in 1937, a move that was rendered meaningless by the fact that its electorate consisted of MPs and local councillors. One relevant factor here was the inability of Irish trade unions to coordinate wage bargaining at this time, which made it difficult for wage restraint to be exchanged for a voice in policy making.

Although in Spain during the 1920s the corporatist system of Primo de Rivera excluded anarchist and communist trade unions, it did allow the socialist unions to participate, but it soon became evident that this system was not real policy concertation because it had little to do with actual policy making. After the Civil War, Franco rendered free policy concertation impossible by outlawing trade unions. In between these two dictatorships, however, the first government of the democratic Second Republic established Mixed Boards in 1931 to manage industrial relations, develop work regulations and make proposals for social legislation, but these failed as employers remained hostile in the face of radical trade unions, and the highly charged political atmosphere made meaningful concertation all but impossible.

To summarise, the configurational theory explains the incidence of broad policy concertation in the 1930s reasonably well. All countries were hit by economic problems, but it was only where a shared economic understanding broadened and implementation was not a significant problem, namely in Sweden, that broad policy concertation became firmly established. The only slight puzzle here is why broad policy concertation was not established prior to the war in the Netherlands, but its establishment after the war, as we shall see, means that this is only a question of timing.

3. The Second World War

As noted in the case of the First World War, the configurational theory predicts that war leads to significant policy concertation in all democratic combatant countries, and this is what we find in the case of the Second World War: the outbreak of war was followed by the establishment of a very extensive system of policy concertation in Britain, the only non-fascist combatant state not to be occupied, as employers and unions were brought into the management of the economy via a proliferation of bipartite and tripartite committees. The extent to which political actors were prepared to sink their differences is shown by the formation for the first time of a grand coalition government to run the war. Implementation does not appear to have been a significant problem. The threat of invasion also led non-combatant Sweden to draw employers and unions further into co-management of the economy during the Second World War.

4. 1945 to the late 1960s

The two decades following the end of the Second World War saw the entrenchment of broad policy concertation in Sweden and its establishment in Austria and the Netherlands, but attempts to introduce it elsewhere were unsuccessful until moves were made in this direction in Britain during the early 1960s.

In Sweden, representatives of employers and trade unions were increasingly included in policy-making commissions, which aimed at reaching agreed positions on policy proposals, and on the governing boards of administrative agencies. Furthermore, between 1949 and 1955 ministers and civil servants met weekly with representatives of business, unions and farmers to discuss and arguably decide economic policy, and top-level consultation continued even after these weekly meetings ceased. The configurational theory holds that the persistence of broad policy concertation is caused by its success in dealing with problems that might reappear if it was abandoned, plus a continuing broad measure of common understanding of the aims and mechanisms of economic policy combined with the capacity to implement agreements. All these conditions were present in Sweden during this period: the country enjoyed economic success that was at least partly attributed to the 'Swedish model' of which broad policy concertation was an integral part; a common economic understanding continued to grow, culminating in the 1960s in the development of an agreed formula for wage growth; and the inclusive and centralised nature of employer and union organisations meant that implementation was not a serious problem, although rank and file resistance to perceived over-centralisation led to tensions towards the end of the decade.

The creation of the Austrian Social Partnership is also consistent with the predictions of the configurational theory. The Soviet occupation of a third of the country in the aftermath of the Second World War led to a shared view that conflict had to be avoided, which implies acceptance of capitalism by trade unions and acceptance of unions and collective bargaining by employers, and the degree of agreement on economic policy was broadened further during the second half of the 1950s when unions adopted a growth-oriented strategy and accepted the need for wage restraint. Broad policy concertation in the form initially of the Parity Commission commenced in 1957, two years after the Soviet troops left, and the problems to which it was oriented were economic, although threatened and actual social unrest in the form of industrial action was also a factor. The encompassing nature of Austria's Chambers and trade union movement meant that implementation was not a significant problem. The perceived success of the Parity Commission's initial economic programme was followed by the entrenchment of broad policy concertation as the dominant policy-making style in Austria, in line with the configurational theory.[7]

The establishment of broad policy concertation in the Netherlands is also consistent with the configurational theory, as the establishment of a set of corporatist institutions designed in part as forums for policy concertation was motivated in large part by the felt urgency of postwar reconstruction and accompanied by growing shared economic understanding, while implementation was not a serious problem. Most prominently, in 1950 the tripartite Social and Economic Council became the government's paramount adviser on economic and social questions: where recommendations were agreed, these were almost invariably accepted by the government. The common understanding of the aims and mechanisms of economic policy was based on the development during the war of a shared conviction that cooperative industrial relations, which implies the acceptance by all political actors of both capitalism and collective bargaining, was indispensable for postwar reconstruction, along with wage restraint and a prominent role for the government. As in Austria, the perceived success of the economic policy that emerged was followed by the entrenchment of broad policy concertation.

In other countries, efforts to establish broad policy concertation were unsuccessful.

Although the postwar system of planning established in France after the war was supposed to have been based on tripartite concertation, in fact it was essentially state-driven despite the creation of concertative institutions such as Planning Commissions, and unions in particular were marginalised. The tripartite Economic and Social Council instituted to be consulted on draft social legislation also failed to operate as a forum for policy concertation. However the 1940s did see the establishment of social security funds managed jointly by employers and trade unions. The failure to establish broader policy concertation can be largely explained in terms of the configurational theory by the domination of the trade union movement by communists, as this meant that a significant degree of shared economic understanding did not exist.

The lack of broad policy concertation in Italy during the postwar period can also be explained in terms of the configurational theory by the lack of common economic understanding consequent on communists being powerful in the trade union movement.

The failure of West German governments to introduce broad policy concertation once the Federal Republic was established in 1949 can be explained by the fact that by this time the economic situation was improving, thus removing the incentive to switch from pluralist policy making (attempts to establish policy concertation in the immediate postwar period had been opposed by employers and vetoed by the Allies). However during the 1950s regular and wide-ranging consultation was institutionalised at all levels.

In Ireland, which had been neutral during the war, the situation was not significantly different to the 1930s: economic problems remained severe, and the views of employers and trade unions were not as polarised as elsewhere, but the inability of trade unions to coordinate collective bargaining meant that it would be difficult if not impossible to implement any wage tradeoffs for policy concertation.

In Britain, the extensive policy concertation of the Second World War was dismantled after the war, consistent with the predictions of the configurational theory that the end of external threat leads to the end of war concertation. The lack of postwar broad policy concertation, beyond a tacit bipartism between the postwar Labour government and the unions, can be explained in terms of the theory by the lack of common economic understanding demonstrated by the resolute opposition of employers to anything other than a return to *laissez faire*.

During the early 1960s, however, the perceived failure of British economic policy, combined with a shared perception that French indicative planning was a success, led to the establishment by a Conservative government of the tripartite National Economic Development Council in 1962, plus sectoral Economic Development Councils, to set targets for production and to influence pay awards. The Labour government of 1964–70 had an even greater commitment to tripartite planning, at least initially, but failed to implement its 1965 Plan. Further broad policy concertation was obstructed by conflict between the government and trade unions over industrial relations reform.

During the period between 1945 and the late 1960s, then, the pattern of broad policy concertation in Western Europe can be readily explained in terms of the configurational theory, although the situation in Britain is not as clear-cut as elsewhere.

5. The late 1960s to late 1980s

After the relative calm and economic prosperity of the two decades following the Second World War, the next two decades were more troubled. One result was renewed consideration of policy concertation in countries dominated by pluralist policy making, at the same time as the efficacy of broad policy concertation was coming into question in two of the three countries in which it had been most important.

In France and Italy it was social unrest that led to a surge of policy concertation.

In France, broad policy concertation was short-lived: the government responded to the student and worker unrest of May 1968 by negotiating the Grenelle Accords – policy concertation – but as soon as the disturbances came to an end, so did this type of policy concertation, just as in 1936 and in line with the configurational theory.

In Italy, however, where concertation over a wide range of public policy also began in response to social unrest in 1968, the trade unions were able to harness worker militancy and use it as a bargaining counter in negotiations with the government for at least a decade. The consequence was that union-dominated broad policy concertation persisted far longer than in France. To this extent the Italian case is consistent with the configurational theory: broad policy concertation persists as long as social unrest, or the threat of social unrest, continues. On the other hand, this occurred despite significant differences in economic views among the political actors, plus the repeated failure of the government to implement its commitments properly.

In 1978, however, the area of shared economic understanding broadened when Italian trade unions accepted the need for wage restraint and the flexible use of labour in the face of a deteriorating economic situation. Agreements were reached in a number of policy areas, and a broad social pact was signed in 1983, but implementation problems remained and effective policy concertation was sporadic rather than continuous. Broad policy concertation finally came to an end in 1984 when the trade union movement split over whether to accept the package being offered by employers and the government.

In Germany, the entry of the Social Democrats into the government in 1966 was followed by the establishment of the so-called 'Concerted Action' of the late 1960s and early 1970s, but although this constituted more intense consultation at national level than before, it did not constitute policy concertation because agreements on public policy were not part of its remit. Moreover, it was terminated in 1977 when the unions walked out over employer opposition to codetermination legislation, although extensive consultation continued in less formal forums.

The rise and fall of the essentially bipartite Social Contract between government and unions in Britain during the 1970s fits the configurational theory well: its beginning in 1974 followed a period of high inflation, leading the government to offer policy concessions in exchange for wage restraint, and it was put in place by a Labour government, the economic views of which were much closer to those of the unions than the views of the preceding Conservative government. In 1978 union leaders were unable to secure the acceptance by their members of the latest agreement, which led to the industrial action of the so-called Winter of Discontent of 1978–9, but another agreement was signed in early 1979, so that broad policy concertation was not in fact terminated until after the Conservatives, led by Margaret Thatcher, came to power following the election of May 1979. In terms of the configurational theory, the sudden end to broad policy concertation can be attributed to the fact that the new government held very different economic views to those of the unions, including the view that unions and collective bargaining obstructed the development of a well-functioning market economy.

In Ireland, too, the rise of significant policy concertation for the first time in the 1970s, and its demise in the early 1980s, fits the predictions of the configurational theory: economic problems had persisted throughout the postwar period, but it was not until the economic views of governments, employers and trade unions converged somewhat, and centralised collective bargaining simplified the problem of implementing wage agreements after 1970, that policy concertation emerged when the government began to facilitate annual wage agreements by offering budgetary concessions. The agreements of 1977 and 1978 were explicitly tripartite in nature, and the National Understandings of 1979 and 1980 contained separate sections for wages and public policy. However the economic problems persisted, leading to disillusionment with the new system and, in accordance with the predictions of the configurational theory in these circumstances, broad policy concertation came to an end in 1982.

Spain's situation in the postwar period was fundamentally different to that of the other countries in that it was only after Franco's death in 1975 that the country moved towards democracy. Nevertheless, the social pact based policy concertation that emerged after 1975 can be explained in terms of the configurational theory. First, not only were there economic problems to motivate consideration of broad policy concertation, but in addition there existed a fear of a reversion to dictatorship that led the political actors to take great care to avoid social unrest. This meant serious efforts to reach agreement on controversial issues, including public policy issues. Second, the area of shared economic understanding was much greater than when policy concertation had last been tried in the 1930s, and included agreement on the need for wage restraint. However this period of broad policy concertation came to an end in the early 1980s following implementation problems plus a divergence of economic views as the government and employers, but not unions, displayed increased interest in deregulation, while the solidification of Spanish democracy removed the fear of a return to authoritarian rule.

Meanwhile, although the Austrian Social Partnership continued to thrive on economic success, during the 1970s policy concertation was running into trouble in both the Netherlands and Sweden, where it was seen to be failing to come to grips with new economic problems at the same time as the economic views of employers, unions and government were diverging.

In the Netherlands the end of broad policy concertation was gradual, but by the 1970s lack of agreement on economic policy meant that the Social and Economic Council was no longer able to deliver meaningful unanimous recommendations to the government: policy concertation was paralysed, and from 1982 the government deliberately bypassed the Council for economic advice. Although the bipartite Wassenaar Accord of the same year led to increased employer-union cooperation, and over the next decade a measure of economic agreement reappeared at a time when economic difficulties continued to be severe, an attempt at resuming broad policy concertation in 1989 with the signing of the Common Course Agreement failed due to implementation problems. All these developments are in line with the predictions of the configurational theory in such circumstances.

In Sweden the economic views of the political actors had started to diverge in certain areas as early as the late 1950s, the development of the agreed EFO wage formula in the 1960s notwithstanding, and growing union radicalism culminated in the 1970s with the Meidner Plan's proposal gradually to transfer the ownership of industry from private capital to union-controlled investment funds. This was interpreted by employers as a deadly threat, and in the 1980s they moved towards a neo-liberal economic position and began a massive ideological counter-attack, even though the watered-down version of this plan that was eventually legislated did not pose any threat to their dominance. In the meantime the Social Democratic governments of the 1980s increasingly came into conflict with the unions on economic policy. By the late 1980s ideological polarisation had led to virtual deadlock in policy concertation.

Drawing this together, it can be seen that the configurational theory explains the incidence of broad policy concertation during the two decades between the late 1960s and late 1980s in all of the countries covered apart from Italy, where broad policy concertation persisted despite the lack of shared understanding of the aims and mechanisms of economic policy up to 1978 and the occurrence of implementation problems throughout the period.

6. From the late 1980s to 1997

Although during most of the postwar period policy concertation was most important in Austria, the Netherlands and Sweden, the three countries in which it was most important between the late 1980s and the end of 1997 were Austria, Ireland and Italy, as shown in Table 23.3.

Although the relevance of the Social Partnership for decision making in Austria did decline somewhat, it still remained important in many policy areas and in numerous formal and informal forums. This persistence of broad policy concertation occurred in the context of an economic performance that compares favourably with most other West European countries plus continued broad consensus on the aims of economic policy and few problems with implementation, just as predicted in such circumstances by the configurational theory.

Table 23.3. *Policy Content and Frequency of Concertation in Western Europe, 1990–1997*

Country	Policy areas covered
Wide-concertation countries with frequent concertation	
Austria	Social policy, fiscal policy, monetary policy, investment policy, industrial policy, social welfare, labour law, job creation and training, employment, EU issues
Wide-concertation countries with sporadic concertation	
Ireland	Overall macroeconomic policy strategy; social welfare, government spending in general; employment policy including active labour market policy; regional policy
Medium-concertation countries with sporadic concertation	
Italy	Taxation, expenditure (especially pensions), labour law
Narrow-concertation countries with frequent concertation	
Netherlands	Social security, employment policy
Sweden	Many sectors until 1992, then restricted to labour market policy and pensions
Germany	Social insurance, labour law, health, reconstruction of the East
Narrow-concertation countries with sporadic concertation	
Spain	Employment law and social security
France	Employment law and social security
Non-concertation countries	
Britain	None

Source: chapters on the politics of policy concertation in the 1990s in Austria, Britain, France, Germany, Ireland, Italy, the Netherlands, Spain and Sweden; communications with the authors.

The resumption of broad policy concertation in Ireland in 1987, in the form of the first of a series of three-year tripartite agreements with provisions on a wide range of public policy, is also in line with the predictions of the theory: in 1987 the economy was still in crisis but the shared understanding of the aims and mechanisms of economic policy had broadened during the 1980s and included agreement on the need for wage restraint. Implementation does not appear to have been a serious problem. Since 1987 broad policy concertation has become well established in a variety of different forums as the country has experienced an unprecedented period of economic success.

The resurgence of social pact based policy concertation in Italy during the early 1990s can also be readily explained in terms of the configurational theory: economic problems were joined by political crisis at the same time as the views of the political actors converged on a common understanding of economic objectives and mechanisms, while potential implementation problems were reduced by increased cooperation among the three trade union confederations. The substantial progress made in tackling Italy's economic problems in recent years has been in part attributed to the social pacts of 1992, 1993 and 1995, so the persistence of this style of broad policy concertation into the late 1990s is consistent with the predictions of the configurational theory in such circumstances.

In most of the remaining countries, policy concertation was restricted mainly to employment and social policy.

Since the failure of the tripartite Common Course agreement of 1989, the prospects of further broad policy concertation in the Netherlands have been impeded by continuing disagreement over economic and social policy plus the fact that the abandonment of broad policy concertation has been accompanied in recent years by considerable economic success. The absence of broad policy concertation is what would be expected by the configurational theory in such circumstances.

In Sweden, decades of policy concertation in the form of the participation of organisational representatives in the decision making of the governing boards of public administrative agencies came to an end in 1992 when the centre-right Bildt government replaced group representatives with lay members selected, at least officially, for their expertise. This followed the unilateral withdrawal of employer representatives in 1991. The only significant policy-making institutions in which this de-concertation process did not occur were pension funds and the Labour Market Board. Other forms of broad policy concertation had already come to an end. From the perspective of the configurational theory this development is hardly surprising, as broad policy concertation had already been virtually paralysed by the divergent economic views of employers and unions, with employers increasingly criticising the economic role of trade unions and collective bargaining even after the unions drew back from their radicalism of the 1970s and early 1980s. However it was not until the arrival of an economic crisis in the early 1990s that policy concertation had patently been unable to prevent, plus the election of a government that saw unions and collective bargaining as an obstacle to economic recovery, that the *coup de grace* was delivered – in accord with the predictions of the configurational theory in such circumstances.

In Germany, on the other hand, where policy concertation normally covers only certain areas of social insurance, labour law and health, mainly as a consequence of the involvement of employers and unions in the administration of these areas of public policy, the economic and social problems created by reunification led to short-term broad policy concertation in the form of the 1993 Solidarity Pact as a means of facilitating reconstruction of the East. This took place in a context of considerable shared understanding of the aims and means of economic policy, plus political actors with a reasonably well-developed capacity to implement agreements, which from the perspective of the configurational theory implies that the lack of broad policy concertation in Germany in the decades prior to reunification is attributable to the relative lack of serious economic or social problems in (the then) West Germany.

In Spain, major reforms to labour law and social security were accomplished by means of negotiations which led to the conclusion of a number of social pacts between 1994 and 1997 that included the government either as a formal participant or as the author of legislation needed to implement the policy contents of bipartite agreements between employers and unions, but, in line with the configurational theory, the broad social pacts of the late 1970s and early 1980s were not repeated due to the previous experience of implementation problems and continuing disagreement on economic policy.

While France lacks the tradition of cooperation between the state and social partners that has characterised most of the above countries, labour law and social provisions are often determined, as in Spain, by means of legislation based on the content of bipartite agreements between employers and trade unions. However governments, employers and trade unions still lack a shared understanding of the goals and mechanisms of economic policy, and, consistent with the configurational theory, broad policy concertation remains non-existent.

There was just one country in which no policy concertation of any sort occurred: Britain, where all forms of policy concertation had been extinguished by the vehemently anti-union Conservative government of 1979–97. Although the views of the new Labour government in 1997 were substantially closer to those of the unions, the economic upturn that was taking place at the time meant that there was no real impetus to switch policy-making styles. In addition, the memory of the Winter of Discontent maintains the view that trade unions would have problems implementing their side of any bargains. This lack of broad policy concertation is in line with the predictions of the configurational theory in such circumstances.

To sum up, the developments in terms of broad policy concertation in the decade since 1987 can without exception be explained in terms of the configurational theory.

Conclusions

The survey of nine countries presented above shows that the incidence of broad policy concertation in Western Europe over the course of the twentieth century can be almost completely explained in terms of the configurational theory. Broad policy concertation arises where there is an external threat, social unrest or economic problems, plus a certain degree of shared understanding among the political actors of the aims and mechanisms of economic policy, plus no serious implementation problems. It persists where it is perceived to be coping with the relevant problem where this is expected to reappear if policy concertation is abandoned, provided that a degree of shared economic understanding continues and implementation problems are not too serious. Otherwise it comes to an end, or, if not already existent, remains non-existent.

The only significant exception to this perfect fit between theory and observations is the episode of broad policy concertation in Italy between 1968 and 1984, as this persisted despite significant differences in economic views during the first part of the period and implementation problems throughout the period. The absence of attempts at policy concertation in Italy following the First World War is also inconsistent with the theory. This means that the configurational theory cannot be considered to be one of deterministic causation, but as a theory of probabilistic causation – which is all that can be expected of most theories of political economy, given the complexity of causation in this area – it is a very successful theory indeed.

Systematic comparison of this explanation with others must await another occasion, but on the evidence presented here the configurational theory provides a parsimonious yet powerful explanation of the incidence of broad policy concertation in Western Europe. The conclusion to be drawn from this is that it may well identify the main proximate causal mechanisms that underlie the political dynamics of broad policy concertation.

Notes

1. For a fuller discussion of the meaning and significance of policy concertation, see the Introduction to this volume.
2. Unless otherwise indicated, all the factual information used in this chapter is drawn from the relevant country chapters in this book.
3. Based on the famous paragraph by Schmitter in which he defines corporatism as 'a system of interest representation in which the constituent elements are organised into a limited number of singular, compulsory, non-competitive, hierarchically ordered and functionally differentiated categories, recognised or licensed (if not created) by the state and granted a deliberate representational monopoly within their respective categories in exchange for observing certain controls on their selection of leaders and articulation of demands and supports.' Philippe C. Schmitter, 'Still the Century of Corporatism?', in *Trends Towards Corporatist Intermediation*, ed. Philippe C. Schmitter and Gerhard Lehmbruch, London: Sage, 1979: 13.
4. Lars Calmfors (1993), 'Centralisation of Wage Bargaining and Unemployment – A Survey', *OECD Economic Studies* 21, 161–91; Mancur Olson, *The Rise and Decline of Nations*, New Haven: Yale University Press, 1982.

5. Gerhard Lehmbruch, 'Liberal Corporatism and Party Government', in *Trends Towards Corporatist Intermediation*, ed. Philippe C. Schmitter and Gerhard Lehmbruch, London: Sage, 1979: 167–8; Hans Slomp, 'European Labor Relations and the Prospects of Tripartism', in *Participation in Public Policy-Making: The Role of Trade Unions and Employers' Associations*, ed. Tiziano Treu, Berlin and New York: Walter de Gruyter, 1992: 163; Colin Crouch, *Industrial Relations and the European State Tradition,* Oxford: Clarendon Press, 1993: 54–5, 289. For a more extensive literature review, see the Introduction to this book.
6. John Kingdon, *Agendas, Alternatives and Public Policies*, 2nd edn, New York: HarperCollins, 1995.
7. Information is also drawn from Emmerich Tálos and Bernhard Kittel, 'Roots of Austro-Corporatism: Institutional Preconditions and Cooperation Before and After 1945', in *Austro-Corporatism: Past, Present, Future*, ed. Günter Bischof and Anton Pelinka, New Brunswick and London: Transaction Publishers, 1996.

Index

Note: Page references in *italic* indicate information contained in tables.